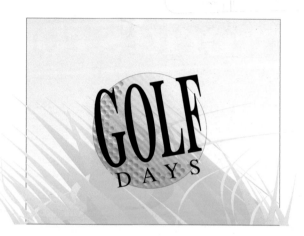

GOLF COURSES IN IRELAND

SEVENTH EDITION

In this book is the priceless heritage of golf throughout Ireland. Three hundred and four courses, most affiliated to the Golfing Union of Ireland, some of which are renowned throughout the world for providing a unique golfing challenge.

Golf Days provides a complete reference to over 300 courses and provides a choice of course to test both high or low handicappers.

The variety of golf courses in Ireland offers almost every conceivable environment and test – the difficulty will be which to choose. Some of the finest courses in Europe are waiting to complete the golfing experience.

The information you need to know is contained in this new updated edition covering so many clubs, from the world famous links courses to the smallest nine holer. GOLF DAYS gives you all the golfing options and now you have the choice — all you have to do is enjoy this great game on some great courses.

The world's round.

HOW TO USE THIS BOOK

GOLF
DAYS

Ireland is divided into four ancient Provinces and these are applied in the administration of golf by the Golfing Union of Ireland. **Golf Days** has adopted the same geographical division. The courses in this book are grouped in Provinces, sub-divided into Counties and then listed alphabetically. The Province appears on the top left hand corner and the County name at the top right of each page.

COURSE INFORMATION

This information has been provided by each club and readers are advised to check details in advance as the publishers cannot guarantee the accuracy. Most clubs will be only too glad to answer queries and telephone numbers for all the courses listed have been included for this purpose.
A telephone call can save a wasted journey.
There are different area dialing codes when calling from the Republic of Ireland to Northern Ireland and vice versa. From N.Ireland dial 00353 & then the code omitting the first zero. From the Republic of Ireland dial 08 then the code including the first zero.

CURRENCY

All green Fees for Northern Ireland *(Counties: Down, Armagh, Antrim, Londonderry, Fermanagh and Tyrone)* are in £ Sterling. Those for the Republic of Ireland are in IR £ (punts). The currencies tend to be within 10% of each other.

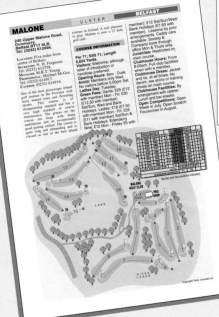

SCORE CARD

Some course cards are marked in metres, some in yards and some have both. Whatever method of distance that is currently used by each course, the same has been adopted in **Golf Days** to maintain the same standard of measurement. Some course lengths differ in text from course cards depending on whether Championship or Medal lengths are on the score card.

COURSE MAP

These are for general information and to provide a layout of the course. They are not intended for interpretation for scoring or competition purposes.

Published by
Tudor Journals Ltd
97 Botanic Avenue,
Belfast BT7 1JN. N. Ireland.
Telephone (01232) 320088.
Fax (01232) 323163.

Original Editorial Committee
Leinster:
Kenneth W. Haughton
Ulster:
Brendan Edwards.
Munster:
J. Percy Shannon.
Connacht:
Michael P. O'Donoghue.

Provincial Introductions:
Jack Magowan.

Sales & Distribution
Lesley Stevenson.

Production
Jacquie Ferguson,
Darrren Downing,
Steven Meredith.

Publisher
Bill Campbell.

QUICK REFERENCE GUIDE

GOLF CLUBS
IN IRELAND
Affiliated To The Golfing Union Of Ireland.

GOLF DAYS

4

LEINSTER

CARLOW
1 Borris
2 Carlow
DUBLIN
3 Balbriggan
4 Ballinascorney
5 Beaverstown
6 Beechpark
7 City West
8 Corballis
9 Donabate
10 Dun Laoghaire
11 Elmgreen
12 Forrest Little
13 Hermitage
14 Hollystown
15 Island
16 Killeny
17 Kilternan
18 Finnstown
19 Lucan
20 Malahide
21 Newlands
22 Old Conna
23 Open Golf Centre
24 Portmarnock
25 Portmarnock Links
26 Rush
27 Skerries
28 Slade Valley
29 Stepaside
30 Westmanstown
31 Woodbrook
DUBLIN CITY
32 Carrickmines
33 Castle
34 Clontarf
35 Deer Park
36 Edmonstown
37 Elm Park
38 Foxrock
39 Grange
40 Hazel Grove
41 Howth
42 Milltown
43 Rathfarnham
44 Royal Dublin
45 St Annes
46 St Margarets
47 Stackstown
48 Sutton
KILDARE
49 Athy
50 Bodenstown
51 Castlewarden
52 Cill Dara
53 The Curragh
54 Kilkea Castle
55 Killeen
56 The "K" Club
57 Knockanally
58 Naas
KILKENNY
59 Callan
60 Castlecomer
61 Kilkenny
62 Mount Juliet
63 Waterford
LAOIS
64 Abbeyleix
65 Heath
66 Mountrath
67 Portarlington
68 Rathdowney
LONGFORD
69 Longford
LOUTH
70 Ardee
71 Co Louth
72 Dundalk
73 Greenore
74 Killinbeg
MEATH
75 The Black Bush
76 Headfort
77 Killock
78 Laytown & Bettystown
79 Royal Tara
80 Trim
OFFALY
81 Birr
82 Edenderry
83 Tullamore
WESTMEATH
84 Glasson
85 Moate
86 Mullingar
WEXFORD
87 Courtown
88 Enniscorthy
89 New Ross
90 Rosslare
91 St. Helen's Bay
92 Wexford
WICKLOW
93 Arklow
94 Ballinglass
95 Blainroe
96 Bray
97 Charlesland
98 Coollattin
99 Delgany
100 Druid's Glen
101 European Club
102 Greystones
103 Powerscourt
104 Rallsallagh
105 Roundwood
106 Tulfarris
107 Wicklow
108 Woodensbridge

ULSTER

ANTRIM
109 Allen Park
110 Ballycastle
111 Ballyclare
112 Ballymena
113 Bushfoot
114 Cairndhu
115 Carrickfergus
116 Cushendal
117 Down Royal Park
118 Gracehill
119 Greenisland
120 Lambeg
121 Larne
122 Lisburn
123 Massereene
124 Royal Portrush
125 Royal Portrush Valley
126 Whitehead
ARMAGH
127 Co Armagh
128 Ashfield
129 Edenmore
130 Lurgan
131 Portadown
132 Silverwood
133 Tandragee
BELFAST CITY
134 Balmoral
135 Belvoir
136 Cliftonville
137 Dunmurry
138 Fort William
139 Knock
140 Knockbracken
141 Malone
142 Ormeau
143 Rockmount
144 Shandon
CAVAN
145 Belturbet
146 Blacklion
147 Cabra Castle
148 Co Cavan
149 Slieve Russell
150 Virginia
DONEGAL
151 Ballybofey & Stranorlar
152 Ballyliffen
153 Bundoran
154 Cruit Island
155 Donegal
156 Dunfanaghy
157 Greencastle
158 Gweedore
159 Letterkenny
160 Narin & Portnoo
161 North West
162 Portsalon
163 Redcastle
164 Rosapenna
DOWN
165 Ardglass
166 Banbridge
167 Bangor
168 Blackwood
169 Bright Castle
170 Carnalea
171 Clandeboye
172 Clandeboye
173 Donaghadee
174 Downpatrick
175 Helens Bay
176 Holywood
177 Kilkeel
178 Kirkistown
179 Mahee Island
180 Ringdufferin
181 Royal Belfast
182 Royal Co Down
183 Scrabo
184 Spa
185 Warrenpoint
FERMANAGH
186 Castlehume
187 Enniskillen
LONDONDERRY
188 Castlerock
189 City of Derry
190 Foyle
191 Moyola
192 Portstewart
193 Roe Park
MONAGHAN
194 Castleblayney
195 Clones
196 Nuremore
197 Rossmore
TYRONE
198 Dungannon
199 Fintona
200 Killymoon
201 Newtown Stewart
202 Omagh
203 Strabane

MUNSTER

CLARE
204 Dromoland Castle
205 East Clare
206 Ennis
207 Kilkee
208 Kilrush
209 Lahinch
210 Lahinch Old Course
211 Shannon
212 Spanish Point
213 Woodstock
CORK
214 Bandon
215 Bantry Park
216 Berehaven
217 Charleville
218 Cobh
219 Coosheen
220 Cork
221 Douglas
222 Dunmore
223 East Cork
224 Fermoy
225 Fota Island
226 Frankfield
227 Glengarriff
228 Harbour Point
229 Kinsale
230 Macroom
231 Mahon
232 Mallow
233 Mitchelstown
234 Monkstown
235 Muskerry
236 Raffeen Creek
237 Skibbereen
238 Youghal
KERRY
239 Ardfert
240 Ballybunion
241 Ballybunion Cashen
242 Beaufort
243 Ceann Sibeal
244 Dooks
245 Kenmare
246 Killarney Killen
247 Killarney O'Mahony's
248 Killorgin
249 Parknasilla
250 Tralee
251 Waterville
LIMERICK
252 Adare
253 Adare Manor
254 Castletroy
255 Killeline
256 Limerick
257 Limerick Country Club
258 Newcastle West
TIPPERARY
259 Ballykisteen
260 Cahir Park
261 Carrick-on-Suir
262 Clonmel
263 Nenagh
264 Roscrea
265 Templemore
266 Thurles
267 County Tipperary
WATERFORD
268 Dungarvan
269 Dumore East
270 Faithlegg
271 Gold Coast
272 Tramore
273 Waterford Castle
274 West Waterford

CONNACHT

GALWAY
275 Athenry
276 Ballinasloe
277 Connemara
278 Galway
279 Galway Bay
280 Gort
281 Loughrea
282 Mount Bellew
283 Oughterard
284 Portumna
285 Tuam
LEITRIM
286 Ballinamore
MAYO
287 Achill
288 Ballina
289 Ballinrobe
290 Ballyhaunis
291 Belmullet
292 Castlebar
293 Claremorris
294 Swinford
295 Westport
ROSCOMMON
296 Athlone
297 Ballaghadereen
298 Boyle
299 Carrick-on-Shannon
300 Castlerea
301 Roscommon
SLIGO
302 Co Sligo
303 Enniscrone
304 Strandhill

THE NUMBERS ABOVE ARE COLOUR CODED IN PROVINCES FOR GEOGRAPHICAL LOCATION ON THE MAP (OPPOSITE). FOR PAGE NUMBERS OF EACH CLUB REFER TO ALPHABETICAL INDEX ON PAGES 350 & 351

'Determination, great effort
nd pure skill. It takes a lot to
produce a winner.

What else but Waterford?"

WATERFORD
CRYSTAL

On the north-east shores lies the famous Royal Portrush course with it's awesome reputation. (below)

Kinsale, in the south offers a gentle 9 holer with superb coastal views. (right)

THE FAR CORNERS
Golf from the north-east to the south-west.

PHOTOGRAPHY BY ESLER CRAWFORD PHOTOGRAPHY.

(Left) Where the Atlantic sweeps in at the west is Lahinch, with the 'Old' course and 'Castle' course.

(Right) Waterville in the extreme south-west enjoys the balmy influence of the Gulf Stream.

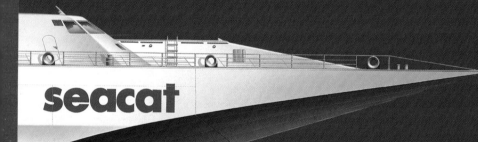

LEINSTER

BY JACK MAGOWAN

Jack Smith was his name, and nobody ever heard of him again. Clearly, the shock of leading a championship field by eight strokes must have been too much for this nervous young Londoner. While George Duncan, his boss at Wentworth, signed for a gale-lashed final-round 74 at Portmarnock, Smith needed seventeen shots more for a butter-fingered score of 91, and fretted all the way home.

This was 1927, the year of the first-ever Irish Open over a course made famous some years before by a couple of high-fliers called Alcock and Brown. These two intrepid aces were in a Vickers-Vimy that glided on to Portmarnock Strand, both fuel tanks empty, after taking off from

A jewel in the Leinster crown is the famous Portmarnock course.

Newfoundland 16 hours before, and were soon to be knighted as the frontrunners of Atlantic aviation.

Overnight, the flagship of Leinster golf had an exciting new identity. Maggie Leonard's cow was no more, but the quickest way to get to this great links was across the estuary from Baldoyle in a row boat or horse and trap, depending on the tide. In those days, no stranger ever left Portmarnock. He may have arrived as a stranger, but by closing time he was a friend. They would ring a ship's bell to signal the departure of the last boat back to the mainland, then came the motor-car and Duncan and Mitchell and Easterbrook and Bobby Locke, all championship winners over the longest, sometimes toughest links course in Europe.

The face of Portmarnock hasn't changed a great deal. Without wind, it may be like Samson shorn of his hair, yet how often do we ever get this Dublin Bay pearl bereft of wind? Even when Sandy Lyle beat a 30 year-old record with a staggering 64 on day one of the 1989 Irish Open, the burly Scot was in a cashmere sweater and cords. In Duncan's day, they usually wore oil-paper under plus-fours as protection against rain or cold.

Locke always waxed eloquent about Portmarnock, and not without reason. Wasn't it there at the age of 21, and in his first season as a professional, that 'Old Muffin Face' won the Irish championship. Two years later (1940) he was flying bombing missions against Rommel in North Africa and didn't touch a golf club again until the War ended. Half-a-century later, the tournament revived by Carrolls Tobacco, and rescued by Murphy's Stout, royally hosts nearly all the game's top players before some of the biggest galleries in Europe.

The Irish love to watch golf as well as play it, and nobody was surprised when Portmarnock had to put up 'house full' notices at the first Walker Cup match ever staged here. That was in 1991 and part of the Golfing Union's centenary celebrations, and you can be certain this glamour fixture will be back

Elm Park – popular city parkland course with many mature trees adding to the test of golf.

in the Emerald Isle before long. If not at Portmarnock, then maybe Royal County Down, Mount Juliet or the K-Club. Out of nearly 20 Irish courses ranked among *Golf World's* choice of the top 100 in Britain, six wear the Leinster label.

Arnold Palmer's baby at Naas, the fashionable K-Club, only comes in at No.93, but don't hold that against it. This is nothing short of a superb course, tailored to a tee and possibly boasting more five-star holes than any other new course in the county. As club pro Ernie Jones said recently, borrowing a phrase from the most celebrated Jones-boy of all.

"There's not a hole here that can't be birdied if you just think. And there's not a hole that can't be double-bogied if you stop thinking!"

County Louth, Royal Dublin, The Island, Rosslare all welcoming hosts and courses that have few equals in a links context. And the same can be said for Pat Ruddy's wonderful new creation

at Brittas Bay, the European Club. This course was only played for the first time in the summer of '94 and needs time to mature. Once it does, we'll be talking about a roller coaster gem in the same breath as Baltray, Portstewart, Ballyliffin, Sligo and others of merit.

Water, in my view, adds greatly to the charm and magnetism of a golf course, and there's an abundance of it at St Margaret's, near Dublin Airport. The eighth there is one of the most genuine par-5's in the business, an exhileratingly difficult long hole that top-girl Laura Davies clearly treated with respectful caution, even in the '95 championship she won there by a runaway 16 strokes. Laura was in orbit that week, surrendering only one shot to par in 72 holes for a World record tally of 25 – under (267) that may never be bettered in a ladies' tourament in Ireland.

St. Margaret's is the brainchild of Ruddy and partner, Tom Caddock, whose eye for what's best in golfing architecture has also put a hideaway hamlet in County Wicklow called Newtownmountkennedy firmly on the map.

Who said Valderrama was the toughest course in Europe?.

It's a pussy-cat (almost) compared to Druid's Glen, where the key is not to play all four short holes in par, but without getting that Titleist wet! The 17th to an Island green is a spectacle hole, a carbon copy of No.17 on Florida's famous Tournament Players' course, only longer.

Druid's Glen is not for everybody, not at an entrance fee of £25,000 + plus, or annual sub. of £1,500, but for sheer drama and challenge, it's something special, an examination in golf for sure.

"Our brief was to build the best inland course in the country," says designer Craddock, once a Walker Cup player. " Clearly, there can't be many better than this."

Golf's magnetism is like the common cold – everybody gets it, but nobody can explain why. There are many permutations for a rewarding, if not inexpensive, tour of Ireland's South-East region, but for one lovely lady from Baltinglass it would begin with a round at the European Club and end at Rathsallagh. Sandwiched between the – two would be a visit to Woodenbridge (Arklow), Rosslare, St Helens Bay, Faithlegg, Mount Juliet and Carlow.

Eight different courses in ten days? Sheer exhaustion, but it would be a never-to-be-forgotten experience!

Every year, nearly 60 top people in golf are invited to rank in merit order Ireland's thirty greatest courses. Portmarnock seems to have found a

THE BALROTHERY INN

The old local Coaching Inn serving the N1 Highway was the first change of horse out of Dublin northwards to Belfast.

*The proprietors, **John McCormack & Family** have developed The Balrothery Inn in a most tasteful manner in keeping with the Norman Tradition and outdoor facilities are excellent and cater for the modern day travellers as of old. With a very good menu and private parking for coach and car alike, the code of the Inn is reflected in one of it's mottos "the place to pause".*

Bar & Lunch Menus 12.00 – 6.30p.m.

Monday – Sunday incl. 6.30p.m. – 10.30p.m.

Credit Cards welcome. Fully licensed.

Balrothery Inn, Balbriggan, Co Dublin. Tel: (01) 8412252, Fax: 8411896.

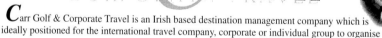

permanent place at No. 1, followed by Royal Portrush and or Ballybunion and Royal County Down.

And how are the others rated? Mount Juliet, which carries the Nicklaus signature, is currently at No.7 and the K-Club at No.9, just in front of Killarney. It will be interesting to see where the critics and Europe's Tour professionals place 'the Glen'.

Here is how Ireland's top courses, North and South, are ranked at home:

1) Portamarock; 2) Royal Portrush; 3) Royal Co. Down; 4) Ballybunion Old; 5) Waterville; 6) The European Club; 7) Mount Juliet; 8) Co. Louth; 9) The K-Club; 10) Co. Sligo; 11) Killarney (Killeen); 12) Lahinch; 13) Royal Dublin; 14) St.Margaret's; 15) Malone; 16) Portstewart; 17) The Island; 18) Carlow; 19) Tralee; 20) Killarney (Mahony); 21) Connemara; 22) Donegal (Murvagh); 23) Slieve Russell; 24) Cork; 25) Tramore; 26) Belvoir Park; 27) Galway Bay; 28) Castlerock; 29) Ballybunion New, and 30) Hermitage.

**Borris Golf Club,
Deerpark, Borris,
Co. Carlow.
Tel: (0503) 73143/73310.**

LOCATION: Outskirts of the town on the road to New Ross.
SECRETARY: Michael Cody.

Picturesque nine hole course, sited in wooded land with an attractive backdrop of hills and mountains.

COURSE INFORMATION

Par 70; SSS 69; Length 5,572 metres.
Visitors: Welcome Mon – Fri.
Opening Hours: 9.30am – 5.30pm.
Avoid: Thursday afternoons, Saturdays and Sundays.
Ladies: Welcome.
Green Fees: £10. (With Members Sun Only).

Juveniles: Welcome. Caddy service available by prior arrangements.
Clubhouse Hours: 10.00am – 11.00pm.
Clubhouse Dress: Casual.
Clubhouse Facilities: Bar food.

NO.	METRES	PAR	S.I.	NO.	METRES	PAR	S.I.
1	297	4	10	10	312	4	7
2	345	4	5	11	311	4	9
3	274	4	16	12	293	4	15
4	117	3	18	13	151	3	14
5	450	5	12	14	346	4	6
6	323	4	8	15	355	4	4
7	152	3	13	16	132	3	17
8	393	4	3	17	430	4	1
9	414	4	2	18	477	5	11
OUT	2,765	35		IN	2,807	35	
				TOTAL	5,572	70	
STANDARD SCRATCH		69					

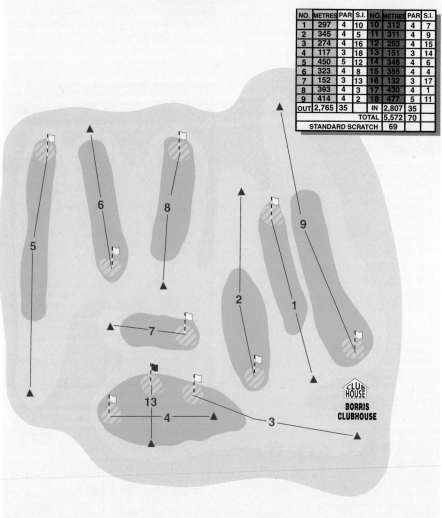

BORRIS
CLUBHOUSE

NO.	MEDAL YARDS	GEN. YARDS	PAR	S.I.	NO.	MEDAL YARDS	GEN. YARDS	PAR	S.I.
1	399	395	4	4	10	277	273	4	11
2	285	275	4	14	11	389	381	4	3
3	133	124	3	17	12	340	334	4	7
4	338	333	4	9	13	154	150	3	16
5	457	450	5	15	14	420	415	4	5
6	167	163	3	12	15	343	334	4	10
7	395	389	4	1	16	396	393	4	2
8	399	390	4	6	17	139	134	3	18
9	344	338	4	8	18	469	460	5	13
OUT	2,917	2,857	35		IN	2,927	2,874	35	
					TOTAL	5,844	5,731	70	
					STANDARD SCRATCH	71	70		

Deerpark, Dublin Road, Co. Carlow.
Tel: (0503) 31695.

Location: Three miles north of Carlow Town on main Dublin Road (N9).
Secretary: Margaret Meaney.
Tel: (0503) 31695. Fax: (0503) 40065.
Professional: Andrew Gilbert.
Tel: (0503) 41745.

Considered one of the best inland courses with fair but tight fairways and good greens. Rarely closed due to water logging. The course has extensive mature woods and many scenic views.

COURSE INFORMATION

Par 70; SSS 71; Length 5,844 metres.
Visitors: Welcome.
Opening Hours: Sunrise – Sunset.
Avoid: Tuesday, Saturday and Sunday.
Ladies: Welcome.
Green Fees: Mon-Fri £20; Groups (12+) £18; Weekends £25. Groups (12+) £12 & £22.
Juveniles: Restricted. Lessons available by prior arrangements. Caddy service available by prior arrangement. Handicap certificate required. Prior arrangement preferred.
Clubhouse Hours: 9.30am – 11.30pm. Full Clubhouse Facilities.
Clubhouse Dress: Casual.
Clubhouse Facilities: Breakfast (summer), lunches, evening meals, snacks all day. Menu available on request.
Open Competitions: Open Week: June; Midland Scratch Cup: Sep.

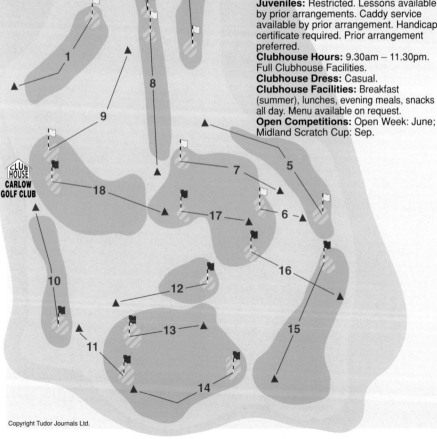

CLUB HOUSE
CARLOW
GOLF CLUB

BALBRIGGAN

Blackhall, Balbriggan, Co. Dublin.
Tel: 8412229. or 8412173.

LOCATION: 1 mile south of Balbriggan on Dublin / Belfast road.

SECRETARY / MANAGER: Michael O'Halloran.
Tel: 8412229.

Expanded to eighteen holes in 1985 and has been developed using an additional 32 acres that the club purchased which allowed for a new clubhouse to be built in 1991 adding to the club's many attractive features. The new layout has made the course more of a formidable challenge.

COURSE INFORMATION

Par 71; SSS 71; Length 5,881 metres.
Visitors: Welcome Monday, Wednesday, Thursday and Friday.
Opening Hours: 8.00am – Sunset.
Avoid: Weekends and Tuesday (Ladies day).
Ladies: Welcome.
Juveniles: Open Week, August.
Green Fees: £14 Mon – Fri; £18 Sat/Sun/Bank Holidays.
Clubhouse Hours: 11.00am – 11.00pm.
Clubhouse Dress: Casual.
Clubhouse Facilities: Snacks available from midday.
Open Competitions: Open Week June; Men's Fourballs, September; Mixed, September; Ladies Open. September.

NO.	METRES	PAR	S.I.	NO.	METRES	PAR	S.I.
1	344	4	6	10	413	5	15
2	501	5	16	11	180	3	9
3	358	4	4	12	364	4	3
4	321	4	18	13	304	4	13
5	397	4	2	14	349	4	5
6	176	3	10	15	392	4	1
7	338	4	14	16	126	3	11
8	170	3	12	17	331	4	9
9	359	4	8	18	454	5	17
OUT	2,968	35		IN	2,913	36	
				TOTAL	5,881	71	
	STANDARD SCRATCH	71					

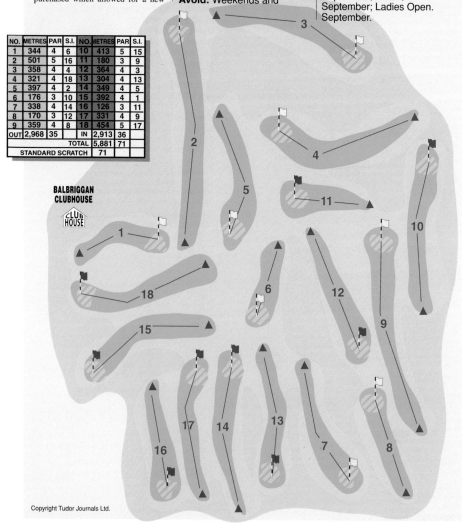

BALBRIGGAN CLUBHOUSE

Ballinascorney, Tallaght, Dublin 24, Co. Dublin.
Tel: 4512775.

LOCATION: Approx. ten miles south west of Dublin.
MANAGER: Mr Francis Bagnall.
Tel: 4512664 / 4516430.

Flat picturesque course in the foothills of the Dublin Mountains. The area has scenic views of the mountains, forests and lakes and overlooks Dublin city and Dublin bay. The course itself offers a varied selection of terrain from level parkland to gentle rolling slopes and some optional terrain of a more difficult nature. The newer section has some interesting water hazards and features holes.

COURSE INFORMATION

Par 71; SSS 67; Length 5,464 metres.
Visitors: Welcome (phone in advance) – societies welcome.
Opening Hours: Sunrise – Sunset.
Avoid: Weekends.
Ladies: Welcome.
Ladies Day: Thursday.

Green Fees: £10 (weekdays) £12 (weekends).
Juveniles: Welcome.
Clubhouse Hours: 8.00am – 11.00pm.
Clubhouse Dress: Smart/ Casual.
Clubhouse Facilities: Snacks – full meals by arrangement.

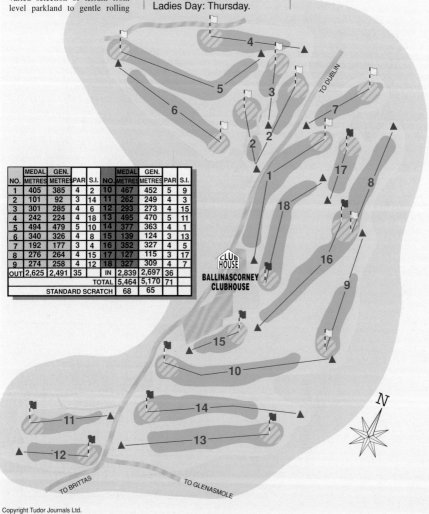

NO.	MEDAL METRES	GEN. METRES	PAR	S.I.	NO.	MEDAL METRES	GEN. METRES	PAR	S.I.
1	405	385	4	2	10	467	452	5	9
2	101	92	3	14	11	262	249	4	3
3	301	285	4	6	12	293	273	4	15
4	242	224	4	18	13	495	470	5	11
5	494	479	5	10	14	377	363	4	1
6	340	326	4	8	15	139	124	3	13
7	192	177	3	4	16	352	327	4	5
8	276	264	4	15	17	127	115	3	17
9	274	258	4	12	18	327	309	4	7
OUT	2,625	2,491	35		IN	2,839	2,697	36	
					TOTAL	5,464	5,170	71	
	STANDARD SCRATCH		68			65			

BALLINASCORNEY CLUBHOUSE

Beaverstown, Donabate, Co. Dublin.
Tel: 8436439.
Fax: 8436721.

LOCATION: 6 miles north of Dublin Airport.
SECRETARY / MANAGER: Eddie Smyth. Tel: 8436721.
ARCHITECT: Eddie Hackett.

Beaverstown is sited in an attractive orchard setting. The main feature of the course is its proximity to deep water which is a hazard on as many as ten of the eighteen holes.

COURSE INFORMATION

Par 72; SSS 71; Length 5,837 metres.
Visitors: Welcome.
Opening Hours: Sunrise – Sunset.

Avoid: Wed afternoon, Sat and Sun mornings.
Ladies: Welcome.
Juveniles: Must be accompanied by an adult. Prior arrangement required; caddy service available by prior arrangements.
Green Fees: £12 Mon – Fri; £20 Sat/Sun.
Clubhouse Hours: 7.30am to closing time.
Clubhouse Dress: Casual.
Clubhouse Facilities: Catering available from 10.30am.
Open Competitions: Various throughout the season.

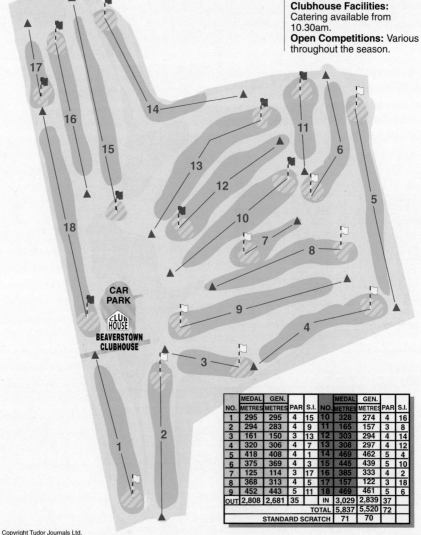

NO.	MEDAL METRES	GEN. METRES	PAR	S.I.	NO.	MEDAL METRES	GEN. METRES	PAR	S.I.
1	295	295	4	15	10	328	274	4	16
2	294	283	4	9	11	165	157	3	8
3	161	150	3	13	12	303	294	4	14
4	320	306	4	7	13	308	297	4	12
5	418	408	4	1	14	469	462	5	4
6	375	369	4	3	15	445	439	5	10
7	125	114	3	17	16	385	333	4	2
8	368	313	4	5	17	157	122	3	18
9	452	443	5	11	18	469	461	5	6
OUT	2,808	2,681	35		IN	3,029	2,839	37	
					TOTAL	5,837	5,520	72	
					STANDARD SCRATCH	71	70		

Johnstown, Rathcoole, Co. Dublin.
Tel: 4580100 / 4580522.

LOCATION: 2 miles from Rathcoole village on Kilteel Road.
SECRETARY / MANAGER: Joe Deally.
ARCHITECT: Eddie Hackett.

The course is in a setting of natural beauty with mature beech trees in abundance. Holes 9, 10, 11, 12 & 13 have a combination of mature trees and water providing difficulty, particularly in the drives.

COURSE INFORMATION

Par 72; SSS 70; Length 6,268 yds; 5,730 metres.
Visitors: Welcome Mon, Thurs & Fri.
Opening Hours: 8.00am – Sunset.
Avoid: Tues, Wed, and weekends.
Ladies Day: Tuesday.
Juveniles: Must be accompanied by an adult. Caddy service available by prior arrangement.

Green Fees: £17, Juveniles £4.
Clubhouse Hours: 9.00am – midnight.
Clubhouse Dress: Collar and tie after 8.00pm. No jeans or sneakers.
Clubhouse Facilities: 11.30am – 10.30pm.
Open Competitions: Open Week June.

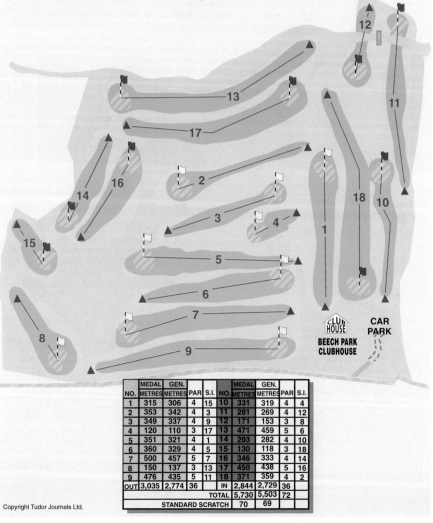

BEECH PARK CLUBHOUSE

CAR PARK

NO.	MEDAL METRES	GEN. METRES	PAR	S.I.	NO.	MEDAL METRES	GEN. METRES	PAR	S.I.
1	315	306	4	15	10	331	319	4	4
2	353	342	4	3	11	281	269	4	12
3	349	337	4	9	12	171	153	3	8
4	120	110	3	17	13	471	459	5	6
5	351	321	4	1	14	293	282	4	10
6	360	329	4	5	15	130	118	3	18
7	500	457	5	7	16	346	333	4	14
8	150	137	3	13	17	450	438	5	16
9	476	435	5	11	18	371	359	4	2
OUT	3,035	2,774	36		IN	2,844	2,729	36	
					TOTAL	5,730	5,503	72	
					STANDARD SCRATCH	70	69		

CITYWEST

LEINSTER

DUBLIN

Citywest Golf Course, Saggart, Co. Dublin.
Tel: (01) 458 8566.
Fax: (01) 458 8565.

LOCATION: 15 minutes from Dublin's City centre (N7 Saggart Village).

SECRETARY/MANAGER:
Eddie Jones. Tel: (01) 458 8566.
Fax: (01) 458 8565.
ARCHITECT: Christy O'Connor Jnr.

The careful construction of the course using the latest technology in drainage and irrigation systems has resulted in a superb playing surface which almost guarantees all year round golf.

COURSE INFORMATION

Par 71; Length 6,822 Yards.
Visitors: Always welcome.
Opening Hours: 7.00am – Sunset.
Green Fees: £25 weekdays; £30 weekends.
Juveniles: Golf clubs, trollies, buggies, locker and caddies available.
Clubhouse Facilities: First class restaurant open 7 days a week, bar food and banqueting/conference facilities available.
Clubhouse Dress: Casual.

TO DUBLIN

DRIVING RANGE

ENTRANCE

CITYWEST CLUBHOUSE

TO NAAS

NO.	CHAMP YARDS	MEDAL YARDS	PAR	S.I.	NO.	CHAMP YARDS	MEDAL YARDS	PAR	S.I.
1	386	366	4	10	10	331	308	4	14
2	197	171	3	16	11	178	156	3	17
3	541	516	5	8	12	536	496	5	7
4	220	211	3	15	13	555	539	5	9
5	398	374	4	4	14	369	349	4	12
6	454	423	4	1	15	400	385	4	13
7	380	367	4	11	16	397	381	4	5
8	457	432	4	3	17	158	139	3	18
9	430	414	4	6	18	435	414	4	2
OUT	3,463	3,274	35		IN	3,359	3,167	36	
					TOTAL	6,822	6,441	71	
					STANDARD SCRATCH				

Bunker and tree positions indicated.
Copyright Tudor Journals Ltd.

CORBALLIS

NO.	YARDS	PAR	S.I.	NO.	YARDS	PAR	S.I.
1	155	3	12	10	132	3	15
2	251	4	18	11	374	4	9
3	465	4	2	12	405	4	3
4	155	3	16	13	264	4	17
5	389	4	4	14	191	3	11
6	183	3	6	15	196	3	5
7	188	3	8	16	392	4	1
8	264	4	14	17	140	3	13
9	494	5	10	18	333	4	7
OUT	2,544	33		IN	2,427	32	
				TOTAL	4,971	65	
	STANDARD SCRATCH	64					

**Corballis Public Golf Course,
Donabate, Co. Dublin.
Tel: 8436583.**

LOCATION: North County Dublin on
the coast.
MANAGER: P. J. Boylan.
Tel: 8436583/8436781.
ARCHITECT: Dublin County Council.

A links course situated adjacent to Corballis
Beach, Donabate. Aquired and redeveloped by
Dublin County Council in 1973. A very
popular and challenging Par 65 course which
attracts large numbers of golfers particularly
during the winter months.

COURSE INFORMATION

**Par 65; SSS 64; Length 4,971 yards.
Visitors:** Welcome.
Opening Hours: Weekends 7.00am;
Weekdays 8.00am.
Ladies: Welcome.
Green Fees: £7 Mon – Fri; £8 Sat/Sun;
Juveniles, Senior Citizens & unemployed
£3 (Mon–Fri before 2.30pm).
Juveniles: Welcome.
Clubhouse Hours: Open normal
hours.
Clubhouse Dress: Casual/neat.
Clubhouse Facilities: Snack and
mineral water.

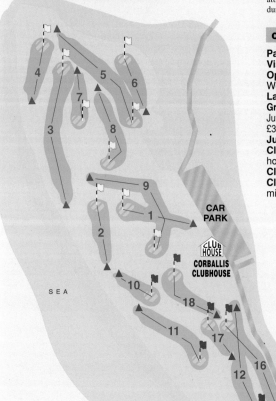

CAR
PARK

CORBALLIS
CLUBHOUSE

SEA

MARTELLO
TOWER

27

Balcarrick, Donabate, Co. Dublin.
Tel: 8436346

LOCATION: 12 miles north of Dublin city.
SECRETARY/MANAGER: Nancy Campion.
Tel: 8436346.
PROFESSIONAL: Hugh Jackson.
Tel: 8436346.

Flat parkland course in a rural setting, best described as a good holiday course.

COURSE INFORMATION

Par 70; SSS 69; Length 5,704 yards.
Visitors: Welcome Mon – Fri.
Opening Hours: 7.30am – Sunset.
Avoid: Wednesday, Saturday, Sunday and Bank Holidays.
Ladies: Welcome.
Green Fees: £18 (weekdays) £9 with member; Sat, Sun, Bank Hols & after 6pm with member £12.

Juveniles: Welcome but restricted. Club hire and caddy service available by prior arrangements.
Clubhouse Hours: 7.00am – midnight.
Clubhouse Dress: Casual / neat.
Clubhouse Facilities: Snacks available at all times; a la carte from 5pm, also a bar.

NO.	MEDAL YARDS	GEN. YARDS	PAR	S.I.	NO.	MEDAL YARDS	GEN. YARDS	PAR	S.I.
1	162	147	3	9	10	375	366	4	2
2	444	435	5	13	11	191	176	3	6
3	375	356	4	3	12	315	296	4	12
4	408	380	4	1	13	322	309	4	15
5	325	314	4	11	14	359	334	4	8
6	356	342	4	5	15	173	164	3	14
7	272	251	4	18	16	316	309	4	10
8	330	315	4	7	17	375	340	4	4
9	154	145	3	16	18	452	438	5	17
OUT	2,826	2,685	35		IN	2,878	2,732	35	
					TOTAL	5,704	5,417	70	
					STANDARD SCRATCH	69	67		

DONABATE CLUBHOUSE

28

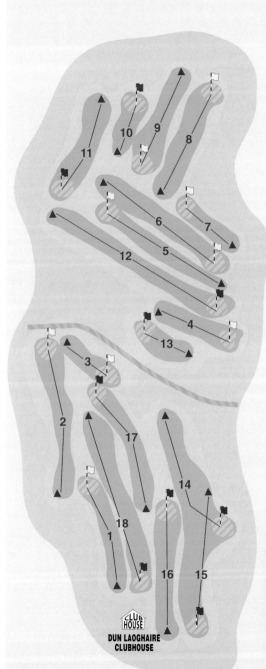

Dun Laoghaire Golf Club, Eglinton Park, Tivoli Road, Dun Laoghaire.
Tel: 01 2803916.

LOCATION: 7 miles South of Dublin.
SECRETARY: Terry Stewart.
Tel: 01 2803916. Fax: 01 2804868.
PROFESSIONAL: Owen Mulhall.
Tel: 01 2801694.

Generally speaking a short course in the quiet suburbs of Dun Laoghaire, but with some interesting holes requiring accurate club selection.

COURSE INFORMATION

Par 70; SSS 68; Length 5,478 Metres.
Visitors: Welcome Mon, Tues, Wed, Friday & Sun.
Opening Hours: 8.00am – Sunset.
Ladies: Welcome.
Green Fees: £25 each day.
Juveniles: Welcome.
Lessons available by prior arrangements. Club Hire available, Caddy service available. Prior arrangement required.
Clubhouse Hours: 10.00am – 11.00pm.
Clubhouse Dress: Casual. Jackets and ties after 8.00pm.
Clubhouse Facilities: 10.00am – 10.00pm snack service April – Oct; 6.00pm – 10.00pm Restaurant April – Oct; 10.00am – 6.00pm Snack service Nov – March.

NO.	METRES	PAR	S.I.	NO.	METRES	PAR	S.I.
1	306	4	11	10	183	3	9
2	333	4	5	11	344	4	6
3	148	3	8	12	438	5	17
4	240	4	18	13	148	3	7
5	392	4	1	14	371	4	2
6	281	4	15	15	343	4	12
7	110	3	14	16	336	4	4
8	368	4	3	17	313	4	13
9	345	4	10	18	479	5	16
OUT	2,523	34		IN	2,955	36	
				TOTAL	5,478	70	
				STANDARD SCRATCH	68		

DUN LAOGHAIRE CLUBHOUSE

CLUB HOUSE

ELMGREEN

L E I N S T E R

DUBLIN

Castleknock, Dublin 15.
Co. Dublin.
Tel: (01) 8200 797.

LOCATION: Situated just off the Navan Road, a minutes drive from Castleknock roundabout.
SECRETARIES: Gerry Carr/ Brian Begley.
Tel: (01) 8200 797.

Located 15 minutes from Dublin City. This is a very pleasant parkland course. The 17th hole Par 3 is an exceptional hole played against the backdrop of the Wicklow Mountains.

COURSE INFORMATION

Par 71; SSS 68; Length 5,300 Yards.
Visitors: Welcome anytime. Telephone for booking.
Opening Hours: Dawn till Dusk.
Avoid: None.
Ladies: Welcome Anytime.
Green Fees: £10.50 Weekdays.
£16.00 Weekends.
Juveniles: Welcome anytime.

Clubhouse Hours: N/A.
Clubhouse Dress: N/A.
Clubhouse Facilities: Changing Rooms / Showers. Coffee Shop.
Open Competitions: Yes.

NO.	YARDS	PAR	S.I.	NO.	YARDS	PAR	S.I.
1	269	4	9	10	300	4	10
2	476	5	13	11	121	3	18
3	118	3	17	12	350	4	12
4	383	4	11	13	401	4	2
5	478	5	5	14	332	4	14
6	308	4	7	15	337	4	8
7	397	4	1	16	509	5	6
8	153	3	15	17	177	3	16
9	289	4	3	18	398	4	4
OUT	2,871	36		IN	2,925	35	
				TOTAL	5,796	71	
				STANDARD SCRATCH	68		

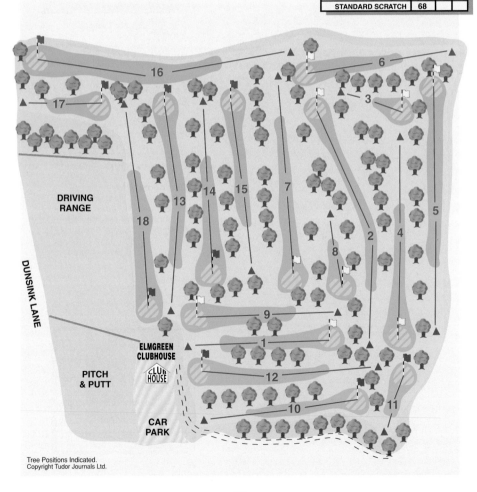

Tree Positions Indicated.
Copyright Tudor Journals Ltd.

Cloghran.
Co. Dublin.
Tel: 8401183 / 8401763.

NO.	MEDAL METRES	GEN. METRES	PAR	S.I.	NO.	MEDAL METRES	GEN. METRES	PAR	S.I.
1	291	278	4	7	10	349	334	4	12
2	377	353	4	5	11	160	143	3	8
3	354	342	4	11	12	324	309	4	4
4	413	374	4	1	13	351	335	4	16
5	171	156	3	9	14	183	170	3	10
6	460	446	5	15	15	450	432	5	18
7	149	126	3	17	16	346	332	4	6
8	400	386	4	3	17	320	304	4	14
9	349	338	4	13	18	418	402	4	2
OUT	2,964	2,799	35		IN	2,901	2,761	35	
					TOTAL	5,865	5,560	70	
		STANDARD SCRATCH				70	69		

LOCATION: Beside Dublin Airport.
SECRETARY / MANAGER: A. J. Greany.
Tel: 8401763.
PROFESSIONAL: Tony Judd.
Tel: 407670.

One of the pre-qualifying courses for the Irish Open. A parkland course sited close to Dublin Airport.

COURSE INFORMATION

Par 70; SSS 70; Length 5,865 metres.
Visitors: Welcome Mon – Fri.
Opening Hours: 8.00am – Sunset.
Avoid: Weekends, Wed & Fri afternoons. Telephone appointment required.
Ladies & Juveniles: Welcome. Handicap certificate required. Lessons, club hire and caddy cars available.
Clubhouse Hours: 8.00am – midnight.
Clubhouse Dress: Casual.
Clubhouse Facilities: Tues & Wed evenings & weekends.
Open Competitions: Open Week June.

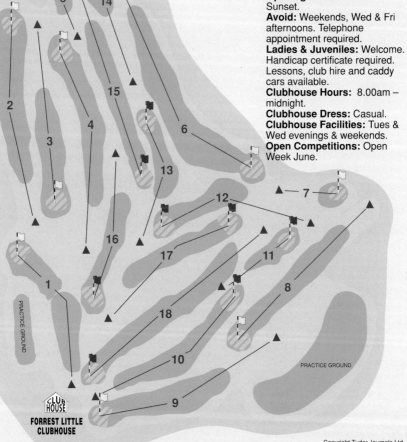

FORREST LITTLE
CLUBHOUSE

Ballydowd, Lucan, Co. Dublin. Tel: 6268491.

LOCATION: 8 miles from Dublin city on main Galway Road.
SECRETARY / MANAGER: Tom Spelman. Tel: 6268491.
PROFESSIONAL: Ciaran Carroll. Tel: 6268072.

This course has a fairly flat front nine and an undulating back nine. The 10th hole is the most scenic, followed by an extremely difficult par 5, bordered on right by the river Liffey and on the left by woodland.

COURSE INFORMATION

Par 71; SSS 71; Length 6,032 metres.
Visitors: Welcome Monday – Friday mornings (except Tuesday).
Opening Hours: 8.00am – Sunset.
Avoid: Weekends.
Ladies: Welcome. Ladies Day Tuesday.
Juveniles: Must be accompanied by an adult, tel. appointment required. Caddy service available; club hire and lessons available by prior arrangement
Green Fees: £25 Mon – Fri. £35 Sat, Sun & Bank Hols.
Clubhouse Hours: 9.00am – midnight
Clubhouse Dress: Casual. No jeans or shorts.
Clubhouse Facilities: Snacks from 10.00am; full restaurant from 12.30pm – 9.30pm.

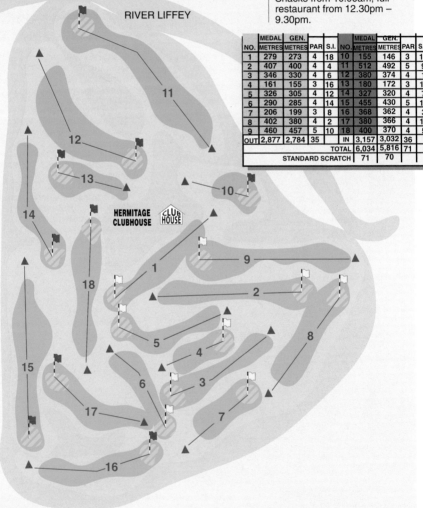

RIVER LIFFEY

NO.	MEDAL METRES	GEN. METRES	PAR	S.I.	NO.	MEDAL METRES	GEN. METRES	PAR	S.I.
1	279	273	4	18	10	155	146	3	15
2	407	400	4	4	11	512	492	5	9
3	346	330	4	6	12	380	374	4	1
4	161	155	3	16	13	180	172	3	11
5	326	305	4	12	14	327	320	4	7
6	290	285	4	14	15	455	430	5	17
7	206	199	3	8	16	368	362	4	3
8	402	380	4	2	17	380	366	4	13
9	460	457	5	10	18	400	370	4	5
OUT	2,877	2,784	35		IN	3,157	3,032	36	
					TOTAL	6,034	5,816	71	
					STANDARD SCRATCH	71	70		

HERMITAGE CLUBHOUSE

Hollystown Golf, Hollystown, Hollywood Rath, Dublin 15.
Tel: (01) 8207444
Fax: (01) 8207447

LOCATION: 10km from Dublin City.
MANAGER: Oliver Barry.
PROFESSIONAL: Adam Whiston.
ARCHITECT: Eddie Hackett.

An inviting green fees only policy gives this new, superb golfing facility a novel attraction. Set in rich natural parkland, well endowed with stately trees, gurgling streams and pleasant ponds, the course has a graceful maturity to please the most discerning golfer. Three testing par 5's, a tricky combination of par 4's and three varying 3's, can make the par 72 an elusive target for those without the right balance of skill, subtlety and aggression.

COURSE INFORMATION

Par72; SSS 70; Length 5,764 metres.
Visitors: Welcome.
Opening Hours: Daylight Hours.
Ladies: Welcome.
Green Fees: £12.50 Weekdays; £16.50 Weekends.
Juveniles: Welcome.
Clubhouse Hours: Daylight Hours.
Clubhouse Dress: Neat.
Clubhouse Facilities: Coffee Shop available.

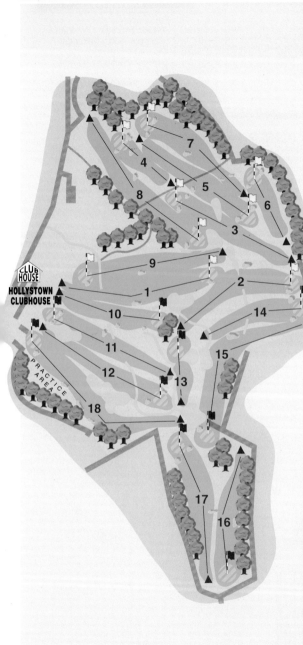

NO.	METRES	PAR	S.I.	NO.	METRES	PAR	S.I.
1	369	4	3	10	291	4	18
2	324	4	11	11	356	4	12
3	307	4	5	12	356	4	2
4	214	3	7	13	147	3	14
5	373	4	1	14	291	4	16
6	134	3	17	15	446	5	6
7	317	4	15	16	322	4	10
8	440	5	9	17	345	4	4
9	283	4	13	18	449	5	8
OUT	2,761	35		IN	3,003	37	
				TOTAL	5,764	72	
	STANDARD SCRATCH			70			

Bunker and tree positions indicated.

Island Golf Club, Corballis, Donabate, Co. Dublin
Tel: 01 8436462.

LOCATION: Corballis.
SECRETARY: Sean Flavin.
Tel: 01 8436205 Fax: 01 8436860.
ARCHITECT: 1990 Redesign, F. Hawtree & E. Hackett.

Enveloped on three sides by the sea, this is a naturally true links course. The 1st, 3rd and 7th are probably the best holes on the outward nine but the most spectacular are to be found on the inward half. The 12th needs an excellent drive while the 13th is a

superb par 3 of 190 metres, requiring a long iron or wood shot to reach a naturally well protected green. The 425 metre par 4 18th offers an excellent challenge with imposing sandhills on both sides.

COURSE INFORMATION

Par 71; SSS 72; Length 6,053 Metres.
Visitors: Welcome Mon, Tues, Wed mornings & Fridays.
Opening Hours: 8.00am – Sunset.

Avoid: Thursday, Wednesday afternoon and weekends except late afternoon.
Ladies: Welcome – Ladies Day Thursday.
Green Fees: £27 Mon – Fri.
Juveniles: Welcome.
Clubhouse Hours: 7.00am – 12.00 midnight (summer); 8.00am – 12.00 midnight (winter).
Clubhouse Dress: Casual. No denims or training shoes.
Clubhouse Facilities: 10.30am – 8.30pm winter. 8.00am - 11.30pm summer.

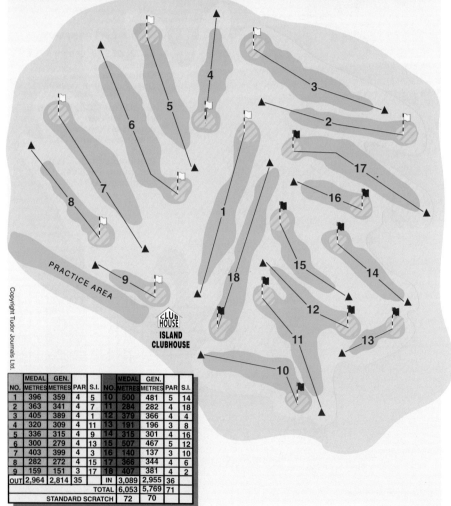

ISLAND CLUBHOUSE

NO.	MEDAL METRES	GEN. METRES	PAR	S.I.	NO.	MEDAL METRES	GEN. METRES	PAR	S.I.
1	396	359	4	5	10	500	481	5	14
2	363	341	4	7	11	284	282	4	18
3	405	389	4	1	12	379	366	4	4
4	320	309	4	11	13	191	196	3	8
5	336	315	4	9	14	315	301	4	16
6	300	279	4	13	15	507	467	5	12
7	403	399	4	3	16	140	137	3	10
8	282	272	4	15	17	366	344	4	6
9	159	151	3	17	18	407	381	4	2
OUT	2,964	2,814	35		IN	3,089	2,955	36	
					TOTAL	6,053	5,769	71	
					STANDARD SCRATCH	72	70		

Killiney Golf Club,
Balinclea Road,
Killiney,
Co. Dublin.
Tel: 01 2851027/2852823.

LOCATION: Killiney.
SECRETARY: Hugh Keegan.
Tel: 01 2852823.
PROFESSIONAL: Paddy O'Boyle.
Tel: 01 2856294.

This parkland course is on the southern side of Killiney Hill, the most scenic area of Co. Dubin. The local terrain while hilly is not too difficult.

COURSE INFORMATION

Par 69; SSS 69; Length 5,626 Metres.
Visitors: Welcome Monday and Tuesday morning; Wednesday, Friday and Sunday afternoons.
Opening Hours: 8.30am – Sunset.
Avoid: Thursdays, Saturdays, Sunday mornings and Tuesday pm.
Ladies: Welcome.
Green Fees: £17 Mon – Fri (£8 with member); £20 Sat/Sun (£10 with member).

Juveniles: Welcome. Lessons available by prior arrangements; Club Hire available; Caddy service available by prior arrangements; Handicap Certificate required.
Clubhouse Hours: 10.00am – 11.00pm. Full clubhouse facilities.
Clubhouse Dress: Casual.
Clubhouse Facilities: Snacks 10.00am – 11.00pm.

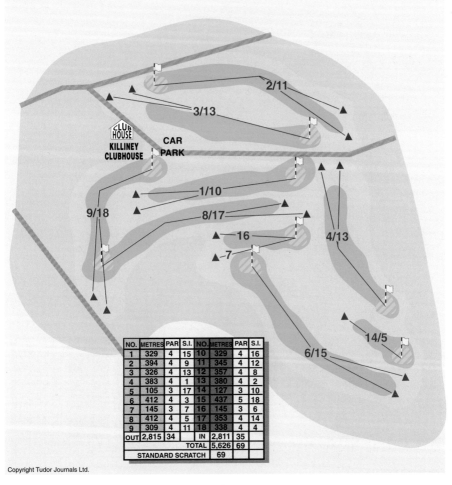

NO.	METRES	PAR	S.I.	NO.	METRES	PAR	S.I.
1	329	4	15	10	329	4	16
2	394	4	9	11	345	4	12
3	326	4	13	12	357	4	8
4	383	4	1	13	380	4	2
5	105	3	17	14	127	3	10
6	412	4	3	15	437	5	18
7	145	3	7	16	145	3	6
8	412	4	5	17	353	4	14
9	309	4	11	18	338	4	4
OUT	2,815	34		IN	2,811	35	
				TOTAL	5,626	69	
STANDARD SCRATCH		69					

KILTERNAN

Kilternan Golf & Country Club Hotel, Enniskerry Road, Kilternan, Co. Dublin.
Tel: 01 2955542
Fax: 2955670.

LOCATION: Kilternan, Co. Dublin.
SECRETARY: Mr Jimmy Kinsella.
Tel: 01 2955542.

A challenging course with spectacular views over Dublin Bay, "Offers every golf shot in the book."

COURSE INFORMATION

Par 68; SSS 67; Length 4,914 Metres.
Visitors: Welcome by booking any time outside competition hours.
Opening Hours: Operates on time sheet only.
Ladies: Welcome.
Green Fees: Mon – Fri £12; Sat/Sun £16 .
Juveniles: Welcome. Lessons available by prior arrangement. Club Hire available. Caddy service

available by prior arrangements.
Clubhouse Hours: Monday – Sunday 8.00am – 11.00pm. Full clubhouse facilities.
Clubhouse Dress: Smart casual, no jeans or training shoes.
Clubhouse Facilities: Mon – Sat 12.30pm – 8.45pm; Sunday 5.30p.m – 8.45pm. Sandwiches are available from 10.30am onwards.

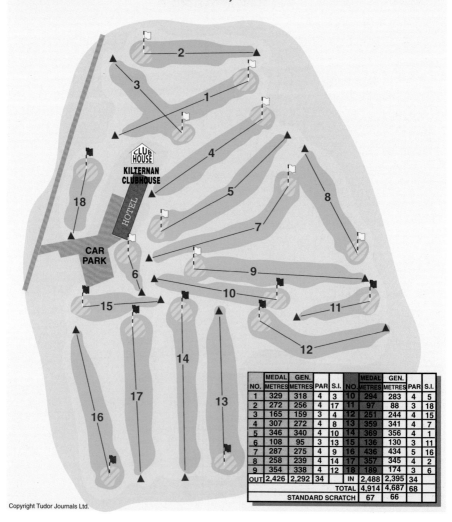

NO.	MEDAL METRES	GEN. METRES	PAR	S.I.	NO.	MEDAL METRES	GEN. METRES	PAR	S.I.
1	329	318	4	3	10	294	283	4	5
2	272	256	4	17	11	97	88	3	18
3	165	159	3	4	12	251	244	4	15
4	307	272	4	8	13	359	341	4	7
5	346	340	4	10	14	369	356	4	1
6	108	95	3	13	15	136	130	3	11
7	287	275	4	9	16	436	434	5	16
8	258	239	4	14	17	357	345	4	2
9	354	338	4	12	18	189	174	3	6
OUT	2,426	2,292	34		IN	2,488	2,395	34	
					TOTAL	4,914	4,687	68	
					STANDARD SCRATCH	67	66		

36

Finnstown Country House Hotel, Newcastle Road, Lucan, Co. Dublin.
Tel: (01) 628 0644.
Fax: (01) 628 1088.

LOCATION: Newcastle Road, Lucan – off the N4.
SECRETARY: Diarmuid Conway.
MANAGER: Elizabeth Duffy.
Tel: (01) 628 0644.
ARCHITECT: Robert Browne.

A parkland 9 hole course where many mature trees have skillfully been brought into play. Many devotees of the game believe Finnstown to be a little gem in the Irish Golfing crown.

It is certainly a challenging course, providing even the best of players with a tough test of golf.

COURSE INFORMATION

Par 66; SSS 66; Length 5,190 metres.
Visitors: Welcome anytime.
Opening Hours: Sunrise – Sunset.
Ladies: Welcome.
Green Fees: £10 Mon – Fri; £12 Sat/Sun/Bank Holidays.
Juveniles: Welcome at certain times. Lessons and club hire available by prior arrangements.

Clubhouse Dress: Neat (no denims allowed).
Clubhouse Facilities: Changing room, bar and restaurant within Finnstown Hotel. Full catering facilities available 7.30am – 9.00pm (booked in advance if possible). Golf buggy available.

NO.	YARDS	PAR	S.I.	NO.	YARDS	PAR	S.I.
1	278	4	11	10	278	4	12
2	313	4	5	11	313	4	6
3	334	4	13	12	334	4	14
4	178	3	15	13	178	3	16
5	165	3	17	14	165	3	18
6	419	4	1	15	419	4	2
7	483	5	9	16	483	5	10
8	230	3	3	17	230	3	4
9	195	3	7	18	195	3	8
OUT	2,595	33		IN	2,595	33	
				TOTAL	5,190	66	
STANDARD SCRATCH		66					

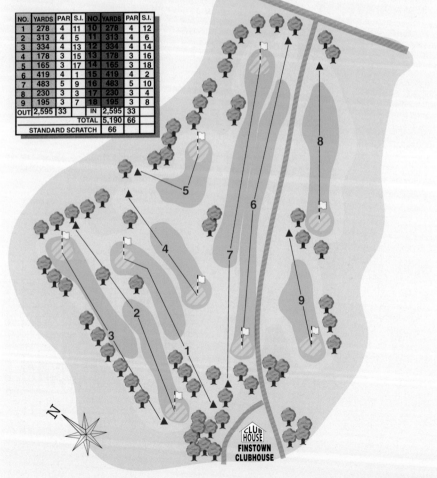

FINNSTOWN
CLUBHOUSE

Tree positions indicated.

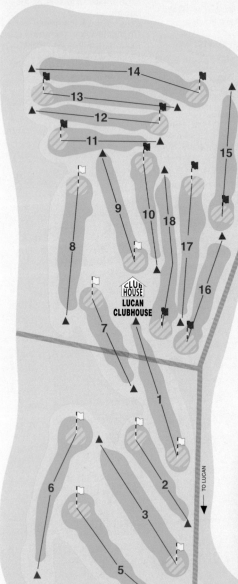

Lucan, Co. Dublin.
Tel: 01 6280106.

LOCATION: 10 miles from Dublin City on Cellbridge Road.
SECRETARY/MANAGER: Tom O'Donnell. Tel: 01 6280106.
CADDYMASTERS: Christy Dobbs/Willie Barr. Tel: 01 6280246.

Lucan Golf Course has an undulating first nine. The first and seventh providing a good test. The back nine which was added in 1988 is fairly flat and has a fine finishing 18th hole of 530 metres.

COURSE INFORMATION

Par 71; SSS 71; Length 5,958 Metres.
Visitors: Monday, Tuesday, Fridays, Wednesdays to 1.00pm.
Opening Hours: Sunrise – Sunset.
Avoid: Weekends.
Ladies: Welcome.
Ladies Day: Thursday.
Green Fees: £16.
Juveniles: Must be accompanied by an adult. Telephone appointment required; Lessons available by prior arrangements; Club Hire available; Caddy service available by prior arrangements.
Clubhouse Hours: 9.00am – 12.00 midnight. Full clubhouse facilities.
Clubhouse Dress: No denims on Course or in Clubhouse.
Clubhouse Facilities: Full bar & resturent facilities. Bar food available.

NO.	MEDAL METRES	GEN. METRES	PAR	S.I.	NO.	MEDAL METRES	GEN. METRES	PAR	S.I.
1	378	369	4	6	10	378	371	4	3
2	336	332	4	8	11	176	169	3	9
3	421	416	4	4	12	299	292	4	17
4	107	107	3	18	13	337	330	4	7
5	440	435	5	14	14	422	415	4	1
6	285	279	4	16	15	341	334	4	13
7	142	138	3	10	16	192	185	3	11
8	369	366	4	2	17	446	439	5	15
9	351	344	4	12	18	538	531	5	5
OUT	2,829	2,786	35		IN	3,129	3,066	36	
					TOTAL	5,958	5,852	71	
					STANDARD SCRATCH	71	70		

Beechwood, The Grange, Malahide, Co. Dublin.

Location: Malahide.
Secretary/Manager: Mr Austin Brogan.
Tel: (01) 8461611/8461270/8461642
Fax: 8461270.
Professional: David Barton.
Tel: 01 8460002.
Architect: E. Hackett.

A championship standard course, which opened to 27 holes in 1990. This parkland course has water as a feature of a number of the holes.

COURSE INFORMATION

Par 70; SSS 72; Length 6,017 metres
Visitors: Welcome.
Opening Hours: Sunrise – Sunset.
Ladies: Welcome. Telephone appointment required.
Green Fees: £25 Mon-Fri; (£9 with member). Weekends & Holidays £35 (£11 with member).
Clubhouse Hours: 9.00am – 12.30am.

Clubhouse Facilities: Full facilities.
Clubhouse Dress: Dining room – jacket and tie after 7.30pm; Lounge and bar – casual.
Open Competitions: August Bank Holiday week.

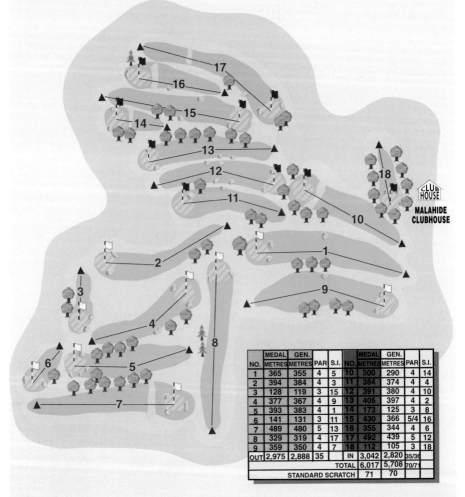

MALAHIDE CLUBHOUSE

	MEDAL METRES	GEN. METRES	PAR	S.I.	NO.	MEDAL METRES	GEN. METRES	PAR	S.I.
1	365	355	4	5	10	300	290	4	14
2	394	384	4	3	11	384	374	4	4
3	128	119	3	15	12	391	380	4	10
4	377	367	4	9	13	405	397	4	2
5	393	383	4	1	14	173	125	3	8
6	141	131	3	11	15	430	366	5/4	16
7	489	480	5	13	16	355	344	4	6
8	329	319	4	17	17	492	439	5	12
9	359	350	4	7	18	112	105	3	18
OUT	2,975	2,888	35		IN	3,042	2,820	35/36	
					TOTAL	6,017	5,708	70/71	
					STANDARD SCRATCH	71	70		

Bunker and tree positions indicated.

39

**Clondalkin,
Dublin, 22.
Tel: 4592903/4593157.
Fax: 4593498.**

LOCATION: Dublin.
SECRETARY / MANAGER:
A.T. O'Neill.
Tel: 4593157/4593498.
ARCHITECT: James Braid.

Attractive, mature parkland course. The careful placing of trees, bunkers and other hazards soon dispels any feeling of complacency, even with the most accomplished of players.

COURSE INFORMATION

Par 71; SSS 70; Length 5,714 metres.
Visitors: Welcome Monday, Wednesday (am), Thursday, Friday.
Opening Hours: 9.00am – Sunset.
Avoid: Tuesday, Saturday, Sunday.
Ladies: Welcome.
Juveniles: Welcome. Must be accompanied by an adult. Lessons available by prior arrangements; club hire available; telephone

appointment required.
Green Fees: £25 Mon – Fri (£9 with member) Societies £23.
Clubhouse Hours: 7.30am – 12.30pm. Full clubhouse facilities.
Clubhouse Dress: Casual. Jacket and tie after 8.00pm.
Clubhouse Facilities: Summer 10.00am – 9.30pm; Winter 10.00am – 6.00pm..
Open Competitions: Husband and wife mixed foursomes.

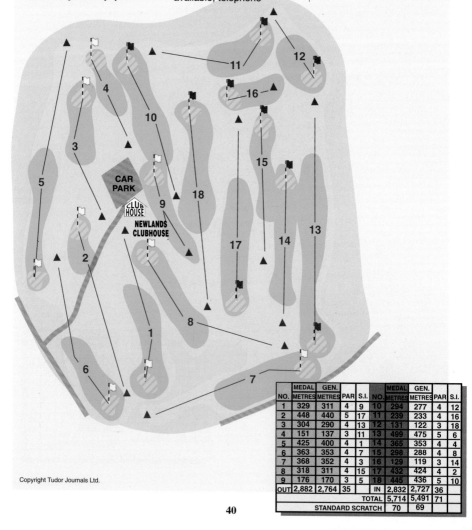

NO.	MEDAL METRES	GEN. METRES	PAR	S.I.	NO.	MEDAL METRES	GEN. METRES	PAR	S.I.
1	329	311	4	9	10	294	277	4	12
2	448	440	5	17	11	239	233	4	16
3	304	290	4	13	12	131	122	3	18
4	151	137	3	11	13	499	475	5	6
5	425	400	4	1	14	365	353	4	4
6	363	353	4	7	15	298	288	4	8
7	368	352	4	3	16	129	119	3	14
8	318	311	4	15	17	432	424	4	2
9	176	170	3	5	18	445	436	5	10
OUT	2,882	2,764	35		IN	2,832	2,727	36	
					TOTAL	5,714	5,491	71	
					STANDARD SCRATCH	70	69		

Old Conna, Ferndale Road, Bray,
Tel: 01 2826055/2826766.
Fax: 01 2825611.

LOCATION: Two miles north of Bray.
SECRETARY: Dave Diviney.
Tel: 01 2826055/2826766.
PROFESSIONAL: Paul McDaid.
Tel: 01 2720022.
ARCHITECT: E. Hackett

The course was recently constructed and will naturally take time to mature. Well laid out and convenient to the south Dublin area. This attractive parkland course, should become one of the regions premier inland courses in the near future.

COURSE INFORMATION

Par 72; SSS 71; Length 6,551 yards.
Visitors: Welcome Mon – Fri 9.00am – 4.00pm (closed 12.30pm – 2.00pm).
Opening Hours: Sunrise – Sunset.
Avoid: Tuesday, Wednesday, Saturday & Sunday.
Ladies: Welcome.
Green Fees: £20 N/A Saturday & Sunday.
Juveniles: Must be accompanied by an adult. Lessons available by prior arrangement; Caddy Service available by prior arrangement.

Clubhouse Hours: 10.30am – 11.30pm; Full clubhouse facilities.
Clubhouse Dress: Neat attire essential.
Clubhouse Facilities: Menu available 12.00 noon – 9.30pm. Phone: Mr. P Coleman 2820038.
Open Competitions: Open Week: June / July.

NO.	MEDAL YARDS	GEN. YARDS	PAR	S.I.	NO.	MEDAL YARDS	GEN. YARDS	PAR	S.I.
1	376	362	4	9	10	344	318	4	17
2	236	221	3	8	11	353	340	4	7
3	320	305	4	16	12	163	149	3	13
4	546	532	5	4	13	565	550	5	5
5	582	574	5	2	14	292	278	4	11
6	373	360	4	10	15	475	461	4	1
7	382	368	4	6	16	437	424	4	3
8	112	127	3	18	17	160	146	3	12
9	336	314	4	14	18	489	476	4	15
OUT	3,273	3,163	36		IN	3,278	3,142	36	
					TOTAL	6,551	6,305	72	
					STANDARD SCRATCH	71	70		

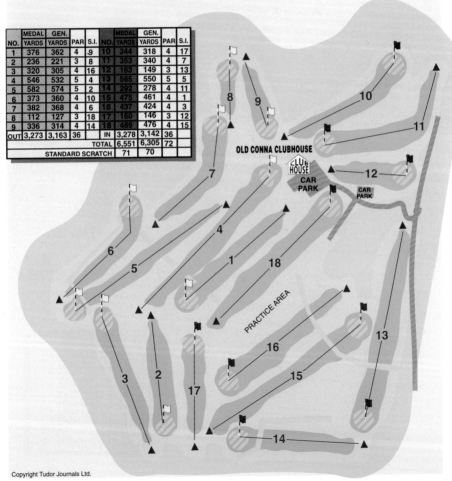

OLD CONNA CLUBHOUSE

**Newtown House,
St. Margaret's, Co. Dublin.
Tel: (01) 8640324.**

LOCATION: Between Derry Rd,
N2 and the St. Margaret's Rd,
by Dublin Airport.
SECRETARY / PROFESSIONAL: Mr
R. Yates.
Tel: (01) 8640324.
ARCHITECT: Martin Hawtree.

Parkland course with large well
guarded greens. Driving range and
large tuition staff – excellent pro shop.
Full range of hire equipment and full
tee time reservation system.

COURSE INFORMATION

**Par 71; SSS 71; Length
6,532 yards.
Visitors:** Welcome at any
time. Bookings may be made
48hrs in advance by telephone.

Ladies: Welcome at any time.
Juveniles: Welcome at any
time.
Green Fees: £7.60 – 18 hole
& £6.50 – 9 hole (mid week).
£11.50 – 18 holes & £8.50 – 9
holes (weekends & Bank
Holidays).
Clubhouse Facilities: Golf
shop & coffee shop.

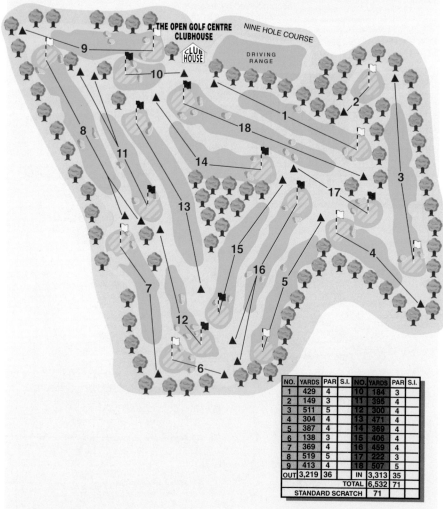

THE OPEN GOLF CENTRE
CLUBHOUSE

NINE HOLE COURSE

DRIVING RANGE

NO.	YARDS	PAR	S.I.	NO.	YARDS	PAR	S.I.
1	429	4		10	184	3	
2	149	3		11	395	4	
3	511	5		12	300	4	
4	304	4		13	471	4	
5	387	4		14	369	4	
6	138	3		15	406	4	
7	369	4		16	459	4	
8	519	5		17	222	3	
9	413	4		18	507	5	
OUT	3,219	36		IN	3,313	35	
				TOTAL	6,532	71	
				STANDARD SCRATCH		71	

Bunker & tree positions indicated.

Portmarnock, Co. Dublin.
Tel: 8462968/Fax: 8462601.

LOCATION: North east of Dublin city.
SECRETARY: John Quigley.
Tel: 8462968.
PROFESSIONAL: Joey Purcell.
Tel: 8462634.

One of the premium links courses in the country. Venue for the Irish Open Championaship and given world championship ranking by many critics. The sandy soil of the Portmarnock peninsula makes it ideal for golf. Now has 27 holes with room for more. Its potential as a golf links was realised in 1894. Within two years of the opening of the 18 hole course, Portmarnock hosted its first tournament, the Irish Open Amateur Championship and has hosted the prestigious Irish Open Championship many times since then and was also host for the Walker Cup.

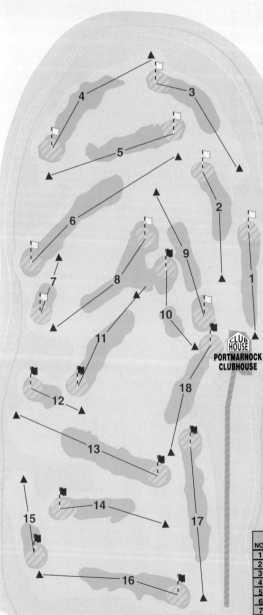

COURSE INFORMATION

Par 72; SSS 75; Length 6,497 metres.
Visitors: No.
Opening Hours: 8.00am – Sunset.
Avoid: Weekends & Bank Holidays.
Ladies: Welcome. Lessons available by prior arrangements. Caddy service available by prior arrangement. Handicap certificate required. Prior arrangement preferred.
Green Fees: Mon – Fri £40 (with member £10); Sat, Sun & Bank Hols £50 (with member £15).
Clubhouse Hours: 8.00am – 10.30pm.
Clubhouse Dress: Jacket and tie to be worn in clubhouse.
Clubhouse Facilities: From 10.30am onwards. Breakfast, lunches & evening meals.

NO.	MEDAL METRES	GEN. METRES	PAR	S.I.	NO.	MEDAL METRES	GEN. METRES	PAR	S.I.
1	355	340	4	13	10	341	333	4	8
2	346	326	4	15	11	392	379	4	2
3	351	345	4	11	12	139	129	3	18
4	403	398	4	1	13	516	502	5	41
5	364	347	4	5	14	350	343	4	6
6	550	533	5	9	15	173	167	3	12
7	168	156	3	17	16	480	470	5	16
8	364	346	4	7	17	429	397	4	4
9	399	381	4	3	18	377	359	4	10
OUT	3,300	3,172	36		IN	3,197	3,079	36	
					TOTAL	6,497	6,251	72	
					STANDARD SCRATCH		75	74	

NEW LISTING

NO.	CHAMP METRES	MEDAL METRES	PAR	S.I.	NO.	CHAMP METRES	MEDAL METRES	PAR	S.I.
1	320	304	4	14	10	329	316	4	5
2	329	305	4	10	11	137	135	3	17
3	178	172	3	12	12	419	406	4	1
4	527	512	5	6	13	484	467	5	15
5	431	409	4	2	14	317	312	4	13
6	486	462	5	18	15	364	352	4	7
7	412	405	4	4	16	371	354	4	11
8	342	323	4	8	17	185	171	3	9
9	156	139	3	16	18	408	365	4	3
OUT	3,181	3,031	36		IN	3,041	2,878	35	
					TOTAL	6,195	5,909	71	
					STANDARD SCRATCH	73	72		

**PORTMARNOCK
HOTEL & CLUBHOUSE**

Portmarnock Hotel & Golf Links, Strand Road, Portmarnock, Co. Dublin.
Tel: (01) 8461800.
Fax: (01) 8461077.

LOCATION: 15 minutes from Dublin Airport, 25 minutes from Dublin City Centre.
GOLF DIRECTOR: Moira Cassidy.
Tel: (01) 8461800.
DESIGNER: Bernhard Langer.
ARCHITECT: Stan Eby.

The first course designed by Bernhard Langer and the only P.G.A. European Tour course in Ireland. The links takes advantage of the natural beauty and immeasurable quality of the landscape. Accommodation is available in the Portmarnock Hotel & Golf Links.

COURSE INFORMATION

Par 71; SSS 73; Length 6,195 Metres.
Visitors: Welcome
Handicap Certificate required.
Opening Hours: 7.30am – Sunset.
Green Fees: Hotel Residents: 18 holes £26.00, Day Ticket £40.00 Mon – Fri. 18 holes £33.00, Day Ticket £48.00 Weekend/Public Holidays.
Non Residents:
18 Holes £35.00, Day Ticket £55.00 Mon – Fri. 18 Holes £45.00, Day Ticket £65.00 Weekend/Public Holidays.
Juveniles: Welcome, must be accompanied by an adult;
Clubhouse Hours: 7.00am – 11.30pm.
Clubhouse facilities:
Catering facilities all day.
Club hire available; Trolley hire available; Caddy service available by prior arrangement.

44

RUSH

L E I N S T E R **DUBLIN**

Rush, Dublin.
Tel: 01 8437548.
Fax: 01 8438177.

LOCATION: Seaside.
SECRETARY: B. Clear
Tel: 01 8438177.

Links course which is playable all year round. Good greens protected by pot bunkers, with undulating fairways. Alternate tees except on two par 3's.

COURSE INFORMATION

Par 70; SSS 69; Length 5,598 Metres.
Visitors: Welcome Monday, Tuesday, Friday.
Opening Hours: 8am – Sunset.
Avoid: Wednesday, Thursday, weekends.
Ladies: Welcome.

Green Fees: £15 (£6 With member).
Juveniles: Welcome.
Clubhouse Hours: 11.00am – 11.00pm.
Clubhouse Dress: Casual. No jeans or shorts allowed.
Clubhouse Facilities: Available on request.
Open Competitions: Seniors only on third Friday in May each year.

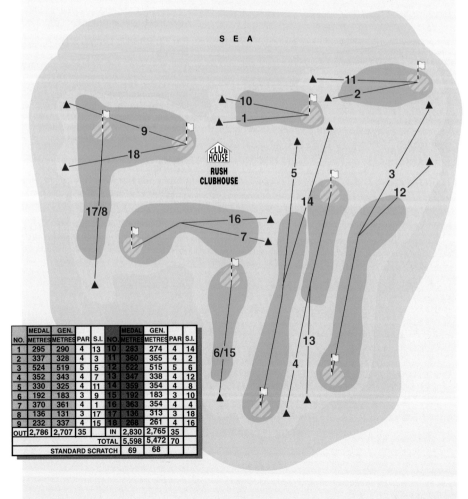

NO.	MEDAL METRES	GEN. METRES	PAR	S.I.	NO.	MEDAL METRES	GEN. METRES	PAR	S.I.
1	295	290	4	13	10	283	274	4	14
2	337	328	4	3	11	360	355	4	2
3	524	519	5	5	12	522	515	5	6
4	352	343	4	7	13	347	338	4	12
5	330	325	4	11	14	359	354	4	8
6	192	183	3	9	15	192	183	3	10
7	370	361	4	1	16	363	354	4	4
8	136	131	3	17	17	136	313	3	18
9	232	337	4	15	18	268	261	4	16
OUT	2,786	2,707	35		IN	2,830	2,765	35	
					TOTAL	5,598	5,472	70	
					STANDARD SCRATCH		69	68	

45

NO.	MEDAL METRES	GEN. METRES	PAR	S.I.	NO.	MEDAL METRES	GEN. METRES	PAR	S.I.
1	379	369	4	5	10	356	346	4	6
2	157	147	3	13	11	266	256	4	16
3	396	386	4	1	12	132	122	3	18
4	420	410	5	17	13	367	357	4	2
5	393	383	4	3	14	448	438	5	12
6	475	465	5	9	15	143	133	3	10
7	145	135	3	7	16	372	362	4	8
8	480	470	5	15	17	491	481	5	14
9	321	311	4	11	18	372	362	4	4
OUT	3,166	3,076	37		IN	2,947	2,857	36	
					TOTAL	6,113	5,933	72	
					STANDARD SCRATCH	72	71		

Hackestown, Skerries, Co. Dublin.
Tel: 8491567/8491204. Fax: 8491591.

LOCATION: 20 miles north of Dublin.
MANAGER: Aiden Burns.
Tel: 8491567.
PROFESSIONAL: Jimmy Kinsella.
Tel: 8490925.

A rolling parkland course with splendid views of the coastline. Many of the holes demand accuracy from the tee to the green. The 12th (par 3) and 18th (par 4) are particularly attractive holes. The newer 4th (par 5), 6th (par 5) and 7th (par 3) have enhanced the course as a good test of golf.

COURSE INFORMATION

Par 72; SSS 72; Length 6,113 Metres.
Visitors: Welcome Mon-Fri.
Avoid: Wednesday afternoons, weekends, Tuesday after 4.30pm. Members hour 1.00pm – 2pm.
Opening Hours: Sunrise – Sunset.
Ladies: Welcome.
Green Fees: £17 weekdays & £22 Weekends (reduction before 8.30am).
Juveniles: Must be accompanied by an adult.
Clubhouse Hours: 9am – 11.30pm.
Clubhouse Dress: Casual.
Clubhouse Facilities: Snacks lunches, dinner available daily.
Open Competitions: Junior Scratch Cup – May; Intermediate scratch cup – June; Open Week – July.

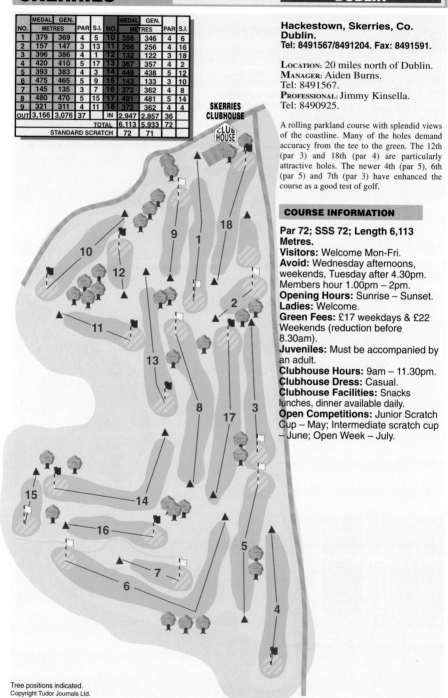

SKERRIES CLUBHOUSE

Tree positions indicated.
Copyright Tudor Journals Ltd.

NO.	MEDAL METRES	GEN. METRES	PAR	S.I.	NO.	MEDAL METRES	GEN. METRES	PAR	S.I.
1	400	369	4	4	10	395	383	4	3
2	168	162	3	12	11	373	371	4	1
3	330	324	4	10	12	330	320	4	15
4	251	243	4	16	13	101	90	3	17
5	119	100	3	14	14	285	279	4	13
6	276	251	4	5	15	335	325	4	9
7	440	423	5	18	16	356	344	4	7
8	280	275	4	8	17	170	164	3	11
9	395	383	4	2	18	384	375	5	5
OUT	2,659	2,530	35		IN	2,729	2,651	34	
					TOTAL	5,388	5,181	69	
					STANDARD SCRATCH	68	67		

**Lynch Park, Brittas,
Co. Dublin.
Tel: 01 4582207/4582183.**

SECRETARY: Pat Maguire.
Tel: 01 4582183.
ARCHITECT: W. Sullivan &
D. O'Brien.

Not a particularly demanding course, but the scenic views make for a very pleasant and relaxing game with some interesting holes. A "take it easy" course.

COURSE INFORMATION

Par 69; SSS 68; Length 5,388 Metres.
Visitors: Welcome Monday, Thursday, Friday.
Opening Hours: Sunrise – Sunset.
Avoid: Weekends.
Ladies: Welcome.
Ladies Day: Tuesday.
Green Fees: Weekdays – £16 (£7 with a member) before noon, £16 (£8 with a member) afternoon; Weekends – £25 (£12.50 with a member).
Juveniles: Welcome.
Clubhouse Hours: 8.30am – 12.00 midnight; Full clubhouse facilities.
Clubhouse Dress: Neat dress.
Clubhouse Facilities: All day.

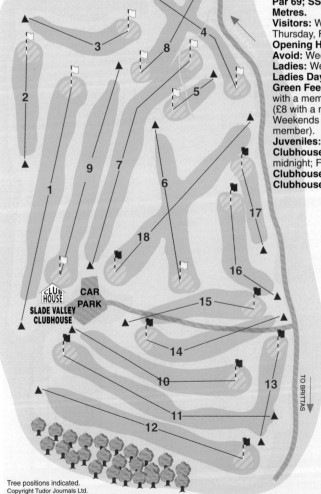

CLUB HOUSE CAR PARK
SLADE VALLEY CLUBHOUSE
TO BRITTAS

Tree positions indicated.
Copyright Tudor Journals Ltd.

STEPASIDE

**Kilternan, Co. Dublin.
Tel: 952859.**

LOCATION: Eight miles south of Dublin City.
SECRETARY: D. Scannell.
Tel: 2952859.
ARCHITECT: E. Hackett.

This course was constructed in 1981 by the joint efforts of the Dublin County Council and G.U.I. who contributed to the construction costs of the course. It is popular both from the availability and the standard of the course.

COURSE INFORMATION

Par 74; SSS 70; Length 5,848 Metres.
Visitors: Welcome.
Opening Hours: 8 o'clock – Sunset.
Ladies: Welcome.
Green Fees: £7 Mon – Fri; £9 Sat/Sun. Senior Citizens, Students and unemployed £3.00.
Juveniles: Welcome.
Clubhouse Hours: 8am – Sunset.

Clubhouse Dress: Casual.
Clubhouse Facilities:
Snacks available.

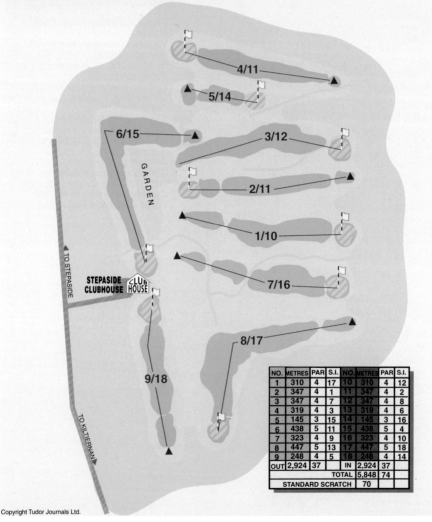

NO.	METRES	PAR	S.I.	NO.	METRES	PAR	S.I.
1	310	4	17	10	310	4	12
2	347	4	1	11	347	4	2
3	347	4	7	12	347	4	8
4	319	4	3	13	319	4	6
5	145	3	15	14	145	3	16
6	438	5	11	15	438	5	4
7	323	4	9	16	323	4	10
8	447	5	13	17	447	5	18
9	248	4	5	18	248	4	14
OUT	2,924	37		IN	2,924	37	
				TOTAL	5,848	74	
STANDARD SCRATCH					70		

Westmanstown, Clonsilla, Dublin 15.
Tel: 8205817.
Fax: 8207891.

LOCATION: Two miles from Lucan Village.
HON. SECRETARY: Jim Tymond.
Tel: 8210562.
ARCHITECT: Mr Eddie Hackett.

Short flat parkland course which has recently undergone additional development.

COURSE INFORMATION
Par 71; SSS 70; Length 5,819 Metres.
Visitors: Welcome except Sat and Sun.
Opening Hours: 8am – Sunset.
Ladies: Welcome.
Green Fees: Weekdays £15; Sat, Sun & Bank Hols £20.
Clubhouse Hours: 7.30am - 12.30pm.

Clubhouse Dress: Neat dress essential on course.
Clubhouse Facilities: Full bar and catering facilities all year.
Open Competitions: Invitation Four Ball every Wednesday.

NO.	MEDAL METRES	GEN. METRES	PAR	S.I.	NO.	MEDAL METRES	GEN. METRES	PAR	S.I.
1	279	260	4	12	10	462	447	5	11
2	333	321	4	8	11	263	254	4	17
3	140	126	3	10	12	170	155	3	7
4	437	427	5	14	13	415	400	4	1
5	368	353	4	6	14	426	411	4	3
6	132	117	3	16	15	493	478	5	9
7	411	396	4	2	16	301	286	4	15
8	371	356	4	4	17	368	353	4	5
9	135	125	3	18	18	315	304	4	13
OUT	2,606	2,481	34		IN	3,213	3,088	37	
					TOTAL	5,819	5,569	71	
	STANDARD SCRATCH					70	69		

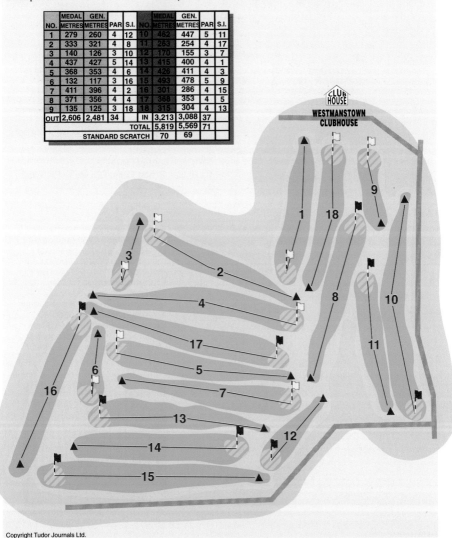

WESTMANSTOWN CLUBHOUSE

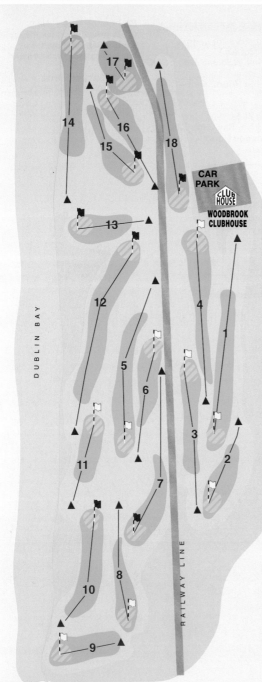

Woodbrook Golf Club, Dublin Road, Bray, Co. Wicklow Tel: 2824799.

LOCATION: Eleven Miles south of Dublin City on N11.
SECRETARY: Derek Smyth.
Tel: 2824799 Fax: 2821950.
PROFESSIONAL: Billy Kinsella.

Whilst the course is beside the sea, it is not a links course. The club prides itself with the standard of the course at all times and is a reasonable test of golf. Well suited to high handicappers.

COURSE INFORMATION

Par 72; SSS 71; Length 5,996 Metres.
Visitors: Welcome weekdays and occasional weekends.
Opening Hours: Sunrise – Sunset.
Avoid: Tuesdays and Bank Holidays.
Ladies: Welcome.
Green Fees: £25 Mon - Fri; £35 Sat/Sun & Public Holidays.
Juveniles: Welcome. Lessons available by prior arrangement; Club hire available; Caddy service available by prior arrangement; Letter of introduction required (if possible); Handicap certificate required; Telephone appointment required.
Clubhouse Hours: 8.00am - 12 midnight.
Clubhouse Dress: Jacket and tie in restaurant after 5.00pm.
Clubhouse Facilities: 10.00am - 9.00pm (with some exceptions in winter); Full restaurant facilities.

NO.	METRES	PAR	S.I.	NO.	METRES	PAR	S.I.
1	457	5	12	10	404	4	1
2	175	3	6	11	195	3	7
3	345	4	8	12	476	5	11
4	360	4	4	13	157	3	13
5	459	5	16	14	475	5	9
6	315	4	10	15	396	4	3
7	397	4	2	16	462	5	15
8	325	4	14	17	127	3	17
9	125	3	18	18	346	4	5
OUT	2,958	36		IN	3,038	36	
				TOTAL	5,996	72	
				STANDARD SCRATCH		71	

**Carrickmines,
Dublin 18.
Tel: 2955972/2955941.**

LOCATION: Carrickmines.
SECRETARY: J.N.S. Pickering.
Tel: 4922960.

Nine hole inland course situated on hilly country approximately six miles from Dublin. Alternate tees are used in summer.

COURSE INFORMATION

**Par 71; SSS 69; Length
6,103 yards.
Visitors:** Welcome.
Opening Hours: 8.30am – Sunset.
Avoid: Saturday and Wednesday.
Ladies: Welcome.
Green Fees: £17 week days; £20 Sundays.

Juveniles: Must be accompanied by a responsible adult.
Clubhouse Hours: 8.30am - 11.30pm.
Clubhouse Dress: Casual.
Clubhouse Facilities: Limited.

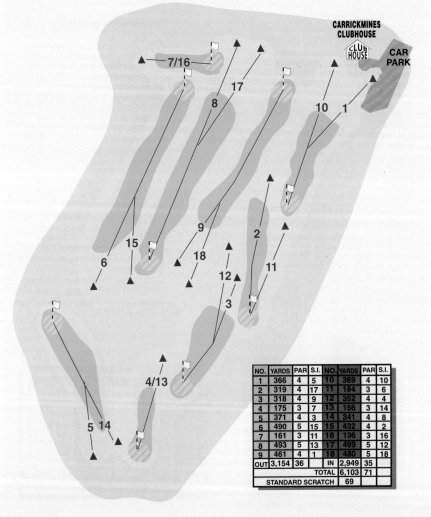

NO.	YARDS	PAR	S.I.	NO.	YARDS	PAR	S.I.
1	366	4	5	10	369	4	10
2	319	4	17	11	184	3	6
3	318	4	9	12	352	4	4
4	175	3	7	13	156	3	14
5	371	4	3	14	341	4	8
6	490	5	15	15	432	4	2
7	161	3	11	16	136	3	16
8	493	5	13	17	499	5	12
9	461	4	1	18	480	5	18
OUT	3,154	36		IN	2,949	35	
				TOTAL	6,103	71	
STANDARD SCRATCH					69		

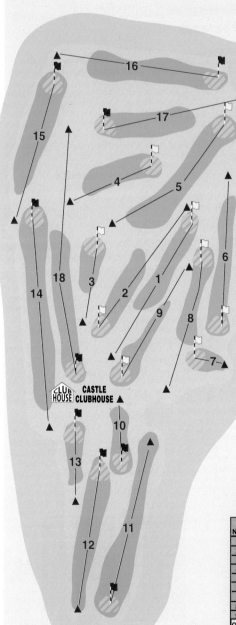

Castle Golf Club, Woodside Drive, Rathfarnham, Dublin 14. Tel: 4904207.

LOCATION: Between Rathfarnham & Churchtown.
SECRETARY: L. Blackburne.
Tel: 4905835.
PROFESSIONAL: D. Kinsella.
Tel: 4920272.
ARCHITECT: Barcroft Pickman & Hood.

Very tight fairways – the Par 4 6th hole regarded as one of the most difficult and yet attractive golf holes. Spectacular views from the Clubhouse.

COURSE INFORMATION

Par 70; SSS 69; Length 5,653 metres.
Visitors: Welcome Monday, Thursday, Friday.
Opening Hours: Sunrise – Sunset.
Avoid: Tuesday, Wednesday afternoons and weekends.
Ladies: As Visitors. Lessons available by prior arrangements; Caddy service available by prior arrangments; Telephone appointment required 4933444.
Green Fees: £25
Juveniles: As Visitors. Lessons available by prior arrangements; Caddy service available by prior arrangements; Telephone appointment required 4933444.
Clubhouse Hours: 8.30am – 11.30pm; Full clubhouse facilities.
Clubhouse Dress: Jacket and tie in Dining Room.
Clubhouse Facilities: 10.00am – 10.30pm, lunch, dinner, snacks.
Open Competitions: Ladies Open; Father & Son.

NO.	MEDAL METRES	GEN. METRES	PAR	S.I.	NO.	MEDAL METRES	GEN. METRES	PAR	S.I.
1	445	436	5	9	10	213	196	3	6
2	391	388	4	5	11	386	361	4	2
3	130	113	3	17	12	315	304	4	10
4	286	276	4	13	13	117	107	3	18
5	333	326	4	7	14	339	328	4	8
6	374	360	4	1	15	166	161	3	16
7	162	150	3	15	16	461	450	5	12
8	308	295	4	11	17	448	440	5	14
9	411	392	4	3	18	376	369	4	4
OUT	2,540	2,736	35		IN	2,803	2,716	35	
						TOTAL	5,653	5,452	70
						STANDARD SCRATCH		69	68	

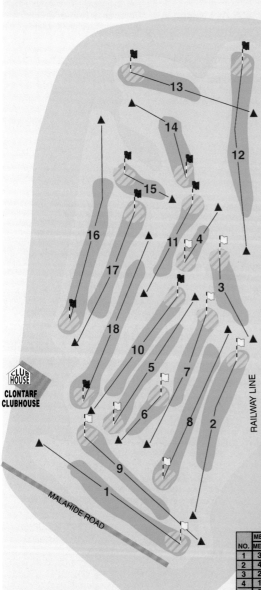

Clontarf Golf Club, Donnycarney House, Malahide Road, Dublin 3. Tel: 8331892.

LOCATION: Two miles from City Centre.
PROFESSIONAL: Joe Craddock. Tel: 331877.
ARCHITECT: Barcroft Pickman & Hood.

A pleasant parkland course with a quarry hole as a special feature. Convenient city course with good access.

COURSE INFORMATION

Par 69; SSS 68; Length 5,459 Metres.
Visitors: Welcome Mon – Fri (telephone first).
Opening Hours: Sunrise – Sunset.
Avoid: Monday.
Ladies: Welcome.
Ladies Day: Wednesday aftrenoon.
Green Fees: £15 (£8 with a member).
Juveniles: Must be accompanied by an adult, if not before 10.00am. Lessons available by prior arrangements; Caddy service available occasionally by prior arrangement.
Clubhouse Hours: 9.00am – 12.00pm; Full clubhouse facilities.
Clubhouse Dress: Casual (no jeans/sneakers). Collar and tie after 8pm.
Clubhouse Facilities: Catering facilities: launches and snacks.
Open Competitions: Mixed Foursomes (Matchplay) May; AIB Lord Mayors Cup (Junior Matchplay) August.

NO.	MEDAL METRES	GEN. METRES	PAR	S.I.	NO.	MEDAL METRES	GEN. METRES	PAR	S.I.
1	324	294	4	10	10	385	351	4	7
2	414	404	4	2	11	187	169	3	11
3	287	272	4	14	12	381	377	4	1
4	151	139	3	12	13	267	361	4	15
5	338	327	4	6	14	329	299	4	3
6	122	112	3	18	15	145	130	3	17
7	339	309	4	8	16	351	336	4	5
8	356	347	4	2	17	356	340	4	9
9	295	272	4	16	18	452	439	5	13
OUT	2,626	2,476	34		IN	2,833	2,702	35	
					TOTAL	5,459	5,178	69	
					STANDARD SCRATCH	68	67		

53

DEERPARK

**Deerpark Hotel,
Howth, Co. Dublin.
Tel: 8322624.**

LOCATION: Howth Head.
SECRETARY: David Tighe.

A busy course with both visitors and holiday-makers, especially during August, well served by the adjacent Deer Park Hotel.

COURSE INFORMATION

**Par 72; SSS 73; Length 6,174 Metres.
Visitors:** Welcome.
Opening Hours: 7.30am – Sunset (weekdays) & 6.30 – Sunset (Weekends).
Ladies: Welcome.
Green Fees: £7.90 Mon – Fri; £9.95 Sat/Sun (18 holes).

Juveniles: Welcome. Club hire available.
Clubhouse Hours: Sunrise – Sunset. Full Hotel facilities.

NO.	MEDAL METRES	GEN. METRES	PAR	S.I.	NO.	MEDAL METRES	GEN. METRES	PAR	S.I.
1	382	367	4	9	10	399	345	4	2
2	197	187	3	5	11	173	158	3	12
3	306	280	4	17	12	360	340	4	8
4	335	315	4	13	13	285	258	4	16
5	372	352	4	3	14	510	490	5	4
6	190	180	3	7	15	153	141	3	18
7	467	452	5	11	16	312	290	4	10
8	395	375	4	1	17	375	363	4	14
9	477	450	5	15	18	488	470	5	6
OUT	3,120	2,959	36		IN	3,084	2,855	36	
					TOTAL	6,174	5,814	72	
					STANDARD SCRATCH	73	71		

Bunker & tree positions indicated.

**Edmondstown Golf Club,
Edmondstown, Dublin 16
Tel: 4932461.**

Hon. Secretary: Peter Kutner.
Tel: 4931082.
Manager: Selwyn S. Davies.
Professional: A. Crofton.
Tel: 4941049.

An elevated parkland course with a fair
but testing reputation, situated in the
Dublin suburbs.

COURSE INFORMATION

**Par 70; SSS 69; Length 6,195
Yards, 5,663 metres.**
Visitors: Welcome to play
Monday – Friday.
Opening Hours: 8.00am –
11.30pm.
Ladies: Welcome.
Green Fees: £20.00 Mon – Fri;
£25 Sat/Sun (by appointment).
Lessons and caddy service
available by prior arrangement.
2nd week in July Festival Week.
Juveniles: Must be
accompanied by an adult.
Clubhouse Hours: 8.00am –
11.30pm.
Clubhouse Dress: Collar and
tie in restaurant. Neat casual
dress on course. No denim
jeans.
Clubhouse Facilities: Coffee
and snacks available 9.00am
onwards. Lunch: 12.30pm –
2pm. Dinner 6.30pm – 11.00pm
to order if later.

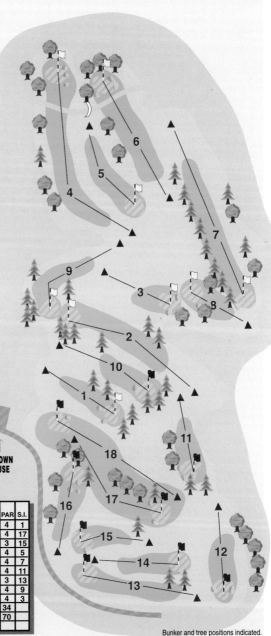

CAR
PARK

EDMONSTOWN
CLUBHOUSE

NO.	MEDAL METRES	GEN. METRES	PAR	S.I.	NO.	MEDAL METRES	GEN. METRES	PAR	S.I.
1	295	280	4	16	10	375	360	4	1
2	339	324	4	8	11	268	253	4	17
3	130	115	3	18	12	143	128	3	15
4	507	492	5	6	13	367	352	4	5
5	391	376	4	2	14	321	306	4	7
6	368	353	4	4	15	319	304	4	11
7	462	447	5	14	16	139	124	3	13
8	181	166	3	12	17	326	311	4	9
9	314	299	4	10	18	418	403	4	3
OUT	2,987	2,852	36		IN	2,676	2,541	34	
					TOTAL	5,663	5,393	70	
				STANDARD SCRATCH		69	68		

Bunker and tree positions indicated.

Elm Park, Nutley House, Nutley Lane, Donnybrook, Dublin 4.

LOCATION: Three miles from City Centre.
SECRETARY: Adrian McCormack.
Tel: 2693438 Fax: 2694505.
PROFESSIONAL: Seamus Green.
Tel: 2692650.

Attractive parkland course, made difficult at times with trees. A stream flows through the course and affects nine holes. Precision rather than distance is required. An interesting course for all levels of golfers.

COURSE INFORMATION

Par 69; SSS 68; Length 5,422 yards.
Visitors: Welcome – please phone for appointment.
Opening Hours: Sunrise – Sunset.
Avoid: Weekends.
Ladies: Welcome.
Green Fees: £40 Mon – Fri; £45 Sat/Sun.
Juveniles: Welcome. Lessons available by prior arrangements; Club Hire available; Caddy Service available; Handicap Certificate required.
Clubhouse Hours: During licensing hours. Full clubhouse facilities.
Clubhouse Dress: Jacket and tie in Dining room.
Clubhouse Facilities: Lunch 12.30 – 2.00pm; Dinner 6.00pm – 9.00pm.
Open Competitions: Open mixed foursomes – Matchplay combined handicap limit 20.

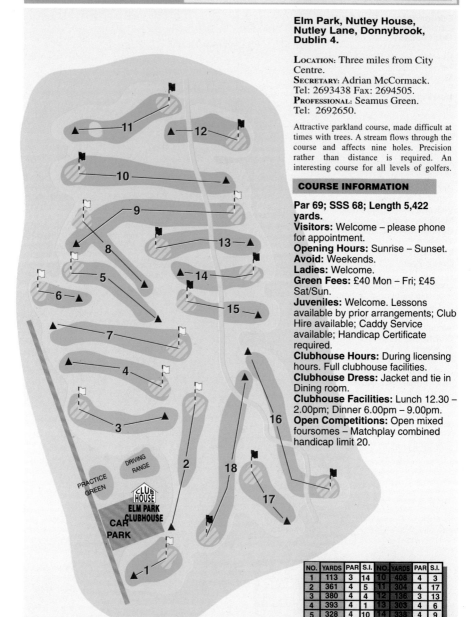

NO.	YARDS	PAR	S.I.	NO.	YARDS	PAR	S.I.
1	113	3	14	10	408	4	3
2	361	4	5	11	304	4	17
3	380	4	4	12	136	3	13
4	393	4	1	13	303	4	6
5	328	4	10	14	338	4	9
6	133	3	16	15	288	4	15
7	436	5	18	16	327	4	2
8	173	3	12	17	198	3	7
9	482	5	8	18	321	4	11
OUT	2,799	35		IN	2,623	34	
				TOTAL	5,422	69	
				STANDARD SCRATCH		68	

FOXROCK

Torquay Road, Foxrock, Dublin 18.
Tel: 2893992/2895668.

LOCATION: South Dublin.
SECRETARY/MANAGER: William Daly.
Tel: 2893992. Fax: 2894943.
PROFESSIONAL: David Walker.
Tel: 2893414.

Foxrock is a very flat course but it nonetheless provides a reasonable test of golf ability.

COURSE INFORMATION

Par 70; SSS 69; Length 5,667 metres.
Visitors: Welcome. Monday, Thursday and Friday mornings.
Opening Hours: 8.00am – Sunset.
Avoid: Tues, Wed, weekends.
Ladies: Welcome. Lessons available by prior arrangement; Club Hire available;

Caddy service available by prior arrangement; Handicap Certificate required for open competition.
Green Fees: £25.
Clubhouse Hours: 8.30am – 11.30pm.
Clubhouse Dress: Casual in the bar, formal in the dining room.
Clubhouse Facilities: Snacks in the bar; meals on Wednesdays and Saturdays.

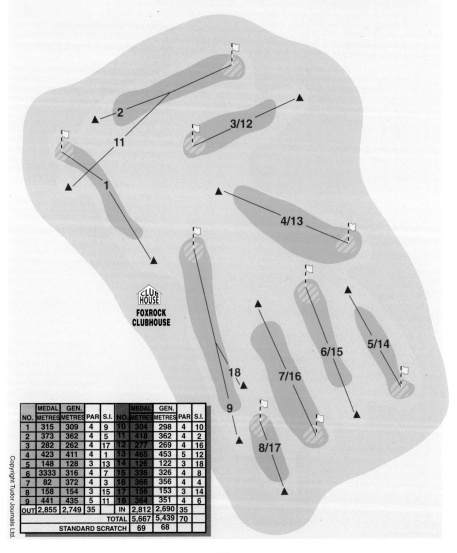

FOXROCK CLUBHOUSE

NO.	MEDAL METRES	GEN. METRES	PAR	S.I.	NO.	MEDAL METRES	GEN. METRES	PAR	S.I.
1	315	309	4	9	10	304	298	4	10
2	373	362	4	5	11	418	362	4	2
3	282	262	4	17	12	277	269	4	16
4	423	411	4	1	13	465	453	5	12
5	148	128	3	13	14	126	122	3	18
6	3333	316	4	7	15	336	326	4	8
7	82	372	4	3	16	366	356	4	4
8	158	154	3	15	17	156	153	3	14
9	441	435	5	11	18	364	351	4	6
OUT	2,855	2,749	35		IN	2,812	2,690	35	
					TOTAL	5,667	5,439	70	
	STANDARD SCRATCH					69	68		

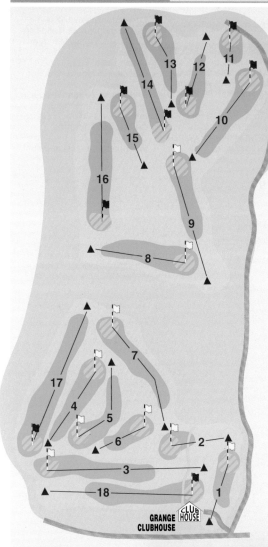

Whitechurch Road, Rathfarnham, Dublin 16. Tel: 4932889.

LOCATION: South West of Dublin City, four miles from City Centre.
SECRETARY: J. A. O'Donaghue. Tel: 4932889.
PROFESSIONAL: Barry Hamill. Tel: 4932299.

Interesting and popular parkland course, with tree-lined fairways being a major feature, which is both attractive yet challenging.

COURSE INFORMATION

Par 68; SSS 69; Length 5,517 Metres.
Visitors: Welcome to play midweek.
Opening Hours: Sunrise – Sunset.
Avoid: Weekends.
Ladies: Welcome.
Green Fees: £28 Mon – Fri. With member only at weekend.
Juveniles: Welcome. Lessons available by prior arrangement; Caddy service available by prior arrangement; Telephone appointment advisable.
Clubhouse Hours: 8.00am – 12.30pm.
Clubhouse Facilities: Full catering facilities.
Clubhouse Dress: Casual, jacket and tie in dining room.

GRANGE CLUBHOUSE

	MEDAL	GEN.				MEDAL	GEN.		
NO.	METRES	METRES	PAR	S.I.	NO.	METRES	METRES	PAR	S.I.
1	203	195	3	7	10	390	385	4	2
2	122	111	3	17	11	182	177	3	8
3	389	384	4	1	12	292	287	4	16
4	383	378	4	5	13	329	324	4	10
5	306	301	4	13	14	487	483	5	14
6	170	165	3	15	15	150	145	3	18
7	388	383	4	3	16	385	380	4	4
8	193	188	3	9	17	467	462	5	12
9	319	315	4	11	18	362	357	4	6
OUT	2,473	2,240	32		IN	3,044	3,000	36	
					TOTAL	5,517	5,420	68	
					STANDARD SCRATCH	69	68		

58

Mount Seskin Road, Jobstown, Tallaght, Dublin 24.
Tel: 4520911/4512020.

LOCATION: Tallaght, Blessington Road.
SECRETARY/MANAGER: James H. Whelan.
Tel: 4520911.
ARCHITECT: Watty Sullivan & Eddie Hackett.

One of the few courses in Dublin which will give you a full panoramic view of the city. This is a course that appears easy on first sight but can be unexpectedly difficult.

COURSE INFORMATION

Par 69; SSS 67; Length 5,225 metres.
Visitors: Welcome.
Opening Hours: 9.00am – Sunset.
Green Fees: Mon – Fri £10 (£7 with member any day); Sat, Sun & Bank Holidays £12.
Avoid: Sundays.
Juveniles: Welcome. Caddy service available by prior arrangements; Telephone appointment required.
Clubhouse Hours: 9.00am – 11.30pm.
Clubhouse Dress: Collar and tie or polo neck after 7pm.
Clubhouse Facilities: Full clubhouse facilities. Catering facilities by prior arrangement.
Open Competitions: Tuesday, Fourballs from April – Sept; Open Week June.

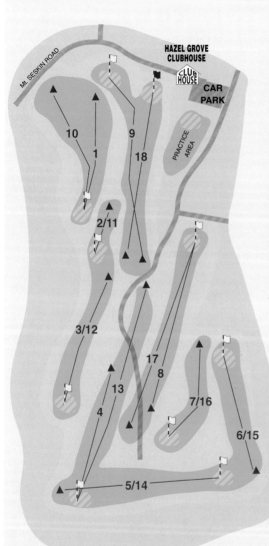

HAZEL GROVE CLUBHOUSE

CAR PARK

PRACTICE AREA

NO.	METRES	PAR	S.I.	NO.	METRES	PAR	S.I.
1	306	4	10	10	292	4	11
2	81	3	18	11	110	3	17
3	300	4	7	12	300	4	8
4	352	4	2	13	390	4	1
5	144	3	9	14	322	4	4
6	200	3	12	15	206	3	13
7	242	4	15	16	242	4	16
8	371	4	5	17	431	4	3
9	507	5	14	18	429	4	6
OUT	2,503	34		IN	2,722	34	
				TOTAL	5,225	69	
				STANDARD SCRATCH	67		

St. Fintan's, Carrickbrack Road, Sutton, Dublin 13. Tel: 8323055.

LOCATION: Nine miles north east of city centre, two miles from Sutton Cross on Sutton side of hill of Howth.
SECRETARY: Ann MacNeice.
Tel: 8323055.
PROFESSIONAL: John McGuirk.
Tel: 8393895.
ARCHITECT: James Braid.

Moorland course with scenic views of Dublin Bay. Very hilly – a challenge for the athletic golfer.

COURSE INFORMATION

Par 71; SSS 69; Length 5,859 yards, 5,607 metres.
Visitors: Welcome weekdays except Wednesday.
Opening Hours: 8.30am – 4.00pm.
Avoid: 1.00pm – 2.00pm; All day Wednesday, Thursday afternoons.
Ladies: Welcome. Lessons available by prior arrangements; Club Hire available; Caddy service available by prior arrangements.
Green Fees: £16, Fri: £18.
Clubhouse Hours: 8.30am – 11.00pm.
Clubhouse Dress: Informal. No denim, training shoes or shorts in Clubhouse.
Clubhouse Facilities: Bar snacks from 11.00am.

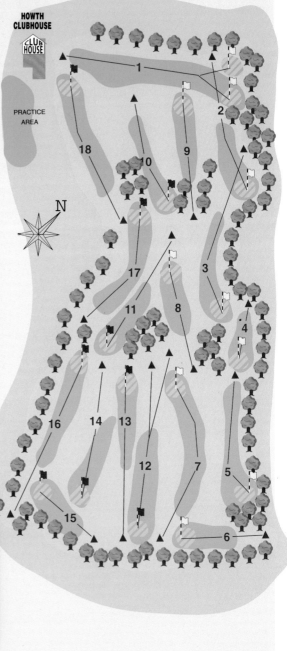

NO.	METRES	PAR	S.I.	NO.	METRES	PAR	S.I.
1	306	4	10	10	309	4	5
2	321	4	4	11	314	4	3
3	408	4	1	12	463	5	15
4	155	3	12	13	397	4	2
5	355	4	6	14	326	4	7
6	269	4	14	15	137	3	17
7	486	5	8	16	296	4	9
8	134	3	18	17	349	4	11
9	252	4	16	18	330	4	13
OUT	2,686	35		IN	2,921	36	
				TOTAL	5,607	71	
	STANDARD SCRATCH				69		

Tree positions indicated.

Lower Churchtown Road, Dublin 14.
Tel: 4976090.

LOCATION: South Dublin three miles from the city centre.
SECRETARY/MANAGER: William Johnston.
Tel: 4976090.
PROFESSIONAL: John Harnett.
Tel: 4977072.
ARCHITECT: Freddie Davis.

Well established parkland course on the suburbs of Dublin. One of the many Dublin clubs that provide convenient locations.

COURSE INFORMATION

Par 71; SSS 69; Length 5,638 Metres.
Visitors: Welcome.
Opening Hours: Sunrise – Sunset.
Avoid: Saturday. Telephone appointment required.
Ladies: Welcome.
Green Fees: £30 Mon – Fri; (£14 with member).
Juveniles: Welcome. Lessons available by prior arrangement; Club hire available; Caddy service

available by prior arrangment; Telephone appointment required.
Clubhouse Hours: 7.30am – 11.30pm (summer); 9.00am – 10.30pm (winter).
Clubhouse Dress: Casual. Jacket & tie after 7.30pm and at all times in dining room.
Clubhouse Facilities: Full clubhouse facilities. Full catering facilities.
Open Competitions: East of Ireland Mixed Foursomes Championship.

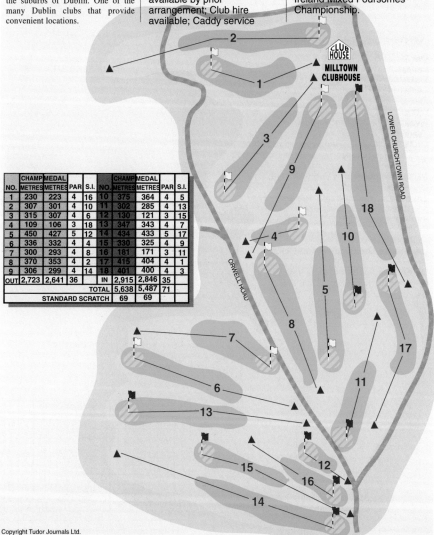

NO.	CHAMP METRES	MEDAL METRES	PAR	S.I.	NO.	CHAMP METRES	MEDAL METRES	PAR	S.I.
1	230	223	4	16	10	375	364	4	5
2	307	301	4	10	11	302	285	4	13
3	315	307	4	6	12	130	121	3	15
4	109	106	3	18	13	347	343	4	7
5	450	427	5	12	14	434	433	5	17
6	336	332	4	4	15	330	325	4	9
7	300	293	4	8	16	181	171	3	11
8	370	353	4	2	17	415	404	4	1
9	306	299	4	14	18	401	400	4	3
OUT	2,723	2,641	36		IN	2,915	2,846	35	
					TOTAL	5,638	5,487	71	
					STANDARD SCRATCH	69	69		

RATHFARNHAM   L E I N S T E R   DUBLIN CITY

**Newtown, Rathfarnham,
Dublin 16
Tel: 4931201.**

LOCATION: Two miles from
Rathfarnham Village.
SECRETARY: P. Lindsay.
Tel: 4931201.
PROFESSIONAL: Brian O'Hara .
Tel: 4931201.
ARCHITECT: John Jacob.

Parkland course, with attractive scenery,
mature trees and spinneys. Greens are
built on the natural lie of the ground.

COURSE INFORMATION

**Par 71; SSS 70; Length 5,824
metres.
Visitors:** Welcome Monday,
Wednesday, Thursday morning &
Friday.
Opening Hours: 8.30am – Sunset.
Avoid: Tues, Sat, Sun & Bank
Holidays.
Ladies: Welcome (Handicap
Certificate required).
Green Fees: £20 Mon – Fri (£25
without member); £10 Sun (with a
member).
Juveniles: Welcome with member
only. Lessons available by prior
arrangements.
Clubhouse Hours: 10.30am –
11.00pm.
Clubhouse Dress: Jacket and tie
after 7.30pm.
Clubhouse Facilities: Light snacks
daily; meals by prior arrangements.

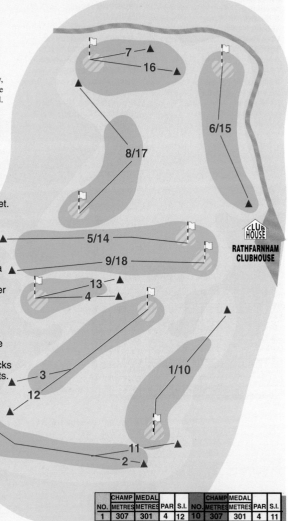

NO.	CHAMP METRES	MEDAL METRES	PAR	S.I.	NO.	CHAMP METRES	MEDAL METRES	PAR	S.I.
1	307	301	4	12	10	307	301	4	11
2	293	287	4	14	11	361	358	4	7
3	452	450	5	16	12	430	425	4	1
4	184	181	3	6	13	146	144	3	15
5	377	370	4	2	14	377	370	4	3
6	336	328	4	4	15	336	328	4	5
7	154	152	3	10	16	137	135	3	13
8	462	454	5	18	17	462	454	5	17
9	356	348	4	8	18	356	348	4	9
OUT	2,921	2,871	36		IN	2,912	2,863	35	
					TOTAL	5,824	5,734	71	
					STANDARD SCRATCH	70	70		

Dollymount, Dublin 3.
Tel: 8336346/8331262.

LOCATION: Three miles north east
from the city centre along the
coast road.
SECRETARY: John A. Lambe.
Tel: 8336346.
PROFESSIONAL: Leonard Owens.
Tel: 8336477.
ARCHITECT: E. S. Colt.

The links is 6,858 yards (6,267 metres) in
length and is laid out in the old traditional
links style resembling St Andrews. Fine
fescue grasses provide an ideal basis for
greens and fairways and a wandering wind
adds that extra hazard. Fine bunkers, close
lies and subtle trapping are all features of
Royal Dublin.

COURSE INFORMATION

Par 72; SSS 73; Length 6,267
Metres.
Visitors: Welcome Monday,
Tuesday, Thursday & Friday.
Please telephone for availability.
Opening Hours: 8.30am – Sunset.
Avoid: Wed. and weekends.
Ladies: Welcome. Lessons
available by prior arrangements;
Club Hire available; Caddy
service available by prior
arrangements. Telephone
appointment required.
Green Fees: £45 Mon – Fri; £55
Sat/Sun.
Clubhouse Hours: 8.00am –
midnight.
Clubhouse Dress: Jacket and
tie in Clubhouse; Casual in Grill
Room.
Clubhouse Facilities: Every
day except Monday.

NO.	METRES	PAR	S.I.	NO.	METRES	PAR	S.I.
1	361	4	7	10	378	4	3
2	445	5	17	11	479	5	13
3	363	4	4	12	188	3	10
4	163	3	12	13	425	4	1
5	423	4	2	14	455	5	15
6	180	3	16	15	397	4	6
7	338	4	9	16	245	4	18
8	465	5	11	17	345	4	8
9	164	3	14	18	453	4	5
OUT	2,902	35		IN	3,365	37	
				TOTAL	6,267	72	
				STANDARD SCRATCH	73		

ROYAL DUBLIN CLUBHOUSE CLUB HOUSE

Copyright Tudor Journals Ltd.

Bunker positions indicated.

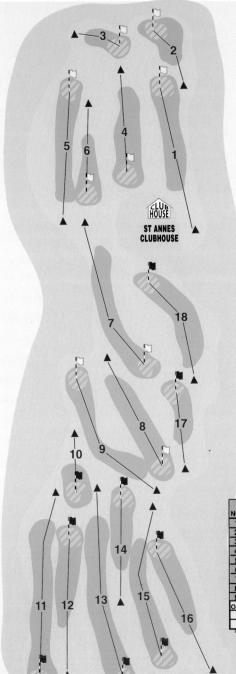

ST ANNES
CLUBHOUSE

**North Bull Island,
Dollymount, Dublin, 5.
Tel: 8336471/8332797.**

LOCATION: Five miles north
east of Dublin.
SECRETARY: J. Carberry.
Tel: 8336471.
PROFESSIONAL: P. Skerritt.
Tel: 8314138.
ARCHITECT: E. Hackett and
Committee.

This is a links course that has recently
undergone the transition from nine holes to
eighteen, which enjoys a very pleasant
seaside location.

COURSE INFORMATION

**Par 70; SSS 70; Length 5,797
metres.**
Visitors: Welcome any time except
during Gents or Ladies
Competitions.
Opening Hours: 9.00am – 7.00pm.
Avoid: Days of Competitions.
Ladies: Welcome. Lessons
available by prior arrangements;
Telephone appointment required.
Green Fees: Weekdays – £20 &
weekends and Bank Holidays –
£25.
Clubhouse Hours: 8.30am –
11.00pm.
Clubhouse Dress: Casual.
Clubhouse Facilities: Snacks
10.30am – 6.30pm; Meals and
snacks 6.30pm - 9.30pm. Bar and
Catering Tel: 332797.
Open Competitions: Open weeks
– June, July & August.

NO.	CHAMP METRES	MEDAL METRES	PAR	S.I.	NO.	CHAMP METRES	MEDAL METRES	PAR	S.I.
1	463	458	5	15	10	148	140	3	16
2	354	349	4	9	11	506	479	5	10
3	150	144	3	13	12	347	339	4	6
4	364	359	4	3	13	440	436	5	8
5	293	290	4	11	14	214	204	3	12
6	140	136	3	17	15	377	369	4	2
7	430	426	4	1	16	284	276	4	18
8	372	360	4	7	17	177	168	3	14
9	360	353	4	5	18	378	366	4	4
OUT	2,926	2,875	35		IN	2,871	2,777	35	
TOTAL						5,797	5,652	70	
STANDARD SCRATCH							70	69	

ST. MARGARET'S   LEINSTER   DUBLIN CITY

**St Margarets Golf &
Country Club, St.
Margarets, Co. Dublin.
Tel: (01) 864 0400.
Fax: (01) 864 0289.**

LOCATION: Eight miles north of
city centre.
SECRETARY: Mr Denis Kane.
GOLF DIRECTOR: Paul Henry.
ARCHITECT: Tom Craddock &
Pat Ruddy

Home to the Women's Irish Open, St
Margaret's measures just under 7,000
yards off the back tees and the

modern design approach makes use of
water hazards and sculptured
mounding on a level new to Irish golf.
Every effort has been made to make
the course a challenge full of variety
and drama but very playable by all
standards of player.

COURSE INFORMATION

**Par 73; SSS 73; Length 6,917
yards.**
Visitors: Welcome everyday.
Opening Hours: Sunrise –
Sunset.

Ladies: Welcome.
Green Fees: Sat/Sun £35;
Weekdays £30.
Juveniles: Welcome.
Clubhouse Hours: 8.30am –
11.00pm.
Clubhouse Dress: Neat.
Clubhouse Facilities: Full
catering facilities available.

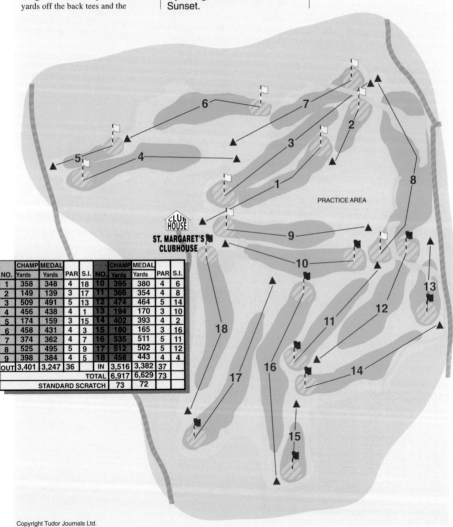

NO.	CHAMP Yards	MEDAL Yards	PAR	S.I.	NO.	CHAMP Yards	MEDAL Yards	PAR	S.I.
1	358	348	4	18	10	395	380	4	6
2	149	139	3	17	11	366	354	4	8
3	509	491	5	13	12	474	464	5	14
4	456	438	4	1	13	194	170	3	10
5	174	159	3	15	14	402	393	4	2
6	458	431	4	3	15	180	165	3	16
7	374	362	4	7	16	535	511	5	11
8	525	495	5	9	17	512	502	5	12
9	398	384	4	5	18	458	443	4	4
OUT	3,401	3,247	36		IN	3,516	3,382	37	
					TOTAL	6,917	6,629	73	
					STANDARD SCRATCH	73	72		

Copyright Tudor Journals Ltd.

**Kellystown Road,
Rathfarnham, Dublin 16.
Tel: 4942338.**

LOCATION: South West Dublin, Six miles from City centre.
SECRETARY: Kieran Lawler.
Tel: 4941993.
ARCHITECT: Shaffreys.

An attractive course on the side of Ticnock Mountain, with marvellous views of Dublin and the Bay.

COURSE INFORMATION

Par 72; SSS 72; Length 5,952 metres.
Visitors: Welcome weekdays.
Opening Hours: Sunrise – Sunset.
Avoid: Weekends and Bank holidays.
Ladies: Welcome.
Green Fees: £14 Mon – Fri; £18 Sat/Sun/Bank Holidays.

Juveniles: Welcome.
Clubhouse Hours: 8.30am – 11.30pm.
Clubhouse Dress: Neat dress required.
Clubhouse Facilities: Catering facilities available.
Open Competitions: May & June.

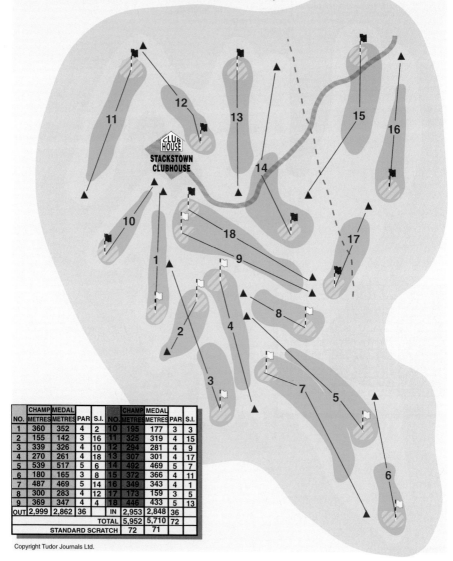

NO.	CHAMP METRES	MEDAL METRES	PAR	S.I.	NO.	CHAMP METRES	MEDAL METRES	PAR	S.I.
1	360	352	4	2	10	195	177	3	3
2	155	142	3	16	11	325	319	4	15
3	339	326	4	10	12	294	281	4	9
4	270	261	4	18	13	307	301	4	17
5	539	517	5	6	14	492	469	5	7
6	180	165	3	8	15	372	366	4	11
7	487	469	5	14	16	349	343	4	1
8	300	283	4	12	17	173	159	3	5
9	369	347	4	4	18	446	433	5	13
OUT	2,999	2,862	36		IN	2,953	2,848	36	
					TOTAL	5,952	5,710	72	
		STANDARD SCRATCH					72	71	

SUTTON

L E I N S T E R ██ **DUBLIN CITY**

**Cush Point, Sutton,
Dublin 13.
Tel: 8323013.**

LOCATION: Ten minutes from City
centre.
HONORARY SECRETARY: P. Bowen.
Tel: 8322965.
PROFESSIONAL: Nicky Lynch.
Tel: 8321703.
ARCHITECT: Donal Steele.

Links course with very narrow fairways and
one of the main features is that the course is
surrounded by water.

NO.	YARDS	PAR	S.I.	NO.	YARDS	PAR	S.I.
1	311	4	13	10	311	4	14
2	300	4	15	11	300	4	16
3	365	4	5	12	365	4	4
4	184	3	7	13	184	3	6
5	487	5	9	14	487	5	12
6	105	3	17	15	105	3	18
7	349	4	11	16	349	4	10
8	382	4	1	17	382	4	2
9	376	4	3	18	376	4	8
OUT	2,859	35		IN	2,859	35	
				TOTAL	5,718	70	
				STANDARD SCRATCH	67		

COURSE INFORMATION

**Par 70; SSS 67; Length 5,718
yards.
Visitors:** Welcome anytime.
Opening Hours: 9.00am – Sunset.
Avoid: Tuesday and Saturday.
Ladies: Welcome.
Green Fees: £15 Mon - Fri (£8 with
member); £20 Sat, Sun & Bank
Hols (£8 with member).
Juveniles: Welcome no weekend
play. Lessons available by prior
arrangments.
Clubhouse Hours: 9,00am
onwards.
Clubhouse Dress: Casual, no
denim.
Clubhouse Facilities: Full
clubhouse facilities, by
arrangement.

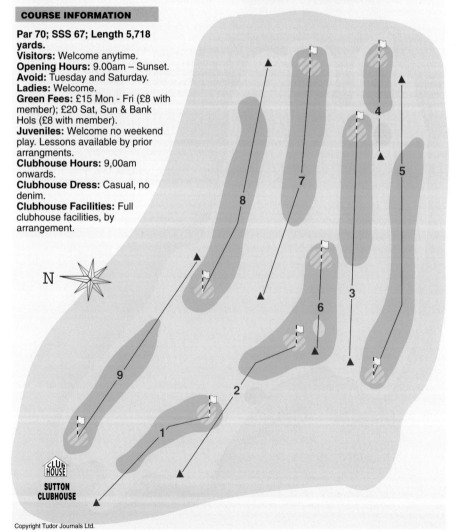

N

SUTTON
CLUBHOUSE

ATHY

LEINSTER · KILDARE

**Geraldine, Athy,
Co. Kildare.
Tel: (01507) 31729.**

LOCATION: Off the Kildare Road.
SECRETARY: Derek O'Donovan.
Tel: (0507) 31729.
PUBLIC RELATIONS OFFICE:
Jim Barry Tel: (0507) 38395.

This is a newly designed 18 hole
course which opened in July 1993.
Among the features of this parkland
course is a river which comes into
play in four holes. All the new greens
are totally sand based. Two of the par
three's are over 200 yards long. The

16th hole has a deep "valley of sin" to
the right and is 420 yards long.
Heading for home the 17th is a unique
dog-leg to the right down a hill to a
two-tier elevated green.

COURSE INFORMATION

**Par 71; SSS 70;
Length 6,340 yards.**
Visitors: Welcome Mon – Fri.
Telephone appointment
required for weekend
Avoid: Weekends and Bank
holidays.

Ladies: Thursday.
Green Fees: £10 Mon – Fri;
£15 Sat/Bank Holidays.
Juveniles: Wed & Fri
mornings during holiday
periods.
Clubhouse Hours: 10.00am
– 11.00pm Mon – Fri;
11.00am – 11.00pm Sat/Sun.
Clubhouse Dress: Casual.
Clubhouse Facilities: By
arrangement.
Open Competitions: Open
Week – mid June; Husband /
Wife – mid July weekend.

NO.	CHAMP YARDS	MEDAL YARDS	PAR	S.I.	NO.	CHAMP YARDS	MEDAL YARDS	PAR	S.I.
1	354	349	4	9	10	402	384	4	7
2	176	162	3	6	11	336	329	4	13
3	301	291	4	18	12	203	188	3	5
4	369	356	4	11	13	487	478	5	17
5	154	147	3	6	14	217	203	3	10
6	421	411	4	4	15	365	356	4	12
7	373	364	4	2	16	423	413	4	1
8	503	499	5	16	17	387	374	4	3
9	362	354	4	14	18	507	501	5	15
OUT	3,013	2,933	35		IN	3,327	3,226	36	
					TOTAL	6,340	6,159	71	
					STANDARD SCRATCH	70	69		

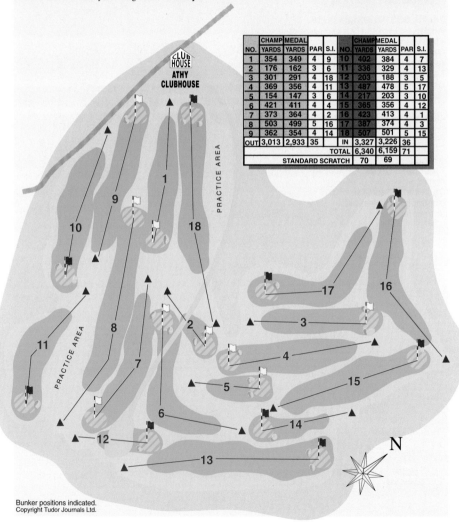

Bunker positions indicated.
Copyright Tudor Journals Ltd.

68

BODENSTOWN

L E I N S T E R

KILDARE

Sallins, Co. Kildare.
Tel: (045) 897096.

LOCATION: Four miles outside Naas near Bodenstown graveyard.
SECRETARY: Bernadette Mather.
Tel: (045) 97096.

The Old Course in Bodenstown, with its ample fairways and large greens, some of which are raised, provides more than a fair test of golf. The

Ladyhill Course, also at Bodenstown, is a little shorter but still affords a fair challenge.

COURSE INFORMATION

Par 72; SSS 73; Length 6,321 yards (Old Course).
Visitors: Welcome.
Opening Hours: Sunrise – Sunset.
Avoid: Main course at weekends. Ladyhill course available.
Ladies: Welcome.

Ladies Day: Thursday.
Green Fees: £10 Main Course; £10 Ladyhill Course.
Juveniles: Welcome.
Clubhouse Hours: 11.00am – 11.00pm. Full clubhouse facilities.
Clubhouse Dress: Informal.
Clubhouse Facilities: Full catering available.
Open Competitions: Open Week – June.

NO.	CHAMP YARDS	MEDAL YARDS	PAR	S.I.	NO.	CHAMP YARDS	MEDAL YARDS	PAR	S.I.
1	364	338	4	11	10	322	317	4	16
2	168	161	3	17	11	379	363	4	4
3	368	366	4	2	12	503	484	5	12
4	355	336	4	7	13	403	382	4	8
5	148	145	3	5	14	398	384	4	1
6	476	476	5	15	15	165	153	3	10
7	359	359	4	9	16	343	336	4	18
8	370	370	4	3	17	205	186	3	6
9	480	468	5	13	18	515	508	5	14
OUT	3,088	3,019	36		IN	3,233	3,113	36	
					TOTAL	6,321	6,132	72	
					STANDARD SCRATCH		73	71	

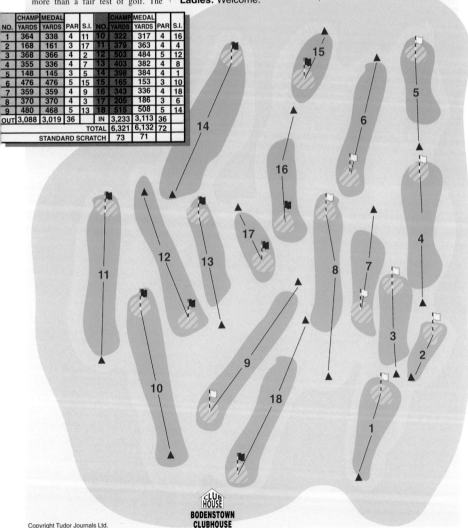

CLUB HOUSE
BODENSTOWN CLUBHOUSE

Castlewarden, Straffan, Co. Kildare.
Tel: Dublin (01) 589254/4588218.

LOCATION: Between Naas and Newlands Cross
SECRETARY: P.J. McCann.
Tel: (01) 4589254.
PROFESSIONAL: Gerry Egan.

Throughout this relatively new course there are several scenic views of both the Dublin and Wicklow mountains. The course features gently-contoured greens, with elevated tees.

COURSE INFORMATION

Par 72; SSS 70; Length 6,642 yards.
Visitors: Welcome to play.
Opening Hours: Daylight to dusk.
Avoid: Saturdays and Sundays.
Ladies: Welcome.
Green Fees: Weekdays – £12 (£7 with a member); Weekend – £16 (£10 with a member). Lessons

available by prior arrangement. Club hire available.
Clubhouse Hours: 1.00pm – 11.30pm (weekdays) & 11.00am – 11.30pm (weekends).
Clubhouse Dress: Neat.
Clubhouse Facilities: Available on request.

NO.	CHAMP YARDS	MEDAL YARDS	PAR	S.I.	NO.	CHAMP YARDS	MEDAL YARDS	PAR	S.I.
1	425	418	4	2	10	262	257	4	15
2	501	496	5	16	11	373	367	4	11
3	321	314	4	12	12	393	387	4	7
4	167	164	3	18	13	161	151	3	13
5	407	395	4	6	14	429	425	4	5
6	418	405	4	4	15	396	382	4	9
7	380	373	4	10	16	418	406	4	1
8	518	480	5	8	17	155	150	3	17
9	347	341	4	14	18	553	548	5	3
OUT	3,484	3,386	37		IN	3,140	3,066	35	
					TOTAL	6,624	6,452	72	
					STANDARD SCRATCH	70			

CASTLEWARDEN CLUBHOUSE

PRACTICE AREA

**Little Curragh, Kildare,
Co. Kildare.
Tel: (045) 521433/521295.**

LOCATION: One mile west of
Kildare town.
SECRETARY: Tony Monahan.
Tel: (45) 521354.
PROFESSIONAL: Jimmy Bolger.

A course which is typical to many in
the area with all the colour of the
gorse and heather. Flat and relatively
straight forward to play. A good
choice for the middle and high
handicappers.

COURSE INFORMATION

**Par 71; SSS 70; Length
5,738 yards.
Visitors:** Welcome.
Opening Hours: Sunrise –
Sunset.
Avoid: Wednesday, Sundays
(Club Competitions).
Ladies: Welcome.

Ladies Day: Wednesday.
Green Fees: £10 Weekday;
£12 Weekend; £7 with a
member.
Juveniles: Welcome. Club
Hire available; Handicap
Certificate preferred;
Telephone appointment
required.
Clubhouse Hours: 11.00am –
11.30pm.
Clubhouse Dress: Casual.
Clubhouse Facilities: 9.00am
– 10.30pm daily (full facilities).

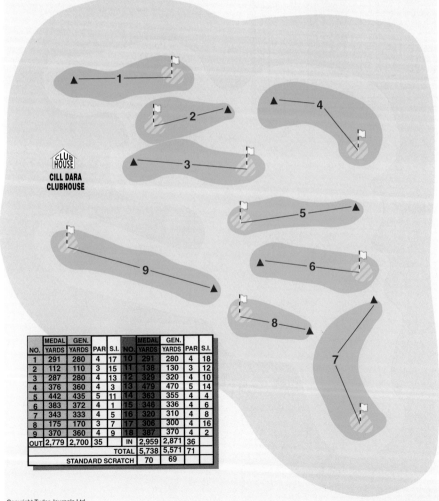

NO.	MEDAL YARDS	GEN. YARDS	PAR	S.I.	NO.	MEDAL YARDS	GEN. YARDS	PAR	S.I.
1	291	280	4	17	10	291	280	4	18
2	112	110	3	15	11	138	130	3	12
3	287	280	4	13	12	329	320	4	10
4	376	360	4	3	13	479	470	5	14
5	442	435	5	11	14	363	355	4	4
6	383	372	4	1	15	346	336	4	6
7	343	333	4	5	16	320	310	4	8
8	175	170	3	7	17	306	300	4	16
9	370	360	4	9	18	387	370	4	2
OUT	2,779	2,700	35		IN	2,959	2,871	36	
					TOTAL	5,738	5,571	71	
					STANDARD SCRATCH	70	69		

71

Curragh, Co. Kildare.
Tel: (045) 441714/441238.

LOCATION: Thiry two miles
south east of Dublin.
SECRETARY: Ann Culleton.
Tel: (045) 441714.
PROFESSIONAL: Phil Lawlor.
Tel: (045) 441896.

A long testing course of over 6,000
metres. Hazards include tree lined
fairways, furze bushes and grazing
sheep. Every hole presents a separate
and distinctive challenge. A scenic
course with panoramic views of
Kildare and the Wicklow Mountains.

COURSE INFORMATION

**Par 72; SSS 71; Length 6,001
metres.**
Visitors: Welcome advance
enquires are essential.
Opening Hours: Sunrise –
Sunset.
Avoid: Tuesdays Sat & Sun.
Ladies: Tuesday.

Green Fees: £14 Mon – Fri;
£18 Sat/Sun/Bank Holidays.
Juveniles: Welcome & must be
accompanied by an adult.
Lessons & club hire available by
prior arrangement with the Club
Professional; Telephone for
appointment.
Clubhouse Hours: 10am–10pm.
(all year).
Clubhouse Dress: Neat Dress.
Clubhouse Facilities:
10.00am–10.00pm.
Open Competitions: June/July.

NO.	MEDAL METRES	GEN. METRES	PAR	S.I.	NO.	MEDAL METRES	GEN. METRES	PAR	S.I.
1	450	436	5	15	10	170	158	3	10
2	335	324	4	5	11	400	392	4	2
3	272	266	4	13	12	391	360	4	6
4	180	174	3	7	13	285	273	4	16
5	322	315	4	11	14	460	449	5	14
6	341	334	4	3	15	459	449	5	12
7	483	473	5	9	16	124	105	3	18
8	166	157	3	17	17	412	403	4	4
9	407	403	4	1	18	344	337	4	8
OUT	2,956	2,882	36		IN	3,045	2,926	36	
					TOTAL	6,001	5,808	72	
					STANDARD SCRATCH	71	70		

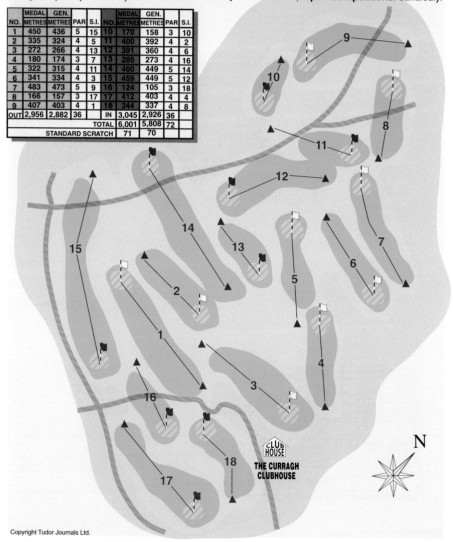

THE CURRAGH
CLUBHOUSE

N

Kilkea Castle, Castledermot, Co. Kildare.
Tel: (0503) 45156.
Fax: (0503) 45187.

LOCATION: 40 miles from Dublin.
SECRETARY: Adeline Molloy.
Tel: (0503) 45156.
Fax: (0503) 45187.

A parkland course which surrounds the oldest inhabited castle in Ireland. The River Griese comes into play on ten of the holes.

COURSE INFORMATION

Par 70; Length 6,100 Metres.
Visitors: Welcome to play every day.
Opening Hours: Sunrise – Sunset.
Ladies: Welcome.
Green Fees: £25 Mon – Thurs. £30 Fri – Sun.
Residents: £20 Mon – Thurs. £25 Fri – Sun.

Juveniles: Welcome only when accompanied by adults.
Clubhouse Hours: 10.00am - 11.30pm.
Clubhouse Dress: Informal but respectable.
Clubhouse Facilities: Bar, restaurant, snooker room, pro-shop, putting green and pitching green.

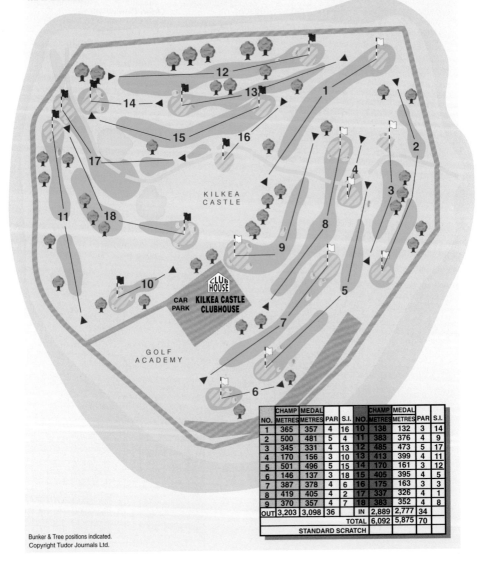

NO.	CHAMP METRES	MEDAL METRES	PAR	S.I.	NO.	CHAMP METRES	MEDAL METRES	PAR	S.I.
1	365	357	4	16	10	138	132	3	14
2	500	481	5	4	11	383	376	4	9
3	345	331	4	13	12	485	473	5	17
4	170	156	3	10	13	413	399	4	11
5	501	496	5	15	14	170	161	3	12
6	146	137	3	18	15	405	395	4	5
7	387	378	4	6	16	175	163	3	3
8	419	405	4	2	17	337	326	4	1
9	370	357	4	7	18	383	352	4	8
OUT	3,203	3,098	36		IN	2,889	2,777	34	
					TOTAL	6,092	5,875	70	
	STANDARD SCRATCH								

**Killeen Golf Club,
Co. Kill, County Kildare,
Co. Galway.
Tel: (045) 866003.
Fax: (045) 875881.**

LOCATION: Two miles west of Kill village, off N7 Dublin – Cork Road.
SECRETARY/MANAGER: Peter Carey. Tel: (045) 866003.
ARCHITECT: Tom Craddock & Pat Ruddy.

1995 saw the introduction of six magnificent holes that feature all the elements associated with Craddock and Ruddy designs in recent years...broad sweeping fairways, boldly shaped and placed fairways, water hazards that are very much in play and also perfectly conditioned greens.

COURSE INFORMATION

Par 71; SSS 70; Length 5,815 Metres.
Visitors: Welcome weekdays and at weekends.
Opening Hours: Summer 7.00am – 12.00pm; Winter 8.00am – 6.00pm.
Avoid: 8.30am – 10.00am & 12.45pm – 2.00pm
At weekends telephone, appointments preferred.
Ladies: Welcome.
Green Fees: £13 Mon – Fri; £15 Sat – Sun.
Caddy car & club hire available.
Clubhouse Hours: Summer 9.00am – 12 midnight; Winter 9.00am – 6.00pm.
Clubhouse Dress: As per golf etiquette.
Clubhouse Facilities: Licensed restaurant.

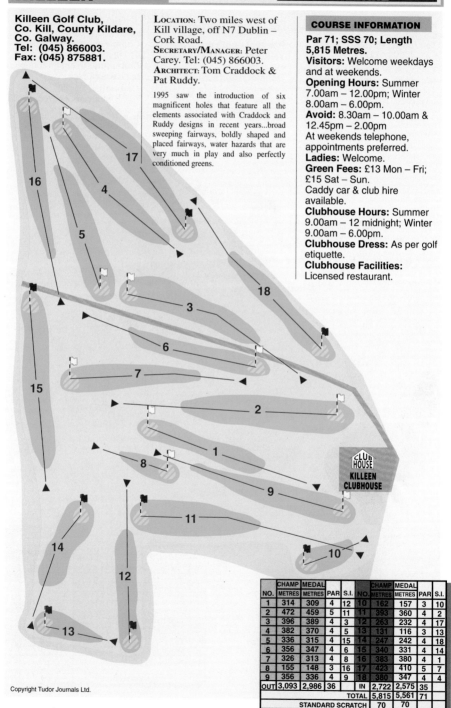

NO.	CHAMP METRES	MEDAL METRES	PAR	S.I.	NO.	CHAMP METRES	MEDAL METRES	PAR	S.I.
1	314	309	4	12	10	162	157	3	10
2	472	459	5	11	11	393	360	4	2
3	396	389	4	3	12	263	232	4	17
4	382	370	4	5	13	131	116	3	13
5	336	315	4	15	14	247	242	4	18
6	356	347	4	6	15	340	331	4	14
7	326	313	4	8	16	383	380	4	1
8	155	148	3	16	17	423	410	5	7
9	356	336	4	9	18	380	347	4	4
OUT	3,093	2,986	36		IN	2,722	2,575	35	
					TOTAL	5,815	5,561	71	
					STANDARD SCRATCH		70	70	

THE 'K' CLUB

L E I N S T E R

Straffan, Co. Kildare.
Tel: (01) 6273111.

LOCATION: Co. Kildare.
GOLF DIRECTOR/MANAGER: Ken Green.
PROFESSIONAL: Ernie Jones.
ARCHITECT: Arnold Palmer.

A world class major championship designed golf course by Arnold Palmer. Eleven man-made lakes, large sand bunkers, large mounds both sides of fairways. The River Liffey runs alongside four holes with the 7th green on the far side of the river. Large quantity of 300 year old trees.

COURSE INFORMATION

Par 72; SSS 74; Length 6,368 metres.
Visitors: Welcome.
Opening Hours: 8.00am (summer), 8.30am (winter).
Avoid: 1.30pm – 2.30pm. Prior arrangement required. Letter of introduction and handicap certificate required.
Ladies: Welcome.
Green Fees: £100 (summer), £75 (winter). Lessons available by prior arrangement. Club hire and caddy service available. No Open Competitions.
Juveniles: Must be accompanied by an adult.
Clubhouse Hours: 8.30am – 10pm (summer) 9pm (winter).
Clubhouse Facilities: Bar, Snack Bar, Restaurant. Snack Bar 9.00am – 9.00pm. Bar & Restaurant 11.00am – 9.00pm.

PRACTICE AREA

NO.	MEDAL YARDS	GEN. YARDS	PAR	S.I.	NO.	MEDAL YARDS	GEN. YARDS	PAR	S.I.
1	529	512	5	5	10	364	364	4	6
2	373	351	4	9	11	361	361	4	12
3	160	148	3	17	12	132	132	3	18
4	368	351	4	7	13	497	497	5	10
5	196	177	3	15	14	358	358	4	2
6	406	376	4	11	15	376	376	4	4
7	553	543	5	3	16	339	339	4	8
8	341	306	4	13	17	160	140	3	16
9	395	392	4	1	18	460	460	5	14
OUT	3,321	3,156	36		IN	3,047	3,027	36	
					TOTAL	6,368	6,183	72	
					STANDARD SCRATCH	74	72		

Donadea, North Kildare.
Tel: (045) 869322.

LOCATION: North Kildare.
SECRETARY: Noel Lyons.
Tel: (045) 869322.
PROFESSIONAL: Peter Hickey.
Tel: (045) 869322.
ARCHITECT: Noel Lyons.

A popular parkland course which is basically flat, and has several water hazards. Christy O'Connor Senior once described the first hole as "the most difficult opening hole in golf".

Home of the Irish International Professional Matchplay Championship. Palladian old world clubhouse is also an interesting feature.

COURSE INFORMATION

Par 72; SSS 72; Length 6,424 yards.
Visitors: Welcome.
Opening Hours: Sunrise – Sunset.
Avoid: Saturday mornings.
Ladies: Welcome.

Green Fees: Mon – Fri £16 (with member £10) Sat, Sun & Bank Hols £20 (with member £10).
Juveniles: Welcome. Lessons available by prior arrangement. Club hire available.
Clubhouse Hours: 8.30am – 12.00 midnight.
Clubhouse Dress: Smart / casual.
Clubhouse Facilities: Available everyday. Members bar, restaurant, professional shop, offices, games rooms.

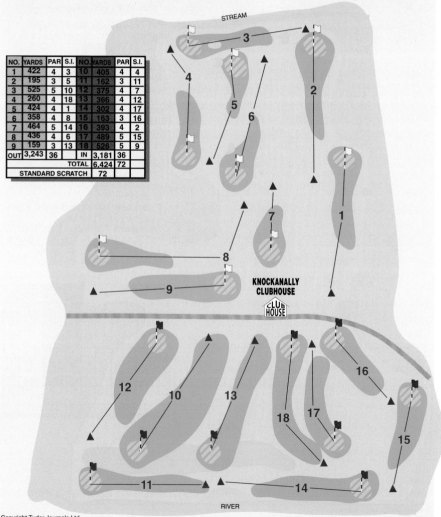

NO.	YARDS	PAR	S.I.	NO.	YARDS	PAR	S.I.
1	422	4	3	10	405	4	4
2	195	3	5	11	162	3	11
3	525	5	10	12	375	4	7
4	260	4	18	13	366	4	12
5	424	4	1	14	302	4	17
6	358	4	8	15	163	3	16
7	464	5	14	16	393	4	2
8	436	4	6	17	489	5	15
9	159	3	13	18	526	5	9
OUT	3,243	36		IN	3,181	36	
				TOTAL	6,424	72	
				STANDARD SCRATCH		72	

STREAM

KNOCKANALLY CLUBHOUSE

RIVER

Copyright Tudor Journals Ltd.

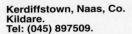

Kerdiffstown, Naas, Co. Kildare.
Tel: (045) 897509.

LOCATION: Beside Naas/Dublin dual carriageway on Johnstown /Sallins road.
SECRETARY: Ken Dermody.
Tel: (045) 877509.

A pleasant parkland course where each hole has its features providing a keen golfing challenge.

COURSE INFORMATION

Par 71; SSS 68; Length 5,660 metres.
Visitors: Welcome Mon, Wed, Fri and Sat.
Opening Hours: Sunrise – Sunset.
Ladies: Welcome.
Green Fees: £12 Mon – Fri; £15 Sat.
Juveniles: Welcome
Clubhouse Hours: 10.30am – 11.30pm.
Clubhouse Dress: Neat.
Clubhouse Facilities: At weekends during summer months.
Open Competitions: April, June & August.

NAAS CLUBHOUSE

NO.	METRES	PAR	S.I.	NO.	METRES	PAR	S.I.
1	403	4	1	10	158	3	11
2	331	4	16	11	367	4	3
3	142	3	10	12	300	4	12
4	372	4	4	13	474	5	8
5	350	4	2	14	149	3	13
6	376	4	6	15	460	5	17
7	450	5	9	16	327	4	5
8	113	3	18	17	154	3	7
9	288	4	15	18	446	5	14
OUT	2,825	35		IN	2,835	36	
				TOTAL	5,660	35	
STANDARD SCRATCH					68	71	

**Geraldine, Callan,
Co. Kilkenny.
Tel: (056) 25136
     (056) 25949.**

LOCATION: One mile from town of Callan on Knocktopher road.
HONORARY SECRETARY:
M. Duggan. Tel: (056) 54362 (056) 22977.

This golf course has a stream 50 yards in front of the 9th tee and 120 yards from the 7th green which proves notorious. In addition there are well placed spinneys to catch wayward drives. There is also a pond left of line of drive on the 6th. All greens are bunkered and well protected.

COURSE INFORMATION

**Par 72; SSS 70; Length
5,721 metres/6259 yards.
Visitors:** Welcome to play.
Opening Hours: Daylight hours.
Avoid: Sundays all day and Saturdays after mid-day. Prior arrangement preferred.
Ladies: Welcome.

Green Fees: £10 all week; £5 with a member. Caddy Service available by prior arrangement.
Juveniles: Welcome
Clubhouse Hours: 9.00am – 11.00pm.
Clubhouse Dress: Casual.
Clubhouse Facilities: Bar open 9.00am – 11.00pm. Catering by prior arrangement. Catering facilities and times, anyday by prior arrangement.

NO.	METRES	PAR	S.I.	NO.	METRES	PAR	S.I.
1	459	5	12	10	459	5	13
2	155	3	14	11	192	3	7
3	329	4	5	12	329	4	6
4	351	4	3	13	351	4	4
5	283	4	15	14	283	4	16
6	345	4	1	15	345	4	2
7	461	5	10	16	461	5	11
8	123	3	17	17	123	3	18
9	333	4	8	18	333	4	9
OUT	2,842	36		IN	2,879	36	
				TOTAL	5,721	72	
				STANDARD SCRATCH		70	

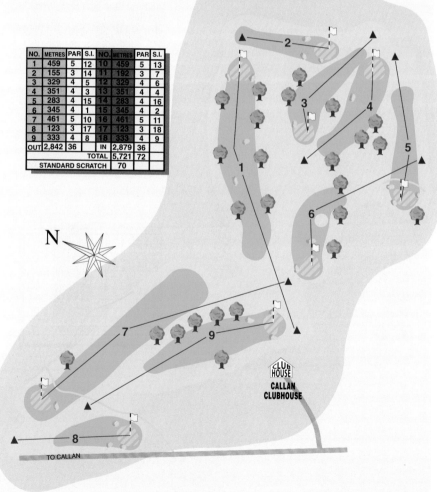

N

CALLAN CLUBHOUSE

TO CALLAN

Bunker and tree positions indicated.

**Drumgoole, Castlecomer,
Co. Kilkenny.
Tel: (056) 41139.**

LOCATION: Edge of town on
Kilkenny road.
HONORARY SECRETARY:
Michael Doheny.
Tel: (056) 33333.
ARCHITECT: Pat Ruddy.

This course is in a sylvan setting bounded on
one side by the River Deen. A long course
considered a good test of golf, it is the third
longest nine hole course in Ireland.

COURSE INFORMATION

**Par 71; SSS 71; Length 5,547
metres.**
Visitors: Welcome.
Opening Hours: Sunrise – Sunset.
Avoid: All Sundays.
Ladies: Welcome.
Green Fees: £10 Mon – Sun (£5
with a member).
Juveniles: Welcome.
Clubhouse Hours: Sunrise –
Sunset.
Clubhouse Dress: Casual.
Clubhouse Facilities: Full
clubhouse facilities (by request for
groups).
Open Competitions: Open Week
July / Aug.

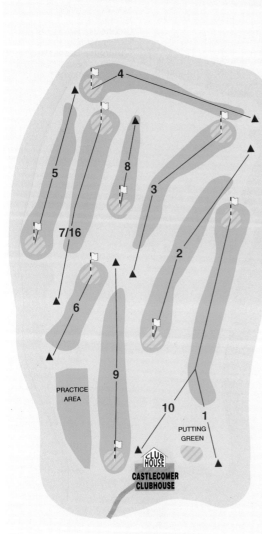

NO.	METRES	PAR	S.I.	NO.	METRES	PAR	S.I.
1	464	5	11	10	375	5	12
2	365	4	7	11	344	4	8
3	363	4	5	12	363	4	6
4	253	4	13	13	253	4	14
5	353	4	3	14	353	4	4
6	132	3	17	15	132	3	18
7	347	4	9	16	368	4	2
8	123	3	15	17	123	3	16
9	396	4	1	18	440	5	10
OUT	2,796	35		IN	2,751	36	
				TOTAL	5,547	71	
				STANDARD SCRATCH		71	

Glendine, Kilkenny.
Tel: (056) 65400.
Members: (056) 22125.

LOCATION: One mile outside the city – off Castlecomer road.
SECRETARY: Mr Sean O'Neill.
Tel: (056) 65400.
PROFESSIONAL: Noel Leahy.
Tel: (056) 61730.
Parkland course with plenty of trees throughout the fairways which provide a good test of golf. GUI Irish finals are held here from time to time.

COURSE INFORMATION

Par 71; SSS 70; Length 5,859 metres.
Visitors: Welcome to play Mon – Fri, weekends by prior arrangement.
Opening Hours: Daylight hours.
Avoid: Saturday and Sunday – prior arrangement preferred.
Ladies: Welcome.
Green Fees: £16 week days

and £18 Weekends. Lessons available by prior arrangement. Club hire available. Caddy service available by prior arrangement.
Clubhouse Hours: As per licensing law.
Clubhouse Dress: Neat.
Clubhouse Facilities: Bar, food, snooker and pool.

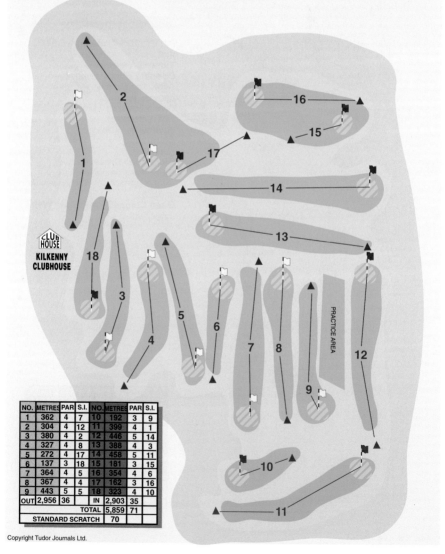

NO.	METRES	PAR	S.I.	NO.	METRES	PAR	S.I.
1	362	4	7	10	192	3	9
2	304	4	12	11	399	4	1
3	380	4	2	12	446	5	14
4	327	4	8	13	388	4	3
5	272	4	17	14	458	5	11
6	137	3	18	15	181	3	15
7	364	4	5	16	354	4	6
8	367	4	4	17	162	3	16
9	443	5	5	18	323	4	10
OUT	2,956	36		IN	2,903	35	
				TOTAL	5,859	71	
STANDARD SCRATCH					70		

KILKENNY CLUBHOUSE

PRACTICE AREA

**Thomastown,
Co. Kilkenny.
Tel: (056) 24725
Fax: (056) 24828.**

LOCATION: Main Dublin – Waterford road, ten miles from Kilkenny.
SECRETARY: Katherine MacCann.
PROFESSIONAL: Todd Poddpyle & Nick Bradley.
ARCHITECT: Jack Nicklaus.

The only Jack Nicklaus designed course in Ireland, it features old specimen trees, water hazards and bunkers. It is set in a beautiful old 1500 acre estate and appeals to all levels and standards of golfers. Accommodation is available in both Mount Juliet House and the clubhouse.

COURSE INFORMATION

Par 72; SSS 72; Length 6,641 yards.
Visitors: Welcome. Prior arrangement required. Handicap certificate required.
Opening Hours: Daily from 8.00am.
Avoid: No restrictions.
Ladies: Welcome.
Green Fees: £40 Mon – Fri & £50 Sat / Sun in Winter. £65 Mon – Fri & £70 Sat/Sun in Summer. Lessons available by prior arrangement. Club hire available. Caddy service available by prior arrangement. Weekend and Three-Day Golf Schools

available. 3 hole Teaching. Academy – lessons available with Todd Poddpyle & Nick Bradley.
Juveniles: Welcome (no reduction in green fees).
Clubhouse Hours: 8.00am – 11.30pm.
Clubhouse Facilities: Changing rooms, Bar, Restuarant. 8.00am – 9.00pm (Must be booked in advance).

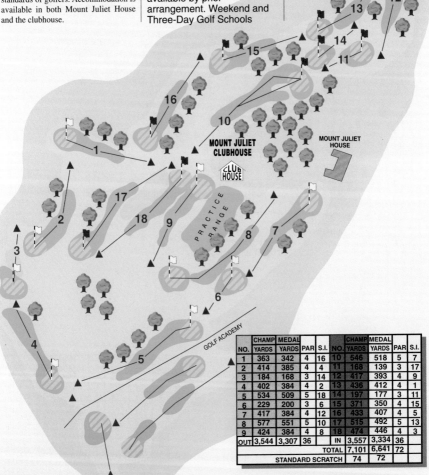

NO.	CHAMP YARDS	MEDAL YARDS	PAR	S.I.	NO.	CHAMP YARDS	MEDAL YARDS	PAR	S.I.
1	363	342	4	16	10	546	518	5	7
2	414	385	4	4	11	168	139	3	17
3	184	168	3	14	12	417	393	4	9
4	402	384	4	2	13	436	412	4	1
5	534	509	5	18	14	197	177	3	11
6	229	200	3	6	15	371	350	4	15
7	417	384	4	12	16	433	407	4	5
8	577	551	5	10	17	515	492	5	13
9	424	384	4	8	18	474	446	4	3
OUT	3,544	3,307	36		IN	3,557	3,334	36	
					TOTAL	7,101	6,641	72	
					STANDARD SCRATCH	74	72		

Tree positions indicated.

Newrath, Waterford.
Tel: (051) 76748.
Fax: (051) 53405.
LOCATION: Newrath.
SECRETARY: Joseph Condon.
Tel: (051) 76748.
PROFESSIONAL: Eamonn Condon.
Tel: (051) 54256.
ARCHITECT: James Braid.

A parkland course with good views of the countryside. The course character is as the undulating countryside around Newrath and will appeal to low and middle handicappers.

COURSE INFORMATION

Par 71; SSS 70; Length 5,722 metres.
Visitors: Welcome by prior arrangement.
Opening Hours: 8.00am – Sunset.
Avoid: Tue/Wed afternoons; all day Sunday.
Ladies: Welcome.
Green Fees: £15 Mon – Fri; £18 Sat/Sun/Bank Holidays.

Juveniles: Welcome Lessons available; Club Hire available; Caddy service available by prior arrangments; Handicap certificate required for open competitions.
Clubhouse Hours: 8.00am – 12.00 midnight.
Clubhouse Dress: Casual.
Clubhouse Facilities: Snacks; full menu from 4pm.
Open Competitions: Open Week July / Aug.

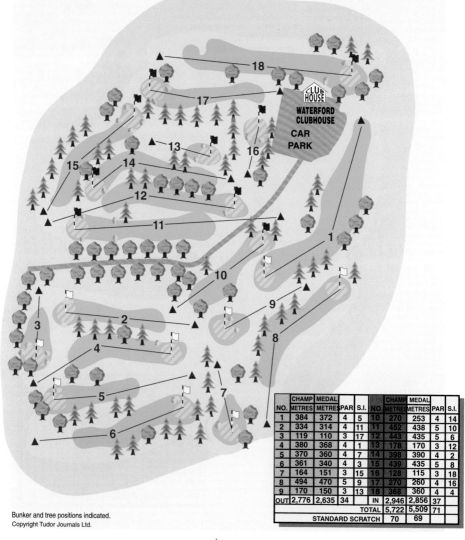

NO.	CHAMP METRES	MEDAL METRES	PAR	S.I.	NO.	CHAMP METRES	MEDAL METRES	PAR	S.I.
1	384	372	4	5	10	270	253	4	14
2	334	314	4	11	11	452	438	5	10
3	119	110	3	17	12	443	435	5	6
4	380	368	4	1	13	178	170	3	12
5	370	360	4	7	14	398	390	4	2
6	361	340	4	3	15	439	435	5	8
7	164	151	3	15	16	128	115	3	18
8	494	470	5	9	17	270	260	4	16
9	170	150	3	13	18	368	360	4	4
OUT	2,776	2,635	34		IN	2,946	2,856	37	
					TOTAL	5,722	5,509	71	
					STANDARD SCRATCH	70	69		

Bunker and tree positions indicated.
Copyright Tudor Journals Ltd.

ABBEYLEIX

L E I N S T E R   **LAOIS**

Rathmoyle, Abbeyleix, Portlaoise, Co Laois
Tel: (0502) 31450

LOCATION: Less than one mile north of the town on Stradbally road.
SECRETARY: James P. Moran
Tel: (0502) 31229/31051.

A parkland course which looks out over the picturesque Slieve Bloom Mountains. Mature trees and new spinneys increase the difficulty factor for most golfers.

COURSE INFORMATION

Par 70; SSS 68; Length 5,626 metres.
Visitors: Welcome to play on weekdays.
Opening Hours: Sunrise – Sunset.
Ladies: Welcome.
Green Fees: £8 Mon – Fri, £10 Sat/Sun, £6 with a member.
Juveniles: Only when accompanied by adults.

Clubhouse Hours: Fri, Sat, Sun in Winter. Most evenings in Summer..
Clubhouse Dress: Informal but respectable.
Clubhouse Facilities: General. Catering facilities and times; by prior arrangement.
Open Competitions: Open Week 2nd weekend & 3rd week of July; Open Hampers October and November.

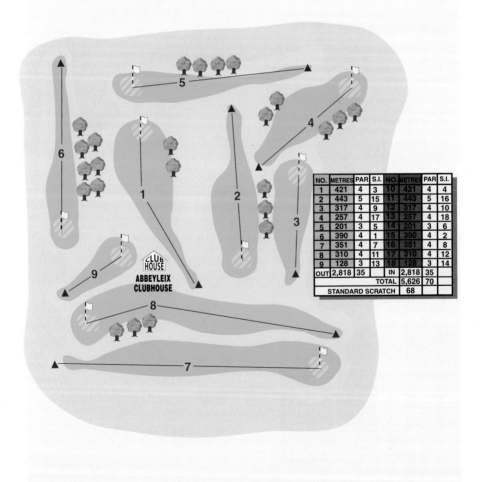

NO.	METRES	PAR	S.I.	NO.	METRES	PAR	S.I.
1	421	4	3	10	421	4	4
2	443	5	15	11	443	5	16
3	317	4	9	12	317	4	10
4	257	4	17	13	257	4	18
5	201	3	5	14	201	3	6
6	390	4	1	15	390	4	2
7	351	4	7	16	351	4	8
8	310	4	11	17	310	4	12
9	128	3	13	18	128	3	14
OUT	2,818	35		IN	2,818	35	
				TOTAL	5,626	70	
				STANDARD SCRATCH	68		

ABBEYLEIX CLUBHOUSE

Tree positions indicated.

The Heath, Portlaoise, Co. Laois.
Tel: (0502) 46533.

LOCATION: Three miles north east
Portlaoise town.
SECRETARY: Pat Malone.
Tel: (0502) 46622.
PROFESSIONAL: Eddie Doyle.
Tel: (0502) 46622 / (0502) 22044.

This Par 71 course is playable all year round
and is exceptionally dry in wintertime. Set in
picturesque surroundings with views of the
rolling hills of Laois, the course incorporates
three natural lakes. Noted for its rough of
heather and gorse furze it is a challenge for
any golfer. The Heath Golf Club is the
seventh oldest Golf Club in Ireland, founded
in November 1889.

COURSE INFORMATION

**Par 72; SSS 70; Length 5,736
metres.**
Visitors: Welcome, please book.
Opening Hours: Sunrise –
Sunset.
Avoid: Weekends unless with
advance booking.
Ladies: Welcome.
Green Fees: £10 Mon – Fri; £16
Sat/Sun/Bank Holidays.
Juveniles: Welcome. Lessons
available by prior arrangement;
Club Hire available; Caddy service
available by prior arrangement;
telephone appointment required.
Clubhouse Hours: 10.30am –
11.30pm Mon-Sat; 10.30am –
11.00pm Sundays.
Clubhouse Dress: Casual (Neat).
Clubhouse Facilities: Full catering
facilities.
Open Competitions: Open Week
May. Other various days.

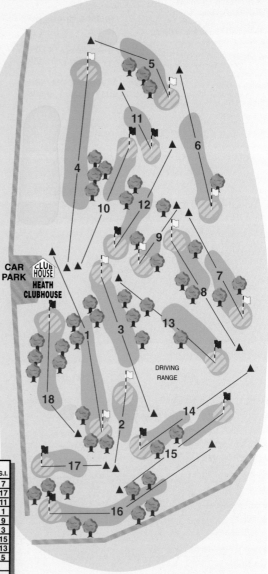

NO.	MEDAL METRES	GEN. METRES	PAR	S.I.	NO.	MEDAL METRES	GEN. METRES	PAR	S.I.
1	456	447	5	16	10	324	296	4	7
2	163	159	3	12	11	138	127	3	17
3	348	332	4	4	12	336	327	4	11
4	437	437	4	10	13	384	378	4	1
5	274	274	4	14	14	352	346	4	9
6	355	322	4	6	15	359	337	4	3
7	342	335	4	8	16	456	449	5	15
8	354	334	4	2	17	162	141	3	13
9	158	148	3	18	18	338	328	4	5
OUT	2,887	2,788	36		IN	2,849	2,729	36	
					TOTAL	5,736	5,517	72	
					STANDARD SCRATCH	70	69		

Tree positions indicated.

84

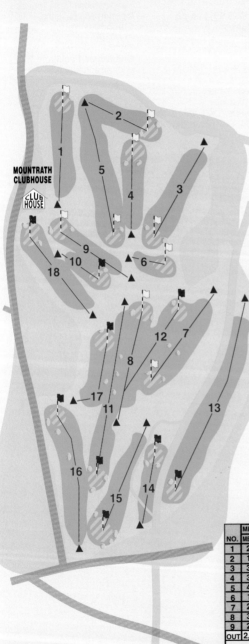

Knockinina, Mountrath, Co. Laois.
Tel: (0502) 32558.

LOCATION: Two miles Limerick side of Mountrath – just off the main Dublin/Limerick road.
SECRETARY: John Mulhare.

Extended to 18 holes in 1994, this is a pleasant course set on gently rolling land with the river Nore and an old Mill stream flowing through and coming into play on a number of holes. Lush fairways and good greens which are well bunkered make it an excellent test of golf.

COURSE INFORMATION

Par 71; SSS 69; Length 5,493 metres.
Visitors: Welcome.
Ladies: Welcome.
Ladies Day: Tuesday.
Opening Hours: Sunrise – Sunset.
Avoid: Saturday or Sunday mornings (check in clubhouse).
Green Fees: £8 per day.
Clubhouse Hours: Evening service only, except for special occasions.
Clubhouse Dress: Casual.
Clubhouse Facilities: Catering facilities by prior arrangment.

NO.	MEDAL METRES	GEN. METRES	PAR	S.I.	NO.	MEDAL METRES	GEN. METRES	PAR	S.I.
1	288	374	4	3	10	127	117	3	17
2	154	142	3	12	11	445	430	5	11
3	352	298	4	1	12	373	350	4	2
4	347	329	4	6	13	463	440	5	8
5	440	418	5	13	14	177	140	3	5
6	111	105	3	16	15	290	268	4	9
7	270	250	4	18	16	378	360	4	4
8	337	320	4	7	17	269	248	4	15
9	287	283	4	10	18	285	265	4	14
OUT	2,686	2,519	35		IN	2,807	2,618	36	
					TOTAL	5,493	5,137	71	
					STANDARD SCRATCH	69	68		

Garryhinch, Portarlington, Co. Laois.
Tel: (0502) 23115.

LOCATION: Three miles from Portarlington.
SECRETARY: James Cannon.
Tel: (0502) 23408.

The course has recently undergone extensive development from a nine hole course to an eighteen hole course. The new course was completed in November 1992 and provides a fresh test of skill and ability.

COURSE INFORMATION

Par 71; SSS 69; Length 5,673 metres.
Visitors: Welcome as members of Societies and as individuals.
Opening Hours: 8.00am – sunset.
Avoid: Weekends.
Ladies: Tuesday.
Green Fees: £10 (+VAT) Mon – Fri; £12 (+VAT) Saturday and Sunday.

Juveniles: Welcome. Handicap certificate required for open competitions.
Clubhouse Hours: 8.00am – 11.00pm.
Clubhouse Dress: Casual.
Clubhouse Facilities: By prior arrangement.

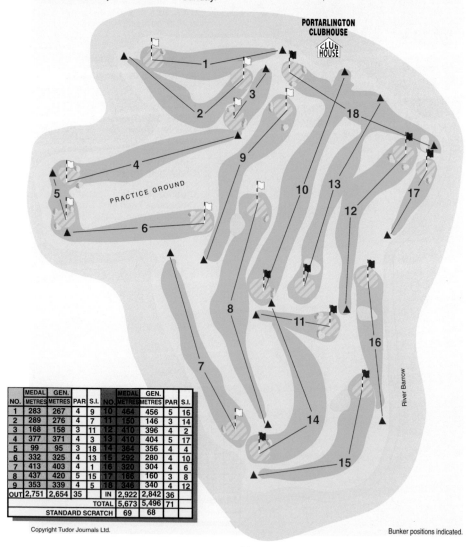

PORTARLINGTON CLUBHOUSE

NO.	MEDAL METRES	GEN. METRES	PAR	S.I.	NO.	MEDAL METRES	GEN. METRES	PAR	S.I.
1	283	267	4	9	10	464	456	5	16
2	289	276	4	7	11	150	146	3	14
3	168	158	3	11	12	410	396	4	2
4	377	371	4	3	13	410	404	5	17
5	99	95	3	18	14	364	356	4	4
6	332	325	4	13	15	292	280	4	10
7	413	403	4	1	16	320	304	4	6
8	437	420	5	15	17	166	160	3	8
9	353	339	4	5	18	346	340	4	12
OUT	2,751	2,654	35		IN	2,922	2,842	36	
					TOTAL	5,673	5,496	71	
	STANDARD SCRATCH					69	68		

Bunker positions indicated.

RATHDOWNEY

LAOIS

Coulnaboul West,
Rathdowney,
Co. Laois.
Tel: (0505) 46170.

LOCATION: Less than one mile
east of Rathdowney.
SECRETARY: Seamus Pyne.
Tel: (0505) 46434.

This is a relatively new course which
is currently being improved. There is
an on-going development of the
course.

COURSE INFORMATION

**Par 70; SSS 69; Length
5,564 metres.**
Visitors: Welcome at all
times.
Opening Hours: Sunrise –
Sunset.
Avoid: Bank Holidays,
sundays, 1st week in July.
Ladies: Welcome.
Green Fees: £6
Juveniles: Welcome.

Clubhouse Hours: 11.00am
– 11.30pm.
Clubhouse Dress: Casual.
Clubhouse Facilities:
Snacks and sandwiches on
order; meals by prior
arrangment.
Open Competitions:
Intermediate Scratch Cup and
Open Week in July; Open
Hampers in November.

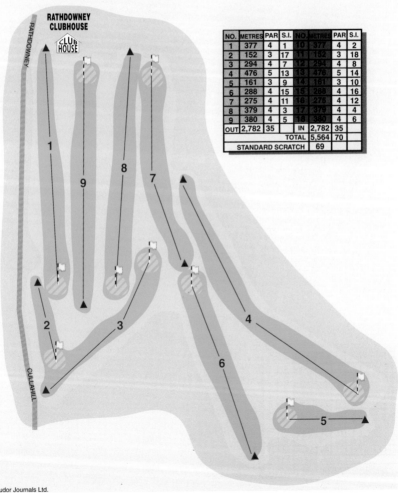

NO.	METRES	PAR	S.I.	NO.	METRES	PAR	S.I.
1	377	4	1	10	377	4	2
2	152	3	17	11	152	3	18
3	294	4	7	12	294	4	8
4	476	5	13	13	476	5	14
5	161	3	9	14	161	3	10
6	288	4	15	15	288	4	16
7	275	4	11	16	275	4	12
8	379	4	3	17	379	4	4
9	380	4	5	18	380	4	6
OUT	2,782	35		IN	2,782	35	
				TOTAL	5,564	70	
STANDARD SCRATCH				69			

COUNTY LONGFORD   L E I N S T E R   LONGFORD

**Glack, Dublin Road,
Longford, Co. Longford
Tel: (043) 46310.**

LOCATION: Dublin Road,
Longford.
SECRETARY: Michael J. Walsh.
ARCHITECT: E. Hackett

An elevated parkland course,
overlooking Longford Town and
surrounding countryside.

COURSE INFORMATION

**Par 70; SSS 69; Length
6,044 yards.**
Visitors: Welcome.
Opening Hours: Sunrise –
Sunset.
Avoid: Weekends and
Tuesdays.
Ladies: Welcome.
Ladies: Tuesday
Green Fees: £10 Mon – Fri
(£8 with member); £12
Sat/Sun (£10 with member on
a one to one basis).

Juveniles: Welcome,
accompanied by an adult.
Clubhouse Hours: 12noon –
11pm.
Clubhouse Dress: Casual.
Clubhouse Facilities: Meals
and snacks.
Open Competitions: Open
week July/August.

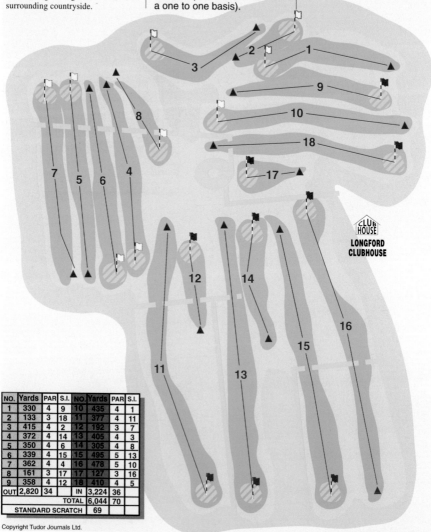

LONGFORD
CLUBHOUSE

NO.	Yards	PAR	S.I.	NO.	Yards	PAR	S.I.
1	330	4	9	10	435	4	1
2	133	3	18	11	377	4	11
3	415	4	2	12	192	3	7
4	372	4	14	13	405	4	3
5	350	4	6	14	305	4	8
6	339	4	15	15	495	5	13
7	362	4	4	16	478	5	10
8	161	3	17	17	127	3	16
9	358	4	12	18	410	4	5
OUT	2,820	34		IN	3,224	36	
				TOTAL	6,044	70	
	STANDARD SCRATCH				69		

Copyright Tudor Journals Ltd.

ARDEE

**Townparks, Ardee,
Co. Louth.
Tel: (041) 53227.**

Location: Just north of Ardee town.
Secretary: Seamus Kelly.
Tel: (041) 53227.
Architect: Mr. Eddie Hackett.

A very fair test of golf and also a very pleasant walk with some beautiful old trees on this parkland course.

COURSE INFORMATION

**Par 69; SSS 69; Length 6,046 yards.
Visitors:** Welcome.
Opening Hours: Sunrise – Sunset.
Avoid: Sun: 8.00am – 11.00am & Weekends.
Ladies: Welcome.
Green Fees: £15 Mon – Fri.
No Green Fees Sat & Sun.

Juveniles: Welcome.
Caddy Service by prior arrangements.
Clubhouse Hours: 10.30am – 11.30pm.
Clubhouse Dress: Casual.
Clubhouse Facilities:
Catering facilities available at all times.
Open Competitions:
Several dates throughout year. Open Week — June.

NO.	MEDAL YARDS	GEN. YARDS	PAR	S.I.	NO.	MEDAL YARDS	GEN. YARDS	PAR	S.I.
1	347	328	4	5	10	389	381	4	4
2	183	157	3	13	11	333	317	4	14
3	308	284	4	18	12	312	300	4	17
4	390	345	4	7	13	165	149	3	16
5	409	394	4	3	14	400	369	4	2
6	443	431	4	1	15	522	489	5	10
7	368	349	4	9	16	167	194	3	12
8	319	303	4	15	17	414	380	4	8
9	192	173	3	11	18	385	353	4	6
OUT	2,959	2,764	34		IN	3,087	2,923	35	
					TOTAL	6,046	5,687	69	
					STANDARD SCRATCH	69	68		

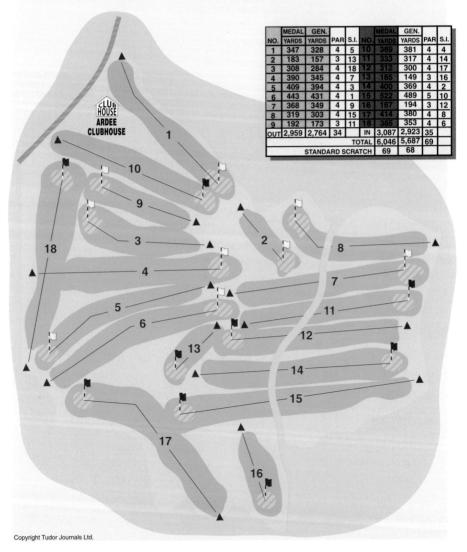

ARDEE CLUBHOUSE

Baltray, Co. Louth.
Tel: (041) 22329.

LOCATION: Five miles north east Drogheda.
SECRETARY: Michael Delany. Tel: (041) 22329.
PROFESSIONAL: Paddy McGuirk. Tel: (041) 22444.
ARCHITECT: Tom Simpson.

A championship links which can be enjoyed by every category of golfer which is not as well known as some of the other links courses. Baltray's demands are stern but its rewards are many not least in the fun and enjoyment it evokes and the sense of freshness that prevails.

COURSE INFORMATION

Par 73; SSS 72; Length 6,783 metres.
Visitors: Welcome by prior arrangement.
Opening Hours: Winter 8.30am – Sunset; Summer 7.30am – Sunset.
Avoid: Weekends and Tuesdays.
Ladies: By prior arrangement.
Green Fees: £35 Mon – Fri; £40 Sat/Sun (£10 with a member).
Juveniles: Restricted.

Lessons available by prior arrangement; Club Hire available; Caddy service available by prior arrangement; Telephone appointment required.
Clubhouse Hours: 10.30am – 12.00 midnight; Clubhouse facilities.
Clubhouse Dress: Casual.
Clubhouse Facilities: 9.00am – 8.00pm (winter); 9.00am – 10.00pm (summer).

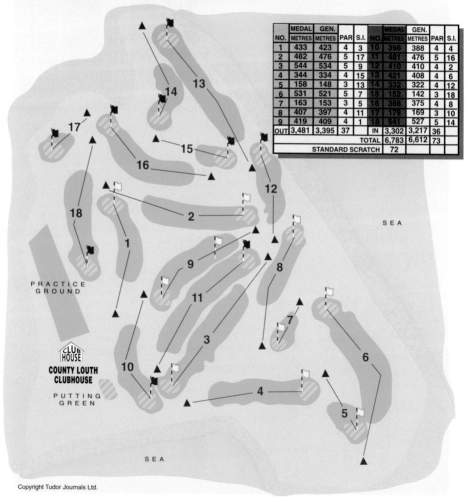

NO.	MEDAL METRES	GEN. METRES	PAR	S.I.	NO.	MEDAL METRES	GEN. METRES	PAR	S.I.
1	433	423	4	3	10	398	388	4	4
2	482	476	5	17	11	481	476	5	16
3	544	534	5	9	12	410	410	4	2
4	344	334	4	15	13	421	408	4	6
5	158	148	3	13	14	332	322	4	12
6	531	521	5	7	15	152	142	3	18
7	163	153	3	5	16	388	375	4	8
8	407	397	4	11	17	179	169	3	10
9	419	409	4	1	18	541	527	5	14
OUT	3,481	3,395	37		IN	3,302	3,217	36	
					TOTAL	6,783	6,612	73	
					STANDARD SCRATCH		72		

**Blackrock, Dundalk,
Co. Louth.
Tel: (042) 21731/22218.
Fax: (042) 22022.**

LOCATION: Three miles south of
Dundalk at Blackrock Village.
SECRETARY: Joe Carroll.
Tel: (042) 21731.
PROFESSIONAL: James Cassidy.
Tel: (042) 22102.
ARCHITECTS: Dave Thomas
& Peter Allis.

A difficult but fair course offering
panoramic views of Dundalk town,
Dundalk Bay with the backdrop of
the Cooley Mountains.

COURSE INFORMATION

**Par 72; SSS 72; Length
6,160 metres.
Visitors:** Welcome.
Opening Hours: Sunrise –
Sunset.
Avoid: Tuesdays and
Sundays. Prior appointment
preferable but not essential.
Ladies: Welcome except
Tuesdays and Sundays.
Green Fees: £16 Mon – Fri;
£20 Sat/Sun/Bank Holidays.
Juveniles: Before 6.00pm,
not Tuesdays or weekends.

Lessons available by prior
arrangement; Club hire
available; Caddy service
available by prior
arrangement.
Clubhouse Hours: Sunrise
to midnight.
Clubhouse Dress: Informal.
Clubhouse Facilities:
Snacks and full meals at
any time.
Open Competitions: May
& July.

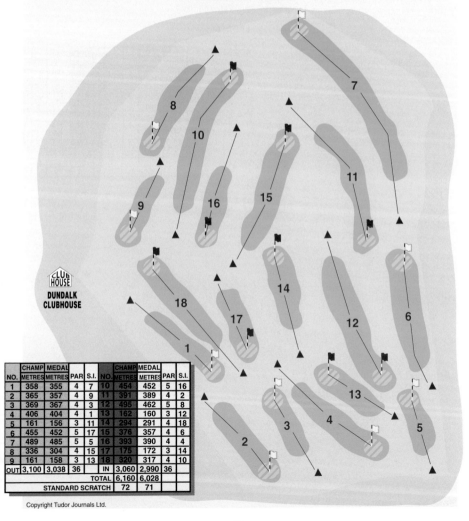

NO.	CHAMP METRES	MEDAL METRES	PAR	S.I.	NO.	CHAMP METRES	MEDAL METRES	PAR	S.I.
1	358	355	4	7	10	454	452	5	16
2	365	357	4	9	11	391	389	4	2
3	369	367	4	3	12	495	462	5	8
4	406	404	4	1	13	162	160	3	12
5	161	156	3	11	14	294	291	4	18
6	455	452	5	17	15	376	357	4	6
7	489	485	5	5	16	393	390	4	4
8	336	304	4	15	17	175	172	3	14
9	161	158	3	13	18	320	317	4	10
OUT	3,100	3,038	36		IN	3,060	2,990	36	
					TOTAL	6,160	6,028		
					STANDARD SCRATCH		72	71	

Copyright Tudor Journals Ltd.

**Greenore, Co. Louth.
Tel: (042) 73212. Fax:
(042) 73678.**

LOCATION: Travelling from
Dublin — proceed through
Drogheda and Dundalk and
take the first turn right on the
Newry road out of Dundalk
and proceed to Greenore —
fifteen miles.
SECRETARY/MANAGER: Roisin
Daly. Tel: (042) 73212.
ARCHITECT: Eddie Hackett.

An inland course with a links nature
on the shores of Carlingford Lough.
The course enjoys scenic views of
both the Lough and the Mountains of
Mourne. An unusual feature are the
tall pine trees, a rare sight on a
semi-links course, which come
into play on seven holes. The 14th
or "pigs back" is the most famous
hole in Greenore, a par 3 to an
elevated green.

COURSE INFORMATION

**Par 71; SSS 71; Length
6,506 yards.**
Visitors: Welcome to play
weekdays and weekends,
but appointment is
recommended for
weekends.
Opening Hours: 8.00am (or
earlier by appointment), to
sunset.
Green Fees: £12 Mon – Fri

(£6 with a member); £18
Sat/Sun/Bank Holidays (£10
with a member); Students –
half price.
Clubhouse Hours:
9.00am-6.00pm (Winter);
8.00am-11.30pm (summer).
Clubhouse Dress:
Informal.
Clubhouse Facilities: All
days.
Open Competitions: Open
Week – July; Irish Assistant
Professionals – July;
Carlingford Lough Classic –
August.

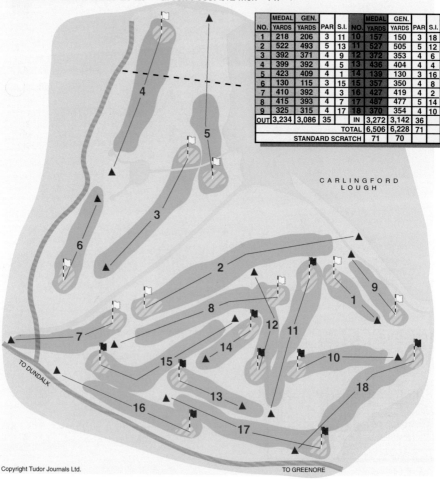

NO.	MEDAL YARDS	GEN. YARDS	PAR	S.I.	NO.	MEDAL YARDS	GEN. YARDS	PAR	S.I.
1	218	206	3	11	10	157	150	3	18
2	522	493	5	13	11	527	505	5	12
3	392	371	4	9	12	372	353	4	6
4	399	392	4	5	13	436	404	4	4
5	423	409	4	1	14	139	130	3	16
6	130	115	3	15	15	357	350	4	8
7	410	392	4	3	16	427	419	4	2
8	415	393	4	7	17	487	477	5	14
9	325	315	4	17	18	370	354	4	10
OUT	3,234	3,086	35		IN	3,272	3,142	36	
					TOTAL	6,506	6,228	71	
					STANDARD SCRATCH	71	70		

CARLINGFORD
LOUGH

TO DUNDALK

TO GREENORE

KILLINBEG

LEINSTER ■ **LOUTH**

Killinbeg, Dundalk, Co. Louth.
Tel: (042) 39303.

LOCATION: Three miles from Killen
town centre — off the
Castleblaney road.
SECRETARY: Michael Donnelly.
Tel: (042) 39303.
ARCHITECT: Eddie Hackett.

Killen Park is a privately owned course
situated in rolling parkland with mature trees
and scenic views of the Mourne mountains.
Bordered by Killin wood and the Castletown
River, this exceptionally free draining course
has American style greens. Noted for its 9th
hole which resembles the 10th at the Belfry,
this course offers a challenge even to the most
experienced golfer.

COURSE INFORMATION

Par 72; SSS 69; Length
5,554 metres.
Visitors: Welcome anytime.
Ladies: Welcome.
Green Fees: £10 Mon – Fri; £14
Sat/Sun/Bank Holidays.
Clubhouse Hours: Sunrise to
Sunset.
Clubhouse Facilities: From
8.30am. Full clubhouse facilities.
Catering facilities every day. Club
hire and caddie cart hire available.

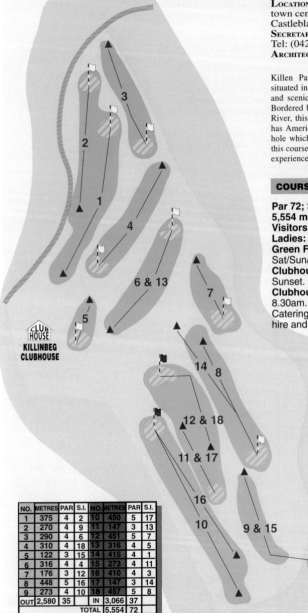

NO.	METRES	PAR	S.I.	NO.	METRES	PAR	S.I.
1	375	4	2	10	450	5	17
2	270	4	9	11	147	3	13
3	290	4	6	12	451	5	7
4	310	4	18	13	316	4	5
5	122	3	15	14	415	4	1
6	316	4	4	15	273	4	11
7	176	3	12	16	410	4	3
8	448	5	16	17	147	3	14
9	273	4	10	18	457	5	8
OUT	2,580	35		IN	3,066	37	
				TOTAL	5,554	72	
				STANDARD SCRATCH		59	

KILLINBEG
CLUBHOUSE

Copyright Tudor Journals Ltd.

Thomastown, Dunshaughlin, Co. Meath.
Tel: (01) 8250021.
Fax (01) 8250400.

LOCATION: 1 mile from Dunshaughlin – off Ratoath road.
HON. SECRETARY: S. Markman. Tel: (01) 8250021.
ARCHITECT: R. J. Browne.
OFFICE MANAGER: MS J. McDermott.

A new 27 hole course which opened in June 1990. It is situated in a beautiful parkland setting, with a memorable 1st hole playing over the lake. There is also a driving range available and a new nine hole course was opened in August 1992.

COURSE INFORMATION

18 Hole: Par 73; SSS 72; Length 6,360 metres. 9 Hole: 2,986 Metres, Par 35.

Visitors: Welcome any day.
Opening Hours: Sunrise – Sunset.
Avoid: Saturday and Sunday mornings (18 hole course only).
Ladies: Welcome.
Green Fees: £13 Mon – Fri; £15 Sat/Sun.
Juveniles: Must be accompanied by an adult. Telephone appointment required for weekend play.
Clubhouse Hours: 8.00am – midnight.
Clubhouse Dress: Casual daylight hours; No shorts or jeans.

Clubhouse Facilities: Dining room, snack bar and a la carte available all day. Pro Shop, Services professional, SOG practice balls, driving range & lessons Tel: 8259793
Open Competitions: Various open days in May, June and July; Open week – August.

COURSE A

NO.	CHAMP YARDS	MEDAL YARDS	PAR	S.I.	NO.	CHAMP YARDS	MEDAL YARDS	PAR	S.I.
1	558	464	5	9	10	503	470	5	18
2	170	153	3	7	11	397	383	4	12
3	580	536	5	5	12	394	383	4	8
4	158	133	3	15	13	164	153	3	16
5	416	383	4	1	14	432	416	4	4
6	383	366	4	11	15	400	388	4	2
7	421	410	4	3	16	186	175	3	10
8	361	328	4	13	17	378	361	4	14
9	462	443	5	17	18	567	525	5	6
OUT	3,509	3,216	37		IN	3,421	3,254	36	
					TOTAL	6,930	6,470	73	
					STANDARD SCRATCH	73	71		

COURSE B

NO.	CHAMP YARDS	MEDAL YARDS	PAR	S.I.	NO.	CHAMP YARDS	MEDAL YARDS	PAR	S.I.
1	503	470	5	18	10	353	332	4	13
2	397	383	4	12	11	184	170	3	7
3	394	383	4	8	12	522	509	5	11
4	164	153	3	16	13	377	344	4	9
5	432	416	4	4	14	437	421	4	1
6	400	388	4	2	15	345	331	4	15
7	186	175	3	10	16	140	132	3	17
8	387	361	4	14	17	394	383	4	3
9	567	525	5	6	18	386	364	4	5
OUT	3,421	3,254	36		IN	3,138	2,986	35	
					TOTAL	6,559	6,240	71	
					STANDARD SCRATCH	71	70		

COURSE C

NO.	CHAMP YARDS	MEDAL YARDS	PAR	S.I.	NO.	CHAMP YARDS	MEDAL YARDS	PAR	S.I.
1	353	332	4	14	10	558	464	4	18
2	184	170	3	8	11	170	153	4	12
3	522	509	5	12	12	580	536	3	8
4	377	344	4	10	13	158	133	5	14
5	437	421	4	2	14	416	383	4	4
6	345	331	4	16	15	383	366	4	10
7	140	132	3	18	16	421	410	3	6
8	394	383	4	4	17	361	328	5	16
9	386	364	4	6	18	462	443	4	2
OUT	3,138	2,986	35		IN	3,509	3,207	36	
					TOTAL	6,647	6,193	72	
					STANDARD SCRATCH	72	70		

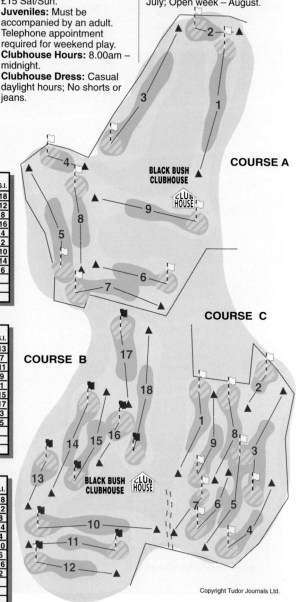

COURSE A

BLACK BUSH CLUBHOUSE

CLUB HOUSE

COURSE C

COURSE B

BLACK BUSH CLUBHOUSE

CLUB HOUSE

Kells, Co. Meath.
Tel: (046) 40146.

LOCATION: Kells/Navan road – within one mile of town.
HON. SECRETARY: Peter McFeely.
Tel: (046) 40146.
PROFESSIONAL: Brendan McGovern.
Tel: (046) 40639.

Generally accepted as a first class parkland course, the Headfort Club is set in the rolling countryside of Kells.

COURSE INFORMATION

Par 72; SSS 69; Length 5,973 metres.
Visitors: Welcome.
Opening Hours: Sunrise – Sunset.
Avoid: Weekends and Tue.
Ladies: Welcome.
Green Fees: £15 Mon – Fri; £18 Sat/Sun/Bank Holidays.
Juveniles: Must be accompanied by an adult (adults with juveniles must give way). Lessons available by prior arrangement; Club hire available; Caddy service available by prior arrangments; Telephone appointment required.
Clubhouse Hours: 10.45am – 11.30pm.
Clubhouse Dress: Casual.
Clubhouse Facilities: Full facilities in new clubhouse.

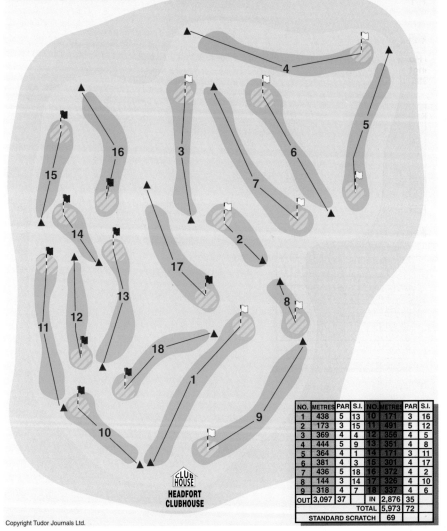

CLUB HOUSE
HEADFORT CLUBHOUSE

NO.	METRES	PAR	S.I.	NO.	METRES	PAR	S.I.
1	438	5	13	10	171	3	16
2	173	3	15	11	491	5	12
3	369	4	4	12	356	4	5
4	444	5	9	13	351	4	8
5	364	4	1	14	171	3	11
6	381	4	3	15	301	4	17
7	436	5	18	16	372	4	2
8	144	3	14	17	326	4	10
9	318	4	7	18	337	4	6
OUT	3,097	37		IN	2,876	35	
				TOTAL	5,973	72	
				STANDARD SCRATCH	69		

KILCOCK

Gallow, Kilcock,
Co. Meath.
Tel: (01) 6287592/6287283.

LOCATION: South Meath.
SECRETARY: Pat McKenna.
PROFESSIONAL: Gerard Canning.
Tel: (01) 6287283.
ARCHITECT: Eddie Hackett.

A relatively easy course for experienced players. Large greens and tees. Generally flat but slopes into a centre stream that features in the course. The club keeps its membership under 200 and therefore all visitors are welcome.

COURSE INFORMATION

Par 71; SSS 68; Length 5,364 metres.
Visitors: Welcome except Sunday morning. Saturday by prior arrangement.
Opening Hours: Sunrise – Sunset.
Ladies: Welcome except Sunday morning & Saturday afternoon.
Green Fees: £9 (+VAT) Mon – Fri; £10 (+VAT) Sat/Sun; £3 (+VAT) Juveniles.
Juveniles: Welcome except Sunday morning (must be accompanied by an adult).
Clubhouse Hours: Sunrise – Sunset.
Clubhouse Dress: Neat.
Clubhouse Facilities: Limited.
Open Competitions: Open Days throughout the summer.

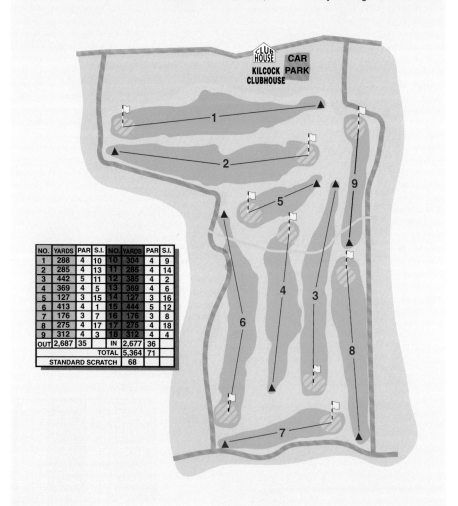

NO.	YARDS	PAR	S.I.	NO.	YARDS	PAR	S.I.
1	288	4	10	10	304	4	9
2	285	4	13	11	285	4	14
3	442	5	11	12	385	4	2
4	369	4	5	13	369	4	6
5	127	3	15	14	127	3	16
6	413	4	1	15	444	5	12
7	176	3	7	16	176	3	8
8	275	4	17	17	275	4	18
9	312	4	3	18	312	4	4
OUT	2,687	35		IN	2,677	36	
				TOTAL	5,364	71	
STANDARD SCRATCH		68					

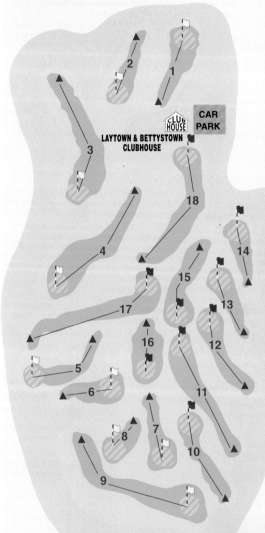

Bettystown, Co. Meath.
Tel: (041) 27170/27534/27563.

LOCATION: Thirty miles north of Dublin.
SECRETARY: Stella Garvey-Hoey.
Tel: (041) 27170.
PROFESSIONAL: Robert J Browne.
Tel: (041) 27563.

This is a traditional links course with the reputation of a tough par of 70. It has produced many fine players, the best known of whom is Des Smyth.

COURSE INFORMATION

Par 70; SSS 69; Length 5,652 metres.
Visitors: Welcome Mon – Fri.
Opening Hours: 8.30am – Sunset.
Avoid: Weekends.
Ladies: Welcome.
Green Fees: £18 Mon – Fri; £22 Sat/Sun.
Juveniles: Welcome. Lessons available by prior arrangement; Club Hire available.
Clubhouse Hours: 10.30am – licencing hours.
Clubhouse Dress: Neat Dress.
Clubhouse Facilities: Catering facilities available from 1.00pm.
Open Competitions: Open week June, July & August .

NO.	MEDAL METRES	GEN. METRES	PAR	S.I.	NO.	MEDAL METRES	GEN. METRES	PAR	S.I.
1	292	272	4	13	10	347	343	4	5
2	310	306	4	10	11	420	420	4	1
3	373	337	4	3	12	357	348	4	4
4	440	433	5	14	13	313	310	4	16
5	335	329	4	8	14	150	143	3	17
6	169	167	3	15	15	359	353	4	7
7	363	363	4	6	16	174	174	3	9
8	164	159	3	11	17	278	274	4	18
9	372	322	4	2	18	436	429	5	12
OUT	2,818	2,688	35		IN	2,834	2,794	35	
					TOTAL	5,652	5,482	70	
					STANDARD SCRATCH	69			

Bellinter, Navan, Co. Meath.
Tel: (046) 25244/25508.
LOCATION: Twenty miles north of Dublin off National Primary Route N 3.
HON. SECRETARY: Mr Paddy O'Brien.
Tel: (046) 25508.
PROFESSIONAL: Mr Adam Whiston.
Tel: (046) 26009.
ARCHITECT: Des Smyth Golf Design Ltd.

Parkland course situated in the heart of Co. Meath adjacent to the Hill of Tara, ancient home of the high kings of Ireland. A pleasant tree-lined course of average length with various degrees of difficulty.

COURSE INFORMATION

Par 70; SSS 71; Length 5,904 metres.
Visitors: Welcome.
Opening Hours: 8.00am-4.00pm.
Avoid: Ladies Day (Tuesday).
Ladies: Welcome.
Green Fees: £14 Mon-Fri; £18 Sat/Sun.
Juveniles: Welcome. Lessons available by prior arrangement; Club Hire available; Caddy service available by prior arrangements; Telephone appointment required.
Clubhouse Hours: 10.30am-11.00pm.
Clubhouse Dress: Casual.
Clubhouse Facilities: 10.00am – 10.30pm (summer); 12.00 noon – 7.00pm (winter).

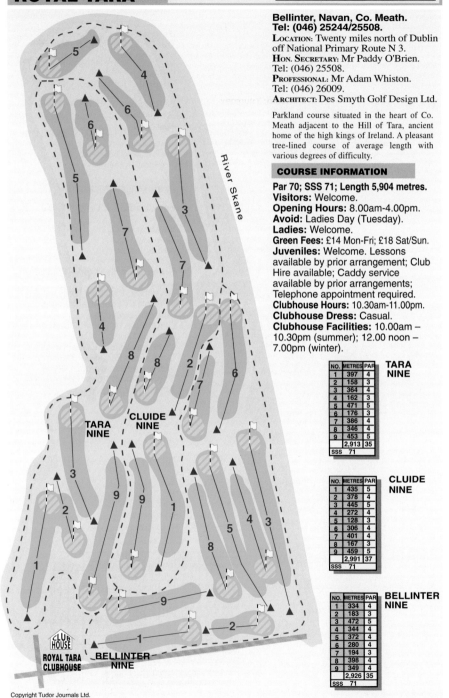

TARA NINE

NO.	METRES	PAR
1	397	4
2	158	3
3	364	4
4	162	3
5	471	5
6	176	3
7	386	4
8	346	4
9	453	5
	2,913	35
SSS	71	

CLUIDE NINE

NO.	METRES	PAR
1	435	5
2	378	4
3	445	5
4	272	4
5	128	3
6	306	4
7	401	4
8	167	3
9	459	5
	2,991	37
SSS	71	

BELLINTER NINE

NO.	METRES	PAR
1	334	4
2	183	3
3	472	5
4	344	4
5	372	4
6	280	4
7	194	3
8	398	4
9	349	4
	2,926	35
SSS	71	

Newtownmoynagh, Trim, Co. Meath.
Tel: (046) 31463.

LOCATION: Three miles from Trim on Longwood road
SECRETARY: Mr John Ennis.
Tel: (046) 31463.
ARCHITECT: E. Hackett.

Originally a pleasing nine hole course which has been recently developed into eighteen holes. Work was completed on the course in 1990.

COURSE INFORMATION

Par 73; SSS 72; Length 6,720 yards.
Visitors: Welcome.
Opening Hours: 8.00am – Sunset.
Avoid: Thursday.
Ladies: Welcome.
Ladies Day: Thursday.
Green Fees: £12 Mon – Fri; £15 Sat/Sun/Bank Holidays. Societies; Mon – Fri £11; Sat/Sun/Bank Holidays £14.

Juveniles: Welcome.
Clubhouse Hours: 10.30am – 11.30pm.
Clubhouse Dress: Casual.
Clubhouse Facilities: Full catering facilities.

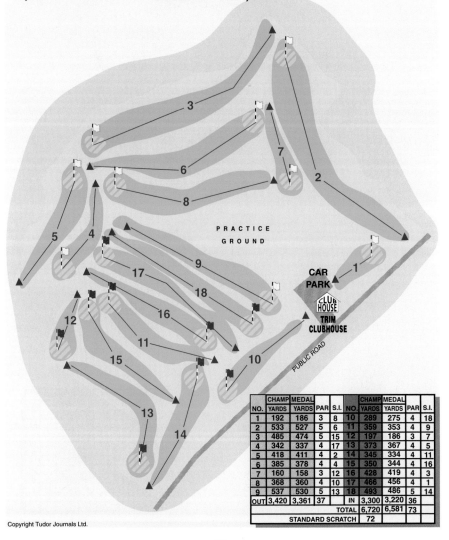

	CHAMP	MEDAL				CHAMP	MEDAL		
NO.	YARDS	YARDS	PAR	S.I.	NO.	YARDS	YARDS	PAR	S.I.
1	192	186	3	8	10	289	275	4	18
2	533	527	5	6	11	359	353	4	9
3	485	474	5	15	12	197	186	3	7
4	342	337	4	17	13	373	367	4	5
5	418	411	4	2	14	345	334	4	11
6	385	378	4	4	15	350	344	4	16
7	160	158	3	12	16	428	419	4	3
8	368	360	4	10	17	466	456	4	1
9	537	530	5	13	18	493	486	5	14
OUT	3,420	3,361	37		IN	3,300	3,220	36	
						TOTAL	6,720	6,581	73
						STANDARD SCRATCH	72		

The Glenns, Birr, Co. Offaly.
Tel: (0509) 20082.

LOCATION: Two miles west of Birr.
SECRETARY: Mr. Jim McMenamin.

Undulating parkland course with sandy sub-soil, the greatest difficulties being "blind" shots and the strategic placing of pines.

COURSE INFORMATION

Par 70; SSS 70; Length 5,727 metres.
Visitors: Welcome, limited to 11.00am – 12.00 noon on Sundays.
Opening Hours: Sunrise – Sunset.
Avoid: Weekends if possible.
Ladies: Welcome.

Green Fees: £10 Mon – Fri; £12 per round Sat/Sun/Bank Holidays.
Juveniles: Welcome.
Clubhouse Hours: 10.00am – 12.00 midnight.
Clubhouse Dress: Casual.
Clubhouse Facilities: By prior arrangement.

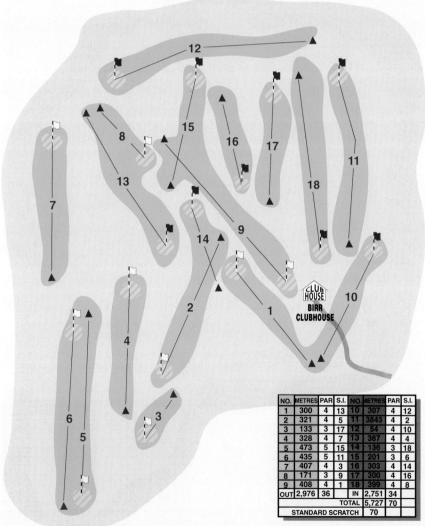

NO.	METRES	PAR	S.I.	NO.	METRES	PAR	S.I.
1	300	4	13	10	307	4	12
2	321	4	5	11	3843	4	2
3	133	3	17	12	54	4	10
4	328	4	7	13	367	4	4
5	473	5	15	14	136	3	18
6	435	5	11	15	201	3	6
7	407	4	3	16	303	4	14
8	171	3	9	17	300	4	16
9	408	4	1	18	399	4	8
OUT	2,976	36		IN	2,751	34	
				TOTAL	5,727	70	
				STANDARD SCRATCH		70	

Copyright Tudor Journals Ltd.

**Kishavanna, Edenderry,
Co. Offaly.
Tel: (0405) 31072.**

LOCATION: Just under a mile from the town centre.
SECRETARY: Tony Smyth.
Tel: (0405) 31534.
ARCHITECT: Havers (original nine hole). E. Hackett (new nine holes).
Unique in so much that it is built almost entirely on fen peat. An attractive 18 hole course, the par 3's in particular being challenging. Trees and traps are ideally located. .

COURSE INFORMATION

Par 73; SSS 72; Length 6,121 yards.
Visitors: Welcome (Weekends Limited).
Opening Hours: 8.30am – Sunset.
Avoid: Thursdays (Ladies Comp. Day).
Ladies: Welcome.
Green Fees: Weekend £10 (£8 with member) Weekday £8 (£6 with member).
Juveniles: Must be accompanied by an adult.
Clubhouse Hours: 11.00am – 11.00pm March – October.
Clubhouse Dress: Casual.
Clubhouse Facilities: Full bar & catering facilities.
Open Competitions: First week in August & most Bank Holidays.

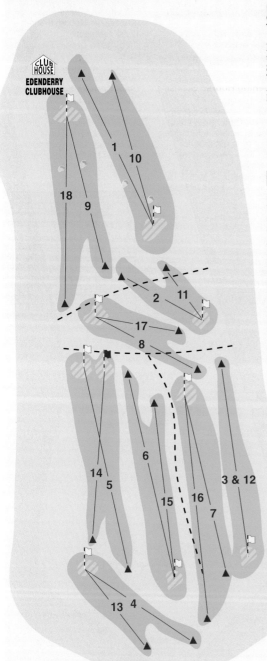

CLUB HOUSE

EDENDERRY CLUBHOUSE

NO.	YARDS	PAR	S.I.	NO.	YARDS	PAR	S.I.
1	332	4	7	10	301	4	14
2	159	3	13	11	118	3	18
3	402	4	1	12	442	5	10
4	231	4	17	13	172	3	8
5	321	4	9	14	436	5	12
6	445	5	11	15	362	4	2
7	346	4	5	16	462	5	6
8	218	3	3	17	162	3	16
9	288	4	15	18	334	4	4
OUT	2,742	36		IN	2,789	37	
				TOTAL	6,121	73	
				STANDARD SCRATCH	72		

Bunker positions indicated.

**Brookfield, Tullamore,
Co. Offaly.
Tel: (0506) 21439.**

LOCATION: Three miles south
west of Tullamore town.
SECRETARY: A. Marsden.
Tel: (0506) 51317.
PROFESSIONAL: Donagh
MacArdle.
Tel: (0506) 51757.
ARCHITECT: James Braid.

Parkland course situated in a very
attractive tree lined setting on the
outskirts of Tullamore.

COURSE INFORMATION

**Par 71; SSS 70; Length
5,779 metres.**
Visitors: Welcome every day
except special event days.
Opening Hours: Sunrise –
Sunset.
Avoid: Tuesday.
Ladies: Tuesday. Lessons
available, Club hire & Caddy
service available, telephone
appointment required for
groups only. (Advised for
other days).
Green Fees: £12 Men, £10
Ladies, Mon - Fri; £15 Men,

£12 Ladies, weekends.
Clubhouse Hours: 8.30am –
12.00 midnight.
Clubhouse Dress: Casual.
No shorts.
Clubhouse Facilities: Full
catering facilities.
Open Competitions: Open
Charity Fourball -
March/August; Open Week -
June; Mixed - July;
Intermediate Sc. Cup –
September; Mixed Hamper –
October; Men's Foursomes
Hamper – November.

NO.	METRES	PAR	S.I.	NO.	METRES	PAR	S.I.
1	281	4	17	10	402	4	2
2	478	5	5	11	201	3	8
3	341	4	7	12	443	5	14
4	168	3	13	13	117	3	18
5	413	4	1	14	348	4	6
6	318	4	9	15	284	4	16
7	162	3	15	16	180	3	12
8	369	4	3	17	354	4	4
9	458	5	11	18	462	5	10
OUT	2,988	36		IN	2,791	35	
				TOTAL	5,779	71	
				STANDARD SCRATCH	70		

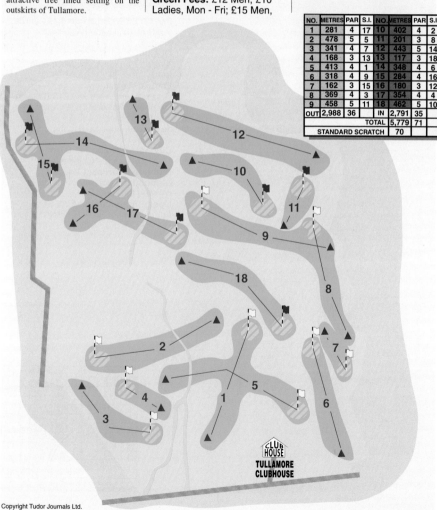

**TULLAMORE
CLUBHOUSE**

Glasson, Golf and Country Club, Glasson. Athlone, Co. Westmeath.
Tel: (0902) 85120. (Office)
Tel: (0902) 85470. (Clubhouse)
Fax: (0902) 85444.

LOCATION: 6 miles north of Athlone Town.
SECRETARY: Fidelma Reid.
Tel: (0902) 85120.
ARCHITECT: Christy O'Connor Jnr.

A Christy O'Connor Jnr. masterpiece that has all golfers talking. Every hole is breathtaking and measuring over 7000 yds from the championship tees it is a true test for all golfing standards.

COURSE INFORMATION

Par 72; SSS 74; Length 7,120 Yards.
Visitors: Welcome anyday.
Opening Hours: Sunrise – Sunset.

Green Fees: £22 (Midweek), £25 (Weekend). Caddies available on request.
Clubhouse Facilities: Catering facilities available at all times.
Open Competitions: Easter weekend, August bank holiday weekend and several other dates throughout the year.

NO.	CHAMP YARDS	MEDAL YARDS	PAR	S.I.	NO.	CHAMP YARDS	MEDAL YARDS	PAR	S.I.
1	396	373	4	15	10	513	476	5	18
2	552	536	5	7	11	183	165	3	14
3	219	190	3	5	12	406	380	4	16
4	406	384	4	9	13	397	369	4	6
5	199	177	3	17	14	566	521	5	12
6	559	535	5	13	15	185	170	3	8
7	410	386	4	1	16	452	417	4	4
8	432	404	4	11	17	450	432	4	2
9	412	377	4	3	18	383	361	4	10
OUT	3,585	3,362	36		IN	3,535	3,291	36	
					TOTAL	7,120	6,653	72	
					STANDARD SCRATCH	74	72		

3

4   5

6

7

2

8

9

2A   1A

3A

1

18

CLUB HOUSE
GLASSON CLUBHOUSE

10

17

12

15   16

13

11

LOUGH REE

14

Bunker and tree positions indicated.
Copyright Tudor Journals Ltd.

Ballinagarby, Moate, Co. Westmeath.
Tel: (0902) 81271.

LOCATION: Less than one mile north of Moate on Mount Temple road.
HON SECRETARY: Joe Creggy.
Tel: (0902) 81270.
PRESIDENT: Michael Glennon.
CAPTAIN: Liam Galvin.

A narrow course which adds to the degree of difficulty. A nine hole parkland course with eighteen tees. It enjoys good drainage which means it is not affected by heavy rainfall and is playable throughout the winter.

COURSE INFORMATION

Par 68; SSS 66; Length 4,879 metres.
Visitors: Welcome.
Opening Hours: Sunrise – Sunset.
Avoid: Sunday.
Ladies: Welcome. Letter of introduction/handicap certificate for open competitions.
Green Fees: Mon - Fri £7 (with member £5); Sat, Sun & Bank Hols £10 (with member £5).
Juveniles: Welcome.
Caddy service available by

prior arrangement; Letter of introduction or handicap certificate required for open competitions; Telephone appointment required.
Clubhouse Hours: 9.00am – 11.00 pm.
Clubhouse Dress: Casual.
Clubhouse Facilities: Catering by arrangement.
Open Competitions: Inter Scratch Cup; Junior Scratch Cup; Open Week; Open Hamper.

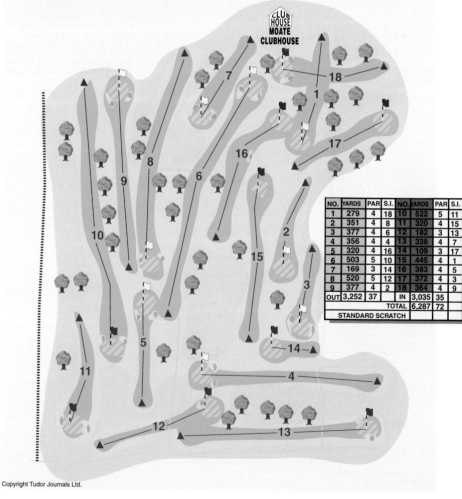

NO.	YARDS	PAR	S.I.	NO.	YARDS	PAR	S.I.
1	279	4	18	10	522	5	11
2	351	4	8	11	320	4	15
3	377	4	6	12	182	3	13
4	356	4	13	13	338	4	7
5	320	4	16	14	109	3	17
6	503	5	10	15	445	4	1
7	169	3	14	16	383	4	5
8	520	5	12	17	372	4	3
9	377	4	2	18	364	4	9
OUT	3,252	37		IN	3,035	35	
				TOTAL	6,287	72	
STANDARD SCRATCH							

**Belvedere, Mullingar,
Co. Westmeath.
Tel: (044) 48629/48366.**

LOCATION: Three miles south of
Mullingar.
HON. SECRETARY: Chris Garry.
Tel: (044) 42753 (H).
SECRETARY/MANAGER:
Charles Mulligan.
Tel: (044) 48366.
Fax: (044) 41499.
PROFESSIONAL: John Burns.
Tel: (044) 40085.

This parkland golf at its most
sublime. Generous, rolling fairways
wind their paths through mature
timbers. It hosts an important
amateur events in Britain and
Ireland annually in the shape of the
Mullingar Scratch Cup.

COURSE INFORMATION

**Par 72; SSS 71; Length
6,200 metres.
Visitors:** Welcome. Prior
arrangement required for
weekends.

Opening Hours: 8.00am –
Sunset.
Avoid: Wednesday and
weekends.
Green Fees: Winter – £10 Mon
– Fri; £15 Weekends. Summer –
£16 Mon – Fri; £23 Weekends.
Ladies: Welcome.
Juveniles: Welcome.
Clubhouse Hours: 10.00am –
11.30pm.
Clubhouse Dress: Casual,
no shorts.
Clubhouse Facilities:
Bar food.

NO.	METRES	PAR	S.I.	NO.	METRES	PAR	S.I.
1	332	4	10	10	420	4	2
2	182	3	7	11	342	4	9
3	378	4	3	12	142	3	18
4	483	5	12	13	360	4	5
5	173	3	11	14	478	5	15
6	315	4	16	15	154	3	17
7	448	4	1	16	485	5	8
8	329	4	6	17	368	4	4
9	330	4	14	18	481	5	13
OUT	2,970	35		IN	3,230	37	
				TOTAL	6,200	72	
STANDARD SCRATCH		71					

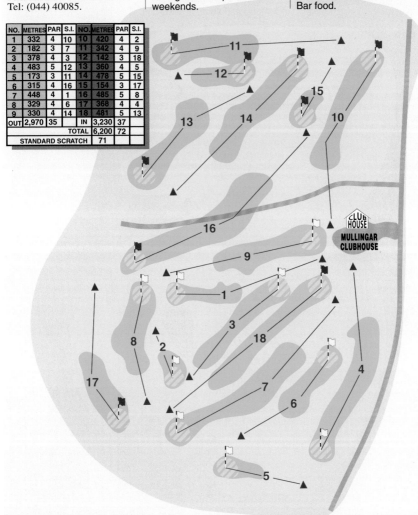

Kiltennel, Gorey,
Co. Wexford
Tel: (055) 25166.
Fax: 055 25553.

LOCATION: 3 miles from Gorey.
SECRETARY / MANAGER: John Finn.
Tel: (055) 25166.
PROFESSIONAL: John Coone.
Tel: (055) 25558/25166.

A tree lined parkland course which enjoys pleasant views overlooking the sea on the outskirts of this Co. Wexford town.

COURSE INFORMATION

Par 71; SSS 71; Length 6,455 yards, 5,898 metres.
Visitors: Welcome except on major competition days and Tuesdays.
Opening Hours: Sunrise – Sunset.
Ladies: Welcome. Lessons available; Club Hire available; Caddy cars available.
Green Fees: Winter – £16 weekdays, £12 weekends & Bank Hols, Summer – £20

weekdays, £16 weekends & Bank Hols; (All plus V.A.T.)
Clubhouse Hours: 10.30am – 11.30pm.
Clubhouse Dress: Casual / neat.
Clubhouse Facilities: Afternoons and evenings June – September. Other times by arrangement.
Open Competitions: Open Week June.

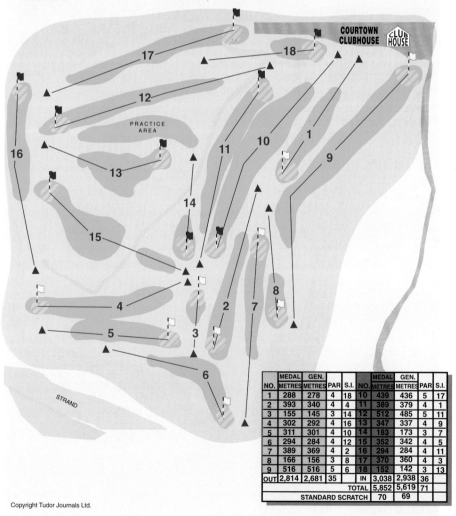

NO.	MEDAL METRES	GEN. METRES	PAR	S.I.	NO.	MEDAL METRES	GEN. METRES	PAR	S.I.
1	288	278	4	18	10	439	436	5	17
2	393	340	4	4	11	389	379	4	1
3	155	145	3	14	12	512	485	5	11
4	302	292	4	16	13	347	337	4	9
5	311	301	4	10	14	183	173	3	7
6	294	284	4	12	15	352	342	4	5
7	389	369	4	2	16	294	284	4	11
8	166	156	3	8	17	370	360	4	3
9	516	516	5	6	18	152	142	3	13
OUT	2,814	2,681	35		IN	3,038	2,938	36	
					TOTAL	5,852	5,619	71	
					STANDARD SCRATCH	70	69		

ENNISCORTHY   L E I N S T E R   WEXFORD

**Knockmarshall, Enniscorthy,
Co. Wexford.
Tel: (054) 33191.**

LOCATION: 2 miles from Enniscorthy
post office off main New Ross Road.
SECRETARY / MANAGER: Ann Byrne.
Tel: (054) 35257.
ARCHITECT: E. Hackett.

Reasonably straight forward course that
will provide little trouble for either the
low or high handicap golfer.

COURSE INFORMATION

**Par 70; SSS 70; Length 5,697
metres.
Visitors:** Welcome.
Opening Hours: Sunrise –
Sunset.
Avoid: Weekends or Telephone
first.
Ladies: Welcome.
Juveniles: Welcome. Telephone
appointment required for open
competitions.
Green Fees: £12 Mon – Fri; £14
Sat / Sun / Bank Holidays.
Clubhouse Hours: 11.00am –
11.00pm; Full clubhouse facilities;
Catering facilities up to
9.00pm daily.
Clubhouse Dress: Casual.

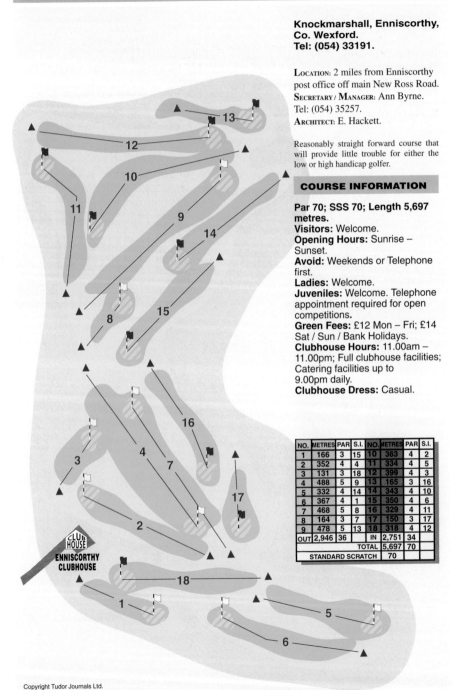

NO.	METRES	PAR	S.I.	NO.	METRES	PAR	S.I.
1	166	3	15	10	363	4	2
2	352	4	4	11	334	4	5
3	131	3	18	12	399	4	3
4	488	5	9	13	165	3	16
5	332	4	14	14	343	4	10
6	367	4	1	15	350	4	6
7	468	5	8	16	329	4	11
8	164	3	7	17	150	3	17
9	478	5	13	18	318	4	12
OUT	2,946	36		IN	2,751	34	
				TOTAL	5,697	70	
				STANDARD SCRATCH		70	

ENNISCORTHY
CLUBHOUSE

Copyright Tudor Journals Ltd.

NEW ROSS

Tinneranny, New Ross, Co. Wexford.

LOCATION: Tinneranny.
HONORARY SECRETARY: Edward Conway.
SECRETARY / MANAGER: Kathleen Daly.
Tel: (051) 21433.

Pleasant, well kept 18 hole golf course. Straight hitting and careful placing of shots is very important as the fairways are tight and allow little room for errors.

COURSE INFORMATION

Par 71; SSS 70; Length 5,751 metres.
Visitors: Welcome weekdays and Saturdays.

Opening Hours: Sunrise – Sunset.
Avoid: Sunday.
Ladies: Welcome.
Juveniles: Welcome.
Green Fees: £10 Mon – Fri; £12 Sat/Sun.
Clubhouse Hours: 8.00am – 11.30pm (summer); 9.00am – 10.30pm (winter). Full clubhouse facilities.
Clubhouse Dress: Casual.
Clubhouse Facilities: By arrangement.

NO.	MEDAL METRES	GEN. METRES	PAR	S.I.	NO.	MEDAL METRES	GEN. METRES	PAR	S.I.
1	334	329	4	6	10	475	465	5	5
2	171	158	3	10	11	169	169	3	9
3	290	272	4	18	12	301	293	4	17
4	420	408	5	14	13	470	434	5	15
5	332	309	4	12	14	163	152	3	11
6	323	309	4	2	15	363	343	4	1
7	335	321	4	8	16	329	309	4	13
8	366	350	4	4	17	357	347	4	7
9	148	139	3	16	18	405	388	4	3
OUT	2,719	2,595	35		IN	3,032	2,900	36	
					TOTAL	5,751	5,495	71	
					STANDARD SCRATCH	70	69		

NEW ROSS CLUBHOUSE

CAR PARK

Bunker & Hedge positions indicated.
Copyright Tudor Journals Ltd.

ROSSLARE

Rosslare, Co. Wexford.
Tel: (053) 32113.
Fax: (053) 32203.

LOCATION: In the village of Rosslare.
SECRETARY: Emily Ward
MANAGER: James F. Hall.
Tel: (053) 32203.
PROFESSIONAL: Austin Skerritt.
Tel: (053) 32238.

Pleasant links which provides a good test of golf. An enjoyable course for both the good and not so good golfer.

COURSE INFORMATION

Par 72; SSS 71;
Length 6,554 yards.
Visitors: Welcome.
Opening Hours: Sunrise – Sunset.
Avoid: No particular day. Telephone first to avoid disappointment.
Ladies: Welcome; Ladies Day Tuesday.
Juveniles: Welcome. Lessons available by prior arrangment; Club Hire available; Caddy service available by prior arrangment; Handicap Certificate required for open competitions.
Green Fees: £20 Mon – Fri; £25 Sat/Sun.
Clubhouse Hours: Sunrise – Sunset; Full clubhouse facilities; Full catering facilities.
Clubhouse Dress: Casual / neat.
Open Competitions: Most Sundays. In high season open to visitor paying green fees.

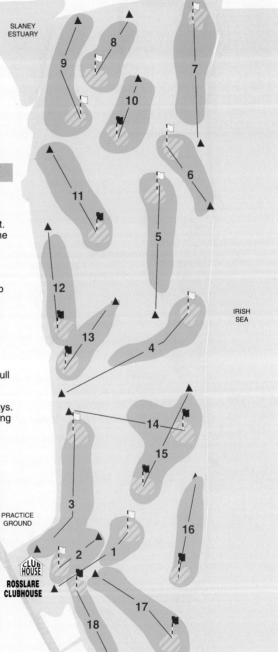

NO.	YARDS	PAR	S.I.	NO.	YARDS	PAR	S.I.
1	356	4	12	10	164	4	8
2	172	3	11	11	469	3	16
3	518	5	9	12	472	4	14
4	373	4	6	13	282	4	6
5	443	4	2	14	160	4	12
6	335	4	18	15	403	3	18
7	554	5	7	16	365	4	2
8	177	3	13	17	418	5	10
9	399	4	4	18	482	4	4
OUT	3,327	36		IN	3,215	35	
				TOTAL	6,554	70	
				STANDARD SCRATCH		71	

SLANEY ESTUARY

IRISH SEA

PRACTICE GROUND

CLUB HOUSE

ROSSLARE CLUBHOUSE

NO.	CHAMP METRES	MEDAL METRES	PAR	S.I.	NO.	CHAMP METRES	MEDAL METRES	PAR	S.I.
1	410	399	5	17	10	488	463	5	4
2	379	367	4	6	11	175	164	3	12
3	192	183	3	10	12	406	386	4	1
4	288	280	4	18	13	419	405	4	5
5	305	298	4	8	14	299	290	4	14
6	308	296	4	16	15	567	482	5	9
7	165	159	3	13	16	368	360	4	11
8	412	400	4	2	17	192	186	3	3
9	478	461	5	7	18	240	234	4	15
OUT	2,937	2,843	36		IN	3,154	2,970	36	
					TOTAL	6,091	5,813	72	
			STANDARD SCRATCH			72	71		

**St. Helen's, Kilrane,
Rosslare Harbour,
Co. Wexford.
Tel: (053) 33234/33669.
Fax: (053) 33803.**

LOCATION: 2 miles from Rosslare Port; 10 miles from Wexford; 90 miles from Dublin.
SECRETARY: Larry Byrne.
Tel: (053) 33234/33669.
Public Tel: (053) 33806.
Fax: (053) 33803.
COURSE DESIGN / ARCHITECT: Philip Walton.

Set in the beautiful location beside St. Helen's Bay, 14 holes of the course overlook the coast and Tuskar Lighthouse. It is a design, by Philip Walton, which takes full advantage of the onshore winds and gently sloping rural land, totally at one with nature. There are nine water features and 5,000 trees, as well as strategically lined bunkers.

COURSE INFORMATION

**Par 72; SSS 72; Length 6,091 Metres.
Type:** Parkland / Links course.
Opening Hours: Daylight Hours
Avoid: None.
Green Fees: Mon – Fri. £17 (High Season), £15 (Low Season). Sat – Sun. £22 (High Season), £18 (Low Season). Club hire available, Caddie Service available.
Clubhouse Hours: Licencing Hours.
Clubhouse Dress: Neat, casual dress.
Clubhouse Facilities & Times: Full catering and clubhouse facilities available. Telephone Caterer: Ext. 21. Accomodation on site.
Open Competitions: Throughout the year and 3 Open Weeks.

ST. HELEN'S BAY CLUBHOUSE

CAR PARK

PUTTING GREEN

Copyright Tudor Journals Ltd.

110

Mulgannon, Co. Wexford.
Tel: (053) 42238.

LOCATION: Wexford Town.
SECRETARY / MANAGER: Pat Daly.
PROFESSIONAL: Paul Roche.
Tel: (053) 46300.
ARCHITECT: H. Stutt & Co.

Parkland course with many mature trees. The location has beautiful views of County Wexford, including the Saltee Islands, Bletchin Mountains and Wexford Harbour.

COURSE INFORMATION

Par 72; SSS 70;
Length 6,306 yards, 5,766 metres.
Visitors: Welcome, should book in advance.
Opening Hours: Sunrise – sunset.
Avoid: Sun 8am – 11am.
Ladies: Weekdays 9.30am – 4.30pm. Thur Ladies Day..
Juveniles: Weekdays 10am – 4.30pm. Lessons available by prior arrangments; Club Hire available; Caddy service available by prior arrangments; Telephone appointment required.
Green Fees: Weekdays £14; Sat, Sun & Bank Hols £15 (with member £8).
Clubhouse Hours: 8am – 11.30pm (summer).
Clubhouse Dress: Casual.
Clubhouse Facilities: Snacks. Scoieties catered for by booking meals in advance.

NO.	YARDS	PAR	S.I.	NO.	YARDS	PAR	S.I.
1	190	3	6	10	340	4	9
2	317	4	14	11	505	5	11
3	395	4	7	12	166	3	12
4	348	4	13	13	491	5	16
5	386	4	4	14	451	4	3
6	151	3	8	15	134	3	17
7	263	4	18	16	399	4	1
8	540	5	10	17	462	5	15
9	433	4	2	18	335	4	5
OUT	3,023	35		IN	3,283	37	
				TOTAL	6,306	72	
	STANDARD SCRATCH					70	

CLUB HOUSE

WEXFORD CLUBHOUSE

111

ARKLOW

**Abbeylands, Arklow,
Co Wicklow.
Tel: (0402) 32492.**

LOCATION: Just south of the town centre.
SECRETARY / MANAGER:
B. Timmons.
Tel: (0402) 32492.
ARCHITECT: Haughtry Taylor.

A typical links course with majestic scenery and the opportunity to play throughout the year. Sited just outside the picturesque townland of Arklow.

COURSE INFORMATION

Par 68; SSS 67; Length 5,404 metres.
Visitors: Welcome.
Opening Hours: 9.00am – 6.00pm in Winter, 8.00am – Sunset in Summer.
Avoid: Weekends. Monday is Ladies Day.

Ladies: Welcome. Monday Ladies Day.
Juveniles: Must by accompanied by an adult. Handicap Certificate required for Open Competitions..
Green Fees: £15 Weekdays; £17 weekends.
Clubhouse Hours: 10.30am – 11.30pm.
Clubhouse Dress: Casual.
Clubhouse Facilities: By prior arrangments.
Open Competitions: Open Week July / August .

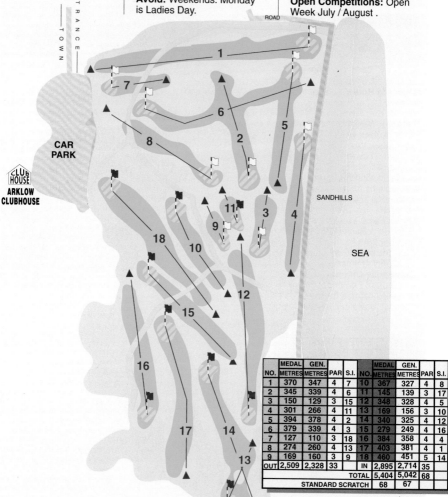

NO.	MEDAL METRES	GEN. METRES	PAR	S.I.	NO.	MEDAL METRES	GEN. METRES	PAR	S.I.
1	370	347	4	7	10	367	327	4	8
2	345	339	4	6	11	145	139	3	17
3	150	129	3	15	12	348	328	4	5
4	301	266	4	11	13	169	156	3	10
5	394	378	4	2	14	340	325	4	12
6	379	339	4	3	15	279	249	4	16
7	127	110	3	18	16	384	358	4	4
8	274	260	4	13	17	403	381	4	1
9	169	160	3	9	18	460	451	5	14
OUT	2,509	2,328	33		IN	2,895	2,714	35	
					TOTAL	5,404	5,042	68	
					STANDARD SCRATCH		68	67	

Baltinglass,
Co Wicklow.
Tel: (0508) 81350.

LOCATION: Baltinglass.
SECRETARY / MANAGER:
Maurice Byrne.
Tel: (0508) 81350.
PROFESSIONAL: Michael Murphy.

Nine hole course with alternate tees
for each nine. A scenic situation
compliments what is a difficult rating
for a nine hole course – par 34.

NO.	METRES	PAR	S.I.	NO.	METRES	PAR	S.I.
1	367	4	3	10	356	4	4
2	325	4	13	11	309	4	11
3	137	3	17	12	133	3	18
4	395	4	5	13	391	4	6
5	366	4	7	14	366	4	8
6	418	4	1	15	409	4	2
7	148	3	16	16	143	3	15
8	339	4	9	17	332	4	10
9	314	4	14	18	301	4	12
OUT	2,809	34		IN	2,740	34	
				TOTAL	5,549	68	
	STANDARD SCRATCH			69			

COURSE INFORMATION

Par 68; SSS 69; Length 6,072 yards, 5,549 metres.
Visitors: Welcome.
Opening Hours: 9.00am – Sunset. Closed in Winter months.
Avoid: Competition dates, weekends & Thursdays.
Ladies: Welcome. Ladies Day Thursday.
Juveniles: Welcome. Caddy service available by prior arrangement, telephone appointment required.
Green Fees: £10 Mon – Fri (£6 with member); £12 Sat/Sun/Bank Holidays (£8 with member).
Clubhouse Hours: 9.00am – 6.00pm (winter; 9.00am – 11.00pm (summer).
Clubhouse Dress: Casual.
Clubhouse Facilities: Catering – prior arrangments except weekends.
Open Competitions: Open Week June / July.

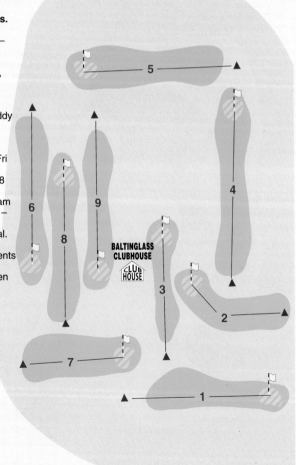

Blainroe, Co Wicklow.
Tel: (0404) 68168.
Fax: (0404) 69369.

LOCATION: 4 miles south of Wicklow Town; 35 miles south of Dublin.
SECRETARY / MANAGER: W. O'Sullivan.
Tel: (0404) 68168.
PROFESSIONAL: J. McDonald.
Tel: (0404) 68168.
ARCHITECT: Charles Hawtree.
This is a parkland course overlooking the sea. Two holes worth noting are the 14th, which is played from the cliff peninsula, and the par 3 15th hole over the lake. There is a total of 58 sand bunkers which makes it a very challenging test to all golfers.

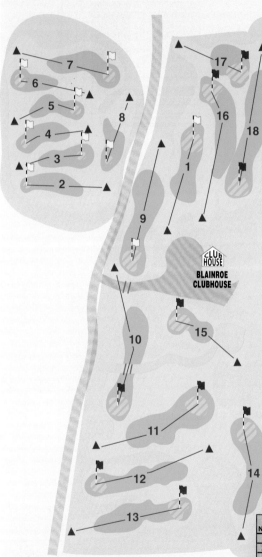

COURSE INFORMATION

Par 72; SSS 72;
Length 6,171 metres.
Visitors: Welcome.
Opening Hours: Sunrise – Sunset.
Avoid: Weekends.
Ladies: Welcome.
Juveniles: Welcome. Lessons available by prior arrangements; Club Hire available; Caddy cars available by prior arrangements.
Green Fees: £20 Mon – Fri; £25 Sat/Sun/Bank Holidays.
Clubhouse Hours: 11.00am – 11.00pm. Full Clubhouse facilities.
Clubhouse Dress: Neat dress essential.
Clubhouse Facilities: Available in season and weekends.

NO.	MEDAL METRES	GEN. METRES	PAR	S.I.	NO.	MEDAL METRES	GEN. METRES	PAR	S.I.
1	330	326	4	15	10	344	336	4	6
2	394	389	4	2	11	356	351	4	12
3	384	378	4	5	12	390	386	4	4
4	480	475	5	13	13	363	357	4	10
5	445	441	5	9	14	303	287	4	17
6	332	328	4	3	15	208	198	3	8
7	338	333	4	11	16	417	408	4	1
8	193	187	3	7	17	112	109	3	18
9	335	329	4	14	18	445	440	5	16
OUT	3,231	3,186	37		IN	2,940	2,800	35	
					TOTAL	6,171	5,986	72	
					STANDARD SCRATCH	72	71		

Ravenswell Road, Bray, Co Wicklow. Tel: 2862092.

LOCATION: Bray Town.
SECRETARY / MANAGER: T. Brennan. Tel: 2862484.
PROFESSIONAL: Michael Walby. Tel: 2760057.

Relatively short nine holes with separate tees for 1st and 2nd nine. A mostly flat inland course, but still a reasonable test of golf.

COURSE INFORMATION

Par 70; SSS 69; Length 5,784 metres.
Visitors: Welcome.
Opening Hours: 8.am – Sunset.
Avoid: Weekends and Mondays.
Ladies: Monday. Lessons available by prior arrangment.
Green Fees: £17.
Clubhouse Hours: 8.30am

– Sunset.
Clubhouse Dress: No Jeans (Course or Clubhouse); proper golf attire on course.
Clubhouse Facilities: By arrangement.

BRAY CLUBHOUSE

NO.	MEDAL METRES	GEN. METRES	PAR	S.I.	NO.	MEDAL METRES	GEN. METRES	PAR	S.I.
1	335	327	4	5	10	357	344	4	3
2	477	453	5	13	11	424	378	4	1
3	339	326	4	6	12	334	311	4	9
4	148	138	3	14	13	138	132	3	17
5	374	351	4	4	14	354	327	4	7
6	155	142	3	11	15	172	162	3	10
7	334	321	4	15	16	312	300	4	16
8	420	392	4	2	17	445	397	5/4	18
9	324	311	4	12	18	340	317	4	8
OUT	2,908	2,761	35		IN	2,876	2,668	35	
					TOTAL	5,784	5,429	70/69	
					STANDARD SCRATCH	70	68		

Tree positions indicated.

Greystones, Co Wicklow.
Tel: (01) 2876764.
Fax: (01) 2873882.

LOCATION: 18 Miles south of Dublin.
GOLF ADMINISTRATION: Madeleine Doherty.
PROFESSIONAL: Paul Heeney.
ARCHITECT: Eddie Hackett.

Parkland course in a superb setting on a delightfully rolling terrain, sweeping towards the Irish Sea. Well bunkered, with water hazards on seven of the holes. An all weather course playable twelve months of the year.

COURSE INFORMATION

Par 72; SSS 72; Length 6,159 metres.
Visitors: Welcome.
Opening Hours: Sunrise – Sunset.
Ladies: Welcome.
Juveniles: Welcome with adult or handicap certificate. Lessons available by prior arrangement.

Green Fees: Mon – Fri £23; Sat / Sun / Bank Holidays £28.
Clubhouse Dress: Neat dress essential.
Clubhouse Facilities: Full facilities available. Bar food menu and Dining Room.
Competitions: Golf Festival, August.

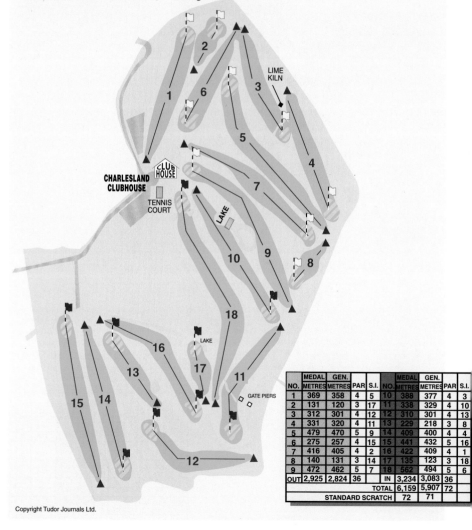

NO.	MEDAL METRES	GEN. METRES	PAR	S.I.	NO.	MEDAL METRES	GEN. METRES	PAR	S.I.
1	369	358	4	5	10	388	377	4	3
2	131	120	3	17	11	338	329	4	10
3	312	301	4	12	12	310	301	4	13
4	331	320	4	11	13	229	218	3	8
5	479	470	5	9	14	409	400	4	4
6	275	257	4	15	15	441	432	5	16
7	416	405	4	2	16	422	409	4	1
8	140	131	3	14	17	135	123	3	18
9	472	462	5	7	18	562	494	5	6
OUT	2,925	2,824	36		IN	3,234	3,083	36	
					TOTAL	6,159	5,907	72	
					STANDARD SCRATCH	72	71		

Shillelagh, Co. Wicklow.
Tel: (055) 29125.

LOCATION: South Wicklow.
SECRETARY: Dick McCrea.
Tel: (055) 26302.

A picturesque parkland course with excellent fairways and greens. The large number of trees of different varieties add greatly to the character of the course. Part of the Old Fitzwilliam Solate, set in a lovely countryside.

COURSE INFORMATION

Par 70; SSS 69; Length 6,221 yards, 5,688 metres.
Visitors: Welcome.
Opening Hours: Sunrise – Sunset.
Avoid: Weekends.
Juveniles: Welcome. Letter of Introduction required.
Green Fees: £10 Mon – Fri.
Clubhouse Hours: 5pm – 11.30pm Mon – Fri; All day Sat/Sun.
Clubhouse Dress: Casual.

Clubhouse Facilities: By prior arrangement.
Open Competitions: Open Week July.

NO.	METRES	PAR	S.I.	NO.	METRES	PAR	S.I.
1	293	4	15	10	289	4	16
2	159	3	8	11	172	3	7
3	342	4	9	12	320	4	13
4	359	4	6	13	372	4	5
5	524	5	11	14	446	5	12
6	345	4	4	15	362	4	3
7	282	4	14	16	284	4	10
8	377	4	1	17	387	4	2
9	139	3	18	18	148	3	17
OUT	3,093	35		IN	2,780	35	
				TOTAL	5,566	70	
				STANDARD SCRATCH	69		

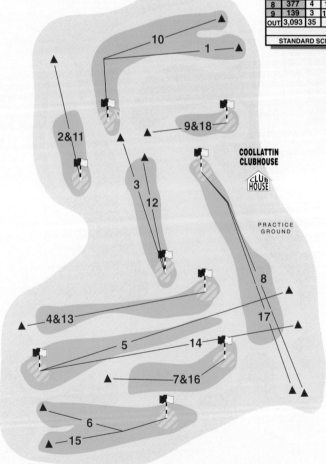

10

1

2&11

9&18

COOLLATTIN
CLUBHOUSE

CLUB
HOUSE

3

12

PRACTICE
GROUND

8

4&13

17

5

14

7&16

6

15

Delgany, Co Wicklow.
Tel: (01) 2874536.

LOCATION: Delgany Village.
SECRETARY / MANAGER:
R.J. Kelly.
Tel: (01) 2874697 (Shop).
PROFESSIONAL: Gavin
Kavanagh.
Tel: (01) 2874697.
RESIDENT PROFESSIONAL:
Paul Thompson.

Slightly hilly parkland course with
beautiful scenery and views, situated
in the attractive village of Delgany.

COURSE INFORMATION

**Par 69; SSS 68; Length
5,414 metres.**
Visitors: Welcome Monday,
Thursday and Friday.
Weekends by arrangment
only.
Opening Hours: 8.30am -
Sunset.
Avoid: Tuesday and
Wednesday afternoon.
Ladies: Welcome.
Juveniles: Welcome.
Lessons available by prior
arrangements; Club hire
available; Caddy service
available prior arrangements;
Telephone appointment
required.
Green Fees: £20 Mon – Fri;
£24 Sat/Sun.
Clubhouse Hours: 8.30am
– Licencing hours.
Clubhouse Dress:
Neat/casual.
Clubhouse Facilities:
Snacks & bar food from
11.00am. Dining room from
1.00pm.

NO.	MEDAL METRES	GEN. METRES	PAR	S.I.	NO.	MEDAL METRES	GEN. METRES	PAR	S.I.
1	367	348	4	4	10	437	331	5	9
2	276	253	4	16	11	159	148	3	7
3	344	330	4	2	12	395	386	4	1
4	352	343	4	14	13	294	285	4	15
5	166	154	3	6	14	163	154	3	11
6	359	348	4	8	15	298	284	4	17
7	302	292	4	12	16	153	142	3	13
8	126	114	3	18	17	367	335	4	5
9	368	354	4	10	18	488	471	5	3
OUT	2,660	2,536	34		IN	2,754	2,536	35	
					TOTAL	5,414	5,072	69	
	STANDARD SCRATCH		69			67			

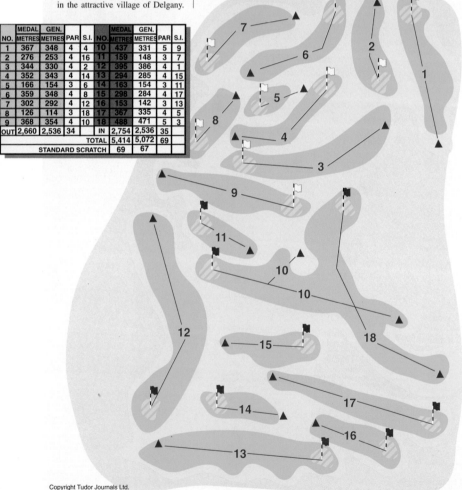

DRUIDS GLEN

LEINSTER | **WICKLOW**

Newtownmountkennedy,
Co. Wicklow.
Tel: (01) 2873600.
Fax: (01) 2873699.

LOCATION: Twenty-three miles south of Dublin City. Two miles east of Newtownmountkennedy off the N11.
GOLF DIRECTOR: Eddie Dunne. Tel: (01) 2873600
PROFESSIONAL: Eamonn Darcy.
COURSE DESIGNERS: Pat Ruddy & Tom Craddock.

Druids Glen situated on the ancestral estate of Sir Thomas Wentworth is already an acknowledged masterpiece and has the honour of hosting the 1996 Murphy's Irish Open Championship.

COURSE INFORMATION

Par 72; Length 7,058 yards.
Visitors: Welcome – tee times by arrangement.
Opening Hours: 8.00am – Sunset.

Green Fees: £75.00
Juveniles: Welcome/ caddies available by prior arrangement.
Clubhouse Hours: 8.00am – onwards.
Clubhouse Dress: Neat Casual.
Clubhouse Facilities: Snacks, Lunch, Dinner available.

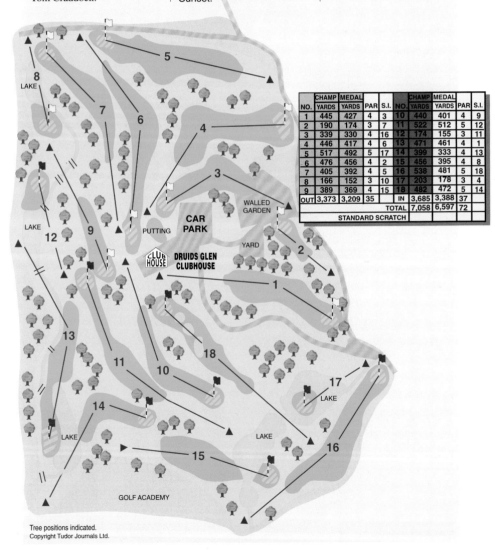

NO.	CHAMP YARDS	MEDAL YARDS	PAR	S.I.	NO.	CHAMP YARDS	MEDAL YARDS	PAR	S.I.
1	445	427	4	3	10	440	401	4	9
2	190	174	3	7	11	522	512	5	12
3	339	330	4	16	12	174	155	3	11
4	446	417	4	6	13	471	461	4	1
5	517	492	5	17	14	399	333	4	13
6	476	456	4	2	15	456	395	4	8
7	405	392	4	5	16	538	481	5	18
8	166	152	3	10	17	203	178	3	4
9	389	369	4	15	18	482	472	5	14
OUT	3,373	3,209	35		IN	3,685	3,388	37	
					TOTAL	7,058	6,597	72	
					STANDARD SCRATCH				

Tree positions indicated.
Copyright Tudor Journals Ltd.

Brittas Bay, Wicklow.
Tel: (0404) 47415.
Fax: (01) 280 8457.

LOCATION: 45 minutes from city centre via the Bray – Shankill Bypass.

SECRETARY / MANAGER: Pat & Sidon Ruddy.

ARCHITECT: Mr Pat Ruddy.

The links offers a rare variety of golf challenges and awesome scenery as the holes plunge into deep valleys in the sand dunes, run on a sand spit through age old marshlands and along and up into the rugged cliffs of Mizen Head. The Irish sea can be seen from every hole on the links and the Wickow Hills complete the scenic cocktail inland.

COURSE INFORMATION

Par 71; SSS 72; Length 6,729 yards.
Visitors: Welcome.
Opening Hours: Summer: 8am – 5pm; Winter: 8.30am – 12.30pm.
Ladies: Welcome.

Juveniles: Must be accompanied by an adult and have playing skills.
Green Fees: £25 Mon – Fri; £30 Weekends and Bank Holidays.
Clubhouse Hours: Open and available to pub closing time.
Clubhouse Dress: Casual.
Clubhouse Facilities: Full clubhouse and catering facilities. Caddy car hire available.

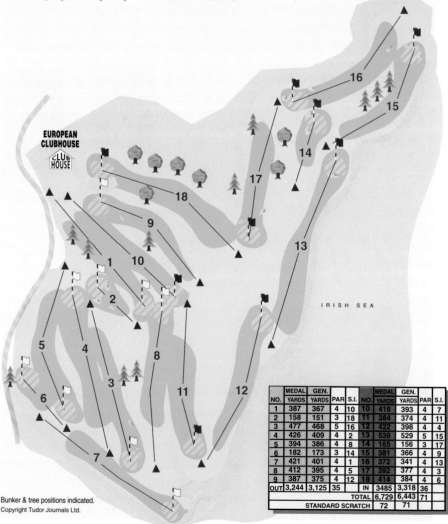

NO.	MEDAL YARDS	GEN. YARDS	PAR	S.I.	NO.	MEDAL YARDS	GEN. YARDS	PAR	S.I.
1	387	367	4	10	10	416	393	4	7
2	158	151	3	18	11	384	374	4	11
3	477	468	5	16	12	422	398	4	4
4	426	409	4	2	13	539	529	5	15
5	394	386	4	8	14	165	156	3	17
6	182	173	3	14	15	381	366	4	9
7	421	401	4	1	16	372	341	4	13
8	412	395	4	5	17	392	377	4	3
9	387	375	4	12	18	414	384	4	6
OUT	3,244	3,125	35		IN	3485	3,318	36	
					TOTAL	6,729	6,443	71	
					STANDARD SCRATCH	72	71		

Bunker & tree positions indicated.
Copyright Tudor Journals Ltd.

NO.	MEDAL METRES	GEN. METRES	PAR	S.I.	NO.	MEDAL METRES	GEN. METRES	PAR	S.I.
1	177	168	3	10	10	400	393	4	1
2	286	284	4	16	11	160	151	3	9
3	377	356	4	4	12	374	360	4	3
4	339	334	4	6	13	321	315	4	7
5	202	194	3	12	14	148	128	3	15
6	284	276	4	2	15	449	437	5	13
7	334	329	4	14	16	127	125	3	17
8	277	254	4	18	17	364	362	4	5
9	455	446	5	8	18	327	263	4	11
OUT	2,731	2,641	35	IN		2,670	2,534	34	
				TOTAL		5,401	5,175	69	
				STANDARD SCRATCH		68	67		

Greystones, Co Wicklow.
Tel: (01) 2876624.

LOCATION: 20 miles south of Dublin.
SECRETARY / MANAGER: Oliver Walsh.
Tel: (01) 2874136.
PROFESSIONAL: Kevin Daly.
Tel: (01) 2875308.

A parkland course with considerable contrasts. The first two holes and the final six are hilly and provide good views which is in stark contrast to the others which are on more level terrain. Since the building of a new clubhouse the club has been experimenting with the course layout which may be altered since our publication date.

COURSE INFORMATION

Par 69; SSS 68; Length 5,401 metres.
Visitors: Welcome Mon, Tues and Frid mornings.
Opening Hours: 9.00am – Sunset.
Avoid: Wed, Thurs and Weekends.
Ladies: Welcome.
Juveniles: Welcome. Lessons available by prior arrangment; Club hire available; Caddy cars available.
Green Fees: £20 weekdays; £24 weekend.
Clubhouse Hours: 9.00am – 12.00 midnight.
Clubhouse Dress: Casual. No jeans or sneakers.
Clubhouse Facilities: By prior arrangment.
Open Competitions: Open Week July; Intermediate Scratch Cup July.

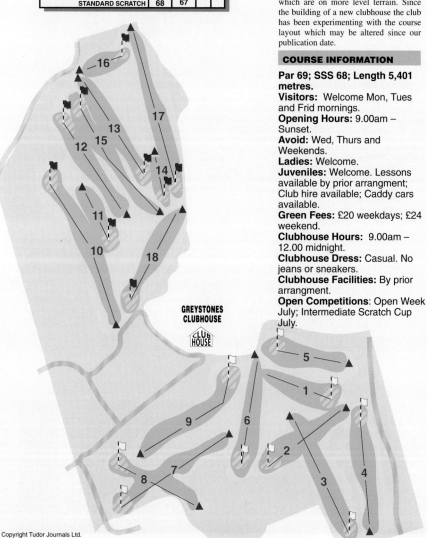

GREYSTONES
CLUBHOUSE

**Powerscourt Golf Club PLC,
Powerscourt Estate, Enniskerry,
Co. Wicklow.
Tel: (01) 286 7676. Fax: (01) 286 3561.**

LOCATION: Set in Powerscourt Estate with its world famous Gardens, 12 miles south of Bray. Powerscourt is 25 minutes from Dublin City Centre adjacent to Enniskerry village.
SECRETARY/MANAGER: Marianne Slazenger.
Tel: (01) 286 7676.

Powerscourt is a free draining course with links characteristics. Built to championship standard, with top quality tees and exceptional tiered greens, it is set in some of Ireland's most beautiful parkland. The course has an abundance of mature trees and natural features, with stunning views to the sea and Sugar Loaf Mountain. Powerscourt is simply an exceptional experience for all golfers.

COURSE INFORMATION

Par 72; SSS 74; Length 6,410 Metres.
Visitors: Welcome
Avoid: Outings restricted to 120 people or less on the course. Please book in advance.
Opening Hours: 8.30am – Sunset
Ladies: Welcome
Juveniles: With handicap welcome,
Caddies, club and trolley hire available, practice range and short game practice area also available
Green Fees: £40 weekdays; £50 weekends; £35 per round for groups of 30 or more people, corporate days (weekdays only).
Clubhouse Hours: 8.30am – 11.30pm
Clubhouse Dress: Casual. No jeans.
Clubhouse Facilities: Pro shop, restaurant and full bar facilities.

POWERSCOURT CLUBHOUSE

NO.	CHAMP METRES	MEDAL METRES	PAR	S.I.	NO.	CHAMP METRES	MEDAL METRES	PAR	S
1	401	384	4	12	10	387	351	4	
2	461	434	5	8	11	382	354	4	
3	154	131	3	14	12	498	485	5	
4	332	295	4	6	13	156	136	3	
5	216	191	3	10	14	350	299	4	
6	484	461	5	16	15	357	333	4	
7	383	336	4	4	16	145	126	3	
8	422	401	4	2	17	544	488	5	
9	348	306	4	18	18	390	347	4	
OUT	3,201	2,939	36		IN	3,209	2,919	36	
					TOTAL	6,410	5,858	72	
					STANDARD SCRATCH	74	71		

Bunkers and trees positions indicated.
Copyright Tudor Journals Ltd.

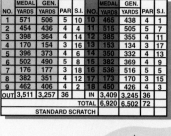

NO.	MEDAL YARDS	GEN. YARDS	PAR	S.I.	NO.	MEDAL YARDS	GEN. YARDS	PAR	S.I.
1	571	506	5	10	10	465	438	4	1
2	454	436	4	4	11	515	505	5	7
3	398	364	4	14	12	385	355	4	11
4	170	154	3	16	13	153	134	3	17
5	396	373	4	6	14	350	332	4	13
6	502	490	5	8	15	382	369	4	9
7	176	177	3	18	16	536	516	5	5
8	382	351	4	12	17	173	170	3	15
9	462	406	4	2	18	450	426	4	3
OUT	3,511	3,257	36		IN	3,409	3,245	36	
					TOTAL	6,920	6,502	72	
STANDARD SCRATCH									

Dunlavin, Co. Wicklow.
Tel: 045 403316.
Fax: 045 403295.

LOCATION: 15 miles southeast of Naas.
GENERAL MANAGER: David O'Flynn.
Tel: 045 403316.
ARCHITECT: Peter McEvoy/Christy
O'Connor Jnr.

Parkland layout on 252 acres with thousands of mature trees, water and spectacular U.S.G.A. specification greens.

COURSE INFORMATION

Par 72; Length 6,920 yards.
Visitors: Welcome (best on week days).
Opening Hours: 8am – 6pm.
Avoid: 9am–11am at weekends.
Ladies: No restrictions.
Green Fees: £20 Sun – Thur; £35 weekends (Fri, Sat & Sun & Bank Hols.).
Juveniles: Restricted.
Clubhouse Dress: Smart/Casual.
Clubhouse Facilities: Temporary showers, shop until clubhouse opens in 1996.

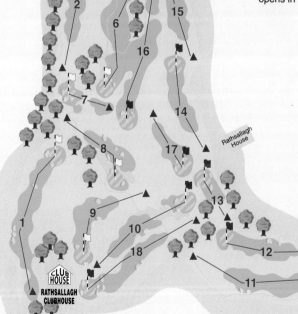

Bunker and tree positions indicated.

ROUNDWOOD

LEINSTER **WICKLOW**

**Newtownmountkennedy,
Co. Wicklow.
Tel: (01) 2818488.**

LOCATION: Accessible from the M11
Dublin to Arklow road.
SECRETARY: Mr Michael McGuirk.
Tel: (01) 2818488.
ARCHITECT: B. Malone, Dr G. Smillie,
Dr A. Morgan & Mr M. Mc Guirk.

All sand greens built to U.S.P.G.A. standards.
Water hazards and forestry.
Heathland/parkland plays like links.
Magnificent views of coast, mountains and
Roundwood lakes.

COURSE INFORMATION

Par 72; Length 6,685 yards.
Visitors: Welcome.
Opening Hours: 7am-8pm.
Ladies: Welcome.
Juveniles: Restricted.
Green Fees: £15 weekdays;
£20 weekends.
Clubhouse Dress: Smart
Casual.
Clubhouse Facilities:
Restaurant, bar facilities and
pro shop.

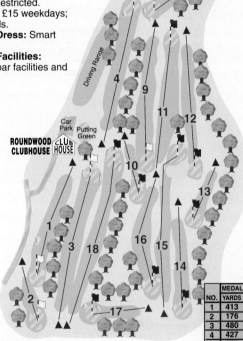

NO.	MEDAL YARDS	GEN. YARDS	PAR	S.I.	NO.	MEDAL YARDS	GEN. YARDS	PAR	S.I.
1	413	379	4	16	10	182	172	3	3
2	176	166	3	14	11	397	382	4	13
3	480	470	5	10	12	435	420	4	17
4	427	383	4	2	13	184	146	3	7
5	556	541	5	8	14	320	300	4	15
6	347	337	4	6	15	501	481	5	1
7	125	119	3	18	16	446	360	4	11
8	381	371	4	4	17	211	183	3	9
9	515	505	5	12	18	589	579	5	5
OUT	3,420	3,271	37		IN	3,265	3,023	35	
					TOTAL	6,685	6,294	72	
STANDARD SCRATCH									

Bunker and tree positions indicated.

Blessington, Co Wicklow.
Tel: (045) 864574.

LOCATION: 5 Miles from Blessington.
SECRETARY / MANAGER: Mr Adrian Williams.
Tel: (045) 864574.
ARCHITECT: Eddie Hackett.

A very interesting course with the added attraction of mature trees, good views of the Blessington Lakes and Wicklow Mountains. The 9th hole is the toughest on the course.

COURSE INFORMATION

Par 72; SSS 69; Length 5,612 metres.
Visitors: Welcome Mon - Fri. Weekends by arrangements.
Opening Hours: 7.00am – 10.00pm.
Ladies: Welcome.
Juveniles: Welcome.
Lessons available by prior arrangment; Club hire available; Caddy service available by prior arrangement; Telephone

appointment required. Under 16s not allowed on the course.
Green Fees: £11 Mon – Fri; £14 Sat / Sun / Bank Holidays; Juveniles £4.50 Mon – Fri; £5.50 Sat / Sun / Bank Holidays.
Clubhouse Hours: 10.00am - 11.00pm; Extensive Clubhouse facilities.
Clubhouse Dress: Neat dress essential.
Clubhouse Facilities: Courtyard Bar Snacks 12.30pm – 10.00pm; Courtyard Restaurant 7.00pm – 9.30pm.

NO.	METRES	PAR	S.I.	NO.	METRES	PAR	S.I.
1	149	3	15	10	149	3	16
2	424	5	9	11	424	5	10
3	362	4	3	12	362	4	4
4	340	4	5	13	340	4	6
5	156	3	13	14	156	3	14
6	415	5	11	15	415	5	12
7	327	4	7	16	327	4	8
8	249	4	17	17	249	4	18
9	384	4	1	18	384	4	2
OUT	2,806	36		IN	2,806	36	
				TOTAL	5,612	72	
				STANDARD SCRATCH	69		

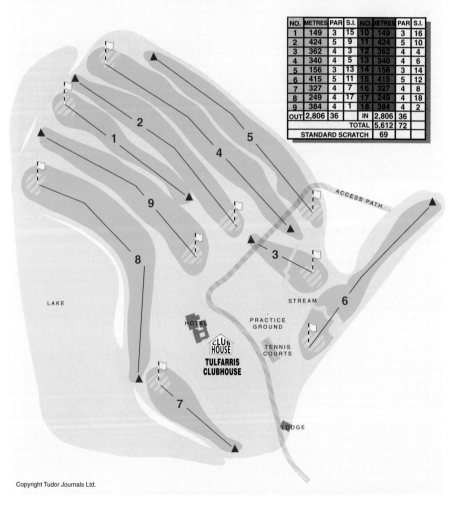

Dunbur Road, Wicklow.
Tel: (0404) 67379

Location: Wicklow town; 30 miles south of Dublin city.
Honorary Secretary: J Kelly.

The course makes full use of the natural contours and features of the terrain, creating a challenging and spectacular test of golf.

COURSE INFORMATION

Par 71; SSS 70; Length 5,695 metres.
Visitors: Welcome.
Opening Hours: Sunrise – Sunset.
Avoid: Wednesday and weekends.
Ladies: Ladies Day Wednesday.
Juveniles: Must be accompanied by an adult.

Green Fees: £15.
Clubhouse Hours: 9.00am Normal Licensing hours.
Clubhouse Dress: Neat, no jeans after 7pm.
Clubhouse Facilities: By prior arrangement. Full facilities every day except Tuesday.
Open Competitions: Regularly throughout the season. Societies welcome with prior arrangement.

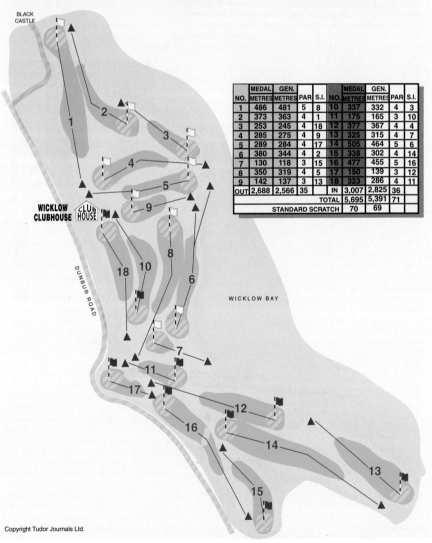

NO.	MEDAL METRES	GEN. METRES	PAR	S.I.	NO.	MEDAL METRES	GEN. METRES	PAR	S.I.
1	486	481	5	8	10	337	332	4	3
2	373	363	4	1	11	175	165	3	10
3	253	245	4	18	12	377	367	4	4
4	285	275	4	9	13	325	315	4	7
5	289	284	4	17	14	505	464	5	6
6	380	344	4	2	15	338	302	4	14
7	130	118	3	15	16	477	455	5	16
8	350	319	4	5	17	150	139	3	12
9	142	137	3	13	18	323	286	4	11
OUT	2,688	2,566	35		IN	3,007	2,825	36	
					TOTAL	5,695	5,391	71	
					STANDARD SCRATCH	70	69		

BLACK CASTLE

WICKLOW CLUBHOUSE   CLUB HOUSE

DUNBUR ROAD

WICKLOW BAY

Woodenbridge, Arklow, Co Wicklow.
Tel: (0402) 35202.

LOCATION: 4 miles west of Arklow town.
HONORARY SECRETARY: Diarmuid Healy.
Tel: (0402) 32116/31571.

A level parkland course, renowned for the quality of its greens; with carefully appointed trees and bunkers demand accurate shots. Sitting scenically in the beautiful Vale of Avoca, crouched under hills of magnificent forests and encircled by the meandering Rivers Avoca & Aughrim, it posses a charm and character very special to Woodenbridge.

COURSE INFORMATION

Par 71; SSS 71; Length 6,316 yards, 5,582 metres.
Visitors: Welcome all week except Thursday and Saturday.
Opening Hours: Sunrise – Sunset.
Avoid: Thursdays and Saturdays.
Ladies: Thursdays.
Juveniles: Welcome.

Green Fees: £25 mid week, £30 Sundays.
Clubhouse Hours: 9.00am – 11.00pm.
Clubhouse Dress: Informal – neat and tidy.
Clubhouse Facilities: Full clubhouse facilities. Midday – 9.00pm. Dinner menu and a la carte. Prior telephone call for special service.

NO.	MTRS	PAR	S.I.	NO.	MTRS	PAR	S.I.
1	338	4	7	10	38	4	8
2	353	4	3	11	353	4	4
3	313	4	11	12	313	4	12
4	167	3	9	13	167	3	10
5	334	4	5	14	334	4	6
6	115	3	17	15	115	3	18
7	398	4	1	16	398	4	2
8	302	4	15	17	302	4	16
9	471	5	13	18	471	5	14
OUT	2,791	35		IN	2,791	35	
				TOTAL	5,582	70	
				STANDARD SCRATCH	71		

WOODENBRIDGE CLUBHOUSE CLUB HOUSE

CAR PARK

Woodenbridge have now extended the course to 18 holes. However at time of going to press a full map of the course was not available.

127

ULSTER

BY JACK MAGOWAN

If they ever strike a medal for the man who sings the loudest praises for Irish golf, then it must go to Peter Dobereiner.

It was this World War II fighter pilot turned law student turned golf-writer who first announced that Royal Co. Down was the best course in the game outside America, and it would hardly flatter him to say he has the front door key to more clubs here than anybody else anywhere.

"Irish golf is informality," smiles Peter. "It's adventure; it's welcoming; and the welcome is genuine because clubs there actually like visitors."

For Dobereiner, author, architect and wine connoisseur, Ireland is where

The Cushendall course in Co. Antrim has strong influence of water with sea on one side and a river on another.

Photo: Esler Crawford Photography.

there are six days in the week, plus one for Guinness and golf.

Peter has told the story a thousand times, yet I never tire of hearing it ..... how the former U.S. Ryder Cup ace, Mike Souchak, lost all awareness of time and place on a visit to Killarney some years ago. For business reasons, Souchak had to be back in New York as quickly as possible after filming ended in one of Shell's 'Wonderful World' matches.

Mike was still in spiked shoes as he set off by taxi for a speedy ride to Shannon Airport. Aer Lingus was alerted and the ground-staff briefed to expect a last-minute VIP. Infact, they even agreed to hold the flight for Mike.

Alas, it was three days later when the burly American checked in. If Dobers says he was singing a song about Rafferty's pig as he boarded the aircraft, you had better believe it.

Nobody ever got to hear exactly what happened to Souchak, but you can be sure that the taxi driver had a hand in it somehow. He could have had a cousin who lived close to Shannon and made only the best poteen in his own private still. Would Mike like to sample

a quick toot? "Sure now, we've plenty of time to spare, and this is a grand car, to be sure."

Life had nothing richer to offer, so Souchak unwittingly said 'yes', a decision he Never regretted.

They say the gifts of the Irish have enriched other nations more than their own, but in golf it's different. Here the game so many of us get a kick out of playing badly has everything going for it, a wide and exciting choice of courses, close to 30 on Dublin's doorstep alone; weather conditions that can be uncharitable but never hazardous, and the kind of friendship and hospitality Souchak and a multitude of

The wooded fairways of Royal Belfast.

One of the top courses in the world — Royal County Down.

others have found so hard to resist.

It was in August 1981 that Royal Belfast celebrated its centenary as Ireland's oldest club. Rasputin was a thorn in the flesh of the Czar and a gallon of whisky cost 24 shillings (£1.20) when the game perfected by Scots was played for the first time over a course at Carnalea.

No competition could begin until the 11 o'clock train arrived from Belfast. The ladies of the club had their own wooden clubhouse built and furnished for less than £100, but without the modern-day luxury of a warm shower. There were rocks nearby, so quite few of the pretty young set would go bathing to cool off after their round. Subject to one condition, that is.

Would ladies kindly refrain from

passing the main clubhouse window in swim attire while the men are at lunch, said a notice bolted to the wooden fence.

It was in the mid-20's that Royal Belfast moved to Craigavad, £6,000 – that's how much they paid for the handsome Victorian manor and 140-acre estate which is now home to one of the most celebrated clubs in the game.

First Royal Belfast. Then Royal Dublin, Royal Curragh, Mullingar, Royal Portrush, Aughnacloy and Royal Co Down. By the time the Golfing Union was born in 1891, there were twenty-one golf clubs in Ireland, half of them Ulster clubs. Infact, the GUI is

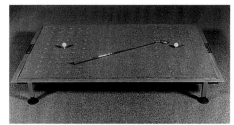

the grandfather of all national golf Unions, older than the United States Golf Association by three years and the Welsh Union by four.

Remarkably, the Scottish Union wasn't formed until 1920, probably because of the Royal and Ancient Club's influence there, and it was four years after that again before England had a ruling body.

What a virtuoso role Royal Portrush has played in the game. Hosts to more major championships and tournaments than they can count, the club's roll-call is dotted with players of distinction, names like Fred Daly, Joe Carr, Catherine Lacoste, Max Faulkner and Garth McGimpsey, not forgetting such legends of the past as Hughie McNeill, Anthony Babington, Rhona Adair, Zara Bolton and the Hezlet sisters.

Like Sir Anthony, P G Stevenson was a pillar of this great club for over half-a-century. And a fine teacher, clubmaker and storyteller, too. Nobody could remember Faulkner's historic 'Open' when Sunday golf there was outlawed as a sin, and the par for Dunluce was 81, repeat 81!. A milestone, surely, in the chequered history of Ulster golf.

A recent poll of Ireland's top 30 courses listed eight in the North with probably only two notable omissions, Clandeboye and Lisburn. Portstewart and Malone were there (naturally !), and Castlerock as well as Slieve Russell, and Donegal leapt out in front of Belvoir Park. Malone came in for a shower of kudos from Gary Player even before his victory in the Irish Seniors' championships of '93, and like good wine, he seems to improve with age.

After the K-Club, Mount Juliet and Druid's Glen, Malone could be the pick of Ireland's best inland courses, and some of them are very good indeed.

It was an American writer of hard-boiled detective stories who compared golf in Ireland to playing poker with nothing wild. "It's the real thing," declared Larry Ferguson after a month-long safari here. "Irish golf is not for players who like to be petted and protected. It's for pulling on a sweater, feeling the spray in your face, then boring long irons under winds that may keep the Coast Guard in port!"

Is it possible that globe-trotter Ferguson may have played Portrush or Newcastle on a bad day in March? As Dobereiner might say, it's not that Irish weather can't be trusted. There's just so much of it, that's all!

There are some places you have to come back to in order to discover them for the first time, wrote Tom Callahan, in GOLF DIGEST after a visit to Ulster, and we know he'll be back to the course he rates the best in Ireland.

" Tom Watson cleaves to Ballybunion," says Callahan. "He agrees the front nine at Newcastle is close to perfection, but suggests that the closing couple of holes are not up to the rest of the course's extreme standard." A view shared by most critics, perhaps, not all of them Americans.

Allen Park Golf Centre, 45 Castle Road (Randalstown Rd), Antrim, BT41 4NA. Tel: (01849) 429001.

LOCATION: 2½ miles from Antrim town centre on the road from Antrim to Randalstown.
CONTACT: Mrs Valerie Richmond (Antrim Borough Council)
Tel: 01849 463113.
ARCHITECT: Mr T. McAuley.

The course is scheduled to open in Spring 1996. This gently undulating parkland course will test the skill and ability of even the more experienced golfer. The shortest hole is 196 yards with the longest being 559 yards. Three lakes provide interesting features in the back nine holes.

COURSE INFORMATION

**Par 72; SSS 72;
Length 6,683 yards.**

Visitors: Welcome.
Opening Hours: Dawn–Dusk.
Ladies: Welcome.
Green Fees: *Mon/Fri* – £10: Adults, £5: Senior Citizen (Over 60), £5:Junior (Under 18). *Weekends & Holidays* – £12: Adults, £6: Senior Citizen (Over 60), £6: Junior (under 18).
Juveniles: Welcome.
Clubhouse Dress: Casual.
Clubhouse Facilities: Locker rooms, Snooker table and catering facilities.

NO.	MEDAL YARDS	GEN YARDS	PAR	S.I.	NO.	MEDAL YARDS	GEN YARDS	PAR	S.I.
1	419	347	4	5	10	427	360	4	3
2	197	175	3	7	11	290	252	4	16
3	396	322	4	9	12	319	277	4	13
4	477	407	5	18	13	306	259	4	15
5	559	479	5	14	14	503	452	5	17
6	196	175	3	6	15	555	463	5	12
7	364	320	4	11	16	203	181	3	8
8	201	179	3	4	17	445	365	4	1
9	388	332	4	10	18	438	373	4	2
OUT	3,197	2,736	35		IN	3,486	2,982	37	
					TOTAL	6,683	5,718	72	
					STANDARD SCRATCH		72		

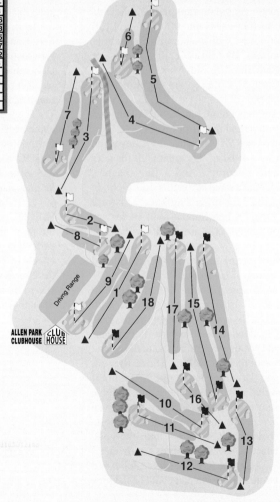

Bunker and tree positions indicated.
Copyright Tudor Journals Ltd.

BALLYCASTLE ULSTER ANTRIM

**Cushendall Road,
Ballycastle, Co. Antrim
BT54 6QP.
Tel: (012657) 62536.**

LOCATION: On the north coast of Antrim at the eastern end of the Causeway Coast — adjacent to the Glens of Antrim.
SECRETARY: Mr. M. Page.
Tel: (012657) 62109.
PROFESSIONAL: Ian McLaughlin.
Tel: (012657) 62506.

The opening five holes are parkland bordered by the Margy and Carey Rivers and played around the ruins of a 13th Century Friary. The Warren area of six holes is true links and the final seven are played in an adjacent upland, giving panoramic views including Mull of Kintyre, Rathlin Island and Ballycastle Bay. Accurate iron play is essential for good scoring.

COURSE INFORMATION

Par 71; SSS 68; Length 5,662 Yards.
Visitors: Welcome.
Opening Hours: Summer 9.00am - 6.00pm; Winter 9.00am - 3.00pm.
Avoid: Sat morning and Sun morning.
Ladies: Friday Ladies day.
Green Fees: £15 (£8 with member) Mon - Fri; £20 (£9 with member) Sat/Sun and public holidays. Juveniles under 18 years — 1/2 rates.
Juveniles: Welcome before 6.00pm in July and August. Lessons by prior arrangement; Club hire available; Caddy service available by prior arrangement.
Clubhouse Hours: 11.30am - 11.00pm (July & August); Restricted in winter.
Clubhouse Dress: Casual dress acceptable.
Clubhouse Facilities: Bar snacks and meals througout the day. Evening meals by prior arrangement.
Open Competitions: Open Week: June; scattered competitions throughout the year.

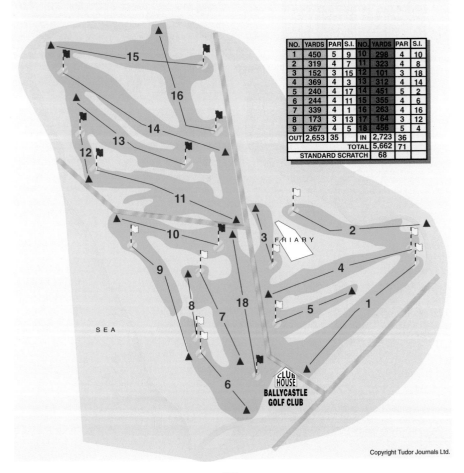

NO.	YARDS	PAR	S.I.	NO.	YARDS	PAR	S.I.
1	450	5	9	10	298	4	10
2	319	4	7	11	323	4	8
3	152	3	15	12	101	3	18
4	369	4	3	13	312	4	14
5	240	4	17	14	451	5	2
6	244	4	11	15	355	4	6
7	339	4	1	16	263	4	16
8	173	3	13	17	164	3	12
9	367	4	5	18	455	5	4
OUT	2,653	35		IN	2,723	36	
				TOTAL	5,662	71	
				STANDARD SCRATCH	68		

25 Springvale Road, Ballyclare, Co. Antrim.
Tel: (01960) 322696.

LOCATION: Two miles north of Ballyclare.
SECRETARY: H. McConnell.
Tel: (01960) 322696.
ARCHITECT: T. McCauley.

Parkland course which makes good use of the local river and streams. The fairways are tree-lined and as expected, accurate driving is required for a good score.

COURSE INFORMATION

Par 72; SSS 71; Length 5,745 Yards.
Visitors: Welcome Mon, Tues, Wed, Fri, & Sun.
Opening Hours: Dawn–Dusk.
Avoid: Sunday mornings, Thursdays from 1.30pm and Saturdays.
Ladies: Welcome.
Green Fees: £15 Mon – Fri; £20 Sunday/Bank Holidays.
Juveniles: Mon – Fri before

4.30pm; Sat/Sun after 4.30pm.
Clubhouse Hours: 12.30 – 11.30pm.
Clubhouse Dress: Jacket and tie after 7.00pm.
Clubhouse Facilities: Snacks, meals from 12.30pm unless by prior arrangement.

NO.	YARDS	PAR	S.I.	NO.	YARDS	PAR	S.I.
1	293	4	13	10	331	4	10
2	458	5	17	11	151	3	8
3	392	4	1	12	435	5	18
4	333	4	5	13	399	4	4
5	345	4	3	14	368	4	12
6	144	3	9	15	117	3	16
7	343	4	7	16	382	4	2
8	322	4	15	17	441	5	14
9	151	3	11	18	340	4	6
OUT	2,781	35		IN	2,964	36	
				TOTAL	5,745	72	
				STANDARD SCRATCH		71	

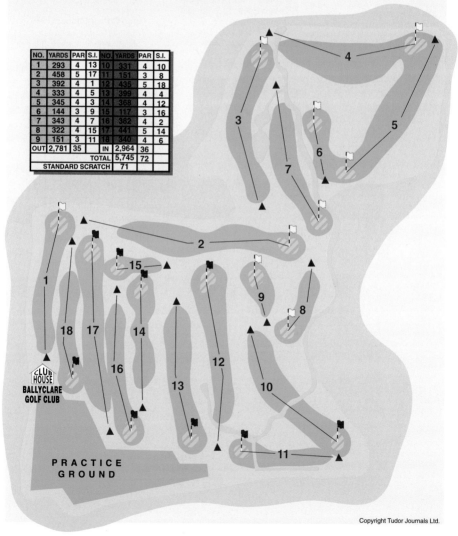

PRACTICE GROUND

CLUB HOUSE
BALLYCLARE GOLF CLUB

BALLYMENA   U L S T E R   ANTRIM

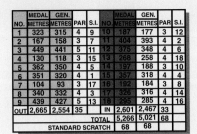

NO.	MEDAL METRES	GEN. METRES	PAR	S.I.	NO.	MEDAL METRES	GEN. METRES	PAR	S.I.
1	323	315	4	9	10	187	177	3	12
2	167	158	3	7	11	404	393	4	2
3	449	441	5	11	12	375	348	4	6
4	130	118	3	15	13	268	258	4	18
5	362	350	4	5	14	197	188	3	10
6	351	320	4	1	15	357	318	4	4
7	104	93	3	17	16	192	184	3	8
8	340	332	4	3	17	326	316	4	14
9	439	427	5	13	18	295	285	4	16
OUT	2,665	2,554	35		IN	2,601	2,467	33	
					TOTAL	5,266	5,021	68	
					STANDARD SCRATCH	68	68		

128 Raceview Road, Ballymena.
Tel: (01266) 861487.

LOCATION: Three miles east of Ballymena.
SECRETARY: Carl McAuley.
Tel: (01266) 861487.

A flat course comprised mainly of heathland with numerous bunkers. The Glens of Antrim lie to the northeast and Slemish Mountain is clearly visible to the east.

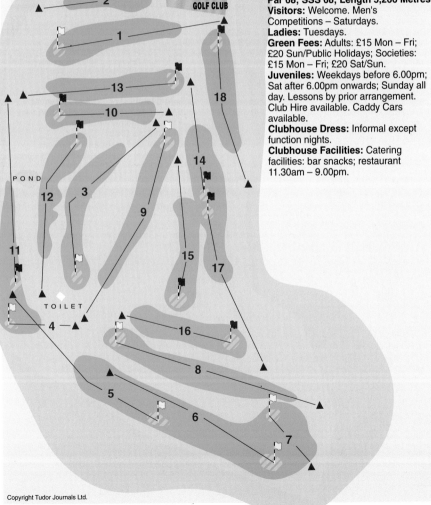

COURSE INFORMATION

Par 68; SSS 68; Length 5,266 Metres.
Visitors: Welcome. Men's Competitions – Saturdays.
Ladies: Tuesdays.
Green Fees: Adults: £15 Mon – Fri; £20 Sun/Public Holidays; Societies: £15 Mon – Fri; £20 Sat/Sun.
Juveniles: Weekdays before 6.00pm; Sat after 6.00pm onwards; Sunday all day. Lessons by prior arrangement. Club Hire available. Caddy Cars available.
Clubhouse Dress: Informal except function nights.
Clubhouse Facilities: Catering facilities: bar snacks; restaurant 11.30am – 9.00pm.

Copyright Tudor Journals Ltd.

141

BUSHFOOT

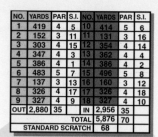

NO.	YARDS	PAR	S.I.	NO.	YARDS	PAR	S.I.
1	419	4	5	10	414	5	6
2	152	3	11	11	131	3	16
3	303	4	15	12	354	4	14
4	347	4	3	13	362	4	4
5	386	4	1	14	386	4	2
6	483	5	7	15	496	5	8
7	137	3	13	16	160	3	12
8	326	4	17	17	326	4	18
9	327	4	9	18	327	4	10
OUT	2,880	35		IN	2,956	35	
				TOTAL	5,876	70	
STANDARD SCRATCH					68		

50 Bushfoot Road, Portballintrae,
Bushmills, Co Antrim.
Tel: (012657) 31317.

LOCATION: Two miles from Bushmills beside Portballintrae village.
SECRETARY/MANAGER: J. Knox Thompson.
Tel: (012657) 31317.

Links course laid around the estuary of the River Bush. Quite a short course with the river playing a prominent part of the challenge. The clubhouse offers good views of the Causeway Coast and on a clear day, Scotland is visible.

COURSE INFORMATION

Par 70; SSS 68; Length 5,876 Yards.
Visitors: Welcome Mon – Fri.
Avoid: Saturday or Sunday unless guest of a member.
Ladies: Welcome any time.
Green Fees: £13 Mon – Fri; £16 Bank & Public Holidays; Sat/Sun £12 with a member only.
Juveniles: Under 10 with an adult. July & August must be off the course by 6.00pm. Handicap Certificate required. Prior arrangement preferable.
Clubhouse Dress: Casual.
Clubhouse Facilities: Full meals, snacks Tue – Sat 12.00 noon – 3.00pm and 5.00pm – 7.30pm.

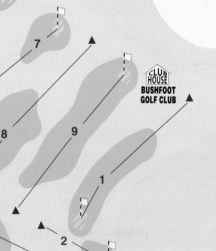

Copyright Tudor Journals Ltd.

142

**192 Coast Road,
Ballygally, Larne.
Tel: (01574) 583324.**

LOCATION: Four miles north
of Larne.
SECRETARY/MANAGER:
Nat Moore
Tel: (01574) 583324.
PROFESSIONAL: Mr R. Walker.
Tel: (01574) 583417.

Parkland course built on the face of a
hill known as Ballygally Head. One
of the more scenic courses in Ireland,
views to Scotland, down the coast to
Carnlough and Antrim Hills. From the
third tee which is 500ft above sea
level beware of the hazardous valley
on the right hand side and the rocks in

front. Your drive has to carry 175
yards to the fairway — apart from
thelevel of difficulty this is one of the
most scenic holes.

COURSE INFORMATION

**Par 70; SSS 69; Length 5,598
Yards.**
Visitors: Welcome any day
except Saturday.
Opening Hours: From 9.00am.
Green Fees: £15 Mon – Fri;
£20 Sat/Sun. Ladies half price;
Juvenilles £3 Mon – Fri, £5
Sat/Sun.
Juveniles: 9.00am – 6.00pm
Monday – Friday; Sat after

7.00pm; Sunday after 6.00pm.
Club Hire available.
Clubhouse Hours: 8.00am –
11.00pm.
Clubhouse Dress: No Denims
or tracksuits. Collar and tie.
Clubhouse Facilities: Catering
facilities: bar and restaurant
5.00pm – 11.00pm. Outside
these hours, by prior
arrangement.
Open Competitions: Open
Week – July.

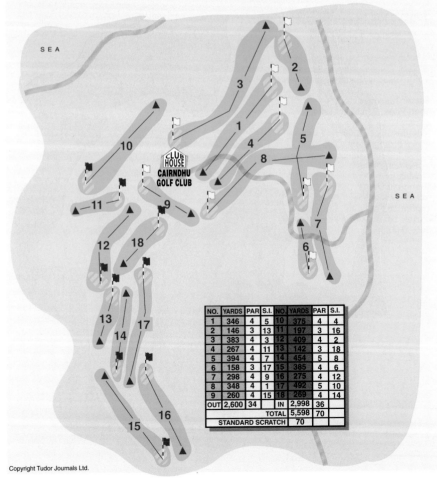

NO.	YARDS	PAR	S.I.	NO.	YARDS	PAR	S.I.
1	346	4	5	10	375	4	4
2	146	3	13	11	197	3	16
3	383	4	3	12	409	4	2
4	267	4	11	13	142	3	18
5	394	4	7	14	454	5	8
6	158	3	17	15	385	4	6
7	298	4	9	16	275	4	12
8	348	4	1	17	492	5	10
9	260	4	15	18	269	4	14
OUT	2,600	34		IN	2,998	36	
				TOTAL	5,598	70	
	STANDARD SCRATCH				70		

**35 North Road, Carrickfergus
BT38 8LP.
Tel: (019603) 63713.**

LOCATION: On outskirts of town.
SECRETARY/MANAGER: R. J. Campbell.
Tel: (019603) 63713.
PROFESSIONAL: Ray Stevenson.
Tel: (019603) 51803.

A parkland course with a spectacular first hole. The first drive, from an elevated tee is over the infamous dam which is full of water and quite intimidating! Although a reasonably flat course there are several demanding holes to be tackled. The Par 4, 6th hole is a dog-leg left playing to a hidden green beside the dam. The course is well maintained throughout the year and there are some very pleasant views across the Belfast Lough to Co. Down.

NO.	MEDAL YARDS	GEN. YARDS	PAR	S.I.	NO.	MEDAL YARDS	GEN. YARDS	PAR	S.I.
1	418	416	4	8	10	444	439	4	1
2	107	104	3	16	11	409	405	4	7
3	384	376	4	4	12	164	154	3	17
4	122	118	3	18	13	436	426	4	3
5	322	312	4	10	14	197	186	3	13
6	426	421	4	2	15	355	353	4	5
7	126	124	3	14	16	301	300	4	15
8	283	273	4	12	17	490	488	5	9
9	440	400	4	6	18	328	320	4	11
OUT	2,628	2,544	33		IN	3,124	3,071	35	
					TOTAL	5,752	5,615	68	
					STANDARD SCRATCH		68		

COURSE INFORMATION

Par 68; SSS 68; Length 5,752 Yards.
Visitors: Welcome any day during the week. Sunday after 11.30am..
Avoid: Tuesday, Saturday and Sunday.
Ladies: Tuesdays.
Green Fees: £14 Mon - Fri; £20 Sat/Sun..
Juveniles: Up to 4.00pm. Lessons by prior arrangement. Club Hire available. Caddy Service available by prior appointment. Caddy cars available.
Clubhouse Dress: Jacket and tie in dinning room after 7.00pm.
Clubhouse Facilities: Catering facilities: bar snacks, meals 12.00 noon - 9.00pm.

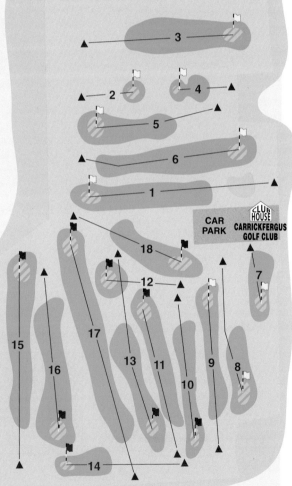

21 Shore Road, Cushendall, Co. Antrim.
Tel: (012667) 71318.

LOCATION: In Cushendall village on road to beach.
SECRETARY: Shaun McLaughlin.
Tel:(012667) 58366.
ARCHITECT: Dan Delargy.

Beautifully situated course where the River Dall winds through the fairways in seven of the nine holes. Cushendall is quite a short course, it has three par 3's and no par 5's, but it requires great accuracy as it is possible to go out of bounds at every hole.

COURSE INFORMATION

Par 66; SSS 63; Length 4,386 Metres.
Visitors: Check with club in advance.
Avoid: Sundays anytime (time sheet).
Ladies: Any time but not Sunday before 1.00pm.
Ladies day – Thursday.

Green Fees: £8.00 Mon – Fri; £10 Sat/Sun/Bank Holidays.
Juveniles: Weekdays up to 6.00pm. Not at weekends.
Clubhouse Dress: Casual.
Clubhouse Facilities: Catering available.
Open Competitions: Most weekends. Handicap certificate required for open competitions.

CLUB HOUSE
CUSHENDALL GOLF CLUB

RIVER DALL

Shore Road

CUSHENDAL VILLAGE

Shore Street

NO.	METRES	PAR	S.I.	NO.	METRES	PAR	S.I.
1	275	4	11	10	275	4	10
2	162	3	13	11	162	3	16
3	291	4	3	12	291	4	6
4	262	4	7	13	262	4	4
5	135	3	15	14	135	3	14
6	244	4	5	15	244	4	8
7	115	3	17	16	115	3	18
8	354	4	1	17	354	4	2
9	355	4	9	18	355	4	12
OUT		33		IN	2,193	33	
				TOTAL	4,386	66	
				STANDARD SCRATCH	63		

Dunygarton Road, Maze, Lisburn BT27 5RT.
Tel: (01846) 621339.

LOCATION: Within the Maze racecourse.
SECRETARY/MANAGER: Mr. J. Tinnion.
Tel: (01846) 621339.
ARCHITECT: Golf Design Associates.

Situated in the Lagan Valley amid pleasant rural surroundings the course is conveniently situated to the city of Belfast and to many of the major provincial towns. Set in 150 acres of rolling heathland within the Down Royal (Maze) Racecourse. The nature of the soil being sandy loam ensures the course is playable all year round. The course is in two loops of nine and a classical Par 72, with four Par 5's, four Par 3's and ten Par 4's.

Visitors: Welcome.
Ladies: Welcome.
Green Fees: £12 Mon - Fri; £14 Sat; £17 Sun/Bank Holidays.
Juveniles: Must be accompanied by an adult.
Clubhouse Facilities: Licensed restaurant nearby.

COURSE INFORMATION

Par 72; SSS Not fixed yet; Length 6,824 Yards.

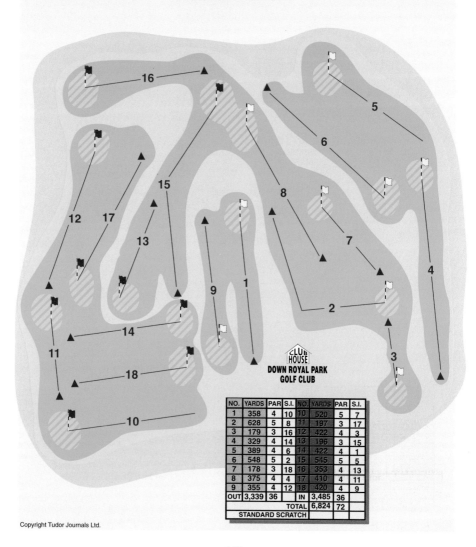

DOWN ROYAL PARK
GOLF CLUB

NO.	YARDS	PAR	S.I.	NO.	YARDS	PAR	S.I.
1	358	4	10	10	520	5	7
2	628	5	8	11	197	3	17
3	179	3	16	12	422	4	3
4	329	4	14	13	196	3	15
5	389	4	6	14	422	4	1
6	548	5	2	15	545	5	5
7	178	3	18	16	353	4	13
8	375	4	4	17	410	4	11
9	355	4	12	18	420	4	9
OUT	3,339	36		IN	3,485	36	
				TOTAL	6,824	72	
STANDARD SCRATCH							

**141 Ballinlea Rd,
Stranocum, Ballymoney,
Co. Antrim, BT53 8PX.
Tel: (012657) 51209.**

Location: Seven miles north of
Ballymoney and ten minutes from
the Causeway Coast.
Proprietors: J&M Gillan.
Tel: 012657 51209.
Architect: Frank Ainsworth.

Gracehill is a new and very
challenging parkland course which
will provide a stern test for even the

best golfers. Six of the first nine holes
are played over water and many
mature trees come into play. As an
added bonus the course has some
excellent views over the surrounding
countryside and is set in a very quiet
rural location near the coast.

COURSE INFORMATION

**Par 70; SSS 70; Length 6,184
yards.**
Visitors: Welcome.
Avoid: Weekends.
Opening Hours: 7.30am–Sunset.

Ladies: Restricted on mens'
competitions days.
Green Fees: £12 weekdays;
£15 weekends.
Juveniles: Must be
accompanied by an adult.
Clubhouse Hours:
8am–Sunset.
Clubhouse Dress:
Smart/Casual.
Clubhouse Facilities: Full
restaurant facilities.

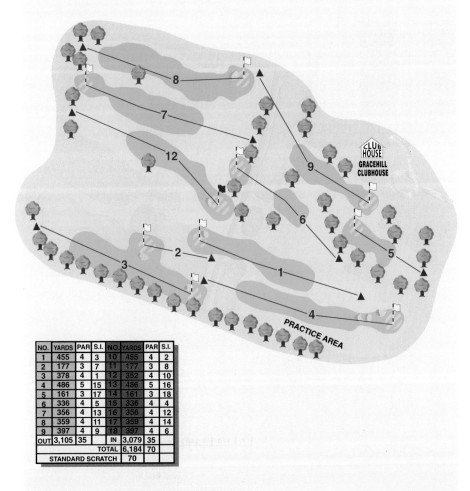

NO.	YARDS	PAR	S.I.	NO.	YARDS	PAR	S.I.
1	455	4	3	10	455	4	2
2	177	3	7	11	177	3	8
3	378	4	1	12	352	4	10
4	486	5	15	13	486	5	16
5	161	3	17	14	161	3	18
6	336	4	5	15	336	4	4
7	356	4	13	16	356	4	12
8	359	4	11	17	359	4	14
9	397	4	9	18	397	4	6
OUT	3,105	35		IN	3,079	35	
				TOTAL	6,184	70	
	STANDARD SCRATCH			70			

Bunker and tree positions indicated.

156 Upper Road,
Greenisland,
Carrickfergus, Co. Antrim.
Tel: (01232) 862236.

LOCATION: Eight miles north of
Belfast, and two miles from
Carrickfergus.
SECRETARY/MANAGER: Jim
Wyness.
Tel: (01232) 862236.

The course is nestled at the foot of the
Knockagh Hill and situated on the
edge of Carrickfergus town. One of
its features is the scenic views over
Belfast Lough.

COURSE INFORMATION

Par 71; SSS 68; Length
5,536 Metres.
Visitors: Welcome.
Opening Hours: Sunrise –
Sunset.
Avoid: Saurdays until 5.30pm
and Club competitions.
Ladies: Saturdays after
5.30pm.
Green Fees: £10 Mon - Fri
(£5 with a member); £15
Sat/Sun/All Public Holidays
(£7.50 with a member).
Juveniles: Saturdays after

5.30pm. Must be
accompanied with an adult.
Prior arrangement is required
for societies.
Clubhouse Hours: 12.00pm
– 11.00pm (summer). Full
clubhouse facilities.
Clubhouse Dress: Bar area
— casual; Dinning room —
jacket, collar and tie.
Clubhouse Facilities:
Tuesday – Sunday: Lunch and
evening meals, bar snacks.
Open Competitions: Men's
Open – June.

NO.	MEDAL METRES	GEN. METRES	PAR	S.I.	NO.	MEDAL METRES	GEN. METRES	PAR	S.I.
1	329	308	4	2	10	312	308	4	3
2	347	337	4	11	11	337	337	4	12
3	458	443	5	8	12	444	443	5	9
4	302	283	4	15	13	302	283	4	16
5	384	374	4	1	14	487	374	5	7
6	163	170	3	10	15	191	170	3	4
7	348	332	4	6	16	342	332	4	5
8	87	97	3	17	17	92	97	3	18
9	304	286	4	13	18	307	286	4	14
OUT	2,722	2,630	35		IN	2,814	2,630	36	
					TOTAL	5,536	5,260	70	
					STANDARD SCRATCH	68	71		

Bunker and tree positions indicated.

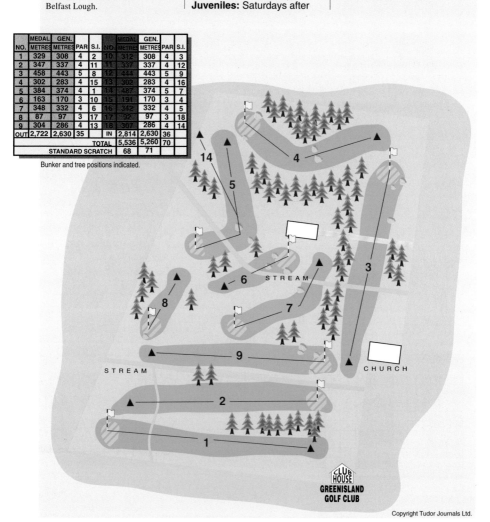

GREENISLAND
GOLF CLUB

Aberdelly, Bells Lane, Lambeg, Lisburn.
Tel: (01846) 662738.

LOCATION: Two miles from Lisburn town centre, off the main Lisburn/Belfast Road.
SECRETARY: Tom Burrell.
Tel: (01846) 662738.
PROFESSIONAL: Ian Murdock.
Tel: (01846) 662738.

This relatively new parkland course is ideal for medium and high handicap golfers. An interesting feature is the Par Three 5th which straddles a reservoir. Plans to extend the course to eighteen holes are planned.

COURSE INFORMATION

Par 66; SSS 65; Length 4,384 Metres.
Visitors: Welcome. Municiple course for public use.
Opening Hours: 8am - dusk.
Avoid: Tuesday, Saturday and Sunday.

Ladies: Welcome.
Green Fees: Mon - Fri £3.30 (18 holes £6.20); Sat/Sun/Public Holidays £3.80 (18 holes £7.00).
Clubhouse Facilities: Limited — no bar. Lessons available by prior arrangement. Club hire available.

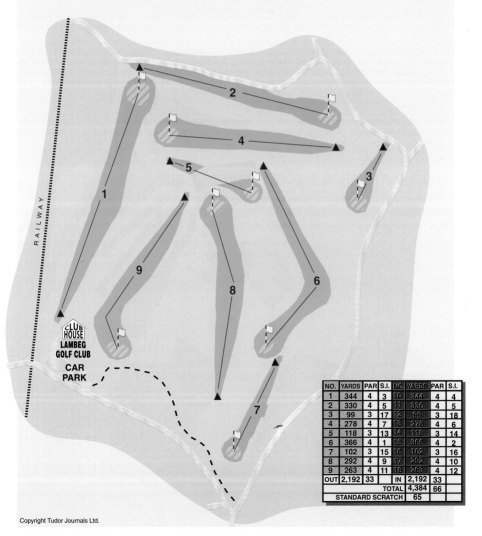

NO.	YARDS	PAR	S.I.	NO.	YARDS	PAR	S.I.
1	344	4	3	10	344	4	4
2	330	4	5	11	330	4	5
3	99	3	17	12	99	3	18
4	278	4	7	13	278	4	6
5	118	3	13	14	118	3	14
6	366	4	1	15	366	4	2
7	102	3	15	16	102	3	16
8	292	4	9	17	292	4	10
9	263	4	11	18	263	4	12
OUT	2,192	33		IN	2,192	33	
				TOTAL	4,384	66	
				STANDARD SCRATCH	65		

Copyright Tudor Journals Ltd.

54 Ferris Bay Road, Islandmagee, Larne, Co. Antrim BT40 3RT. Tel: (01960) 382228.

LOCATION: Six miles north of Whitehead.
HONORARY SECRETARY: Mr Ken Headly.
Tel: (01232) 382228.
ARCHITECT: G. L. Bailie.

This course is part links, meadowland with good views of Larne Lough to the Maidens. The first five holes are fairly 'open', and from the 6th the course becomes tighter with the 7th, 8th and 9th being 'sterner' tests along the shore. Greens are varied. The 8th is the most difficult, spoiling many good cards.

COURSE INFORMATION

Par 70; SSS 70; Length 6,114 Yards.
Visitors: Welcome.
Opening Hours: Sunrise - Sunset.
Avoid: Friday & Saturday.
Ladies: Friday.
Green Fees: £8 Mon - Fri (with member £4); £15 Sat/Sun/Bank Hols (w/m £6).

Saturdays — members only.
Juveniles: Mon - Fri before 5.00pm. Not at weekends.
Clubhouse Hours: Mon - Fri 1pm - 11.00pm; Sat 12 noon - 11pm, Sun 12.30pm - 2.30pm and 5.00pm - 8pm. Full clubhouse facilities.
Clubhouse Dress: Casual, (no denims). Jacket and tie for evening.
Clubhouse Facilities: Mon - Fri bar snacks after 5.00pm by arrangement. Sunday — as bar hours.

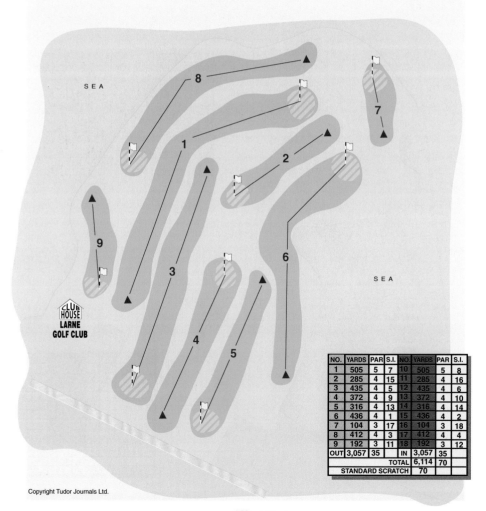

NO.	YARDS	PAR	S.I.	NO.	YARDS	PAR	S.I.
1	505	5	7	10	505	5	8
2	285	4	15	11	285	4	16
3	435	4	5	12	435	4	6
4	372	4	9	13	372	4	10
5	316	4	13	14	316	4	14
6	436	4	1	15	436	4	2
7	104	3	17	16	104	3	18
8	412	4	3	17	412	4	4
9	192	3	11	18	192	3	12
OUT	3,057	35		IN	3,057	35	
				TOTAL	6,114	70	
			STANDARD SCRATCH		70		

68 Eglantine Road, Lisburn, Co. Antrim. Tel: (01846) 677216.

LOCATION: Two miles south of Lisburn off A1 to Hillsborough.
SECRETARY/MANAGER: George McVeigh.
Tel: (01846) 677216.
PROFESSIONAL: B.R. Campbell.
Tel: (01846) 677217.
ARCHITECT: F. Hawtree.

Mixture of parkland and meadowland with reasonbly flat terrain which has an abundance of trees, some of which have not yet reached maturity. Landscaped in recent years, many shrubs are beginning to feature and enhance the course. Again, this is a course of championship standard with a very difficult finish at 16, 17 and 18, with the last hole being a spectacular downhill Par 3 of 195 metres.

COURSE INFORMATION

Par 72; SSS 72; Length 6,647 Yards.
Visitors: Welcome. Mon, Wed, Thurs, Fri, Sun. Must commence before 3.00pm. Members only Tue & Sat.
Green Fees: £25 Mon - Fri (with member £9); £30 Sat/Sun/Bank Holidays (with member £11).
Juveniles: Mon - Fri £12.50 (with member £4.50), Sat/Sun/Bank Holidays £15 (with member £5.50). Must be off course by 5.30pm. Lessons by prior arrangements. Club Hire available. Caddy cars available prior arrangement required. Full clubhouse facilities.
Clubhouse Dress: Jacket and tie after 7.30pm.
Clubhouse Facilities: Snacks and meals all day.

NO.	MEDAL YARDS	GEN. YARDS	PAR	S.I.	NO.	MEDAL YARDS	GEN. YARDS	PAR	S.I.
1	479	465	5	6	10	461	448	4	3
2	360	344	4	16	11	401	385	4	5
3	375	330	4	10	12	493	484	5	11
4	157	140	3	18	13	160	152	3	17
5	349	344	4	4	14	505	488	5	13
6	164	150	3	12	15	367	358	4	15
7	465	449	4	1	16	375	355	4	7
8	500	488	5	8	17	449	379	4	2
9	370	335	4	14	18	217	200	3	9
OUT	3,219	3,045	36		IN	3,428	3,249	36	
					TOTAL	6,647	6,294	72	
					STANDARD SCRATCH	72	70		

PRACTICE GROUND

CLUB HOUSE

LISBURN GOLF CLUB

151

51 Lough Road, Antrim BT41 4DQ.
Tel: (01849) 428096.

LOCATION: Two miles from Antrim town centre.
SECRETARY/MANAGER: Mrs. Marie Agnew.
Tel: (01849) 428096
PROFESSIONAL: Jim Smyth.
Tel: (01849) 464074.
ARCHITECT: Mr F. Hawtree.

The first nine holes could be described as parkland in character with trees and indigenous scrub. The second nine holes are adjacent to the shore of Lough Neagh and are sandy in nature resembling a links course. The most difficult holes on the course are the long Par 4's at the 6th and 17th. A true golf shot from the tee is essential at the Par 3, 11th which is well bunkered. The view from the course takes in Lough Neagh and Shanes Castle.

COURSE INFORMATION

Par 72; SSS 71; Length 6,614 Yards.
Visitors: Welcome.
Opening Hours: 7.30am – 8.00pm (summer); 8.00am – 4.00pm (winter).
Avoid: Sat & Fri mornings.
Ladies: Fridays.
Green Fees: £18 Mon – Fri; £23 Sat/Sun; Ladies £12 Mon – Fri; £15 Sat/Sun; Juveniles £4 Mon – Fri; £5 Sat/Sun.
Juveniles: Mon – Fri; no teeing off after 4.45pm unless with an adult. Lessons available by prior arrangement. Club hire available. Societies only need prior arrangement.
Clubhouse Hours: 11.30am – 11.00pm. Full clubhouse facilities.
Clubhouse Dress: Casual – no denims.
Clubhouse Facilities: Catering facilities: snack meals and dinning room meals 10.30am – 9.30pm (summer); 11.30am – 5.00pm (winter).
Open Competitions: Open Week: first week in June; Open Stroke: September.

NO.	MEDAL YARDS	GEN. YARDS	PAR	S.I.	NO.	MEDAL YARDS	GEN. YARDS	PAR	S.I.
1	374	350	4	5	10	510	480	5	14
2	400	384	4	3	11	205	189	3	10
3	130	118	3	17	12	341	329	4	8
4	363	346	4	7	13	415	425	4	2
5	376	360	4	9	14	135	126	3	18
6	460	436	4	1	15	392	377	4	6
7	554	538	5	11	16	496	480	5	16
8	196	187	3	15	17	438	420	4	4
9	329	313	4	13	18	502	487	5	12
OUT	3,182	3,032	35		IN	3,432	3,313	37	
					TOTAL	6,614	6,345	72	
					STANDARD SCRATCH	72	71		

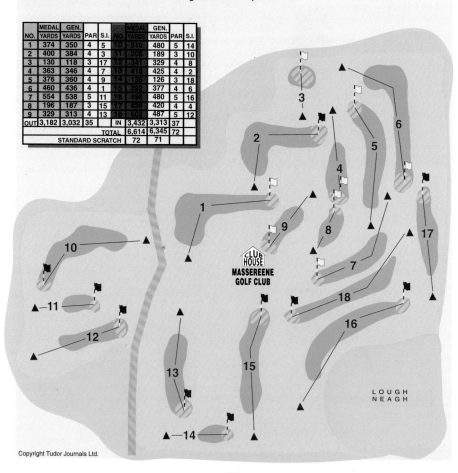

MASSEREENE GOLF CLUB

LOUGH NEAGH

Bushmills Road, Portrush, Co. Antrim BT56 8JQ.
Tel: (01265) 822311.

LOCATION: Two miles from Portrush town towards Bushmills.
SECRETARY/MANAGER: Wilma Erskine.
Tel: (01265) 822311. Fax: (01265) 823139.
PROFESSIONAL: Dai Stevenson.
Tel: (01265) 823335.
ARCHITECT: Harry Colt.

One of Ireland's most famous links courses. The course is laid out in a marvellous stretch of natural golfing country. Through a tangle of sandhills the course threads its way, with the sweeping contours of dunes lending infinite variety of the game. Situated east of Portrush occupying a triangle of giant sandhills, from the highest point of which is an amazing varied prospect. The hills of Donegal in the west, the Isle of of Islay and southern Hebrides in the north with the Giants Causeway and the Skerries to the east.

COURSE INFORMATION

Par 72; SSS 73; Length 6,782 yards.
Visitors: Welcome on any week day.
Opening Hours: Sunrise – Sunset.
Avoid: Wed, Fri pm, Saturday.
Ladies: Valley Links reserved.
Green Fees: £45 Mon - Fri; £55 Sat/Sun/Bank Hols (w/m £15).
Juveniles: Play with a member. Lessons by prior arrangements.

Club hire available; Caddy service available by prior arrangement. A letter of introduction is required. Prior arrangement is required.
Clubhouse Hours: 7.00am - 11.00pm. Full clubhouse facilities.
Clubhouse Dress: Casual acceptable; jacket & tie for functions.
Clubhouse Facilities: Limited snacks, a la carte and group bookings.
Open Competitions: Antrim Cup: May (Mixed foursomes); Lifeboat Trophy: June; Irish Cup: August (Mixed foursomes); Scott Cup: Sept (Mixed foursomes).

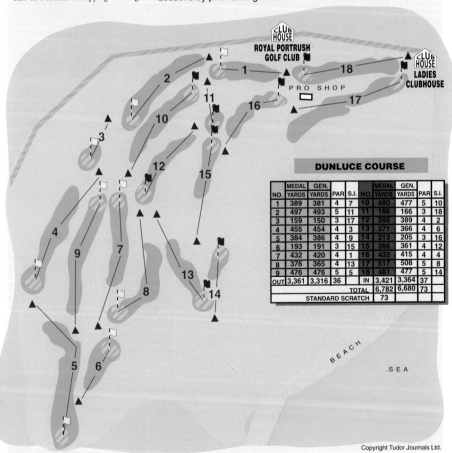

ROYAL PORTRUSH GOLF CLUB

DUNLUCE COURSE

NO.	MEDAL YARDS	GEN. YARDS	PAR	S.I.	NO.	MEDAL YARDS	GEN. YARDS	PAR	S.I.
1	389	381	4	7	10	480	477	5	10
2	497	493	5	11	11	166	166	3	18
3	159	150	3	17	12	395	389	4	2
4	455	454	4	3	13	371	366	4	6
5	384	386	4	9	14	213	205	3	16
6	193	191	3	15	15	366	361	4	12
7	432	420	4	1	16	432	415	4	4
8	376	365	4	13	17	517	508	5	8
9	476	476	5	5	18	481	477	5	14
OUT	3,361	3,316	36		IN	3,421	3,364	37	
					TOTAL	6,782	6,680	73	
					STANDARD SCRATCH		73		

LADIES CLUBHOUSE

PRO SHOP

BEACH

.SEA

**Bushmills Road, Portrush, Co. Antrim. BT56 8JQ.
Tel: (01265) 822311.**

LOCATION: One - two miles from Portrush town towards Bushmills.
SECRETARY: Wilma Erskine. Tel: (01265) 822311. Fax: (01265) 823139.
PROFESSIONAL: Dai Stevenson. Tel: (01265) 823335.
ARCHITECT: Harry Colt.

The Valley lies between the East Strand and the Dunluce course. It is the home of Royal Portrush Ladies Club and the affiliated Rathmore Club. Its characteristics are very much that of a links, undulating sandhills, remarkably dry and in some places below sea level.

COURSE INFORMATION

Par 70; SSS 71: Length 6,273 Yards.
Visitors: Welcome every day except mornings and weekends.
Opening Hours: Dawn — Dusk.
Avoid: Thurs (pm); Sat. & Sun. (am).

Ladies: Saturday mornings.
Green Fees: £18 Mon-Fri (with Member £8); £20 Sat/Sun/Bank Hols (w/m £10).
Juveniles: Play with a member.
Clubhouse Hours: 7.00am - 11.00pm.
Clubhouse Dress: Smart casual at all times. Jacket and tie required for functions.
Clubhouse Facilities: Full clubhouse facilities. Catering facilities: snacks. R.P.G.C.

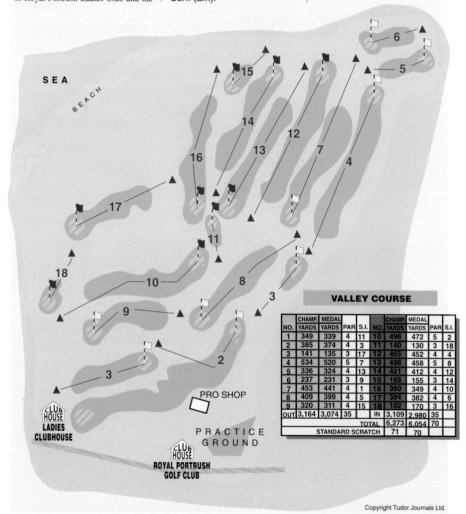

	CHAMP.	MEDAL				CHAMP.	MEDAL		
NO.	YARDS	YARDS	PAR	S.I.	NO.	YARDS	YARDS	PAR	S.I.
1	349	339	4	11	10	496	472	5	2
2	385	374	4	3	11	140	130	3	18
3	141	135	3	17	12	465	452	4	4
4	534	520	5	7	13	486	458	5	8
5	336	324	4	13	14	421	412	4	12
6	237	231	3	9	15	165	155	3	14
7	453	441	4	1	16	360	349	4	10
8	409	399	4	5	17	384	382	4	6
9	320	311	4	15	18	192	170	3	16
OUT	3,164	3,074	35		IN	3,109	2,980	35	
					TOTAL	6,273	6,054	70	
					STANDARD SCRATCH	71	70		

VALLEY COURSE

SEA

BEACH

PRO SHOP

PRACTICE GROUND

CLUB HOUSE
LADIES CLUBHOUSE

CLUB HOUSE
ROYAL PORTRUSH GOLF CLUB

Copyright Tudor Journals Ltd.

WHITEHEAD

**McCrae's Brae,
Whitehead, Carrickfergus,
Co. Antrim BT38 9NZ.
Tel: (01960)
353631/353792.**

Location: County Antrim coast. 18 miles north of Belfast, midway between Carrickfergus and Larne.
Secretary: J. M. Niblock.
Tel: (01960) 353631 (Mon – Fri; 9am – 1pm).
Clubhouse: T. Loughran.
Tel: (01960) 353792.
Pro Shop: T. Loughran.
Tel: (01960) 353118.

Parkland course overlooking Blackhead and the Irish Sea. The views from the 4th tee are superb and include Fairhead in the north, the Mourne Mountains to the south and Ailsa Craig to the east.

COURSE INFORMATION

Par 72; SSS 71; Length 6,362 Yards.
Visitors: Welcome Mon – Fri, Sunday with a member only.
Opening Hours: 9am – 6pm (April & Sept); 9am - 5pm (Winter).
Avoid: Saturdays.
Ladies: Mon – Fri unrestricted except 4.15pm – 7.00pm Wed & Fri. Sat after 6.00pm. Sun. unrestricted. Competition Day – Thursday.
Green Fees: £11 Mon – Fri (£6 with a member) £17 Sun, & Public Hols (only with member).
Juveniles: Mon – Fri before 4.15pm. Must be off by

6.00pm. Sunday after 2.30pm. (under 18) £6 Mon – Fri (£4 with a member); £8 Sat/Sun/All public holidays (£4 with a member). Parties 25 plus: £6 Mon – Fri; £17 Sat/Sun/all public holidays.
Clubhouse Hours: Summer: 12am – 11.30pm; Sun 12.30am – 8.30pm. Winter 6pm – 11.30pm. Sun. restricted.
Clubhouse Dress: Casual, except on Sat after 8.00pm – jacket and tie.
Clubhouse Facilities: Mon 12 – 2pm; Tues closed; Wed – Fri 12 – 2pm & 5pm – 9pm.
Open Competitions: August – McKenna Scratch & Open mixed foursomes Open week June/July .

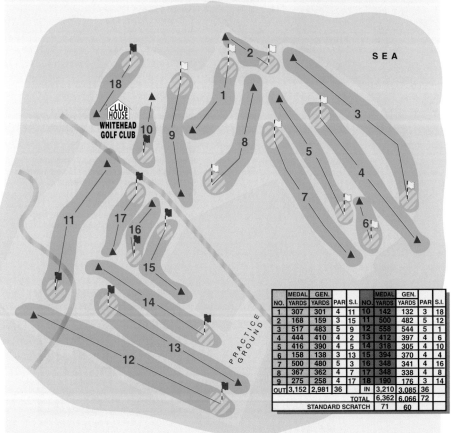

	MEDAL	GEN.				MEDAL	GEN.		
NO.	YARDS	YARDS	PAR	S.I.	NO.	YARDS	YARDS	PAR	S.I.
1	307	301	4	11	10	142	132	3	18
2	168	159	3	15	11	500	482	5	12
3	517	483	5	9	12	558	544	5	1
4	444	410	4	2	13	412	397	4	6
5	416	390	4	5	14	318	305	4	10
6	158	138	3	13	15	394	370	4	4
7	500	480	5	3	16	348	341	4	16
8	367	362	4	7	17	348	338	4	8
9	275	258	4	17	18	190	176	3	14
OUT	3,152	2,981	36		IN	3,210	3.085	36	
					TOTAL	6,362	6.066	72	
					STANDARD SCRATCH	71	60		

155

The Demense, Newry Road, Armagh.
Tel: (01861) 522501.

LOCATION:
SECRETARY: Philip Reid.
Tel: (01861) 525861.
PROFESSIONAL: Alan Rankin.
Tel: (01861) 525864.

This wooded parkland course, established in 1893, has nice views from the Obelisk built by Primate Robinson in 1700's. While the 16th might be considered the most difficult, the fifth requires an accurate drive and then an even more accurate second shot down an alley of mature trees, which should remain the most rewarding to play well.

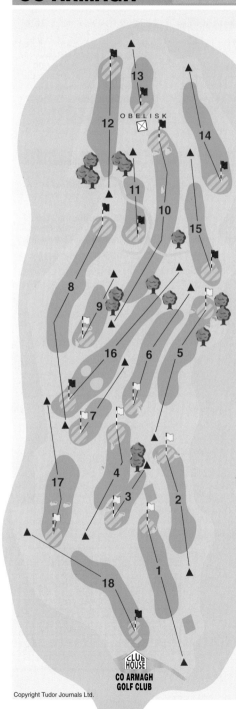

COURSE INFORMATION

Par 70; SSS 69; Length 5,649 Metres.
Visitors: Welcome Mon – Fri (contact Secretary's office for weekends).
Opening Hours: Sunrise - Sunset.
Avoid: Tues evenings and Thurs.
Green Fees: £12 weekdays. £18 weekends & holidays. Prior arrangement required if possible. Lessons available by prior arrangement. Caddy cars available. Full Clubhouse facilities.
Juveniles: Monday - Friday with adult evenings and weekends.
Clubhouse Hours: 9.30am – 11.30pm. Full Clubhouse facilities.
Clubhouse Dress: Informal.
Clubhouse Facilities: Closed Monday, bar snacks and a la carte available until 9.00pm.
Open Competitions: Open Stableford: May; Open Mixed Greensums: May; Lonsdale Cup: June; Open Mixed Team Competition: June; Open Mixed Greensums: July; Open Family Greensums: Aug; Open Mixed Greensums: Aug; Wood-Webster: Sep; Joshua White Stroke: Sep; Open Mixed Greensums: Sep.

NO.	METRES	PAR	S.I.	NO.	METRES	PAR	S.I.
1	365	4	3	10	473	5	4
2	313	4	10	11	162	3	12
3	133	3	14	12	439	5	17
4	349	4	6	13	164	3	13
5	384	4	1	14	335	4	9
6	308	4	18	15	297	4	15
7	130	3	16	16	402	4	2
8	486	5	7	17	350	4	5
9	170	3	11	18	389	4	8
OUT	2,638	34		IN	3,011	36	
				TOTAL	5,649	70	
				STANDARD SCRATCH	69		

Bunker and tree positions indicated.

CO ARMAGH
GOLF CLUB

Freeduff, Cullyhanna, Co. Armagh.
Tel: (01693) 868180.
Fax:(01693) 868611.

LOCATION: Two miles from Crossmaglen.
SECRETARY: James and Elizabeth Quinn.
PROFESSIONAL: Erill Maney.
ARCHITECT: Frank Ainsworth.

An interesting eighteen hole course situated in attractive rural surroundings. Advance notice is recommended before turning up at weekends. There are over one hundred new trees of mature variety and a man-made lake, and bunkers on the 17th, 4th, 1st 3rd and 8th.

COURSE INFORMATION

Par 69; SSS 70; Length 5,616 Yards.
Visitors: Welcome. Telephone appointment preferred.
Opening Hours: Summer 8.00am - 10.00pm.

Green Fees: £10 Mon - Fri; £12 Sat/Sun. Special reductions for school children, students, senior citizens, handicapped persons and unemployed persons.Special rates for societies.
Juveniles: Welcome.
Lessons by prior arrangment.
Club Hire available.
Clubhouse Hours: 8.00am - 10.00pm.
Clubhouse Dress: Informal.
Clubhouse Facilities: Meals and snacks available.

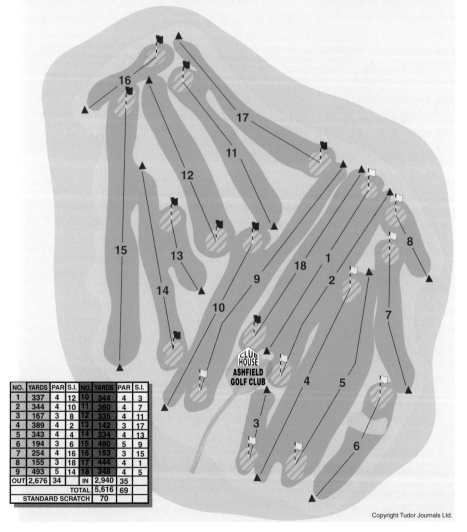

NO.	YARDS	PAR	S.I.	NO.	YARDS	PAR	S.I.
1	337	4	12	10	344	4	3
2	344	4	10	11	360	4	7
3	167	3	8	12	335	4	11
4	389	4	2	13	142	3	17
5	343	4	4	14	334	4	13
6	194	3	6	15	480	5	9
7	254	4	16	16	153	3	15
8	155	3	18	17	444	4	1
9	493	5	14	18	348	4	5
OUT	2,676	34		IN	2,940	35	
				TOTAL	5,616	69	
STANDARD SCRATCH		70					

ASHFIELD GOLF CLUB

NO.	MEDAL YARDS	GEN YARDS	PAR	S.I.	NO.	MEDAL YARDS	GEN YARDS	PAR	S.I.
1	530	502	5	8	10	550	531	5	5
2	186	160	3	10	11	426	368	4	1
3	284	270	4	16	12	358	330	4	17
4	481	470	5	12	13	168	148	3	7
5	401	380	4	2	14	311	285	4	15
6	424	380	4	4	15	342	322	4	9
7	289	269	4	18	16	382	372	4	11
8	184	174	3	6	17	195	170	3	3
9	330	320	4	14	18	403	373	4	13
OUT	3109	2925	36	IN		3135	2899	35	
TOTAL						6244	5824	71	
STANDARD SCRATCH						70			

Drumnabreeze Road,
Magheralin,
Craigavon, Co. Armagh.
Tel: (01846) 611310 /
619199.

Location: Twenty miles from
Belfast, five minutes from
Moira roundabout. Signposted
from Magheralin on main
Moira - Lurgan Road
Architect: Frank Ainsworth.

COURSE INFORMATION

Par 71; SSS 70; Length
6,244 yds.
Visitors: Very Welcome.
Opening Hours: 8am –
Sunset.
Avoid: Saturday Mornings.
Members only Sundays.
Ladies: Welcome
Green Fees: Weekdays £10.
Fridays £12. Saturdays £15.
Juveniles: Welcome.
Clubhouse Dress: Smart and
Casual.
Clubhouse Facilities:
Restaurant, Showers etc. Old
Yard Restaurant closed
Sundays.

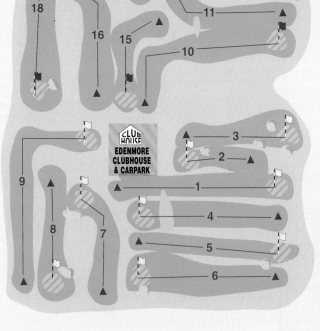

NO.	MEDAL METRES	GEN. METRES	PAR	S.I.	NO.	MEDAL METRES	GEN. METRES	PAR	S.I.
1	258	233	4	13	10	298	272	4	14
2	214	194	3	5	11	158	143	3	15
3	113	107	3	18	12	355	345	4	2
4	371	354	4	3	13	448	430	5/4	12
5	387	374	4	9	14	376	365	4	8
6	504	490	5	7	15	394	374	4	4
7	390	368	4	1	16	410	395	4	6
8	152	150	3	16	17	125	114	3	17
9	528	513	5	11	18	355	340	4	10
OUT	2,917	2,783	35		IN	2,919	2,778	35/34	
					TOTAL	5,836	5,561	70/69	
					STANDARD SCRATCH	70	69		

**The Demense, Lurgan BT67 9BN.
Tel: (01762) 322087.**

LOCATION: One to two miles from the town centre.
HONORARY SECRETARY: Mr S. McClean.
SECRETARY/MANAGER: Mrs G. Turkington.
Tel: (01762) 322087.
PROFESSIONAL: Des Paul.

Parkland course bordering on Lurgan Lake. Well wooded and greens well trapped. Pond on 7th and 17th fairways, internal out-of-bounds (on some holes), quite a few dog-legs, long straight driving essential. Considered quite a difficult course and well suited for low and middle handicappers.

COURSE INFORMATION

Par 70; SSS 70; Length 5,836 Metres.
Visitors: Welcome, Mon – Fri.
Opening Hours: 9.00am – 6.00pm.
Avoid: Wednesday (playing by arrangement) and Saturday.
Ladies: £12 (£6 with member).
Green Fees: £15 Mon – Fri (£7.50 with member); £20 Sat/Sun/Bank Holidays (£10 with member).
Juveniles: £5 Must give way to adult members and visitors.
Student: £10 (£5 with member).
Clubhouse Hours: 8.00am – 11.30pm. Professional shop open 9.00am – 6.00pm.
Clubhouse Dress: Smart/casual.
Clubhouse Facilities: Catering facilities: Bar snacks and full menu. Mon: closed; Tues & Thurs 12.00 – 9.00pm; Wed, Fri, Sat and Sun 12.00 – 9.00pm.
Open Competitions: Open week normally May. Handicap certificate required for Open Competition only.

PARK
LAKE

CLUB HOUSE
LURGAN GOLF CLUB

PORTADOWN

192 Gilford Road, Portadown.
Tel: (01762) 355356.

LOCATION: On Gilford Road out of
Portadown, approx. 34 miles from Belfast.
SECRETARY: Mrs. Holloway.
Tel: (01762) 355356.
PROFESSIONAL: Mr. Paul Stevenson.
Tel: (01762) 334655.
ARCHITECT: Clive Henning.

Situated on the edge of Portadown this parkland
course has one of the holes actually played over
the River Bann (9th). Trees come into play on
many of the holes, and the course is generally flat.

COURSE INFORMATION

Par 70; SSS 70; Length 5,621 Metres.
Visitors: Welcome.
Opening Hours: 9.00am – 9.30pm.
Ladies: Monday, Tuesday, Wednesday
& Friday up to 4.00pm. No green fees on
Tuesdays).
Green Fees: £16 Mon – Fri (£10 with
member); £20 Sat/Sun, Bank Holidays
(£10 with member); Ladies: £14 Mon –
Fri (£10 with member); £18 Sat/Sun (£10
with member); Juveniles: 50% off listed
price.
Juveniles: Mon, Wed, Fri until 5.00pm;
Thur/Sat restricted. Club hire available.
Clubhouse Hours: Office: 9.00am –
5.00pm. Bar: 12.00noon – 11.00pm. Full
Clubhouse facilities.
Clubhouse Dress: Neat dress essential.
No jeans, shorts or sleeveless shirts both
on the course or clubhouse.
Clubhouse Facilities: Full catering, a
la carte, snacks and functions 12.00 –
9.00pm. Closed Mondays.
Open Competitions: Open Week:
beginning of August.

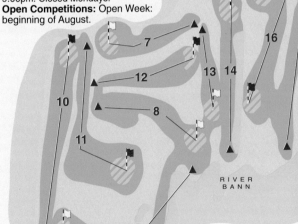

NO.	METRES	PAR	S.I.	NO.	METRES	PAR	S.I.
1	247	4	18		334	4	12
2	297	4	14		376	4	9
3	392	4	1		378	4	4
4	150/143	3	13		173	3	7
5	398	4	3		259	4	15
6	113	3	17		129	3	16
7	346	4	8		329	4	10
8	371	4	5		504	5	6
9	452	5	11		401	4	2
OUT	2,766	35		IN	2,883	35	
				TOTAL	5,621	70	
				STANDARD SCRATCH		70	

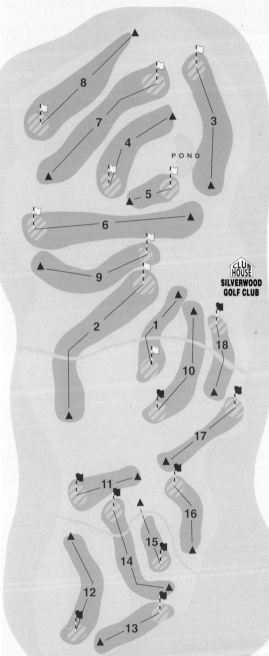

**Tormoyra Lane, Silverwood,
Lurgan, BT66 6NG.
Tel: (01762) 326606.**

LOCATION: The Golf/Ski Centre is located at Silverwood, just off the M1 Lurgan roundabout.
MANAGER: Vincent P. McCorry.
PROFESSIONAL: Part-time, Mr D. Paul.
Tel: (01762) 326606.

The course has sand-based, well irrigated greens making ideal winter putting conditions and is ideally suited for the middle and high handicap golfers. One of it's main features are the lakes which are incorporated into the third and tenth holes. The course has already proved extremely popular with golfing societies for tournaments.

COURSE INFORMATION

**Par 72; SSS 72; Length 6,496 Yards.
Visitors:** Welcome to play: municipal course for public use.
Opening Hours: Daylight hours.
Green Fees: £9.50 Mon – Fri; £12.50 Sat, Sun & Bank Hols. Club hire available.
Clubhouse Hours: Monday – Sunday 9.00am – 7.00pm.
Clubhouse Facilities: New clubhouse open. Full restaurant available. Driving range Par 3 Course.
Open Competitions: June/July.

SILVERWOOD
GOLF CLUB

NO.	YARDS	PAR	S.I.	NO.	YARDS	PAR	S.I.
1	401	4	5	10	484	5	11
2	529	5	9	11	188	3	10
3	390	4	8	12	369	4	6
4	320	4	16	13	284	4	17
5	161	3	18	14	464	4	1
6	433	4	4	15	212	3	3
7	444	4	2	16	321	4	13
8	387	4	7	17	326	4	15
9	477	5	12	18	306	4	14
OUT	3,542	37		IN	2,954	35	
				TOTAL	6,496	72	
	STANDARD SCRATCH			72			

Markethill Rd, Tandragee.
Tel: (01762) 840727.

LOCATION: Six miles from Portadown, 15 miles from Newry.
SECRETARY/MANAGER: B. Carson. Tel: (01762) 841272.
PROFESSIONAL: Paul Stevenson. Tel: (01762) 841761.
ARCHITECT: C. Henning.

Parkland course — complete with beautiful old trees and pleasant views of the Mourne Mountains and South Armagh hills.

COURSE INFORMATION

Par 69; SSS 68; Length 5,446 Metres.
Visitors: Welcome.
Opening Hours: Dawn – Dusk.
Avoid: After 4.00pm Mon – Fri. Sat and Sun to be accompanied by a member.
Green Fees: £18 Weekdays; £21 Sat/Sun all Public Holidays.
Juveniles & Ladies: £10 weekdays; £18 weekends and Public Holidays.

Ladies Day: Thursday.
Clubhouse Hours: 9.00am – 11.00pm. Full clubhouse facilities.
Clubhouse Dress: Casual; jacket & tie on function nights.
Clubhouse Facilities: Full catering from 12.30pm. Last orders 9pm.
Open Competitions: May Holiday, August Bank Holiday and Dixon Cup – June (one day). Handicap certificate required for competitions.

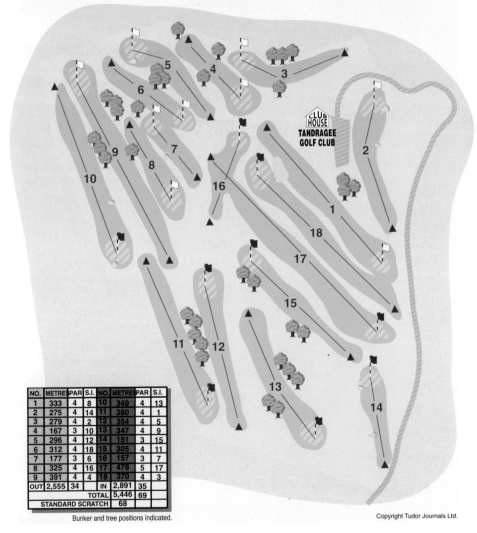

NO.	METRES	PAR	S.I.	NO.	METRES	PAR	S.I.
1	333	4	8	10	349	4	13
2	275	4	14	11	380	4	1
3	279	4	2	12	354	4	5
4	167	3	10	13	347	4	9
5	296	4	12	14	151	3	15
6	312	4	18	15	305	4	11
7	177	3	6	16	157	3	7
8	325	4	16	17	478	5	17
9	391	4	4	18	370	4	3
OUT	2,555	34		IN	2,891	35	
				TOTAL	5,446	69	
				STANDARD SCRATCH	68		

Bunker and tree positions indicated.

Copyright Tudor Journals Ltd.

**518 Lisburn Road,
Belfast BT9 6GX.
Tel: (01232) 381514.**

LOCATION: Two to three miles
south of Belfast City Centre
on main Lisburn Road, next
to King's Hall.
MANAGER: R. McConkey.
PROFESSIONAL: G. Bleakley.
Tel: (01232) 667747.

A flat undulating course with thirty
plus bunkers, and a stream to
contend with when playing. The
greens are generally excellent and
approached by tree-lined fairways.

Situated beside the Royal Ulster
Agricultural Society, the course is
particularly convenient to Belfast
city centre.

COURSE INFORMATION

**Par 69; SSS 70;
Length 5,702 Metres.**
Visitors: Welcome.
Green Fees: £20 Mon – Fri
(£24 Wed.) £10 with member.
£30 weekends & public
holidays (£10 with amember).
Ladies: £12.50 Mon - Fri; £15
weekends/Public holidays.
Juveniles: £7 and restricted on
weekends. Lessons by prior
arrangement.

Clubhouse Hours: 9.00am -
11.00pm
Clubhouse Dress: Smart
casual (no jeans) up to
8.00pm. After 7.30pm jacket and
tie for gentlemen.
Catering Facilities: Lunch
12.30pm - 2.30pm; Evening meal
6.30pm - 10.00pm. Full a la carte
menu. (Last orders 9.30pm).
Open Competitions: Several
throughout the golfing season.
Convenient Hotel: Dukes Hotel,
Belfast. Tel: (01232) 236666.

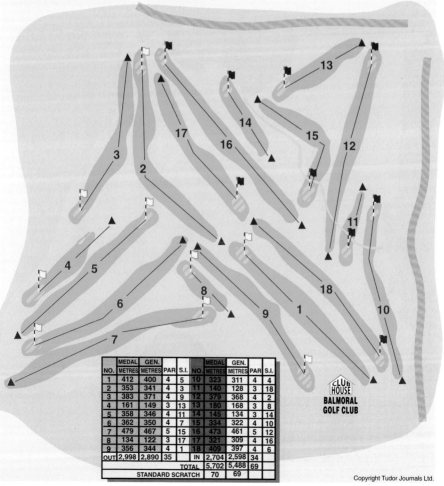

BALMORAL
GOLF CLUB

NO.	MEDAL METRES	GEN. METRES	PAR	S.I.	NO.	MEDAL METRES	GEN. METRES	PAR	S.I.
1	412	400	4	5	10	323	311	4	4
2	353	341	4	3	11	140	128	3	18
3	383	371	4	9	12	379	368	4	2
4	161	149	3	13	13	180	168	3	8
5	358	346	4	11	14	145	134	3	14
6	362	350	4	7	15	334	322	4	10
7	479	467	5	15	16	473	461	5	12
8	134	122	3	17	17	321	309	4	16
9	356	344	4	1	18	409	397	4	6
OUT	2,998	2,890	35		IN	2,704	2,598	34	
					TOTAL	5,702	5,488	69	
					STANDARD SCRATCH	70	69		

Newtownbreda, Belfast BT8 4AN.
Tel: (01232)491693 / 646113.

LOCATION: Four miles south of city centre.
SECRETARY: K.H. Graham.
Tel: (01232) 491693.
Fax: (01232) 646113.
PROFESSIONAL: Maurice Kelly.
Tel: (01232) 646714.

Considered one of the best inland courses with fair but tight fairways and good greens. Rarely closed due to water logging. The course has extensive mature woods and many scenic views.

COURSE INFORMATION

Par 71; SSS 71; Length 6,476 Yards.
Visitors: Welcome.
Opening Hours: 8am – dusk.
Avoid: Wednesday & Saturday. Friday is Ladies Day, prior arrangement is preferred.
Ladies: Welcome.
Ladies Day: Friday.
Green Fees: Weekdays excluding Wed. – £27. Weekends and Bank Holidays – £32.
Clubhouse Hours: 10am – 11pm.

Clubhouse Dress: Jacket, collar and tie after 7.30pm.
Clubhouse Facilities: Catering facilities 10.30am – 9.30pm.
Open Competitions: Mixed foursomes in June; Open week – August.

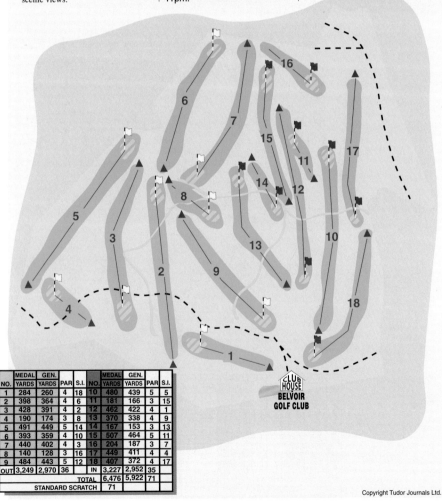

BELVOIR
GOLF CLUB

NO.	MEDAL YARDS	GEN. YARDS	PAR	S.I.	NO.	MEDAL YARDS	GEN. YARDS	PAR	S.I.
1	284	260	4	18	10	480	439	5	5
2	398	364	4	6	11	181	166	3	15
3	428	391	4	2	12	462	422	4	1
4	190	174	3	8	13	370	338	4	9
5	491	449	5	14	14	167	153	3	13
6	393	359	4	10	15	507	464	5	11
7	440	402	4	3	16	204	187	3	7
8	140	128	3	16	17	449	411	4	4
9	484	443	5	12	18	407	372	4	17
OUT	3,249	2,970	36		IN	3,227	2,952	35	
					TOTAL	6,476	5,922	71	
	STANDARD SCRATCH		71						

CLIFTONVILLE

U L S T E R

BELFAST

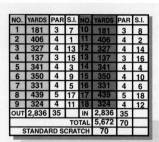

NO.	YARDS	PAR	S.I.	NO.	YARDS	PAR	S.I.
1	181	3	7	10	181	3	8
2	406	4	1	11	406	4	2
3	327	4	13	12	327	4	14
4	137	3	15	13	137	3	16
5	341	4	3	14	341	4	4
6	350	4	9	15	350	4	10
7	331	4	5	16	331	4	6
8	439	5	17	17	439	5	18
9	324	4	11	18	324	4	12
OUT	2,836	35		IN	2,836	35	
				TOTAL	5,672	70	
				STANDARD SCRATCH	70		

Bunker and tree positions indicated.

44 Westland Road, Belfast
BT14 6NH.
Tel: (01232) 744158.

LOCATION: Situated between Cavehill Road and Cliftonville Circus.
SECRETARY: J. M. Henderson.
Tel: (01232) 746595.

Parkland course on rising ground with extensive views of Belfast Lough. Course is played around the waterworks complex.

COURSE INFORMATION

Par 70; SSS 70; Length 5,672 Yards.
Visitors: Welcome to play up to 5.00pm.
Opening Hours:
Avoid: Tuesday afternoons and Sunday mornings. Members only —
Saturday, (visitors can only be accompanied by a member after 6.00pm.
Ladies: Tuesday.
Green Fees: £12 weekdays (w/m £8); £15 Sat, Sun/Bank Holidays (w/m £10).
Juveniles: £3 weekdays only. Full clubhouse facilities.
Clubhouse Hours:
Clubhouse Dress: No denims. Jacket and tie in lounge after 9.00pm.
Clubhouse Facilities: Snacks, meals 12.00 - 3.00pm and a la carte 5.00pm - 9.00pm. No catering on Monday except by arrangement.

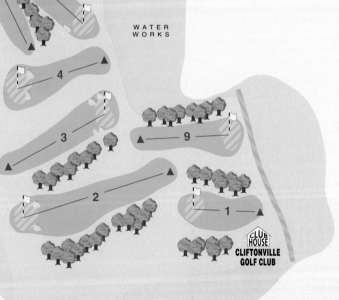

WATER WORKS

CLUB HOUSE
CLIFTONVILLE
GOLF CLUB

91 Dunmurry Lane, Dunmurry, Belfast.
Tel: (01232) 610834.

LOCATION: Between Upper Malone Road and Lisburn Rd.
SECRETARY/MANAGER: Ian McBride.
Tel: (01232) 610834.
PROFESSIONAL: P. Leonard.
ASSISTANT: T. Andrews.
Tel: (01232) 621314.

The course lies astride Dunmurray Lane and consists of rolling parkland in all directions. Since its opening in 1983 it has matured well and is a popular venue for many golfers. The lake at the tenth makes it a very interesting hole.

COURSE INFORMATION

Par 69; SSS 68; Length 5,832 Yards.
Visitors: Welcome weekdays by arrangement.
Opening Hours: Dawn to dusk.
Ladies: Welcome.
Green Fees: £17 weekdays; £26.50 weekends.

Juveniles: Must be accompanied by an adult. Lessons by prior arrangements. Full clubhouse facilities.
Clubhouse Dress: Jacket and tie after 7.00pm and all day Sunday.
Clubhouse Facilities: Snacks and meals: Tue – Fri 12.00 – 2.30pm and 6.00pm – 9.30pm; Sat 12.00 – 9.00pm; Sun 12.00 – 2.30pm and 5.30pm – 8.00pm.

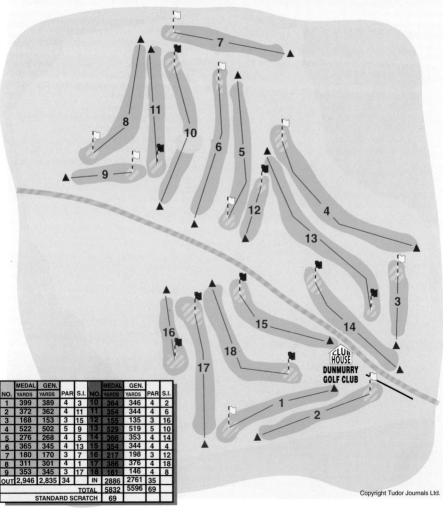

NO.	MEDAL YARDS	GEN. YARDS	PAR	S.I.	NO.	MEDAL YARDS	GEN. YARDS	PAR	S.I.
1	399	389	4	3	10	364	346	4	2
2	372	362	4	11	11	354	344	4	6
3	168	153	3	15	12	155	135	3	16
4	522	502	5	9	13	529	519	5	10
5	276	268	4	5	14	366	353	4	14
6	365	345	4	13	15	354	344	4	4
7	180	170	3	7	16	217	198	3	12
8	311	301	4	1	17	386	376	4	18
9	353	345	3	17	18	161	146	4	8
OUT	2,946	2,835	34		IN	2886	2761	35	
					TOTAL	5832	5596	69	
					STANDARD SCRATCH		69		

Copyright Tudor Journals Ltd.

166

**Downview Avenue,
Belfast BT15 4EZ.
Tel: (01232) 370770.**

LOCATION: Off Antrim Rd, Belfast.
HONORARY SECRETARY: Michael Purdy.
Tel: (01232) 370770.
PROFESSIONAL: Peter Hanna.
Tel: (01232) 770980.
ARCHITECT: H. Colt.

The course is dominated by the picturesque and heavily wooded 'Cavehill' which rises to over 1,000 feet above sea level, making an attractive background to many

shots throughout the round. There is quite a height difference between the top and bottom of the course, which in itself is divided into two parts by Grays Lane.

COURSE INFORMATION

Par 70; SSS 69; Length 5,973 Yards.
Visitors: Welcome Mon - Fri.
Opening Hours: 8.30 – Dusk.
Ladies: £17 Monday; £21 Sat/Sun.
Ladies Day: Friday.
Green Fees: £19 Mon - Fri; £25 Saturday/Sunday.

Juveniles: Must commence play before 4.00pm Monday – Friday. Must commence play before 12.00pm Wed.
Clubhouse Hours: 9.00am – 11.30pm everyday.
Clubhouse Dress: October – March jacket and tie after 9.00pm. April - September casual smart dress (no denims).
Open Competitions: Open Week – August.

NO.	YARDS	PAR	S.I.	NO.	YARDS	PAR	S.I.
1	421	4	7	10	195	3	10
2	329	4	9	11	378	4	8
3	437	4	1	12	131	3	18
4	314	4	17	13	377	4	2
5	474	5	11	14	502	5	12
6	169	3	15	15	315	4	14
7	311	4	3	16	345	4	4
8	421	4	5	17	150	3	16
9	272	4	13	18	432	4	6
OUT	3,148	36		IN	2,825	34	
				TOTAL	5,973	70	
STANDARD SCRATCH			69				

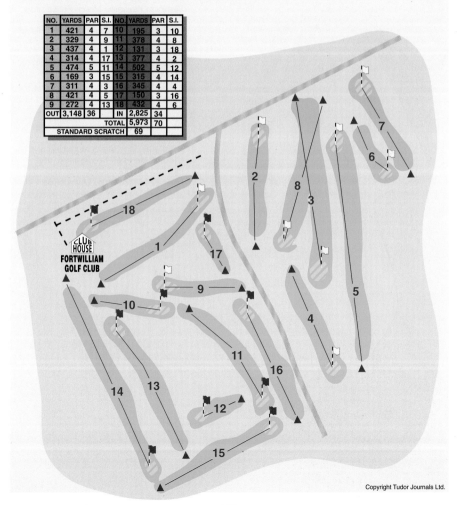

FORTWILLIAM
GOLF CLUB

Summerfield, Dundonald, Belfast. BT16 OQX.
Tel: (01232) 482249.

NO.	MEDAL YARDS	GEN. YARDS	PAR	S.I.	NO.	MEDAL YARDS	GEN. YARDS	PAR	S.I.
1	328	312	4	11	10	493	483	5	12
2	379	370	4	16	11	417	410	4	5
3	457	452	4	2	12	147	135	3	15
4	136	115	3	17	13	377	367	4	10
5	377	367	4	9	14	447	442	4	1
6	453	447	4	3	15	400	390	4	4
7	402	374	4	7	16	185	178	3	14
8	410	397	4	6	17	270	260	4	18
9	359	349	4	13	18	398	389	4	8
OUT	3,301	3,183	35		IN	3,134	3,054	35	
					TOTAL	6,435	6,237	70	
					STANDARD SCRATCH	71	70		

LOCATION: Five miles east of Belfast on the Upper Newtownards Road.
SECRETARY/MANAGER: Mr Managh.
Tel: (01232) 483251.
PROFESSIONAL: Gordon Fairweather.
Tel: (01232) 483825.

Parkland course with numerous large and small trees with the additional hazard of several deep bunkers. The 8th is an interesting hole with a river immediately fronting the green. The course is situated on the eastern suburbs of the city adjacent to Dundonald village.

COURSE INFORMATION

Par 70; SSS 71; Length 6,435 Yards.
Visitors: Welcome Mon – Fri & Sun.
Avoid: Tues & Sat.
Ladies: Anytime except after 4pm Wed & before 4pm Sat.
Ladies Day: Tuesday.
Green Fees: £20 Mon – Fri; £25 Sun & Public Holidays.
Juveniles: Anytime except after 4pm Wed & before 4pm Sat. Lessons by prior arrangement. Club hire available. Full clubhouse facilities.
Clubhouse Dress: Casual – men's lounge and Copper Room; jacket in main room until 7pm; thereafter jacket and tie.
Clubhouse Facilities: Snacks and meals available all day.
Open Competitions: Open week – June.

KNOCK GOLF CLUB
CLUB HOUSE

Mount Ober Golf and Country Club, 24 Ballymaconaghy Road, Knockbracken, Belfast. Tel: (0232) 792108.

LOCATION: 15 minutes from the city centre, off the Saintfield Road.
SECRETARY/MANAGER: P. Laverty. Tel: (0232) 792108.
PROFESSIONAL: David Jones. Tel: (0232) 792108.

This is an excellent test of golf. It has several other sporting facilities on location. There is a large Golf Driving Range at the complex, which is ideal for practice and a Golf Academy with shop and three top teaching professionals.

COURSE INFORMATION

Par 67; SSS 68; Length 5,321 Metres.
Visitors: Welcome anytime.
Avoid: Saturday all day and Sunday 8am – 10.30am.
Ladies: Welcome anytime.
Green Fees: £10 Mon - Fri; £12 Sat & Sun.

£11 Sat/Sun.
Juveniles: Weekdays and after 2.00pm Sat & Sun. Lessons by prior arrangements. Club hire available. Caddy cars are also available. Full clubhouse facilities.
Clubhouse Dress: Smart casual wear after 7.30pm.
Clubhouse Facilities: Snacks and meals all day for up to 100 people. Also all weather barbecue available,

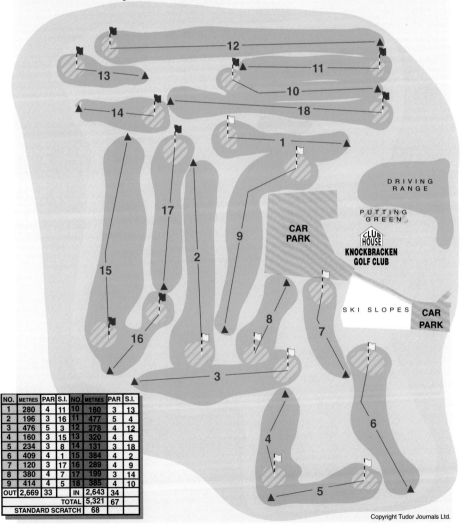

NO.	METRES	PAR	S.I.	NO.	METRES	PAR	S.I.
1	280	4	11	10	180	3	13
2	196	3	16	11	477	5	4
3	476	5	3	12	278	4	12
4	160	3	15	13	320	4	6
5	234	3	8	14	131	3	18
6	409	4	1	15	384	4	2
7	120	3	17	16	289	4	9
8	380	4	7	17	199	3	14
9	414	4	5	18	385	4	10
OUT	2,669	33		IN	2,643	34	
				TOTAL	5,321	67	
				STANDARD SCRATCH		68	

240 Upper Malone Road, Dunmurry, Belfast BT17 9LB. Tel: (01232) 612695.

LOCATION: Five miles from centre of Belfast.
SECRETARY: N. H. Ferguson. Tel: (01232) 612758.
MANAGER: : R. P. Price.
PROFESSIONAL: Michael McGee. Tel: (01232) 614917.
CATERER: (01232) 614916.

One of the most picturesque inland golf courses in the Province with many mature trees and flowering shrubs. This course is of championship standard and has a very high standard of course maintenance. The greens on the course are large with many undulations and an exceptionally good putting surface. The course is quite long and demanding and is classed as one of the best inland

courses in Ireland. A real pleasure to play. Malone is now a 27 hole golf club.

COURSE INFORMATION

Par 71; SSS 71; Length 6,654 Yards.
Visitors: Welcome, although letter of introduction or handicap preferred.
Opening Hours: 8am - Dusk.
Avoid: Members only Wed. No visitors before 5.00pm Sat.
Ladies Day: Tuesday.
Green Fees: £28 Mon - Fri (£11 with member); £33 Sat/Sun, Wed & Bank Holidays (£12.50 with member). Lessons by prior arrangements. Caddy cars available. Society & Company book through office Mon & Thurs only.

member); £12 Sat/Sun/Wed/ Bank Holidays (£7.60 with member). Lessons by prior arrangements. Caddy cars available. Society & Company book through office Mon & Thurs only.
Juveniles: Restricted on main course.
Clubhouse Hours: From 8.00am. Full club facilities when with a member.
Clubhouse Dress: Jacket and tie, at all times. No denim, tee shirts or training shoes on main course.
Clubhouse Facilities: By arrangement with caterer. Lunch and bar snacks.
Open Competitions: Open Week in July. Open Scratch Foursomes in August.

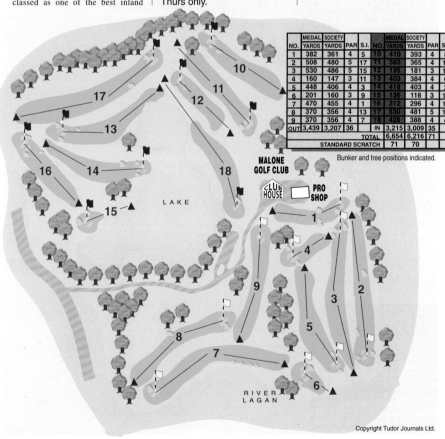

NO.	MEDAL YARDS	SOCIETY YARDS	PAR	S.I.	NO.	MEDAL YARDS	SOCIETY YARDS	PAR	S.I.
1	382	361	4	5	10	410	393	4	8
2	508	480	5	17	11	383	365	4	10
3	530	486	5	15	12	195	181	3	12
4	160	147	3	11	13	403	384	4	6
5	448	406	4	3	14	418	403	4	2
6	201	160	3	9	15	136	118	3	16
7	470	455	4	1	16	312	296	4	18
8	370	356	4	13	17	530	481	5	14
9	370	356	4	7	18	428	388	4	4
OUT	3,439	3,207	36		IN	3,215	3,009	35	
					TOTAL	6,654	6,216	71	
					STANDARD SCRATCH	71	70		

MALONE GOLF CLUB

Bunker and tree positions indicated.

CLUB HOUSE   PRO SHOP

LAKE

RIVER LAGAN

Copyright Tudor Journals Ltd.

50 Park Road,
Belfast
BT7 2FX.
Tel: (01232) 641069.
Fax: (01232) 646250.

LOCATION: Alongside Ravenhill
Road and Park Road, adjacent
to Ormeau Road.
SECRETARY/MANAGER: Robin
Kirk.
SHOP MANAGER: Bert Wilson.
Tel: (0232) 640999.

Set in picturesque, parkland setting
on the edge of Ormeau Park, this
course is tree-lined on all holes, with
a realistic out of bounds on eight of
the nine holes. Nearest golf course to
Belfast city centre, although situated
in a quiet residential area. New
clubhouse recently constructed.

COURSE INFORMATION

**Par 68; SSS 65; Length
5,308 Yards, 4,850 Metres.**
Visitors: Welcome except
Tuesday evening, (Ladies
competition) and Saturdays
until 4.30pm.
Opening Hours: 9.00am –
11.00pm seven days per week.
Avoid: Visitors play up to 5pm
every day except Tuesday.
Ladies: Can play up to 5.00pm
every day except Sat.
Ladies Day: Tuesday.
Green Fees: £11 Weekdays;
£13.50 Weekends. Telephone
for special offers.

Juveniles: Can play up to
5.00pm every day. Wednesday
must be accompanied by
senior members after 5.00pm.
Clubhouse Hours: Mon – Sat
11.30am – 11.00pm. Sun
12.30pm – 2.00pm and
5.00pm – 8.00pm (6pm – 9pm
summer).
Clubhouse Dress: Informal
jacket, collar and tie after
7.30pm - 8.00pm.
Clubhouse Facilities: Lounge
bar. Restaurant & Snooker.

NO.	METRES	PAR	S.I.	NO.	METRES	PAR	S.I.
1	261	4	15	10	261	4	16
2	265	4	13	11	265	4	14
3	465	5	3	12	465	5	4
4	92	3	17	13	92	3	18
5	414	4	1	14	414	4	2
6	173	3	7	15	173	3	8
7	274	4	9	16	274	4	10
8	202	3	5	17	202	3	6
9	279	4	11	18	279	4	12
OUT	2,425	34		IN	2,425	34	
				TOTAL	4,850	68	
STANDARD SCRATCH		65					

Bunkers and tree positions indicated.

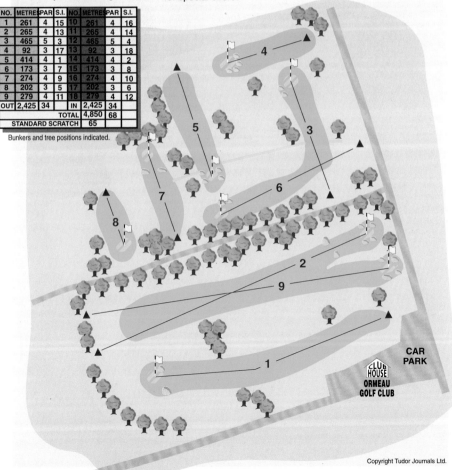

CAR
PARK

CLUB
HOUSE
ORMEAU
GOLF CLUB

ROCKMOUNT

U L S T E R

DOWN

28 Drumalig Road,
Carryduff,
Co.Down.
Tel: (01232) 812279

LOCATION: Seven miles south of Belfast.

SECRETARY: R & D. Patterson.
Tel: (01232) 812279.

18 hole Drumlin Course set in the beauty and quiet of the countryside with scenic views of the Mourne Mountains. The course has been cleverly designed to ensure that the land's natural features are incorporated throughout the 18 holes.

COURSE INFORMATION

Par 72; SSS 72; Length 6,215 Yards.
Visitors: Welcome any day.
Opening Hours: 8am – Dusk.
Avoid: Saturday (members only).
Ladies: Welcome.
Green Fees: Mon – Thurs £16, Fri – £18 & Sun – £22.
Juveniles: Welcome, must be accompanied by an adult.
Clubhouse Hours: 8.00am – 11.30pm. (Seasonal).
Clubhouse Dress: Proper dress (smart / casual).

Clubhouse Facilities:
Restaurant open to the public. Grill & Table D'Hote menu available. Function room & professional shop.

NO.	CHAMP METRES	MEDAL METRES	PAR	S.I.	NO.	CHAMP METRES	MEDAL METRES	PAR	S.I.
1	301	289	4	15	10	358	345	4	5
2	496	485	5	4	11	381	374	4	3
3	213	182	3	8	12	150	144	3	11
4	287	280	4	16	13	346	340	4	9
5	540	513	5	6	14	347	336	4	13
6	489	473	5	14	15	511	501	5	7
7	392	384	4	2	16	170	157	3	17
8	344	334	4	10	17	336	327	4	12
9	129	121	3	18	18	425	412	4	1
OUT	3191	3061	37		IN	3024	2936	35	
					TOTAL	6215	5997	72	
					STANDARD SCRATCH	72	72		

CAR PARK
CLUB HOUSE
ROCKMOUNT CLUBHOUSE

**73 Shandon Park,
Belfast
BT5 6NY.
Tel: (01232) 793730.**

LOCATION: Three miles from
city centre.
GENERAL MANAGER: M. Corsar.
Tel: (01232) 401856.
PROFESSIONAL: B. Wilson.
Tel: (01232) 797859.

Situated in eastern suburbs of Belfast
this is a well known lush parkland
course with true greens. Irrespective
of handicap, golfers will find that it
offers an enjoyable challenge to their
golfing prowness. The course is
generally flat and trees come into
play on some of the holes.

COURSE INFORMATION

**Par 70; SSS 70; Length 6,261
Yards.
Visitors:** Welcome.
Opening Hours: 8.00am –
Sunset.
Avoid: Saturdays.
Ladies: Welcome. Ladies Day
Tuesday.
Green Fees: £22 Mon – Fri;
£27 Sat/Sun/All Public
Holidays.
Juveniles: Accompanied by an
adult. Lessons by prior
arrangement.
Clubhouse Hours: 12 noon –
11.00pm Mon – Sat; 12.30pm –
2.00pm; 4.30pm – 8.00pm

Sun. Full clubhouse facilities.
Clubhouse Dress: Jacket and
tie. Casual in Men's Bar.
Clubhouse Facilities: 12.00 –
3.00pm all week, 5.30pm –
10.00pm Mon – Sat and 5.30pm
– 9.30pm High tea (Sun).
Open Competitions: Open
Mixed Foursomes (May); Open
18 Holes Stroke (June); Open
Week (July); Open 36 Holes
Stroke (July); Open Mixed
Greensomes (Sep).

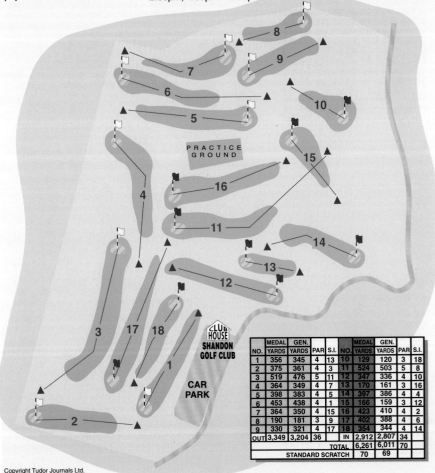

NO.	MEDAL YARDS	GEN. YARDS	PAR	S.I.	NO.	MEDAL YARDS	GEN. YARDS	PAR	S.I.
1	356	345	4	13	10	129	120	3	18
2	375	361	4	3	11	524	503	5	8
3	519	476	5	11	12	347	336	4	10
4	364	349	4	7	13	170	161	3	16
5	398	383	4	5	14	397	386	4	4
6	453	438	4	1	15	166	159	3	12
7	364	350	4	15	16	423	410	4	2
8	190	181	3	9	17	402	388	4	6
9	330	321	4	17	18	354	344	4	14
OUT	3,349	3,204	36		IN	2,912	2,807	34	
					TOTAL	6,261	6,011	70	
					STANDARD SCRATCH	70	69		

**Erne Hill, Belturbet,
Co. Cavan.
Tel: (049) 22287.**

LOCATION: Just outside town on main Cavan Road.
SECRETARY: Peter Coffey.
Tel: (049) 22498.

Most of the holes at Belturbet are played to elevated greens. Out of the eighteen holes the 5th, 7th and 9th holes are considered to be the toughest on the whole course.

COURSE INFORMATION

Par 72; SSS 65; Length 5,180 Yards.
Visitors: Welcome any day, including weekends.
Opening Hours: 9.00am - dusk each day.
Avoid: Major club competitions and selected Open Competitions.
Green Fees: £7 Mon - Fri; £8 Sat/Sun. Letter of introduction required, or handicap certificate required

if wishing to compete in Open Competitions.
Clubhouse Hours: Normal bar hours except mornings.
Clubhouse Dress: Informal.
Clubhouse Facilities: Snooker, darts. Catering facilities by arrangement.
Open Competitions: 17/18 April; 8/9 May; Open week: 18 - 25 July inclusive; 20 - 22 August inclusive; 18/19 September.

NO.	YARDS	PAR	S.I.	NO.	YARDS	PAR	S.I.
1	277	4	15	10	277	4	16
2	378	4	3	11	378	4	4
3	477	5	11	12	477	5	12
4	175	3	7	13	175	3	8
5	340	4	5	14	340	4	6
6	115	3	17	15	115	3	18
7	415	4	1	16	415	4	2
8	272	4	13	17	272	4	14
9	141	3	9	18	141	3	10
OUT	2,590	34		IN	2,590	34	
				TOTAL	5,180	72	
STANDARD SCRATCH					65		

CLUB
HOUSE
BELTURBET
GOLF CLUB

**Toam, Blacklion,
Co. Cavan.
Tel: (072) 53024.**

LOCATION: At Blacklion
Village on the main
Enniskillen – Sligo Road
(A4/N15).
SECRETARY: Robert Thompson.
Tel: (0365) 348796.
ARCHITECT: E. Hackett.

The course is bordered on two sides
by Lough McNean which can come
into play on three holes. Typical
inland course, which is playable all
year. Out of bounds on two holes,
some thick shrubbery comes into play

on two holes. Reasonably easy for
the straight hitter!

COURSE INFORMATION

**Par 72; SSS 69; Length
6,136 Yards, 5,614 Metres.**
Visitors: Welcome any day,
but prior arrangement is
preferred.
Opening Hours: Sunrise –
Sunset.
Avoid: Sunday morning and
early afternoon. Certain club
competitions, which are
posted in clubhouse.
Ladies: Welcome.

Green Fees: £8 weekdays
(£6 with member); £10.00
Sat/Sun and all public
holidays (£8 with member).
Juveniles: Welcome when
accompanied by an adult.
Lessons available by prior
arrangement.
Clubhouse Hours: 2pm –
10pm.
Clubhouse Dress: Informal.
Clubhouse Facilities:
Meals for small parties by
prior arrangement.
Open Competitions: 1st
Monday in June; Open Week
in mid June.

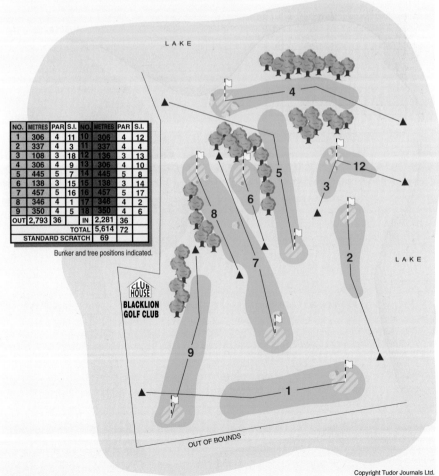

NO.	METRES	PAR	S.I.	NO.	METRES	PAR	S.I.
1	306	4	11	10	306	4	12
2	337	4	3	11	337	4	4
3	108	3	18	12	136	3	13
4	306	4	9	13	306	4	10
5	445	5	7	14	445	5	8
6	138	3	15	15	138	3	14
7	457	5	16	16	457	5	17
8	346	4	1	17	346	4	2
9	350	4	5	18	350	4	6
OUT	2,793	36		IN	2,281	36	
				TOTAL	5,614	72	
	STANDARD SCRATCH	69					

Bunker and tree positions indicated.

**CLUB HOUSE
BLACKLION
GOLF CLUB**

LAKE

LAKE

OUT OF BOUNDS

CABRA CASTLE
ULSTER

CAVAN

**Kingscourt, Co. Cavan.
Tel: (042) 67030.**

LOCATION: Kingscourt, Co Cavan.
SECRETARY: Jean Smith.
Tel: (042) 67030. Fax: (0232) (042) 67039.

Cabra Castle Golf Club may not be the hardest course that you will play, but it can be surprisingly difficult and will provide a reasonable test of golf.

COURSE INFORMATION

Par 70; SSS 68; Length 5,308 Metres.
Visitors: Welcome to play at all times.
Opening Hours: Daylight.
Avoid: Sunday morning.
Green Fees: £9 Mon – Fri; £9 Sat/Sun.
Clubhouse Hours: Cabra Castle Hotel 7am – 12 midnight.

Clubhouse Dress: Casual.
Clubhouse Facilities: Full catering facilities.
Open Competitions: Open Week – June.

NO.	METRES	PAR	S.I.	NO.	METRES	PAR	S.I.
1	315	4	7	10	315	4	8
2	186	3	11	11	186	3	12
3	346	4	5	12	346	4	6
4	114	3	15	13	114	3	16
5	347	4	1	14	347	4	2
6	275	4	17	15	275	4	18
7	452	5	9	16	452	5	10
8	275	4	13	17	275	4	14
9	344	4	3	18	344	4	4
OUT	2,654	35		IN	2,654	35	
				TOTAL	5,308	70	
				STANDARD SCRATCH	68		

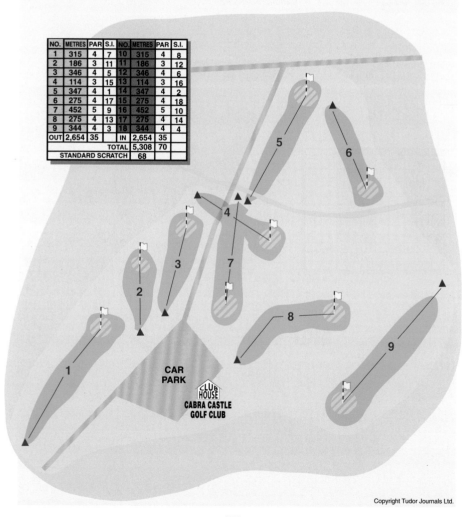

CAR PARK

CABRA CASTLE GOLF CLUB

**Arnmore House,
Drumelis, Cavan,
Co. Cavan.
Tel: (049) 31283.**

LOCATION: One mile from
Cavan town, on the
Killeshandra Road.
SECRETARY: J. Sheridan.
Tel: (049) 32045.

A Parkland course in the suburbs of
Cavan town that offers a good test of
golf, with several interesting holes a
feature of the course.

COURSE INFORMATION

**Par 70; SSS 69; Length
5,519 Metres.**

Visitors: Welcome to play at
any time.
Opening Hours: Daylight
hours.
Avoid: Sundays and
Wednesdays.
Ladies: Welcome. Ladies Day
– Wednesday.
Green Fees: £10 Mon – Fri;
£12 Sat/Sun & Public
Holidays.
Juveniles: To be
accompanied. Caddy cars
available by prior
arrangement.
Clubhouse Hours: Normal
licensing hours.
Clubhouse Dress: Casual.
Clubhouse Facilities: Bar,
meals and snooker room.

Catering facilities; available —
prior arrangements may be
made with resident steward or
caterer.
Open Competitions: Open
Week – July; Open Junior
Scratch Cup – Aug; Open
Intermediate Scratch Cup –
Sept; Handicap Certificate
required if competing in
competitions.

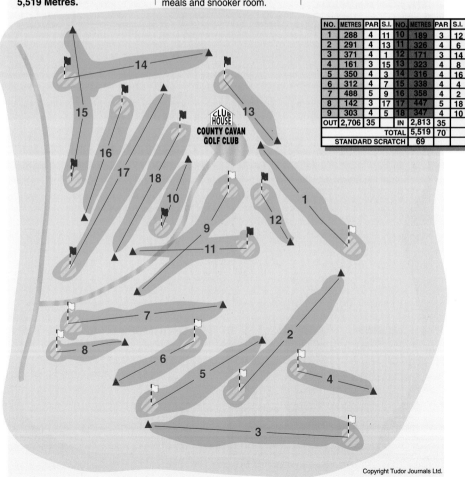

NO.	METRES	PAR	S.I.	NO.	METRES	PAR	S.I.
1	288	4	11	10	189	3	12
2	291	4	13	11	326	4	6
3	371	4	1	12	171	3	14
4	161	3	15	13	323	4	8
5	350	4	3	14	316	4	16
6	312	4	7	15	338	4	4
7	488	5	9	16	358	4	2
8	142	3	17	17	447	5	18
9	303	4	5	18	347	4	10
OUT	2,706	35		IN	2,813	35	
				TOTAL	5,519	70	
				STANDARD SCRATCH	69		

COUNTY CAVAN
GOLF CLUB

Copyright Tudor Journals Ltd.

The Slieve Russell, Golf and Country Club, Ballyconnell, Co. Cavan. Tel: (049) 26444, Fax: (049) 26474/26511.

LOCATION: Two hours from both Dublin and Belfast.

GOLF DIRECTOR: Mr P.J. Creamer.

ARCHITECT: Paddy Merrigan.

PROFESSIONAL: Liam McCool.

18 hole championship course is set in 300 acres of parkland including 50 acres of lake. The unique style of the Slieve Russell fits and complements the Cavan Drumlin landscape multiple tee positions facilitate all categories of golfer.

COURSE INFORMATION

Par 72; Length 7,013 yards.
Visitors: Welcome.
Opening Hours: 8am–11pm (seasonal opening times).
Avoid: Saturday.
Ladies: Welcome.
Juveniles: Over 12yrs full green fees payable.
Green Fees: Non-resident rates rates –£27 (Sun– Fri) & £35 (Sat).
Clubhouse Hours: 10.30am–11pm.
Clubhouse Dress: Dress code in operation.
Clubhouse Facilities: Attached to the Slieve Russell Hotel, Clubhouse restaurant and bar also available.

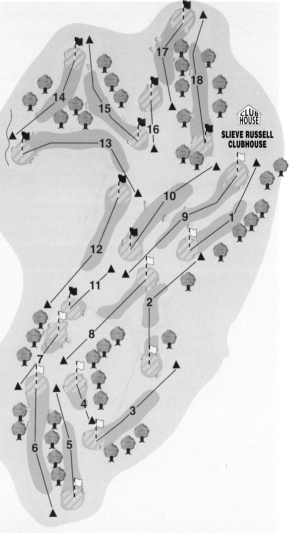

SLIEVE RUSSELL CLUBHOUSE

NO.	CHAMP YARDS	MEDAL YARDS	PAR	S.I.	NO.	CHAMP YARDS	MEDAL YARDS	PAR	S.I.
1	382	355	4	8	10	376	360	4	2
2	397	373	4	1	11	178	154	3	13
3	364	339	4	6	12	404	397	4	4
4	152	145	3	18	13	484	459	5	12
5	399	377	4	3	14	342	326	4	16
6	468	449	5	15	15	414	390	4	5
7	201	179	3	10	16	161	151	3	9
8	356	309	4	14	17	338	315	4	17
9	505	466	5	11	18	494	474	5	7
OUT	3,224	2,992	36		IN	3,189	3,026	36	
					TOTAL	6,413	6,018	72	
					STANDARD SCRATCH	74	72		

Bunker & tree positions indicated.

Virginia, Co Cavan.
Tel: (049) 48066.

LOCATION: Fifty miles N.W. of Dublin on Virginia – Ballyjamesduff Road on the grounds of the Park Hotel.
SECRETARY: Joe Greene.
Tel: (049) 40223.
PROFESSIONAL: Victor Nesbitt.

A compact nine hole course situated adjacent to the picturesque Lough Ramor. Fairways are narrow and divided by trees. Involves accuracy and a delicate touch around the greens. The course is located in the grounds of the Park Hotel.

COURSE INFORMATION

Par 64; SSS 62; Length 4,139 Metres.
Visitors: Welcome to play on any day except Ladies Day on Thurs.
Opening Hours: Daylight hrs.

Avoid: Sunday (am) of Men's competitions.
Ladies: Welcome except on Competition Days.
Green Fees: £8 (£4 with a member).
Juveniles: Not allowed after 5.00pm or on Sun. or Thur.
Clubhouse Hours:
Clubhouse Facilities: Available in the Park Hotel.

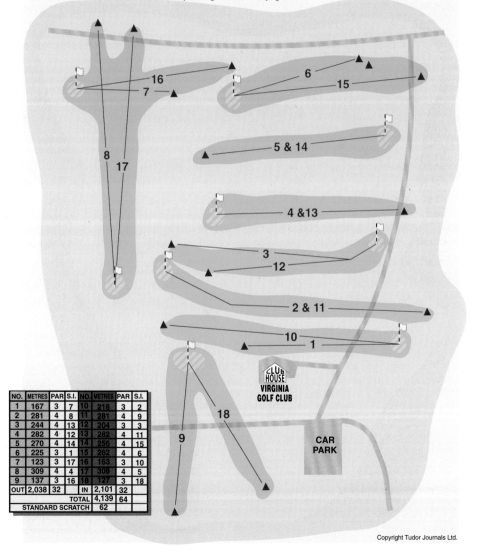

NO.	METRES	PAR	S.I.	NO.	METRES	PAR	S.I.
1	167	3	7	10	218	3	2
2	281	4	8	11	281	4	9
3	244	4	13	12	204	3	3
4	282	4	12	13	282	4	11
5	270	4	14	14	256	4	15
6	225	3	1	15	262	4	6
7	123	3	17	16	163	3	10
8	309	4	4	17	308	4	5
9	137	3	16	18	127	3	18
OUT	2,038	32		IN	2,101	32	
				TOTAL	4,139	64	
STANDARD SCRATCH		62					

VIRGINIA GOLF CLUB

CAR PARK

Ballybofey, Co. Donegal.
Tel: (074) 31093.

LOCATION: Lough Alan, Stranorlar, off Strabane/Stranorlar main road.
SECRETARY: A. Harkin.
Tel: (074) 31228.
ARCHITECT: P.C. Carr.
CAPTAIN: Peter Byrne.

Undulating parkland course with picturesque views of the Donegal Hills and Valley of River Finn. The course is located on the shores of Lough Alan, yet follows the rolling contours of the surrounding countryside. A satisfying course and one that is popular with societies.

COURSE INFORMATION

Par 68; SSS 69; Length 5,366 yards.
Visitors: Welcome. Booking essential for weekends. Please telephone (074) 31033.
Opening Hours: 9am – Sunset.

Avoid: Mon & Tue evenings from 5pm.
Green Fees: £12.00 per day Mon – Fri; £12 per round Sat/Sun; £10 Societies.
Clubhouse Hours: 9am – 12pm.
Clubhouse Dress: Informal.
Clubhouse Facilities: A new clubhouse with improved facilities.
Open Competitions: Annual Open Week 1st week in June & 1st – 2nd weekends; Scratch Cup annually in July.

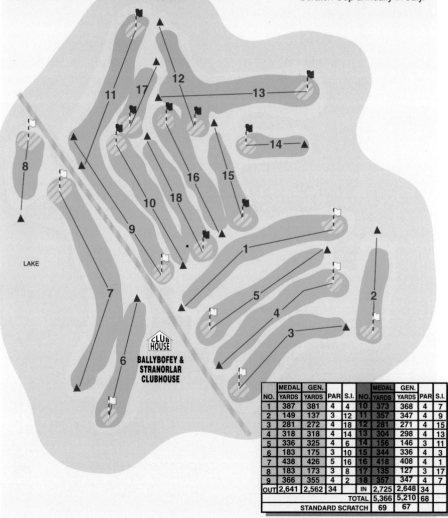

LAKE

CLUB HOUSE

BALLYBOFEY & STRANORLAR CLUBHOUSE

NO.	MEDAL YARDS	GEN. YARDS	PAR	S.I.	NO.	MEDAL YARDS	GEN. YARDS	PAR	S.I.
1	387	381	4	4	10	373	368	4	7
2	149	137	3	12	11	357	347	4	9
3	281	272	4	18	12	281	271	4	15
4	318	318	4	14	13	304	298	4	13
5	336	325	4	6	14	156	146	3	11
6	183	175	3	10	15	344	336	4	3
7	438	426	5	16	16	418	408	4	1
8	183	173	3	8	17	135	127	3	17
9	366	355	4	2	18	357	347	4	7
OUT	2,641	2,562	34		IN	2,725	2,648	34	
					TOTAL	5,366	5,210	68	
					STANDARD SCRATCH		69	67	

Copyright Tudor Journals Ltd.

180

BALLYLIFFIN
U L S T E R — DONEGAL

Ballyliffin, Carndonagh,
Co. Donegal.
Tel: (077) 76119
Fax: 7667222.

LOCATION: Carndonagh six miles; Buncrana 12 miles; L'Derry 20 miles; Coleraine 30 miles.

SECRETARY: Karl O'Doherty. Tel: (077) 74417.

Generous fairways give way to breathtaking views. "A real jewel", commented the late Fred Daly. Very difficult 3rd hole with narrow fairway and sloping green with magnificent

Glashedy Island in the background. The course also has an interesting par 3 5th holes known locally as the "Tank".

COURSE INFORMATION

Par 71; SSS 72; Length 6,524 yards, 6158 metres.
Visitors: Welcome .
Opening Hours: Daylight.
Avoid: Sat & Sun afternoons.
Ladies: Tues only and 4.00pm – 6.00pm Sat & Sun.

Green Fees: £20. Mon – Fri; £25 Weekends (£1 less with members).
Juveniles: By arrangement. Caddy service available by prior arrangement.
Clubhouse Hours: 9.00am – 11.30pm.
Clubhouse Facilities: Bar, snacks, showers, meals by arrangment. Catering facilities by arrangement & most weekends.
Open Competitions: Open Week June / July.

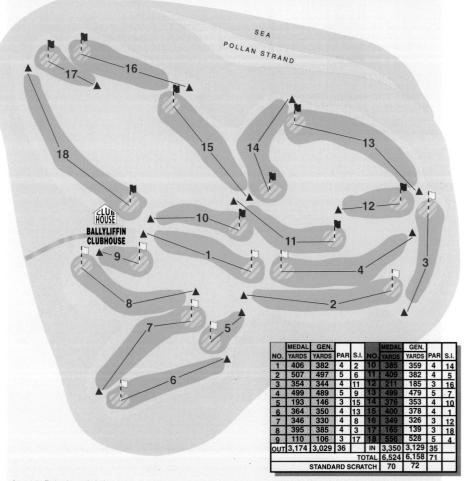

NO.	MEDAL YARDS	GEN. YARDS	PAR	S.I.	NO.	MEDAL YARDS	GEN. YARDS	PAR	S.I.
1	406	382	4	2	10	385	359	4	14
2	507	497	5	6	11	409	382	4	5
3	354	344	4	11	12	211	185	3	16
4	499	489	5	9	13	499	479	5	7
5	193	146	3	15	14	376	353	4	10
6	364	350	4	13	15	400	378	4	1
7	346	330	4	8	16	349	326	3	12
8	395	385	4	3	17	165	139	3	18
9	110	106	3	17	18	556	528	5	4
OUT	3,174	3,029	36		IN	3,350	3,129	35	
					TOTAL	6,524	6,158	71	
					STANDARD SCRATCH	70	72		

Ballyliffin have extended another 18 holes. However at time of going to press a full map of the course was not available.

181

**Bundoran, Co. Donegal.
Tel: (072) 41302.**

Location: 25 miles North of Sligo on coast.
Secretary: John McGagh.
Tel: (072) 41302.
Professional: David Robinson.
Tel: (072) 41302.
Architect: Harry Vardon.

A combination of links and a treeless parkland course in undulating terrain. The greens and approaches are well protected by bunkers. A picturesque course with the middle holes playing alongside the impressive Atlantic coast and beautiful strands. The course is sited on the edge of Bundoran and literally surrounds the Great Northern Hotel.

COURSE INFORMATION

Par 69; SSS 70; Length 5,689 metres.
Visitors: Welcome to play especially on weekdays.
Opening Hours: 9.00am – 6.00pm (winter) 8.00am – 8.00pm (summer).
Green Fees: £14 Mon – Fri; £16 at weekends. Club hire available.
Clubhouse Hours: Bar 4.30pm – 11.30pm (winter) 12noon – 11.30pm (summer).
Clubhouse Dress: Casual.
Clubhouse Facilities: Snacks only. Open all day, snacks available. Hotel on course.
Open Competitions: All weekends from May to October. Open Week – July & Centenary – 7 to 14 August. Letter of introduction required for competitions.

NO.	CHAMP METRES	MEDAL METRES	PAR	S.I.	NO.	CHAMP METRES	MEDAL METRES	PAR	S.I.
1	327	327	4	8	10	364	358	4	1
2	459	437	5	16	11	384	374	4	5
3	117	107	3	18	12	316	316	4	11
4	331	291	4	6	13	212	179	3	9
5	197	156	3	10	14	366	343	4	7
6	180	180	3	2	15	390	371	4	3
7	325	276	4	12	16	142	132	3	17
8	356	324	4	4	17	453	453	5/4	15
9	356	333	4	13	18	324	291	4	14
OUT	2,738	2,431	34		IN	2,951	2,817	35/34	
					TOTAL	5,689	5,248	69/68	
					STANDARD SCRATCH	70	68		

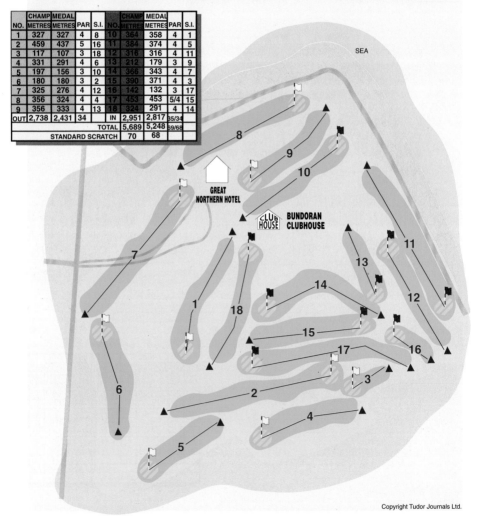

SEA

GREAT NORTHERN HOTEL

CLUB HOUSE BUNDORAN CLUBHOUSE

Kincasslagh, Co Donegal.
Tel: (075) 43296.

LOCATION: Two miles outside village of Kincasslagh.
SECRETARY: D. Devenney.
Tel: (075) 48151.

A breathtaking 9 hole links course perched precariously on the edge of the Atlantic Ocean and accessible only by a bridge which joins it to the mainland and the village of Kincasslagh. The crowning glory of the course is the magnificent Par 3 6th hole where nerves of steel are required to hit over a deep cove and land on a small green which as a sheer drop into the sea behind for anyone who over clubs it.

COURSE INFORMATION

Par 68; SSS 66; Length 4,860 Metres.
Visitors: Welcome anytime. Prior arrangement required for parties in excess of 12 people.
Avoid: Club Competitions Sunday mornings; Ladies Competitions Saturday mornings.
Ladies: Welcome.
Ladies Day: Thursday.

Green Fees: £7 (£5 with a member); £9 July/August (Subject to change).
Juveniles: Welcome. No restrictions. Lessons available Friday evenings.
Juveniles: Welcome. No restrictions. Lessons available Friday evenings.
Clubhouse Hours: June/Sept 10.00am – dusk.
Clubhouse Facilities: Bar, locker rooms. Catering facilities, meals available. Prior arrangement required for larger parties.

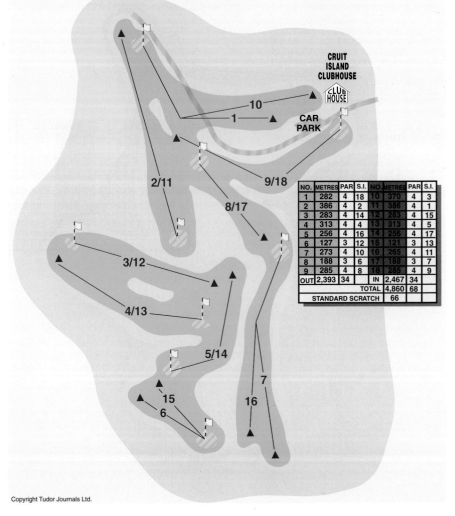

NO.	METRES	PAR	S.I.	NO.	METRES	PAR	S.I.
1	282	4	18	10	370	4	3
2	386	4	2	11	386	4	1
3	283	4	14	12	283	4	15
4	313	4	4	13	313	4	5
5	256	4	16	14	256	4	17
6	127	3	12	15	121	3	13
7	273	4	10	16	265	4	11
8	188	3	6	17	188	3	7
9	285	4	8	18	285	4	9
OUT	2,393	34		IN	2,467	34	
					TOTAL	4,860	68	
				STANDARD SCRATCH		66	

**Murvagh, Laghey,
Ballintra, Co Donegal
Tel: (073) 34054
Fax: (073) 34377.**

LOCATION: Halfway between
Rossnowlagh & Donegal
Town.
ADMINISTRATOR: John McBride.
ARCHITECT: Eddie Hackett.

Challenging links course fit to test the
best. Superbly scenic between sea
and mountains, the holes are a mixture
of testing Par 5's, tricky Par 4's and
memorable Par 3's.

COURSE INFORMATION

**Par 73; SSS 73; Length
6,243 Metres.
Visitors:** Welcome. Every day
except special events as per
fixture card.
Opening Hours: Dawn –
Dusk.
Avoid: Sunday.
Ladies: Welcome. Ladies Day
Monday.
Green Fees: £17 weekdays;
£22.50 Weekends and
holidays. Husband & wife
weekday rate £27 inc. vat.

Juveniles: Welcome 1/2 price
– restrictions at weekends.
Clubhouse Hours: 9am –
11pm.
Clubhouse Dress: Informal
but neat.
Clubhouse Facilities:
Available to visitors, include
buggy hire £20 per round,
caddy carts £1.50, bar,
snooker, locker rooms and
showers. Snacks available at
all times full meals by prior
arrangement with caterer.
Open Competitions: Phone
and check.

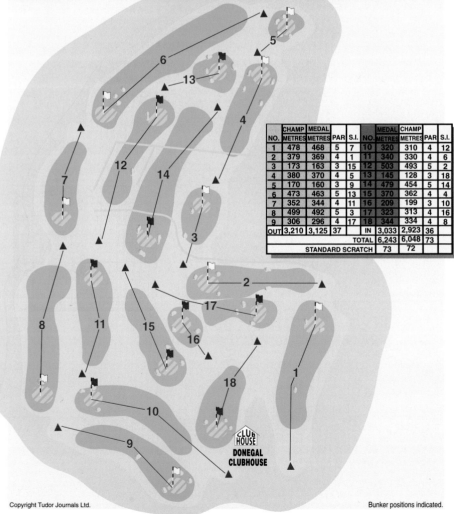

NO.	CHAMP METRES	MEDAL METRES	PAR	S.I.	NO.	MEDAL METRES	CHAMP METRES	PAR	S.I.
1	478	468	5	7	10	320	310	4	12
2	379	369	4	1	11	340	330	4	6
3	173	163	3	15	12	503	493	5	2
4	380	370	4	5	13	145	128	3	18
5	170	160	3	9	14	479	454	5	14
6	473	463	5	13	15	370	362	4	4
7	352	344	4	11	16	209	199	3	10
8	499	492	5	3	17	323	313	4	16
9	306	296	4	17	18	344	334	4	8
OUT	3,210	3,125	37		IN	3,033	2,923	36	
					TOTAL	6,243	6,048	73	
					STANDARD SCRATCH	73	72		

DONEGAL
CLUBHOUSE

Bunker positions indicated.

Kill, Dunfanaghy.
Tel: (074) 36335.

LOCATION: Less than a mile from Dunfanaghy on the main road to Letterkenny.
SECRETARY/MANAGER: Sam Sterritt.
Tel: (074) 36335.

This is a course suited for high and middle handicappers. It improves each year and provides a fair test. The most notable improvement of recent years is the removal of fences and sheep from the course and a notable feature is the view from the 7th tee, looking west across the bay to Horn Head.

COURSE INFORMATION

Par 68; SSS 66; Length 5,066 Metres.
Visitors: Welcome anytime.
Opening Hours: 9.00am – 10.00pm.
Ladies: Wednesday.
Green Fees: Mon – Fri £11 (£7 with a member); £13 Sat, Sun & Bank Hols (£7 with a member).
Juveniles: Not before 6.00pm weekends.
Clubhouse Hours: 9.00am onwards.
Clubhouse Dress: Informal.
Clubhouse Facilities: Bar and snacks.
Open Competitions: Shandon Open Classic, Singles, May. Hickey Clarke & Largan Open Stablefored June. Open Week July / Aug. Carrig Rua Classic September.

DUNFANAGHY CLUBHOUSE

NO.	METRES	PAR	S.I.	NO.	METRES	PAR	S.I.
1	306	4	12	10	228	4	13
2	143	3	15	11	280	4	17
3	351	4	1	12	332	4	2
4	336	4	4	13	141	3	14
5	325	4	11	14	322	4	3
6	305	4	8	15	358	4	7
7	205	3	5	16	466	5	6
8	277	4	16	17	156	3	9
9	120	3	18	18	325	4	10
OUT	2,336	33		IN	2,638	35	
				TOTAL	5,066	68	
				STANDARD SCRATCH		66	

185

Maghergallon, Derrybeg, Letterkenny.
Tel: (075) 31140/81013.

LOCATION: North west of Letterkenny.
SECRETARY: Bryan Gormley.
Tel: (075) 82280.
ARCHITECT: E. Hackett.

A scenic course sited along the very pleasant shores of the Insihowen Pennisula in the north of Donegal.

NO.	MEDAL METRES	GEN. METRES	PAR	S.I.	NO.	MEDAL METRES	GEN. METRES	PAR	S.I.
1	312	312	4	11	10	488	474	5	6
2	386	344	4	1	11	165	155	3	8
3	138	138	3	13	12	311	299	4	10
4	428	414	4	3	13	440	420	5	16
5	319	264	4	7	14	350	350	4	4
6	285	285	4	9	15	103	103	3	18
7	119	119	3	15	16	366	350	4	2
8	265	265	4	17	17	277	255	4	14
9	294	279	4	5	18	165	153	3	12
OUT	2,546	2,420	34		IN	2,665	2,559	35	
					TOTAL	5,211	4,979	69	
					STANDARD SCRATCH	66	66		

COURSE INFORMATION

Par 69; SSS 66; Length 5,211 metres.
Visitors: Welcome.
Opening Hours: Daylight.
Ladies: Welcome.
Green Fees: £10 Mon-Fri, (£8 with member); £15 Sat/Sun & Bank Hols (£10 with member).
Juveniles: Welcome.
Clubhouse Hours: 11.00am – 11.00pm.
Clubhouse Dress: Informal.
Clubhouse Facilities: Available Thurs & Weekends in summer. Full Clubhouse Facilities.
Open Competitions: Open week June. Open Competitions various weekends.

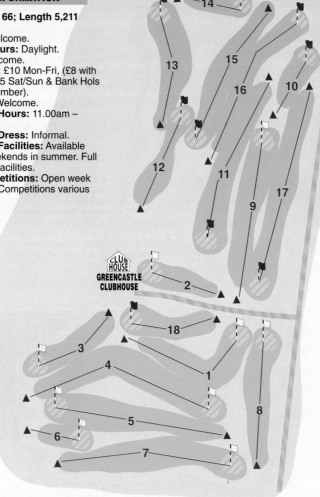

Maghergallon, Derrybeg, Letterkenny, Co Donegal.
Tel: (075) 31140.

LOCATION: North west of Letterkenny.

SECRETARY/MANAGER: Eamonn McBride.

An attractive nine hole, seaside course which is quite challenging for players of all handicaps. The course is not physically taxing and the setting is attractive.

COURSE INFORMATION

Par 71; SSS 69; Length 6,201 metres.
Visitors: Welcome.
Opening Hours: All day.
Ladies: Welcome.
Green Fees: Mon - Fri £7; Sat, Sun & Bank Hols £8 (with member £5). Caddy service available by prior arrangement.

Juveniles: Sat mornings.
Clubhouse Hours: Normally 10am – 12 midnight.
Clubhouse Dress: Informal.
Clubhouse Facilities: Showers, Cloakrooms. Catering facilities; daily during summer months. Weekends for remainder of the year.

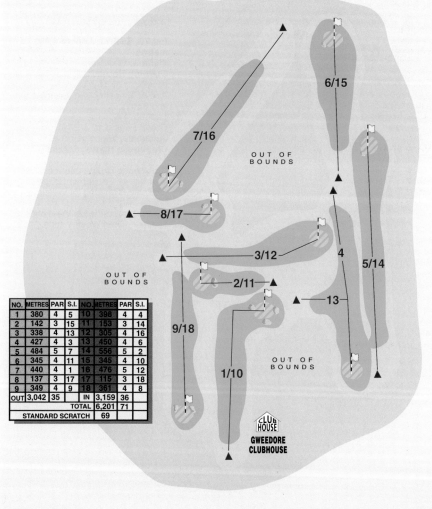

NO.	METRES	PAR	S.I.	NO.	METRES	PAR	S.I.
1	380	4	5	10	398	4	4
2	142	3	15	11	153	3	14
3	338	4	13	12	305	4	16
4	427	4	3	13	450	4	6
5	484	5	7	14	556	5	2
6	345	4	11	15	345	4	10
7	440	4	1	16	476	5	12
8	137	3	17	17	115	3	18
9	349	4	9	18	361	4	8
OUT	3,042	35		IN	3,159	36	
				TOTAL	6,201	71	
	STANDARD SCRATCH	69					

GWEEDORE CLUBHOUSE

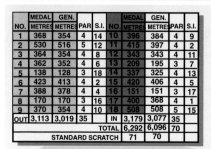

NO.	MEDAL METRES	GEN. METRES	PAR	S.I.	NO.	MEDAL METRES	GEN. METRES	PAR	S.I.
1	368	354	4	14	10	396	384	4	9
2	530	516	5	12	11	415	397	4	2
3	364	354	4	8	12	343	343	4	11
4	362	352	4	6	13	209	195	3	7
5	138	128	3	18	14	337	325	4	13
6	423	413	4	2	15	420	406	4	5
7	388	378	4	4	16	151	151	3	17
8	170	170	3	16	17	400	368	4	1
9	370	354	4	10	18	508	508	5	15
OUT	3,113	3,019	35		IN	3,179	3,077	35	
					TOTAL	6,292	6,096	70	
					STANDARD SCRATCH	71	70		

**Barnhill Golf Club,
Letterkenny Co Donegal.
Tel: (074) 21150.**

LOCATION: One – two miles from outskirts of Letterkenny town.
SECRETARY: Barry Ramsey.
Tel: (074) 21150.
PROFESSIONAL: J. Gallagher.

An attractive eighteen hole golf course in which the first eleven holes are played on relatively flat ground, the remaining seven holes are played on a plateau above the others. The course is a good challenge with a demanding finishing hole.

COURSE INFORMATION

Par 70; SSS 71; Length 6,292 metres.
Visitors: Welcome.
Opening Hours: Call in advance to check.
Avoid: Timesheets in use most Sat and Sun.
Ladies: Welcome.
Green Fees: £10 & £7 for societies.
Juveniles: Welcome.
Clubhouse Hours: 3.00pm – 11.30pm.
Clubhouse Dress: Informal.
Clubhouse Facilities: Snacks available. Catering for visiting teams.
Open Competitions: Weekends in summer. Open Week – June.

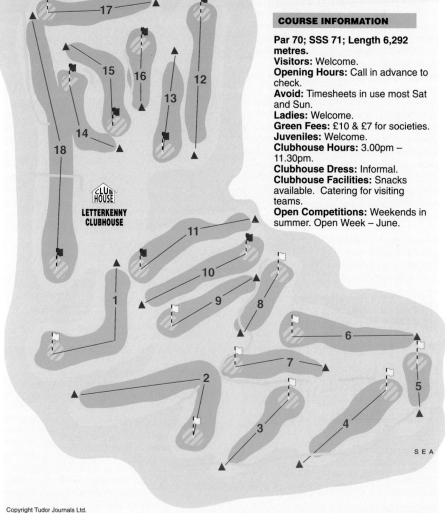

LETTERKENNY
CLUBHOUSE

SEA

NARIN & PORTNOO

ULSTER | DONEGAL

Narin, Portnoo, Co Donegal.
Tel: (074) 45107.

LOCATION: Narin / Portnoo, Co Donegal.
SECRETARY: Edna Bonner.
Tel: (074) 24668.
PROFESSIONAL: None.
ARCHITECT: P Carr, Ballybofey.

Beautiful scenery and a quiet course, although it is particularly popular in the summer months as it is located in a holiday area. Set amidst beautiful scenery on the extreme west coast of Donegal, providing well deserved praise from both low and high handicappers. A very popular location with the best of links and inland characteristics.

COURSE INFORMATION

Par 69; SSS 68; Length 5,766 yards.
Visitors: Welcome.
Opening Hours: Daylight hours.
Avoid: Sunday (sometimes available – ring before).
Ladies: Welcome.
Green Fees: £10 daily, £14 weekends. £10 Societies (twenty plus).
Juveniles: Welcome.
Clubhouse Hours: 9.00am – 12.00pm.
Clubhouse Dress: Casual.
Clubhouse Facilities: Bar and light refreshments.
Open Competitions: Open Week – August; Open Competitions evey second weekend during July & August.

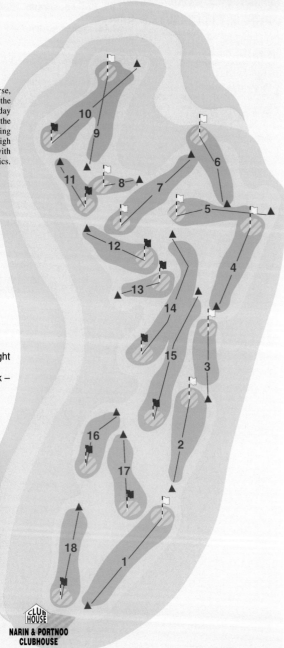

NARIN & PORTNOO
CLUBHOUSE

NO.	YARDS	PAR	S.I.	NO.	YARDS	PAR	S.I.
1	313	4	17	10	386	4	2
2	486	5	6	11	195	3	5
3	185	3	12	12	328	4	11
4	450	4	1	13	184	3	16
5	386	4	7	14	516	5	10
6	202	3	9	15	488	5	8
7	316	4	3	16	120	3	18
8	140	3	13	17	402	4	4
9	319	4	15	18	348	4	14
OUT	2,801	34		IN	2,965	35	
				TOTAL	5,766	69	
	STANDARD SCRATCH				68		

Copyright Tudor Journals Ltd.

189

**Lisfannon, Fahan,
Co. Donegal.
Tel: (077) 61027/61715.**

LOCATION: At Lisfannon which is two miles from Buncrana and eight miles from Derry.
SECRETARY: Tom Crossam.
PROFESSIONAL: Seamus McBriarty.

The course lies between the sea and the picturesque Mouldy Mountain. The holes are varied, with many sandy knolls and pleasing undulations, but the general tendency is flattish. There are two loops of nine holes, each loop terminating at the Clubhouse.

COURSE INFORMATION

Par 69; SSS 68; Length 6,203 yards.
Visitors: Welcome Mon-Fri and Weekends by arrangement.
Opening Hours: 8.00am till dark.
Avoid: Weekends during October – March, 12.00 – 2.00pm Saturday and 8.30am – 11pm Sunday's.
Ladies: Welcome.
Green Fees: £10 Mon - Fri (£8 with member); £15 Sat, Sun & Bank Hols

(£12 with member). Caddy cars available by prior arrangement. Lesson available by prior arrangement.
Juveniles: Welcome.
Clubhouse Dress: Casual.
Clubhouse Facilities: Locker room, showers. Catering facilities all week at 1.00pm.
Open Competitions: Whit Open May; Open Week July. Handicap certificate required.

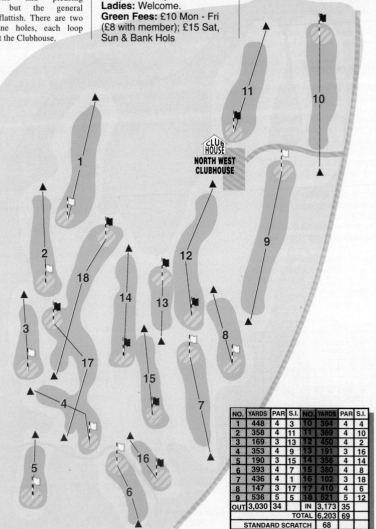

NO.	YARDS	PAR	S.I.	NO.	YARDS	PAR	S.I.
1	448	4	3	10	394	4	4
2	358	4	11	11	369	4	10
3	169	3	13	12	450	4	2
4	353	4	9	13	191	3	16
5	190	3	15	14	356	4	14
6	393	4	7	15	380	4	8
7	436	4	1	16	102	3	18
8	147	3	17	17	410	4	6
9	536	5	5	18	521	5	12
OUT	3,030	34		IN	3,173	35	
				TOTAL	6,203	69	
	STANDARD SCRATCH			68			

Copyright Tudor Journals Ltd.

Portsalon, Letterkenny, Co. Donegal.
Tel: (074) 59459.

LOCATION: Twenty miles north of Letterkenny on western shore of Lough Swilly.
SECRETARY: Cathal Toland. Tel: (074) 59459.

A popular seaside links with quite narrow fairways. Greens are well protected with bunkers, streams and natural sand dunes all coming into play. Course runs in clockwise direction, so the out-of-bounds is generally on left. The club celebrated its Centenary in 1991 and in the same year built a new clubhouse.

COURSE INFORMATION

Par 69; SSS 68; Length 5,379 metres.
Visitors: Welcome (ring in advance).
Opening Hours: Sunrise – Sunset.
Ladies: Welcome.
Green Fees: £10.00 (weekdays), £12 (weekends): £50.00 per week.

Juveniles: Should be accompanied by an adult.
Clubhouse Hours: 8.30 – 11.30pm.
Clubhouse Facilities: Snacks and meals available by arrangement with caterer.
Open Competitions: Open Week – July. Last weekend of each month. Normal clubhouse facilities.

NO.	METRES	PAR	S.I.	NO.	METRES	PAR	S.I.
1	334	4	4	10	321	4	5
2	180	3	12	11	296	4	15
3	326	4	14	12	170	3	13
4	315	4	6	13	394	4	1
5	191	3	18	14	142	3	11
6	324	4	10	15	355	4	9
7	470	5	2	16	261	4	17
8	159	3	16	17	481	5	7
9	290	4	8	18	370	4	3
OUT	2,589	34		IN	2,790	34	
				TOTAL	5,379	69	
				STANDARD SCRATCH		68	

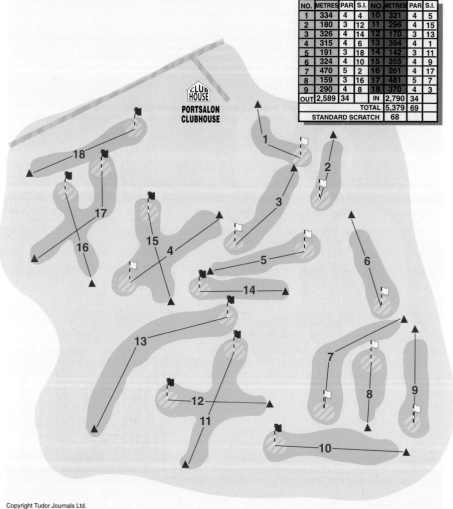

PORTSALON
CLUBHOUSE

REDCASTLE   U L S T E R   ■ DONEGAL

Redcastle, Moville, Co. Donegal.
Tel: (077) 82073.

LOCATION: Beside hotel.
SECRETARY: Brian McQuaid.
Tel: (077) 350510.
A difficult course set in a very picturesque area on the shores of Lough Foyle, with the advantage of its own hotel. The two Par 3 holes are quite difficult and should be approached with the necessary respect.

COURSE INFORMATION

Par 72; SSS 69; Length 6,046 yards.
Visitors: Welcome to play midweek.
Opening Hours: All day, all year.
Avoid: Weekends – May, June, July and August.
Ladies: Welcome.
Green Fees: £7 Mon/Fri (£5 with member); £10 Sat/Sun &

Bank Hols (£9 with member).
Juveniles: Welcome.
Clubhouse Hours: 9.00am – 11.30pm.
Clubhouse Dress: Casual.
Clubhouse Facilities: Bar food from 11.30am – 7pm.
Open Competitions: On request.

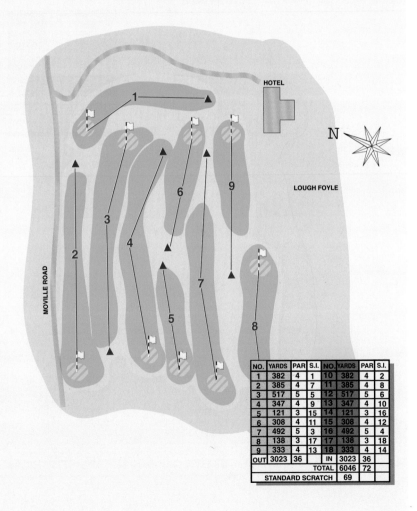

NO.	YARDS	PAR	S.I.	NO.	YARDS	PAR	S.I.
1	382	4	1	10	382	4	2
2	385	4	7	11	385	4	8
3	517	5	5	12	517	5	6
4	347	4	9	13	347	4	10
5	121	3	15	14	121	3	16
6	308	4	11	15	308	4	12
7	492	5	3	16	492	5	4
8	138	3	17	17	138	3	18
9	333	4	13	18	333	4	14
OUT	3023	36		IN	3023	36	
				TOTAL	6046	72	
				STANDARD SCRATCH	69		

**Rosapenna Golf Club,
Downings.
Co. Donegal.
Tel: (010 353) 7455301.**

LOCATION: Two miles north of
Carrigart.
SECRETARY: Mr J. Gallagher.
ARCHITECT: Original Course (1893)
– Tom Morris.

This championship length links course is
set in north west Donegal at Downings.
The first nine are played along a majestic
stretch of beach and have many large
sandhills and bunkers. The second nine
begins and ends with a second shot over
the main Downings–Carrigart Road.
Looping around a large bluff the second
nine have inland characteristics. Very
popular with visiting societies as the
Rosapenna Golf Hotel is situated on the
course and offers special golf breaks.

COURSE INFORMATION

**Par 70; SSS 71; Length 5,719
metres.
Visitors:** Welcome.
Opening Hours: Dawn to Dusk.
Ladies: Welcome.
Green Fees: £15 every other day;
£18 Saturday and Sunday.
Juveniles: Must be accompanied
by an adult.
Clubhouse Facilities: Full
catering facilities at Rosapenna
Golf Hotel.

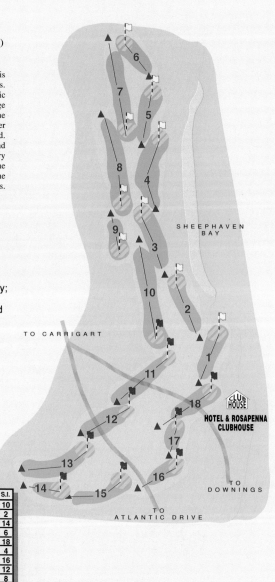

NO.	YARDS	PAR	S.I.	NO.	YARDS	PAR	S.I.
1	298	4	11	10	543	5	10
2	428	4	5	11	427	4	2
3	446	4	1	12	342	4	14
4	386	4	9	13	455	4	6
5	255	4	15	14	128	3	18
6	167	3	17	15	418	4	4
7	367	4	3	16	216	3	16
8	485	5	7	17	358	4	12
9	185	3	13	18	367	4	8
OUT	3,017	35		IN	3,254	35	
				TOTAL	6,271	70	
	STANDARD SCRATCH			71			

Castle Place, Ardglass.
Co. Down.
Tel: (01396) 841219.

LOCATION: Approx 7 miles from Downpatrick on B1.
PROFESSIONAL: Philip Farrell.
Tel: (01396) 841022.
SECRETARY: Debbie Polly..
Tel: (01396) 841219.

A seaside course with superb views over St. Johns Point, Killough Harbour and lying to the west, the Mourne Mountains. The 2nd (Howds) hole a 147 Metres, Par 3 is played over a gaping gorge to an elevated green. Another Par 3, the 11th is played from an elevated tee looking down to Coney Island. Both provide two memorable golf holes.

CLUB HOUSE

ARDGLASS CLUBHOUSE

IRISH SEA

COURSE INFORMATION

Par 70; SSS 69; Length 5,498 metres.
Visitors: Welcome Monday, Tuesday, Thursday & Friday.
Avoid: Holiday periods by arraangement only Wednesday, Saturday, Sunday.
Green Fees: £15 Mon – Fri; £20 weekends.
Ladies Day: Wednesday.
Clubhouse Dress: Smart dress.
Clubhouse Facilities: Snacks are available during the day. Evening meals by prior arrangement.

NO.	MEDAL METRES	GEN. METRES	PAR	S.I.	NO.	MEDAL METRES	GEN. METRES	PAR	S.I.
1	297	267	4	10	10	401	393	4	1
2	147	158	3	6	11	130	115	3	11
3	305	246	4	14	12	363	339	4	5
4	332	321	4	4	13	349	331	4	7
5	123	123	3	12	14	448	439	5	13
6	452	443	5	16	15	358	351	4	3
7	470	463	5	18	16	330	330	4	9
8	369	359	4	2	17	109	104	3	17
9	200	187	3	8	18	315	293	4	15
OUT	2,695	2,567	35		IN	2,803	2,695	35	
					TOTAL	5,498	5,262	70	
					STANDARD SCRATCH	69	68		

Bunker positions indicated.
Copyright Tudor Journals Ltd.

BANBRIDGE

Huntly Road, Banbridge. Co. Down.
Tel: (018206) 62342 / 62211.

LOCATION: 1 mile from town centre on Huntly Road.
HON/SECRETARY: Bert Wilson.
ADMINISTRATOR: Mrs J. A. Anketell.
Tel: (018206) 62211.

The course has been extended to 18 holes the new holes designed by Frank Ainsworth and include a very exciting 'pond hole', 6th. The redesigned Par 5, 14th calls for an accurate shot over a ravine. The Par 3, 10th is tricky primarily as it is quite long at 201 metres and secondly, the green is very close to the boundary hedge.

COURSE INFORMATION

Par 69; SSS 67; Length 5,003 metres.
Visitors: Welcome to play

On most days contact office to make arrangements.
Avoid: Sun morning, members only on ladies day, Tuesday and Saturday.
Green Fees: £15 Mon – Fri (£8 with member); £20 weekends (£10 with member).
Ladies Day: Tuesday.
Clubhouse Dress: Casual.
Clubhouse Facilities: By arrangement.
Open Competitions: Civic week, June.

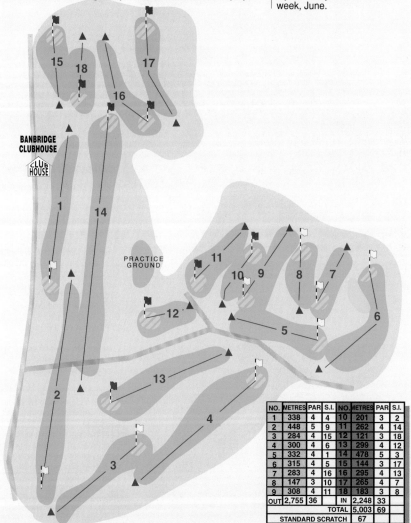

NO.	METRES	PAR	S.I.	NO.	METRES	PAR	S.I.
1	338	4	4	10	201	3	2
2	448	5	9	11	262	4	14
3	284	4	15	12	121	3	18
4	300	4	6	13	299	4	12
5	332	4	1	14	478	5	3
6	315	4	5	15	144	3	17
7	283	4	16	16	295	4	13
8	147	3	10	17	265	4	7
9	308	4	11	18	183	3	8
OUT	2,755	36		IN	2,248	33	
				TOTAL	5,003	69	
STANDARD SCRATCH		67					

BANBRIDGE CLUBHOUSE

PRACTICE GROUND

BANGOR   ULSTER   DOWN

NO.	MEDAL YARDS	GEN. YARDS	PAR	S.I.	NO.	MEDAL YARDS	GEN. YARDS	PAR	S.I.
1	353	343	4	14	10	437	416	4	3
2	494	482	5	10	11	319	309	4	15
3	359	349	4	18	12	186	176	3	7
4	471	461	5	6	13	384	374	4	5
5	473	465	4	2	14	175	163	3	13
6	353	353	4	16	15	415	405	4	1
7	191	181	3	12	16	509	481	5	11
8	411	401	4	4	17	160	150	3	17
9	392	384	4	8	18	342	326	4	9
OUT	3,497	3,419	37		IN	2,927	2,800	34	
	TOTAL	6,424	6,219	71					
	STANDARD SCRATCH		71	70					

Bunker and tree positions indicated.

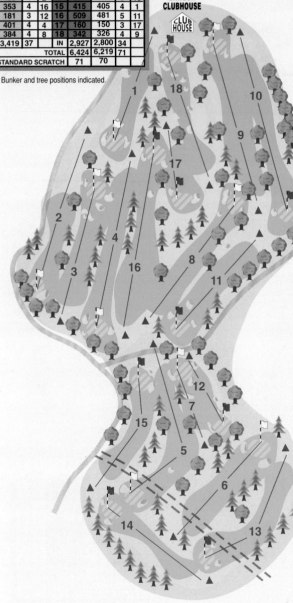

BANGOR CLUBHOUSE

**Broadway, Bangor.
Co. Down.
Tel: (01247) 270922.**

LOCATION: 1 mile from town centre off Donaghadee Road.
SECRETARY: David Ryan.
Tel: (01247) 270922.
PROFESSIONAL: N. V. Drew.
Tel: (01247) 462164.
ARCHITECT: James Braid.

Bangor Golf Course is a pleasant, well-groomed, scenic parkland course. The four 'pitch' holes balance the three Par 5's, and the long and difficult Par 4, 5th hole. Recent improvements in fairway drainage and in the treatment of greens have resulted in the course returning to its previous year-round excellence. A major tree planting programme has been undertaken. It remains a challenge and a pleasure to both 'single-figure' and less serious players.

COURSE INFORMATION

Par 71; SSS 71; Length 6,424 yards.
Visitors: Welcome, Monday, Wednesday, Thursday, Friday & Sunday.
Avoid: 1.00pm – 2.00pm everyday; Wednesday, Friday after 4.00pm; Sunday morning. Members only Tuesday and Saturday.
Green Fees: £21 Mon – Fri (£10.50 with member); £27 Sun/all bank holidays. Weekends (£13.50 with member).
Ladies: No visitors after 4.00pm Monday and Wednesday or Saturday all day.
Juveniles: Weekdays up to 12 noon only. Lessons by prior arrangements. Golf trolleys available.
Clubhouse Facilities: Bar snacks up to 7.30pm. Lunch and evening meal – booking is essential. No catering on Mondays from Oct – Mar. Tel: (01247) 270483.
Clubhouse Dress: Jacket and tie in dining room. No denim at any time.

**Crawfordsburn Rd,
Clandeboye, Co. Down,
BT19 1GB.
Tel: (01247) 852706.**

LOCATION: Ten miles from Belfast –
three miles from Bangor, Co. Down.
GENERAL MANAGER: Richard Gibson.
Tel: (01247) 853581.
PROFESSIONAL: Tony White.
Tel: (01247) 852706.
ARCHITECT: Simon Gidman.

Blackwood Golf Centre is Ulster's foremost pay and play golf facility. Opened in 1994, the centre comprises Hamilton course – an eighteen hole championship standard course, Temple course – an eighteen hole, par 3 course, plus a twenty bay covered, floodlit driving range. The centre also boasts Shanks Restaurant, bar & grill and a salon privé (private function room) sponsored by Guinness Northern Ireland.

NO.	MEDAL YARDS	GEN. YARDS	PAR	S.I.	NO.	MEDAL YARDS	GEN. YARDS	PAR	S.I.
1	354	343	4	12	10	436	421	4	3
2	540	529	5	4	11	354	341	4	15
3	212	206	3	6	12	166	152	3	9
4	306	295	4	18	13	436	415	4	1
5	419	398	4	2	14	491	475	5	11
6	332	321	4	14	15	404	385	4	7
7	165	165	3	16	16	180	164	3	5
8	325	305	4	10	17	355	340	4	13
9	480	471	5	8	18	349	331	4	17
OUT	3,133	3,033	36		IN	3,171	3,024	35	
					TOTAL	6,304	6,057	71	
STANDARD SCRATCH									

COURSE INFORMATION

**HAMILTON COURSE
Par 71; Length 6,304 yards.**
Visitors: Welcome.
Opening Hours: 8am–10pm.
Green Fees: £12 midweek & £16 weekends and bank holidays (booking advised).

**TEMPLE COURSE
Par 54; Length 2,492 yards.**
Greens Fees: £7 midweek & £9 weekends and bank holidays.
Opening hours: 8am –10pm.4
Golf Centre Hours: 10am–11pm.
Golf Centre Dress: Smart /Casual.
Golf Centre Facilities: Top rated restaurant (telephone booking for evening service is recommended), bar and grill (with lunch menu) and private function room – available for private hire.

ARDS	PAR	S.I.	NO.	YARDS	PAR	S.I.
75	3	16	10	185	3	1
82	3	6	11	101	3	13
08	3	14	12	176	3	3
83	3	18	13	129	3	15
16	3	8	14	154	3	7
16	3	12	15	125	3	11
47	3	4	16	163	3	9
77	3	2	17	129	3	17
32	3	10	18	174	3	5
136	27		IN	1,356	27	
			TOTAL	2,492	54	
ANDARD SCRATCH						

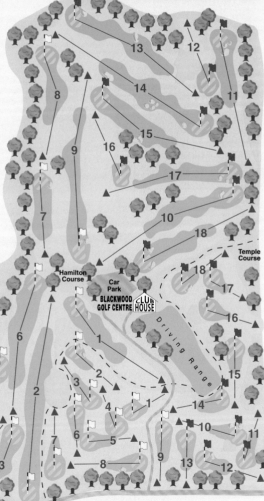

Hamilton
Course

Car
Park

BLACKWOOD
GOLF CENTRE

CLUB
HOUSE

Temple
Course

Driving Range

Bunker and tree positions indicated.

14 Coniamstown Road, Bright, Downpatrick, Co. Down.
Tel: (01396) 841319.

LOCATION: 5 miles south of Downpatrick off B1 to Ardglass, take road to Bright.
SECRETARY: John McCaul.
Tel: (01396) 841319.
ARCHITECT: Mr A. Ennis (Sen).

Inland course on high ground with splendid views of the Mourne Mountains from the 2nd green. A long course with five Par 5's including the 16th (735 yards from championship tee) and with an abundance of young trees which are maturing well. Stamina is important on this course.

COURSE INFORMATION

Par 74; SSS 74; Length 7,143 Yards.

Visitors: Welcome anytime.
Opening Hours: Sunrise – sunset.
Green Fees: £10 Mon – Fri; £12 Sat/Sun/Bank Holidays
Clubhouse Dress: Casual.
Clubhouse Facilities: Changing rooms only. snacks from 9am – 8pm, golfers frys available, fish & chips, sausage bacon, chips ets...
Open Competitions: Open week Aug.

NO.	YARDS	PAR	S.I.	NO.	YARDS	PAR	S.I.
1	550	5	8	10	565	5	13
2	560	5	2	11	345	4	11
3	475	4	6	12	455	4	1
4	440	4	4	13	455	4	5
5	285	4	16	14	320	4	7
6	340	4	12	15	210	3	15
7	330	4	14	16	735	6	3
8	355	4	10	17	395	4	9
9	140	3	18	18	188	3	17
OUT	3,475	37		IN	3,668	37	
				TOTAL	7,143	74	
				STANDARD SCRATCH	74		

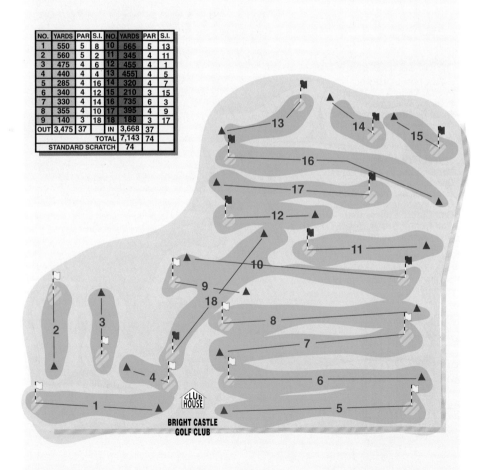

BRIGHT CASTLE GOLF CLUB

CARNALEA

U L S T E R

DOWN

Station Road, Bangor, Co. Down.
Tel: (01247) 465004.

LOCATION: 2 Miles West of Bangor.
SECRETARY: J.H. Crozier.
Tel: (01247) 270368.

The course is situated on rising ground by the shores of Belfast Lough and the turf is of inland variety. The railway line runs parallel and adjacent to the 1st hole so one has to be careful not to be playing three off the tee! If your game is not working on all cylinders you can enjoy the scenery instead.

COURSE INFORMATION

Par 68; SSS 67; Length 5,574 yards.
Visitors: Welcome any day.
Avoid: Tuesday and Saturday.

Ladies: Welcome.
Green Fees: £12 Mon - Fri; £16 Sat./Sun.
Juveniles: Must be accompanied by an adult. Lessons available by prior arrangement. Club hire and caddy cars available.
Clubhouse Dress: Informal except Saturday night. Jacket and tie after 8.00pm.
Clubhouse Facilities: Full facilities. Lunches, snacks 11.30am - 2.30pm. Snacks, high tea, a la carte 5.00pm - 10.00pm.

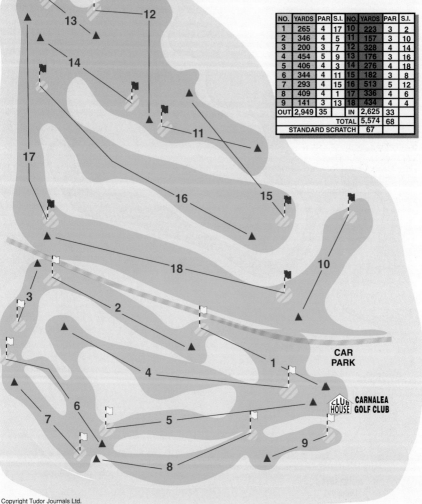

NO.	YARDS	PAR	S.I.	NO.	YARDS	PAR	S.I.
1	265	4	17	10	223	3	2
2	346	4	5	11	157	3	10
3	200	3	7	12	328	4	14
4	454	5	9	13	176	3	16
5	406	4	3	14	276	4	18
6	344	4	11	15	182	3	8
7	293	4	15	16	513	5	12
8	409	4	1	17	336	4	6
9	141	3	13	18	434	4	4
OUT	2,949	35		IN	2,625	33	
				TOTAL	5,574	68	
				STANDARD SCRATCH		67	

CAR PARK

CARNALEA GOLF CLUB

Tower Road, Conlig,
Co. Down. BT23 3PN.
Tel: (01247) 271767.

LOCATION: Above Conlig Village off A21 between Bangor and Newtownards.
PROFESSIONAL: Peter Gregory.
Tel: (01247) 271750.
ARCHITECT: William Rennick Robinson, Dr Von Limburger.

The second course at Clandeboye, the Ava, although much shorter, has probably the best hole of either course. The second shot on the Par 5, 2nd requires great accuracy as the course narrows significantly only to widen out again for a simple pitch to the green.

NO.	MEDAL YARDS	GEN. YARDS	PAR	S.I.	NO.	MEDAL YARDS	GEN. YARDS	PAR	S.I.
1	346	335	4	9	10	175	150	3	12
2	524	506	5	1	11	432	421	4	2
3	166	156	3	7	12	178	167	3	10
4	319	274	4	5	13	495	479	5	14
5	310	303	4	17	14	359	345	4	4
6	183	171	3	15	15	131	120	3	18
7	312	305	4	3	16	317	303	4	6
8	542	496	5	13	17	329	315	4	16
9	309	294	4	11	18	328	317	4	8
OUT	3,011	2,840	36		IN	2,744	2,625	34	
					TOTAL	5,755	5,465	70	
					STANDARD SCRATCH	68	67		

COURSE INFORMATION

Par 70; SSS 68; Length 5,755 yards.
Visitors: Welcome on Weekdays. Must be with member at weekends.
Green Fees: £17 Mon - Fri (W/M £9). Lessons available by prior arrangments. Club Hire available. Caddy Cars Available. Letter of Introduction required if possible for open competition.
Clubhouse Facilities: Full facilities. Prior arrangement required. Snacks, meals 10.00am - 10.00pm.
Open Competitions: Numerous throughout the year.

AVA COURSE

CLANDEBOYE CLUBHOUSE

**Tower Road, Conlig,
Co. Down.
BT23 3PN.
Tel: (01247) 271767.**

LOCATION: Above Conlig
Village off A21 between
Bangor and Newtownards.
PROFESSIONAL: Peter Gregory.
Tel: (01247) 271750.
ARCHITECT: William Rennick
Robinson, Dr Von Limburger.

One of North Down's most popular
golf clubs Clandeboye has two
courses – the Ava and the Dufferin.
The latter being the Championship

one, the short Par 4, 1st giving no
indication of the stern test ahead. The
course is laid out on the hills above
Conlig village and has good views
over Belfast Lough and the Irish Sea.

COURSE INFORMATION

**Par 71; SSS 71; Length
6,548 yards.**
Visitors: Welcome on
weekdays. Must be with
member at weekends.
Green Fees: £21 Mon – Fri
(w/m £10). Lessons available
by prior arrangements. Club
Hire available. Caddy Cars
Available. Letter of

Introduction required if
possible for open competition.
Clubhouse Facilities: Full
facilities. Prior arrangement
required. Snacks, meals
10.00am – 10.00pm.
Open Competitions:
Numerous throughout the
year.

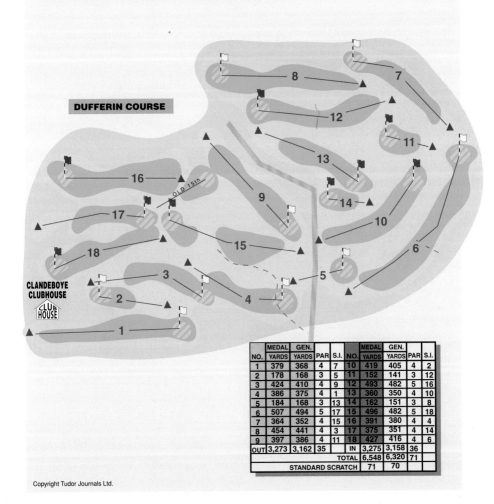

NO.	MEDAL YARDS	GEN. YARDS	PAR	S.I.	NO.	MEDAL YARDS	GEN. YARDS	PAR	S.I.
1	379	368	4	7	10	419	405	4	2
2	178	168	3	5	11	152	141	3	12
3	424	410	4	9	12	493	482	5	16
4	386	375	4	1	13	360	350	4	10
5	184	168	3	13	14	162	151	3	8
6	507	494	5	17	15	496	482	5	18
7	364	352	4	15	16	391	380	4	4
8	454	441	4	3	17	375	351	4	14
9	397	386	4	11	18	427	416	4	6
OUT	3,273	3,162	35		IN	3,275	3,158	36	
					TOTAL	6,548	6,320	71	
					STANDARD SCRATCH	71	70		

**84 Warren Road,
Donaghadee,
Co. Down.
Tel: (01247) 883624.**

LOCATION: 5 miles south of Bangor on A2 on Coast Road.
SECRETARY: Mr K. Patton.
Tel: (01247) 883624.
PROFESSIONAL: Gordon Drew.
Tel: (01247) 882392.

A part links and part inland open course with little rough but several water hazards which can catch the unthinking shot. The 18th with out-of-bounds on both left and right can be intimidating. Lovely views over the Copeland Islands to the Scottish Coast, particularly from the 16th tee. Well appointed clubhouse.

COURSE INFORMATION

Par 71; SSS 69; Length 6,000 yards, 5,561 metres.
Visitors: Welcome on any weekday and Sunday, Special rates for societies. Members only until 4pm on Saturday.
Avoid: Bank Holidays.
Ladies: Welcome. Ladies Day: Tuesday.
Green Fees: £14 Mon – Fri; £18 Sunday. Societies: Special rates.
Juveniles: Mon – Fri and Sun. Must be accompanied by an adult. Lessons available by prior arrangement. Club Hire available. Caddy Cars available.
Clubhouse Dress: Informal except Saturday after 8.00pm in mixed lounge and dining room.
Clubhouse Facilities: Full facilities. Tues – Sun 11.00am – 9.00pm.
Open Competitions: Open week, June.

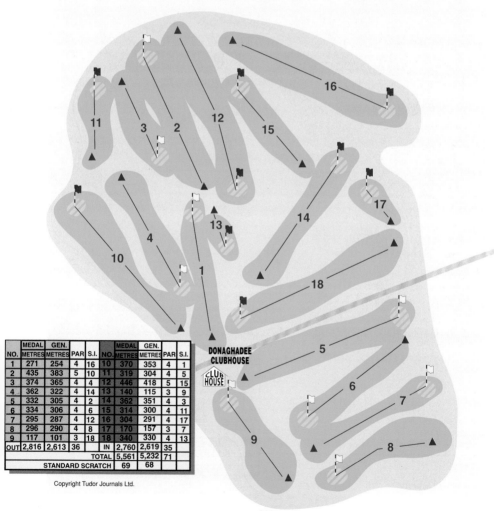

NO.	MEDAL METRES	GEN. METRES	PAR	S.I.	NO.	MEDAL METRES	GEN. METRES	PAR	S.I.
1	271	254	4	16	10	370	353	4	1
2	435	383	5	10	11	319	304	4	5
3	374	365	4	4	12	446	418	5	15
4	362	322	4	14	13	140	115	3	9
5	332	305	4	2	14	362	351	4	3
6	334	306	4	6	15	314	300	4	11
7	295	287	4	12	16	304	291	4	17
8	296	290	4	8	17	170	157	3	7
9	117	101	3	18	18	340	330	4	13
OUT	2,816	2,613	36		IN	2,760	2,619	35	
					TOTAL	5,561	5,232	71	
					STANDARD SCRATCH		69	68	

DONAGHADEE CLUBHOUSE

CLUB HOUSE

**43 Saul Road,
Downpatrick, Co. Down
BT30 6PA
Tel: (01396)
612152/615947.**

LOCATION: 25 miles south of Belfast on (A7) and 1 1/2 miles south east of Downpatrick town centre.
SECRETARY: Mr J. P. McCoubrey.
Tel: (01396) 615947.
ARCHITECT: Martin Hawtree.
Recently upgraded, challenging parkland course. 5th hole particularly challenging. Excellent drainage so open all year round.

COURSE INFORMATION

Par 69; SSS 69; Length 6,100 yards.
Visitors: Welcome any day by prior arrangment.
Ladies: Anyday except Sunday.
Green Fees: £15 Mon – Fri; £20 Sat/Sun.
Juveniles: No non - members allowed on course. Lessons available. Club Hire available. Caddy Cars available.
Clubhouse Hours: 11.00am – 11.00pm.

Clubhouse Dress: Jacket and tie after 7pm.
Clubhouse Facilities: Full facilities snooker, bowls, TV lounge. Meals available all day; everyday (except Monday) during season. Winter months 12pm – 3pm.
Open Competitions: Bank of Ireland & Senior Scratch, June; Guinness Open, July; Heart of down, Sept.

NO.	MEDAL YARDS	GEN. YARDS	PAR	S.I.	NO.	MEDAL YARDS	GEN. YARDS	PAR	S.I.
1	374	368	4	3	10	362	326	4	10
2	298	293	4	17	11	181	170	3	12
3	506	500	5	11	12	544	538	5	4
4	176	166	3	13	13	390	379	4	6
5	457	457	4	5	14	424	390	4	2
6	330	324	4	9	15	171	168	3	16
7	437	427	4	1	16	364	338	4	14
8	135	129	3	15	17	278	270	4	18
9	337	325	4	7	18	336	330	4	8
OUT	3050	2989	35		IN	3050	2909	35	
TOTAL	6100	5898	70						
STANDARD SCRATCH	69								

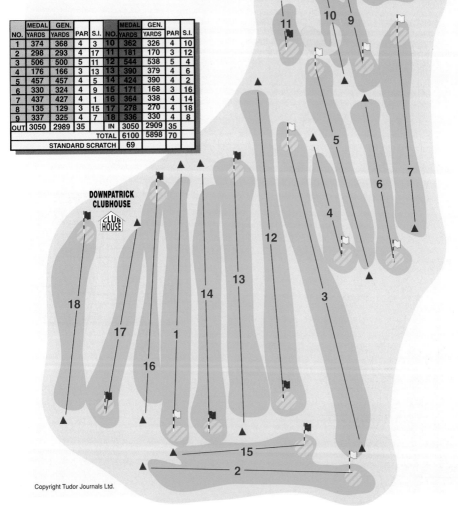

DOWNPATRICK CLUBHOUSE

CLUB HOUSE

Golf Road, Helens Bay, Bangor, Co Down. Tel: (01247) 852601.

LOCATION: 9 miles east of Belfast on A2.
SECRETARY: L. W. L. Mann. Tel: (01247) 852815.

This popular course is compact with the layout encircling the Clubhouse. The turf is of the inland variety, greens are small making scoring more difficult than first impressions would suggest. There are extensive views of the Antrim Hills across Belfast Lough. The 4th hole, a short pitch over trees to a green protected by bunkers on three sides, is a particularily interesting one.

COURSE INFORMATION

Par 68; SSS 67; Length 5,176 metres.
Visitors: Welcome to play; Mon, Wed, Thurs up to 5.00pm. Fri and Sun.
Avoid: Tue, Thur (after 2.30pm) Sat before 6.00pm..
Ladies: Tuesday - members only.
Green Fees: £12 Mon Fri (£6 with member); £15 Sun.Public

Holidays (£7.50 with member).
Juveniles: Under 18 Must be accompanied by an adult.
Clubhouse Hours:
Clubhouse Dress: Smart casual dress is permitted until 7.30pm. After 7.30pm gentlemen must wear a jacket, collar and tie. Tee shirts or denim jeans are not acceptable on the course or in the Clubhouse.
Clubhouse Facilities: Full facilities. Last order 9.00pm.
Open Competitions: Open week, July 9th - 15th (incl).

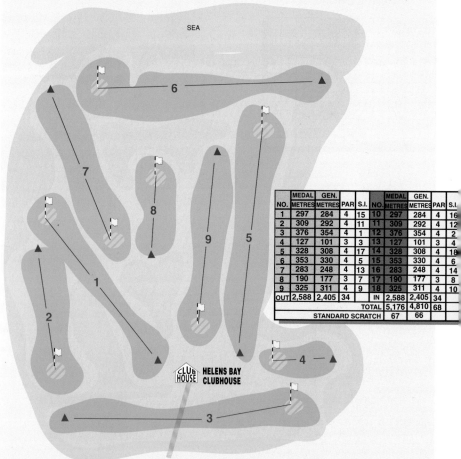

NO.	MEDAL METRES	GEN. METRES	PAR	S.I.	NO.	MEDAL METRES	GEN. METRES	PAR	S.I.
1	297	284	4	15	10	297	284	4	16
2	309	292	4	11	11	309	292	4	12
3	376	354	4	1	12	376	354	4	2
4	127	101	3	3	13	127	101	3	4
5	328	308	4	17	14	328	308	4	18
6	353	330	4	5	15	353	330	4	6
7	283	248	4	13	16	283	248	4	14
8	190	177	3	7	17	190	177	3	8
9	325	311	4	9	18	325	311	4	10
OUT	2,588	2,405	34		IN	2,588	2,405	34	
					TOTAL	5,176	4,810	68	
					STANDARD SCRATCH		67	66	

HELENS BAY CLUBHOUSE

**Demense Road,
Holywood, Co Down.
Tel: (01232) 422138.**

LOCATION: 5 miles east of
Belfast on A2.
SECRETARY: D. Jenkins
Tel: 423135.
PROFESSIONAL: Michael Bannon.
Tel: 425503.

Hilly parkland course over-looking
Holywood, and with excellent views
over Belfast Lough. The first nine play
on the slopes of the Holywood Hills,
whilst the back nine are more varied
with some interesting tee shots and
some steep hills and valleys. Most of
the greens run toward the sea. The
back nine are a strenuous test
beginning with a very steep climb to
the 10th green.

COURSE INFORMATION

**Par 69; SSS 68; Length
5,425 metres.**
Opening hours: Sunrise -
Sunset.
Visitors: Welcome to play;
Mon, Tue, Wed, Fri and Sun
after 2.15pm. (members only
1.30pm - 2.15pm.)
Avoid: Public holidays.
Ladies: Thursday - Ladies
Day.
Green Fees: £15 Mon/Fri,
£21 Sun; Ladies £9 Mon/Fri,
£21 Sun.
Juveniles: Accompanied by
an adult. Sundays and
evenings after 5.00pm.
Lessons available by prior
arrangments. Club Hire

available.
Clubhouse Hours: 9.00am
11.30pm.
Clubhouse Dress: Informal,
no denims or training shoes
on course. Jacket and tie in
mixed lounge after 7pm.
Clubhouse Facilities: Full
facilities. Snacks, evening
meals all day Tue - Sun.
Open Competitions: Several,
week in June.

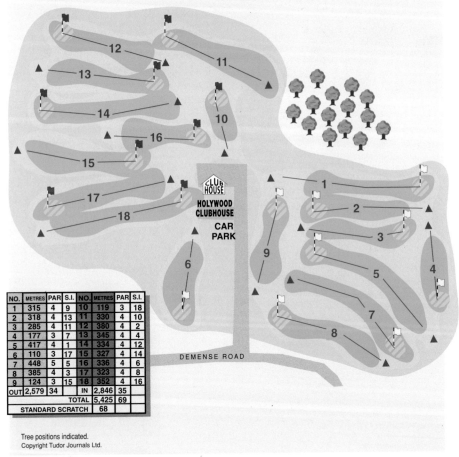

NO.	METRES	PAR	S.I.	NO.	METRES	PAR	S.I.
1	315	4	9	10	119	3	18
2	318	4	13	11	330	4	10
3	285	4	11	12	380	4	2
4	177	3	7	13	345	4	4
5	417	4	1	14	334	4	12
6	110	3	17	15	327	4	14
7	448	5	5	16	336	4	6
8	385	4	3	17	323	4	8
9	124	3	15	18	352	4	16
OUT	2,579	34		IN	2,846	35	
				TOTAL	5,425	69	
STANDARD SCRATCH		68					

Tree positions indicated.
Copyright Tudor Journals Ltd.

Mourne Park, Ballyardle, Kilkeel, Co Down.
Tel: (016937) 62296.

LOCATION: Three miles from Kilkeel on main Newry Road.
SECRETARY: S. C. McBride.
Tel: (016937) 62296.
ARCHITECT: Lord Justice Babington (original nine holes); Mr. E. Hackett (new development).

Situated at the foot of Knockcree Mountain, the course is ringed by woodlands and masses of rhododendron shrubs in an area that might well be described as the Garden of Mourne. The course was enlarged in 1993 from seven old holes to 18 holes.

COURSE INFORMATION

Par 72; SSS 72; Length 6,615 yards.
Opening hours: Sunrise – Sunset.
Visitors: Welcome Mon, Wed, Thurs, Fri and Sun.
Avoid: Tues & Sat.
Ladies: Tuesday.

Green Fees: £16.00 Mon – Fri; £18.00 Weekends.
Juveniles: up to 5.00pm.
Caddy cars available by prior arrangment. A Handicap Certificate is required for open competitions.
Clubhouse Dress: Jacket and tie in main lounge.
Clubhouse Facilities: Full facilities. Snacks, evening meals all day during summer or by prior arrangment.
Open Competitions: Several throughout the year.

KILKEEL CLUBHOUSE

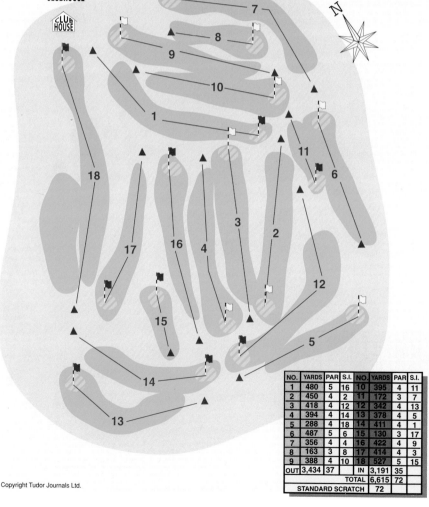

NO.	YARDS	PAR	S.I.	NO.	YARDS	PAR	S.I.
1	480	5	16	10	395	4	11
2	450	4	2	11	172	3	7
3	418	4	12	12	342	4	13
4	394	4	14	13	378	4	5
5	288	4	18	14	411	4	1
6	487	5	6	15	130	3	17
7	356	4	4	16	422	4	9
8	163	3	8	17	414	4	3
9	388	4	10	18	527	5	15
OUT	3,434	37		IN	3,191	35	
				TOTAL	6,615	72	
			STANDARD SCRATCH		72		

142 Main Road,
Cloughey, Newtownards,
Co Down.
Tel: (01247) 71233

LOCATION: 16 miles south east
of Newtownards on A2.
SECRETARY: George Graham.
Tel: (012477) 71233.
PROFESSIONAL: J. Peden.
Tel: (012477) 71004.
ARCHITECT: J Braid.

Eighteen hole links course having
the distinct advantage due to its
dryness of being open for play
when many other courses are
closed due to inclement weather.
An open course that offers much
forgiveness for errant shots.
Adjacent to the Irish Sea coastline.

COURSE INFORMATION

Par 69; SSS 69; Length
5,596 metres.
Opening hours: 8am - Dusk.
Visitors: Welcome any
weekday.
Avoid: Friday mornings.
Green Fees: £13 Mon – Fri;
(£9 with a member); £25
Sat/Sun/All public holidays
(£12 with a member).
Juveniles: £3 Mon – Fri; £8 –
Sat/Sun, must be accompanied
by an adult. Can play anytime.
Clubhouse Hours: 8am –
11.30pm.
Clubhouse Dress: Casual,
jacket and tie after 7.30pm.
Clubhouse Facilities: Full
facilities up to 5.00pm and
evening meals must be
ordered before commencing
play.
Open Competitions:
Throughout the season. Open
Week July/August.

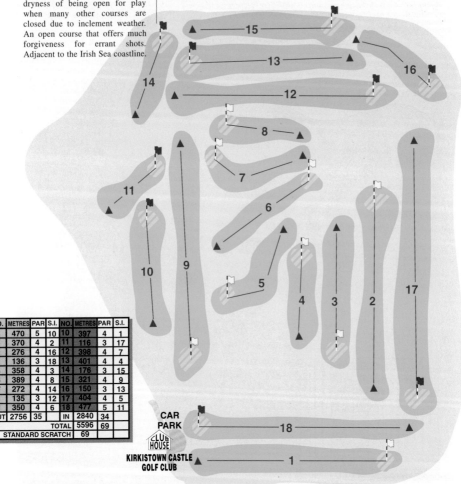

NO.	METRES	PAR	S.I.	NO.	METRES	PAR	S.I.
1	470	5	10	10	397	4	1
2	370	4	2	11	116	3	17
3	276	4	16	12	398	4	7
4	136	3	18	13	401	4	4
5	358	4	3	14	176	3	15
6	389	4	8	15	321	4	9
7	272	4	14	16	150	3	13
8	135	3	12	17	404	4	5
9	350	4	6	18	477	5	11
OUT	2756	35		IN	2840	34	
				TOTAL	5596	69	
	STANDARD SCRATCH	69					

CAR
PARK

CLUB
HOUSE
KIRKISTOWN CASTLE
GOLF CLUB

Comber, Newtownards, Co Down.
Tel: (01238) 541234.

LOCATION: Take Killyleagh Road from Comber, in less than a mile take a road to left, signposted Ardmillan. Bear left for 6 miles to Mahee Island.
SECRETARY: John McMillen.
Tel: (01247) 878219.
SHOP: A McCracken.
Tel: (01238) 541234.
ARCHITECT: Mr Robinson, Bangor.

A nine hole course sited on an island in Strangford Lough with excellent views for 360 degrees. The course is parkland with luscious fairways and well manicured greens. The undulating fairways and tricky approach shots make this a good test of golf. The course record stands at 65 so it is no pushover. One to visit, not only for the golf enthusiast, but for the views.

COURSE INFORMATION

Par 68; SSS 67; Length 5,588 Yards 5,108 metres.
Opening hours: 9.00am – 9.00pm.
Visitors: Welcome to play.
Avoid: Sat before 4.30pm and Wed after 4.30pm.

Ladies: Ladies Day Monday.
Green Fees: £10 Mon – Fri; £15 Sat/Sun/All public holidays.
Juveniles: Play Thur. Not Sat. Club Hire available. Handicap Certificate required for Open competition only. Prior arrangement required.
Clubhouse Hours: 9am – 5.30pm.
Clubhouse Dress: Casual to 7pm. Jacket and tie at all functions.
Clubhouse Facilities: Meals by prior arrangement. No bar.
Open Competitions: July each year.

NO.	METRES	PAR	S.I.	NO.	METRES	PAR	S.I.
1	308	4	7	10	308	4	10
2	231	4	17	11	231	4	18
3	283	4	13	12	283	4	14
4	227	3	3	13	227	3	2
5	359	4	9	14	359	4	6
6	296	4	11	15	296	4	12
7	404	4	1	16	404	4	4
8	123	3	15	17	123	3	16
9	323	4	5	18	323	4	8
OUT	2,554	34		IN	2,554	34	
					TOTAL	5,108	68
STANDARD SCRATCH		67					

SEA

CLUB HOUSE

MAHEE ISLAND CLUBHOUSE

Bunker and tree positions indicated.

NO.	MEDAL METRES	GEN. METRES	PAR	S.I.	NO.	MEDAL METRES	GEN. METRES	PAR	S.I.
1	322	309	4	7	10	322	309	4	9
2	252	252	4	15	11	252	252	4	16
3	309	309	4	8	12	309	309	4	10
4	176	162	3	5	13	176	162	3	6
5	427	383	5	1	14	427	383	5	4
6	313	291	4	3	15	313	291	4	2
7	277	277	4	11	16	277	277	4	14
8	121	121	3	17	17	121	121	3	18
9	291	273	4	12	18	291	273	4	13
OUT	2,488	2,377	35		IN	2,488	2,377	35	
					TOTAL	4,976	4,754	70	
					STANDARD SCRATCH	67			

Ringdufferin Road, Toye, Killyleagh, Co Down.
Tel: (01396) 828812.

LOCATION: Three miles north of Killyleagh on Comber Road.
SECRETARY: Helen Lindsay.
Tel: (01396) 828812.

A nine hole course with excellent views of Strangford Lough. The course is a drumlin (rounded hills) course with a wildlife refuge included in the course. The undulating fairways and tricky approach shots make this a testing course to play on. Enjoy an excellent days golf with idyllic views of Strangford Lough.

COURSE INFORMATION

Par 70; SSS 67; Length 5,424 yards, 4,976 metres.
Visitors: None.
Opening Hours: 8.00am – 9.00pm.
Avoid: Telephone for available tee times (Sat).
Ladies: Welcome.
Green Fees: £4 Mon – Fri (9 holes), £7 (18 holes); Sat & Sun £5 (9 holes), £10 (18 holes).
Juveniles: Permitted.
Clubhouse Hours: 8.00am – 9.00pm.
Clubhouse Dress: Casual.
Clubhouse Facilities: Light snacks and society meals by prior arrangement.

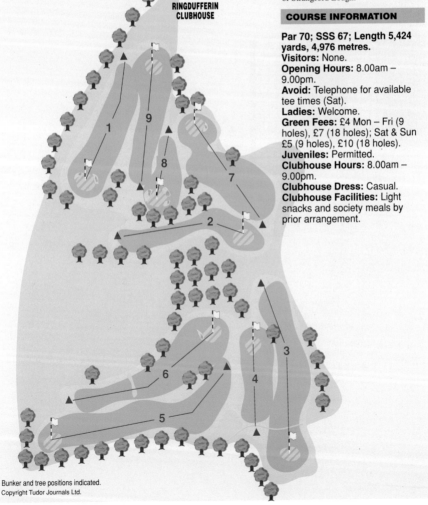

RINGDUFFERIN
CLUBHOUSE

Bunker and tree positions indicated.
Copyright Tudor Journals Ltd.

209

**Station Road, Craigavad,
Holywood,
Co Down.
Tel: (01232) 428165.**

LOCATION: 7 miles east of
Belfast on A2.
SECRETARY: T. H. Young.
Tel: (01232)428165.
PROFESSIONAL: David. H.
Carson. Tel: (01232) 428586
ARCHITECT: H. C.Colt

Eighteen hole parkland course rolls
gently to the shores of Belfast Lough.
The course is very picturesque with
many mature trees and many carefully
placed bunkers. The greens are
undulating and generally run towards
the sea. A very pleasant course that
presents a challenge to any handicap of
golfer.

COURSE INFORMATION

**Par 70; SSS 71; Length 6,274
yards.**
Visitors: Welcome any day
except Wednesday and
Saturday before 4.30pm.
Opening Hours: 8.30am –
7.30pm.

Avoid: Wednesday.
Ladies: Avoid Wednesday and
Saturdays before 4.30pm.
Green Fees: £30 Mon – Fri;
£35 Sat/Sun/all public holidays.
Juveniles: May play with
member only. Lessons available
by prior

NO.	MEDAL YARDS	GEN. YARDS	PAR	S.I.	NO.	MEDAL YARDS	GEN. YARDS	PAR	S.I.
1	417	414	4	7	10	303	299	4	14
2	404	400	4	3	11	165	162	3	8
3	372	359	4	13	12	433	430	4	4
4	143	140	3	15	13	360	357	4	12
5	555	550	5	9	14	187	184	3	10
6	351	348	4	11	15	410	407	4	2
7	184	164	3	17	16	485	476	5	16
8	394	392	4	5	17	193	190	3	18
9	409	406	4	1	18	509	506	5	6
OUT	3,229	3,173	35		IN	3,045	3,011	35	
					TOTAL	6,274	6,184	70	
					STANDARD SCRATCH	71	70		

CLUB
HOUSE
**ROYAL BELFAST
CLUBHOUSE**

NO.	MEDAL YARDS	GEN. YARDS	PAR	S.I.	NO.	MEDAL YARDS	GEN. YARDS	PAR	S.I.
1	506	500	5	13	10	200	200	3	14
2	424	374	4	9	11	440	429	4	8
3	473	473	4	3	12	501	476	5	10
4	217	217	3	15	13	445	422	4	2
5	440	418	4	7	14	213	213	3	12
6	396	368	4	11	15	445	445	4	4
7	145	129	3	17	16	265	265	4	18
8	428	428	4	1	17	400	376	4	16
9	486	431	4	5	18	545	528	5	6
OUT	3,515	2,338	35		IN	3,454	3,354	36	
					TOTAL	6,969	6,692	71	
					STANDARD SCRATCH	73	72		

ROYAL COUNTY DOWN GOLF CLUB

CLUB HOUSE

PRO SHOP

10
9
1
18
11
2
8 12
17
5 6
7
16
3
13
4 15
14

Copyright Tudor Journals Ltd.

Newcastle, Co. Down.
Tel: (013967) 23314.
Fax: (013967) 26281.

LOCATION: 30 miles south of Belfast, 1 mile from Newcastle.
HON/SECRETARY: I. W. L. Webb.
SECRETARY: P. E. Rolph.
Tel: (013967) 23314.
PROFESSIONAL: Kevan J. Whitson.
Tel: (013967) 22419.
ARCHITECT: Tom Morris.

Founded in 1889, the course offers an exhilerating challenge to even the most experienced golfers. The setting of this links course is continually remarked upon for its outstanding beauty. The Mountains of Mourne in all their glory rise up from the Irish Sea. The fact that this course has five blind tee shots and several partially obscured approach shots makes it all the more formidable challenge to play. This is in addition to its well positioned bunkers. Professional golfers from all over the world rate Royal County Down as one of the best.

COURSE INFORMATION

Par 71; SSS 73; Length 6,969 yards.
Visitors: Welcome to play every weekday, except Wed; (limited hours) Sat & Sun, make prior arrangements.
Opening Hours: Daylight.
Avoid: Wed & weekends. Prior arrangement preferred. Sat (members only).
Ladies: Welcome.
Green Fees: £50 Mon – Fri; £60 weekends. Reduced green fees with a member. club hire available, caddy service available by prior arrangement and caddy cars available. No open competitions.
Juveniles: With a member only.
Clubhouse Hours: 9am – 7pm except at weekends when members only.
Clubhouse Dress: Jacket and tie at all times except in the Centenary Room where casual dress is permitted.
Clubhouse Facilities: Available in the Centenarary Room from 9.30am – 6.30pm weekdays.
Convenient Hotels: Enniskeen Hotel, Newcastle. Tel: (013967) 22392. Glassdrumman Lodge, Co. Down. Tel: (013967) 68451. Fax: (013967) 67041.

THE DONARD HOTEL
Close proximity to R.C.D.
Special rates for golf groups.
Tel: (013967) 22203.
Fax: (013967) 23970.

233 Scrabo Road, Newtownards, Co Down. BT23 4SL.
Tel: (01247) 812355.
Fax: (01247) 822919.

LOCATION: 10 miles from Belfast off the main Belfast to Newtownards carriageway.
SECRETARY: James Fraser.
Tel: (01247) 812355.
PROFESSIONAL: Allister Cardwell.
Tel: (01247) 817848.

The course winds its way around Scrabo Hill and Tower, one of the well-known Co Down landmarks. Fabulous views over Strangford Lough and Mourne Mountains (the 2nd hole is called Mourne View). Narrow fairways bordered by health and gorse call for accurate driving. The terrain around Scrabo Hill makes it a strenuous course for golfers.

COURSE INFORMATION

Par 71; SSS 71; Length 5,699 metres.
Visitors: Welcome.
Opening Hours: 9.00am – sunset.
Avoid: Saturday & Wednesday afternoons.
Ladies: Wednesday (ladies day).
Green Fees: £15.00 Mon – Fri; £20.00weekend.

Societies: Special rates.
Juveniles: Not to play after 5.30pm. Must be accompanied by an adult member. Lessons by prior arrangements. Club hire available. Caddy service available by prior arrangements.
Clubhouse Hours: 8.30am – 12 midnight. Full clubhouse facilities.
Clubhouse Dress: Informal except Saturday after 8.00pm in mixed lounge and dining room.
Clubhouse Facilities: Tues 11.30am – 2.30pm; Wed – Fri 11.30am – 2.30pm & 6pm – 9.30pm. Sat/Sun 11.30am – 9.30pm. Excellent Cuisine.

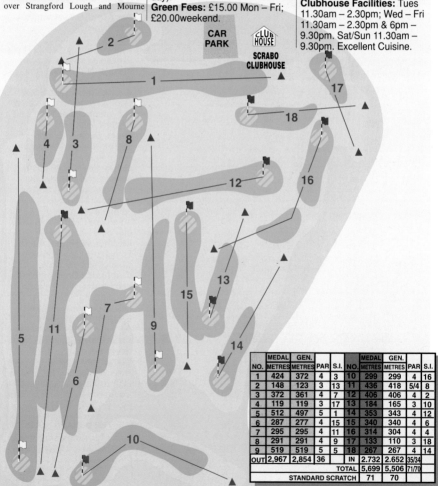

NO.	MEDAL METRES	GEN. METRES	PAR	S.I.	NO.	MEDAL METRES	GEN. METRES	PAR	S.I.
1	424	372	4	3	10	299	299	4	16
2	148	123	3	13	11	436	418	5/4	8
3	372	361	4	7	12	406	406	4	2
4	119	119	3	17	13	184	165	3	10
5	512	497	5	1	14	353	343	4	12
6	287	277	4	15	15	340	340	4	6
7	295	295	4	11	16	314	304	4	4
8	291	291	4	9	17	133	110	3	18
9	519	519	5	5	18	267	267	4	14
OUT	2,967	2,854	36		IN	2.732	2.652	35/34	
					TOTAL	5,699	5,506	71/70	
					STANDARD SCRATCH	71	70		

20 Grove Road, Ballynahinch, Co. Down.
Tel: (01238) 562365.

LOCATION: 11 miles south of Belfast on the main road to Newcastle.
HON. SECRETARY: N. Morrow.
Tel: (01238) 562365.

Each fairway is lined with trees, and several high points on the course give scenic views of the countryside. The 8th and 17th give panoramic views of the Mourne Mountains. This is a newly created eighteen hole golf course which has been laid out adjacent to the Monalto

Estate. Not physically demanding and many of the views on the course overlook the Mourne Mountains. Wildlife is also a great feature of the course.

COURSE INFORMATION

Par 72; SSS 72; Length 6,003 metres.
Visitors: Welcome any day.
Green Fees: £14.00 Mon – Fri; £18.00 Sun & Bank Holidays.
Ladies: Welcome.
Ladies: Competition – Friday.

Juveniles: Must be accompanied by an adult.
Clubhouse Hours: 8.30am – 11.30pm.
Clubhouse Facilities: Full clubhouse facilities. Bar snacks from 12noon – 3.00pm. Arrangements for parties.
Clubhouse Dress: Casual – no denims.
Open Competitions: Open Week – July.

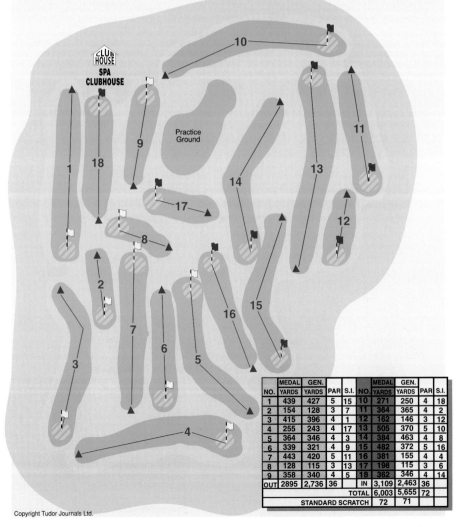

	MEDAL	GEN.				MEDAL	GEN.		
NO.	YARDS	YARDS	PAR	S.I.	NO.	YARDS	YARDS	PAR	S.I.
1	439	427	5	15	10	271	250	4	18
2	154	128	3	7	11	364	365	4	2
3	415	396	4	1	12	162	146	3	12
4	255	243	4	17	13	505	370	5	10
5	364	346	4	3	14	384	463	4	8
6	339	321	4	9	15	482	372	5	16
7	443	420	5	11	16	381	155	4	4
8	128	115	3	13	17	198	115	3	6
9	358	340	4	5	18	362	346	4	14
OUT	2895	2,736	36		IN	3,109	2,463	36	
					TOTAL	6,003	5,655	72	
					STANDARD SCRATCH		72	71	

Lower Dromore Road, Warrenpoint, Co. Down.
Tel: (01693) 753695.

SECRETARY / MANAGER: John McMahon.
Tel: (01693) 753695.
PROFESSIONAL: Nigel Shaw.
Tel: (01693) 752371.

The course is set in parkland with picturesque views of the Carlingford Mountains. Although not a long course, it demands from the golfer straight driving and skill around the greens. There are five par 3's and four par 5's so it offers plenty of variety.

COURSE INFORMATION

Par 71; SSS 70; Length 5,618 metres.
Visitors: Welcome Mon, Thurs & Fri. By arrangement Wed & Sun. Avoid: Tues & Sat.
Green Fees: £17 Mon – Fri; £23 Sat, Sun & Bank Holidays.
Juveniles: Must be accompanied by an adult. Lessons available by prior arrangement. Club hire available. Caddy cars available by prior arrangement.
Clubhouse Hours: 8.30am – 12midnight.
Clubhouse Facilities: Full clubhouse facilities. Catering 11.30am – 9.30pm.
Clubhouse Dress: Casual. Jacket and tie after 7.30pm.
Open Competitions: Open Week June. Handicap certificate is required for open competitions.

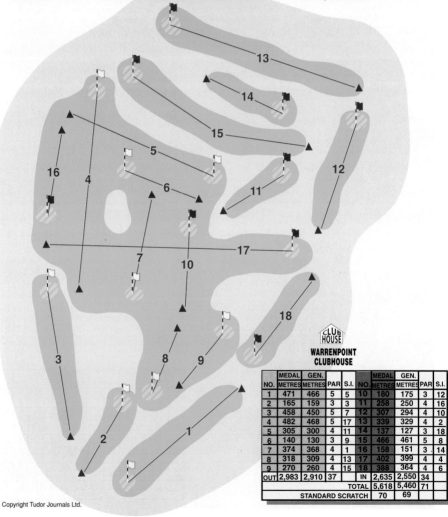

WARRENPOINT CLUBHOUSE

NO.	MEDAL METRES	GEN. METRES	PAR	S.I.	NO.	MEDAL METRES	GEN. METRES	PAR	S.I.
1	471	466	5	5	10	180	175	3	12
2	165	159	3	3	11	258	250	4	16
3	458	450	5	7	12	307	294	4	10
4	482	468	5	17	13	339	329	4	2
5	305	300	4	11	14	137	127	3	18
6	140	130	3	9	15	466	461	5	8
7	374	368	4	1	16	158	151	3	14
8	318	309	4	13	17	402	399	4	4
9	270	260	4	15	18	388	364	4	6
OUT	2,983	2,910	37		IN	2,635	2,550	34	
					TOTAL	5,618	5,460	71	
					STANDARD SCRATCH		70	69	

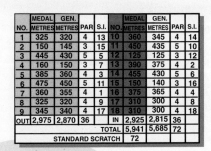

NO.	MEDAL METRES	GEN. METRES	PAR	S.I.	NO.	MEDAL METRES	GEN. METRES	PAR	S.I.
1	325	320	4	13	10	360	345	4	14
2	150	145	3	15	11	450	435	5	10
3	445	430	5	5	12	125	125	3	12
4	160	150	3	7	13	390	375	4	2
5	385	360	4	3	14	455	430	5	6
6	475	450	5	11	15	150	140	3	16
7	360	355	4	1	16	375	365	4	4
8	325	320	4	9	17	310	300	4	8
9	345	340	4	17	18	310	300	4	18
OUT	2,975	2,870	36		IN	2,925	2,815	36	
					TOTAL	5,941	5,685	72	
					STANDARD SCRATCH		72		

Castle Hume, Enniskillen, Co. Fermanagh.

LOCATION: Four miles from Enniskillen on the Belleek Road.
SECRETARY: Dessie Donegan.
Tel: (01365) 327077.
CLUB STEWARD: Mark Conway.
Tel: (01365) 327077.
ARCHITECT: Tony Carroll.

The Castle Hume course has been constructed and designed to high standards. In addition to the two water hazards running through the course, there are five man-made hazards and the course has over 6,000 trees, numerous and various shrubs and over 30 bunkers. These obstacles, however, in no way detract from the well drained fairways, the generous tees and the large rolling greens, specifically designed and grown with imported fescue and bent grass.

COURSE INFORMATION

Par 72; SSS 72; Length 5,900 metres.
Visitors: Welcome all day.
Opening Hours: Dawn – Dusk.
Ladies: Welcome any day.
Green Fees: Mon – Fri £10; Sat/Sun £12; Juveniles £4.
Juveniles: Welcome.
Clubhouse Dress: Casual.
Clubhouse Facilities: Snacks available everyday. Meals available by prior arrangement.
Open Competitions: Open competitions on most weekends from April - December.

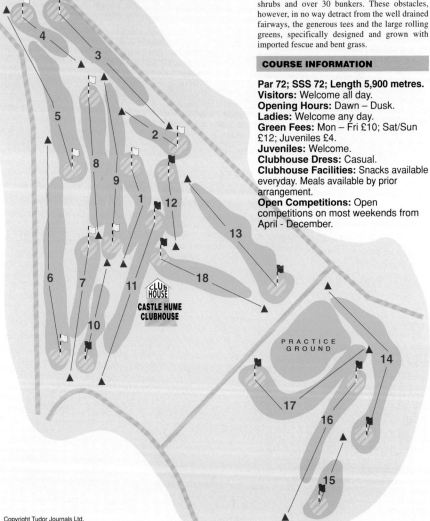

CASTLE HUME
CLUBHOUSE

PRACTICE GROUND

ENNISKILLEN

U L S T E R **FERMANAGH**

Castlecoole Rd, Enniskillen, Co. Fermanagh.
Tel: (01365) 325250.

LOCATION: Beside Castlecoole Estate.
SECRETARY: Mr. Raymond Millar.
Tel: (01365) 324562.

The first nine holes of this course are developing well with plenty of new young trees, shrubs and new drainage while the back nine offers a different challenge with a more mature landscape.

COURSE INFORMATION

Par 71; SSS 69; Length 5,588 metres (medal).
Visitors: Welcome to play.
Opening Hours: Daylight hours.
Avoid: Tuesday – all day, and Saturday afternoons.
Green Fees: £12 Weekdays; £15 weekends and bank holidays. Concessions with member, one visitor per member.

Juveniles: Not allowed on course after 6pm, unless accompanied by an adult.
Clubhouse Hours: 9.00am – 11.00pm.
Clubhouse Facilities: All refurbished. Snooker and table-tennis. Snacks and catering available by prior arrangement.
Open Competitions: On a regular basis.

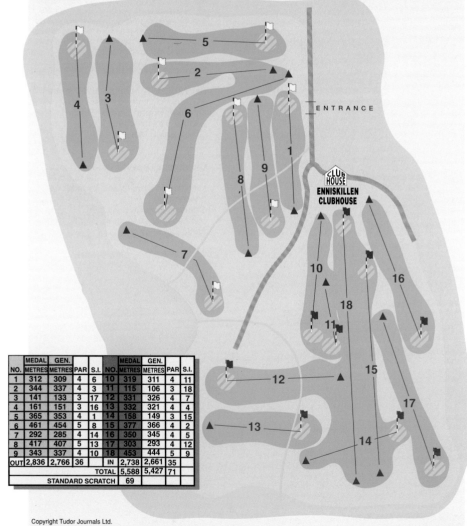

NO.	MEDAL METRES	GEN. METRES	PAR	S.I.	NO.	MEDAL METRES	GEN. METRES	PAR	S.I.
1	312	309	4	6	10	319	311	4	11
2	344	337	4	3	11	115	106	3	18
3	141	133	3	17	12	331	326	4	7
4	161	151	3	16	13	332	321	4	4
5	365	353	4	1	14	158	149	3	15
6	461	454	5	8	15	377	366	4	2
7	292	285	4	14	16	350	345	4	5
8	417	407	5	13	17	303	293	4	12
9	343	337	4	10	18	453	444	5	9
OUT	2,836	2,766	36		IN	2,738	2,661	35	
					TOTAL	5,588	5,427	71	
					STANDARD SCRATCH		69		

65 Circular Road, Castlerock.
Tel: (01265) 848314.

LOCATION: Six miles north-west of Coleraine.
SECRETARY: G. McBride.
Tel: (01265) 848314.
PROFESSIONAL: Mr Bobby Kelly.
Tel: (01265) 848314.
ARCHITECT: Ben Sayers.

A true links course, with two courses — eighteen holes and nine holes. Main feature is the 4th hole with a burn on left and a railway on the right! The club claims the best greens in Ireland twelve months of the year. Castlerock can sometimes be underestimated, or not appreciated for the magnificent links course that it is. There are also superb views to Donegal and over to Scotland.

COURSE INFORMATION

Par 73; SSS 72; Length 6,499 Yards.
Visitors: Welcome.
Opening Hours: Sunrise – Sunset.
Avoid: Weekends.
Ladies Day: Friday. Can play on Sat & Sun afternoons.
Green Fees: Mon – Fri £17; Sat/Sun £25; Ladies £8; Juveniles £5.
Juveniles: Cannot play before 4.30pm. Must be accompanied by an adult. Lessons by prior arrangements; Club hire available. Caddy service available by prior arrangements.
Clubhouse Hours: 8 am – 12 midnight.
Clubhouse Facilities: Full clubhouse facilities; Snacks; meals by arrangement.
Clubhouse Dress: Neat (no denims/trainers; jacket & tie for functions.
Open Competitions: Open Week – July.

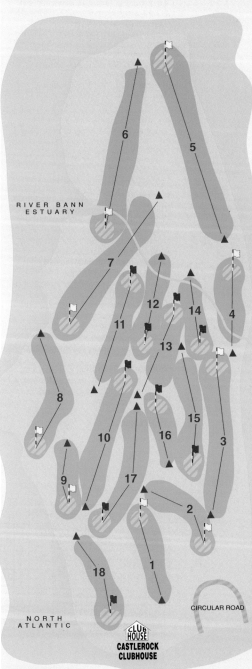

RIVER BANN ESTUARY

NORTH ATLANTIC

CIRCULAR ROAD

CLUB HOUSE

CASTLEROCK CLUBHOUSE

NO.	MEDAL YARDS	COMP YARDS	PAR	S.I.	NO.	MEDAL YARDS	COMP YARDS	PAR	S.I.
1	343	348	4	5	10	386	391	4	4
2	366	375	4	13	11	485	509	5	16
3	493	509	5	11	12	420	430	4	1
4	184	200	3	8	13	363	379	4	14
5	472	477	5	15	14	182	192	3	9
6	336	347	4	7	15	510	518	5	6
7	407	409	4	2	16	145	157	3	18
8	400	411	4	3	17	485	493	5	12
9	193	200	3	17	18	330	342	4	10
OUT	3,194	3,276	36		IN	3,305	3,411	37	
					TOTAL	6,499	6,687	73	
					STANDARD SCRATCH	72	71		

CITY OF DERRY ULSTER L/DERRY

49 Victoria Road, Londonderry BT47 2PU.
Tel: (01504)311610.

LOCATION: Three miles from city centre on A5 to Strabane, turn left.
SECRETARY: Mr Patrick J. Doherty.
Tel: (01504)46369.
PROFESSIONAL: Michael Doherty.
Tel: (01504) 311496.

Parkland course overlooking River Foyle with views towards Donegal. Undulating terrain well lined by plenty of trees. There is also an easy nine hole course which is very suitable for those beginning golf.

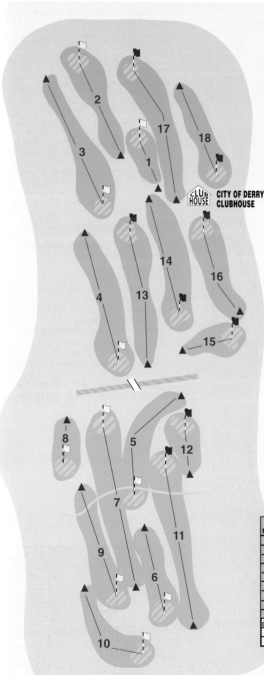

CITY OF DERRY CLUBHOUSE

COURSE INFORMATION

Par 71; SSS 71; Length 6,406 yards.
Visitors: Welcome anytime.
Weekends – please check with the club professional.
Opening Hours: Sunrise – Sunset.
Avoid: Tuesday (ladies day).
Ladies Day: Welcome (Tuesday).
Green Fees: £11 Monday – Friday; Saturday, Sunday & Bank Holidays £13. Handicap certificate required.
Juveniles: Handicap 12 and under anytime, otherwise with adult only. Lessons by prior arrangement. Full clubhouse facilities.
Clubhouse Hours: 8.00am –12.00 midnight.
Clubhouse Facilities: Bar snacks, full meals everyday except Monday. A Handicap Certificate is required for Open competitions.
Clubhouse Dress: Jacket and tie after 7.00pm.

NO.	MEDAL YARDS	GEN. YARDS	PAR	S.I.	NO.	MEDAL YARDS	GEN. YARDS	PAR	S.I.
1	222	212	3	12	10	362	342	4	13
2	381	374	4	4	11	507	495	5	7
3	540	516	5	8	12	175	166	3	11
4	441	431	4	2	13	412	404	4	3
5	370	362	4	6	14	435	427	4	1
6	338	328	4	16	15	142	130	3	17
7	488	478	5	10	16	299	289	4	15
8	165	154	3	18	17	401	393	44	5
9	379	369	4	14	18	349	341	35	9
OUT	3,324	3,224	36		IN	3,082	2,987	71	
					TOTAL	6,406	6,211		
					STANDARD SCRATCH		71	70	

Copyright Tudor Journals Ltd.

218

**Foyle Golf Centre,
12 Alder Road,
Londonderry. Bt48 8DB.
Tel: (01504) 3522.
Fax: (01504) 353967.**

LOCATION: One mile from Foyle Bridge heading for Moville turn left.
SECRETARY: Margaret Lapsley.
Tel: (01504) 352222.
ARHITECT: Frank Ainsworth.

The Foyle Golf Centre consists of an 18 hole par 72 course, nine hole par three course and a driving range. The parkland course is designed at championship standard with water coming into play on three of the 18 holes. It is well worthy of a visit by the discerning golfer.

COURSE INFORMATION

Par 72; SSS 72; Length 6,678 Yards.
Visitors: Welcome at any time. Guaranteed a tee time due to computerised booking system.
Opening Hours: Dawn – Dusk.
Juveniles: Handicap 12 and under anytime otherwise with an adult.

Green Fees: £11 week day, £13 weekends & Bank Hols.
Clubhouse Hours: 8.00am – midnight
Clubhouse Dress: Informal.
Clubhouse Facilities: Fully licensed restaurant with food available every day including lunch, bar snacks & a la carte.

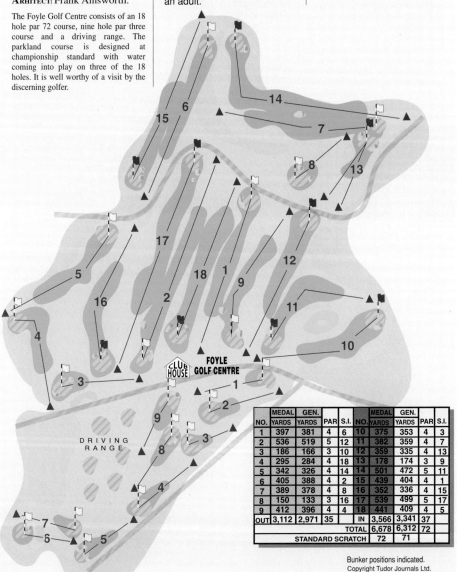

NO.	MEDAL YARDS	GEN. YARDS	PAR	S.I.	NO.	MEDAL YARDS	GEN. YARDS	PAR	S.I.
1	397	381	4	6	10	375	353	4	3
2	536	519	5	12	11	382	359	4	7
3	186	166	3	10	12	359	335	4	13
4	295	284	4	18	13	178	174	3	9
5	342	326	4	14	14	501	472	5	11
6	405	388	4	2	15	439	404	4	1
7	389	378	4	8	16	352	336	4	15
8	150	133	3	16	17	539	499	5	17
9	412	396	4	4	18	441	409	4	5
OUT	3,112	2,971	35		IN	3,566	3,341	37	
					TOTAL	6,678	6,312	72	
					STANDARD SCRATCH	72	71		

Bunker positions indicated.
Copyright Tudor Journals Ltd.

Shanemullagh,
Castledawson,
Co. Londonderry.
Tel: (01648) 468468.

LOCATION: 40 miles north of Belfast.
HONORARY SECRETARY: Laurence Hastings.
Tel: (01648) 468468.
PROFESSIONAL: Vivian Teague.
Tel: (01648) 468830.
Catering Tel: (01648) 468392.
ARCHITECT: Don Patterson.

The course demands long accurate driving on most holes and the strategic use of large mature trees emphasises the need for well placed approach shots. The 8th hole is a ninety degree dog-leg which features a difficult pitch shot to the green across the Moyola River.

COURSE INFORMATION

Par 71; SSS 71; Length 6,517 yards.
Visitors: Welcome mid-week. Weekends by prior arrangement.
Opening Hours: Dawn – Dusk Monday – Saturday.
Avoid: Tuesday, Wednesday evenings in Summer; Saturday in Winter.
Ladies Day: Wednesday. None after 4.30pm; weekends by arrangement.
Green Fees: £12 Monday –

Friday (£8 with member); £22 Saturday/Sunday/Public Holidays (£12 with member).
Juveniles: Mon – Fri; after 4.30pm on Sat/Sun. Lessons by prior arrangement. Caddy cars available by prior arrangement.
Clubhouse Hours: 11.00am – 11.00pm. Full clubhouse facilities.
Clubhouse Facilities: 11.00am – 9.00pm. A la carte by prior arrangement.
Clubhouse Dress: Casual, no denims.
Open Competitions: Open Week – July; usually monthly in Summer.

NO.	YARDS	PAR	S.I.	NO.	YARDS	PAR	S.I.
1	437	4	3	10	352	4	8
2	414	4	7	11	382	4	4
3	347	4	13	12	202	3	14
4	159	3	17	13	493	5	12
5	528	5	15	14	102	3	18
6	430	4	5	15	424	4	2
7	395	4	11	16	315	4	16
8	412	4	1	17	182	3	10
9	379	4	9	18	564	5	6
OUT	3,501	36		IN	3,016	35	
				TOTAL	6,517	71	
	STANDARD SCRATCH					71	

Bunker positions indicated.

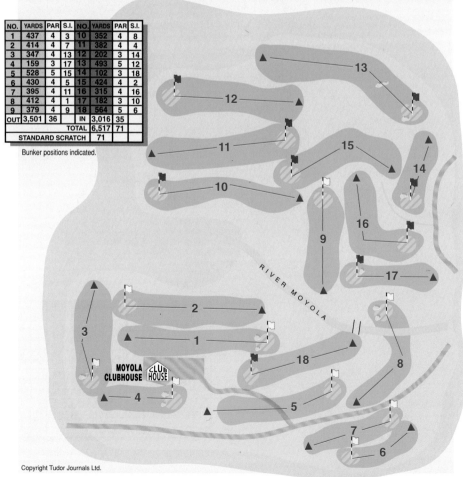

117 Strand Road, Portstewart, Co. L/Derry. Tel: (01265) 832015.

LOCATION: Four miles north west of Coleraine on the north coast.
SECRETARY: Michael Moss.
Tel: (01265) 832015/833839.
PROFESSIONAL: Alan Hunter.
Tel: (01265) 832601.
Fax: (01265) 834097.

Difficult, but open links course giving magnificent views of Donegal Hills, the rolling Atlantic, Strand Beach and the River Bann, especially from the 1st, 5th and 12th tees. Greens are fast and true. The 18th hole links course is of championship standard with more than 40 holes on offer. Held qualifying rounds of 'Open' in 1951. Has hosted other events such as the Irish Professionals and Irish Amateur Close 45 Holes on offer.

COURSE INFORMATION

Par 72; SSS 73; Length 6,784 yards (Strand Course).
Par 72; SSS 73; Length 6,784 yards (Old Course).
Par 72; SSS 73; Length 6,784 yards (Riverside Course).
Visitors: Welcome.
Avoid: Weekends and Bank Holidays.
Ladies Day: Priority on Wednesdays. Lady visitors by prior arrangement. Saturdays after 3.00 pm.
Green Fees: Strand Course – £25 Mon – Fri (£10 with member); £30 – Sat & Sun (£12 with member. Ladies/Juveniles – same fees.
Juveniles: Restricted. Lessons by prior arrangements. Club Hire & Caddy Cars available.
Clubhouse Hours: Oct – March 8.00 am – 6.00 pm; April – Sept 8.00 am – Dark.
Clubhouse Facilities: Full clubhouse facilities. Oct – March catering facilities: 12 noon – 2.30 pm/5.00 pm – 8.00 pm; April – Sept: 12 noon 2.30 pm/5.00 pm – 9.00 pm.
Clubhouse Dress: Jacket and tie in function lounge after 8.00pm on function nights only.
Clubhouse Dress: Open Week – July.

STRAND COURSE

NO.	YARDS	PAR	S.I.	NO.	YARDS	PAR	S.I.
1	425	4	7	10	393	4	10
2	366	4	15	11	370	4	4
3	207	3	11	12	166	3	18
4	535	5	5	13	500	5	12
5	456	4	1	14	485	5	14
6	140	3	17	15	169	3	16
7	476	5	13	16	422	4	6
8	384	4	9	17	434	4	2
9	352	4	3	18	434	4	8
OUT	3,341	36		IN	3,373	36	
				TOTAL	6,714	72	
				STANDARD SCRATCH	73		

RIVER BANN

PORTSTEWART STRAND

SEA

PORTSTEWART CLUBHOUSE

CLUB HOUSE

**Radisson Roe Park Hotel and Golf Resort,
Roe Park. Limavady,
Co. Londonderry.
BT49 9LB.
Tel: (015 047) 60105.
Fax: (015 047) 22313.**

LOCATION: In the picturesque Roe Valley, one mile west of Limavady, adjacent to Roe Valley Country Park.
GOLF ADMINISTRATOR: Don Brockerton.
Tel: (015 047) 60105.
ARHITECT: Frank Ainsworth.
PROFESSIONAL: Seamus Duffy.
Tel: (015 047) 60105.

Roe Park is an outstanding feature of Radisson Roe Park Hotel and Golf Resort, where superb accommodation and amenities combine in an historic riverside estate. The 18 hole parkland course takes full advantage of this beautiful setting, with Lough Foyle and the Inishowen Peninsula providing a dramatic backdrop. Water comes into play on five holes, and with a challenging par four 18th to finish, the golfer can enjoy the game to the full.

COURSE INFORMATION

**Par 70; SSS 71; Length
6,318 Yards.
Visitors:** Welcome.
Opening Hours: 8am – Dusk.

Avoid: No restrictions of prohibited times.
Ladies: Welcome.
Juveniles: Permitted.
Green Fees: £16 Weekdays ans £20 Weekends.
Coach House Hours: Open every day from 10.00am until late.
Coach House Dress: Smart casual.
Coach House Facilities: International menu available all day in the Coach House.

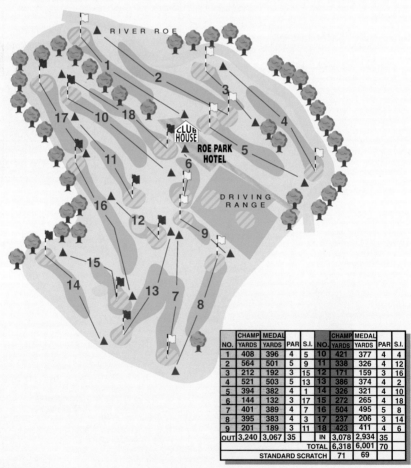

NO.	CHAMP YARDS	MEDAL YARDS	PAR	S.I.	NO.	CHAMP YARDS	MEDAL YARDS	PAR	S.I.
1	408	396	4	5	10	421	377	4	4
2	564	501	5	9	11	338	326	4	12
3	212	192	3	15	12	171	159	3	16
4	521	503	5	13	13	386	374	4	2
5	394	382	4	1	14	326	321	4	10
6	144	132	3	17	15	272	265	4	18
7	401	389	4	7	16	504	495	5	8
8	395	383	4	3	17	237	206	4	14
9	201	189	3	11	18	423	411	4	6
OUT	3,240	3,067	35		IN	3,078	2,934	35	
					TOTAL	6,318	6,001	70	
					STANDARD SCRATCH		71	69	

Tree positions indicated.

CASTLEBLAYNEY ULSTER MONAGHAN

Onomy, Castleblayney,
Co. Monaghan.
Tel: (042) 40197.

LOCATION: Hope Castle Estate,
Castleblayney.
SECRETARY: Aiden McNally.
Tel: (042) 46570.
ARCHITECT: R.J. Browne.

The course enjoys a scenic setting beside lake and forest. Hilly in character yet convenient (approx. 500 yards) to town centre the course is enjoyable for all levels of handicappers.

COURSE INFORMATION

Par 68; SSS 66; Length 5,378 yards.
Visitors: Welcome at all times.
Opening Hours: Sunrise – Sunset.
Ladies: Thursday – Ladies Day.
Green Fees: £5 Mon – Fri; £8 Sat/Sun/all Public Holidays.
Juveniles: Monday, Tuesday, Thursday, Friday up to 5.00pm; weekends after 6.00pm.

Clubhouse Hours: Normal. Full clubhouse facilities.
Clubhouse Dress: Casual.
Clubhouse Facilities: Restaurant and bar facilities opened mid 1992 in clubhouse, in Hope Castle..
Open Competitions: Open weekend May ; Open Week July/ August.

NO.	YARDS	PAR	S.I.	NO.	YARDS	PAR	S.I.
1	336	4	6	10	356	4	5
2	186	3	10	11	170	3	11
3	302	4	12	12	335	4	7
4	381	4	4	13	381	4	3
5	315	4	14	14	325	4	13
6	389	4	2	15	389	4	1
7	126	3	18	16	126	3	17
8	317	4	16	17	317	4	15
9	311	4	8	18	316	4	9
OUT	2,663	34		IN	2,715	34	
				TOTAL	5,378	68	
				STANDARD SCRATCH	66		

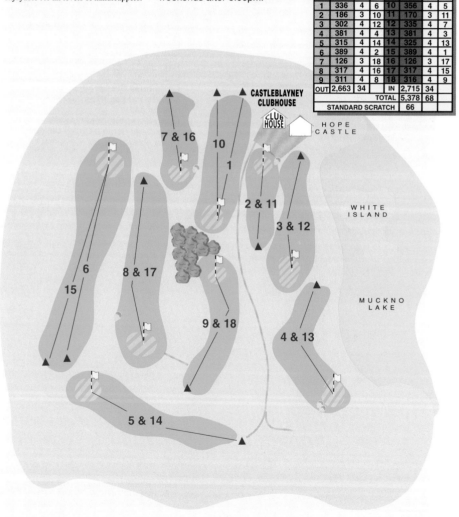

CASTLEBLAYNEY CLUBHOUSE

HOPE CASTLE

WHITE ISLAND

MUCKNO LAKE

223

**Hilton Park, Clones,
Co. Monaghan.
Tel: (047) 56017.**

LOCATION: Scotshouse Road, Clones.
SECRETARY: Martin Taylor.

The course is usually playable all year round. It is parkland and set in Hilton Park estate and with its hills, forts, lakes and streams provides a very scenic backdrop for a good test of golf.

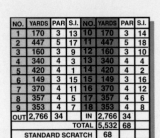

NO.	YARDS	PAR	S.I.	NO.	YARDS	PAR	S.I.
1	170	3	13	10	170	3	14
2	447	5	17	11	447	5	18
3	160	3	9	12	160	3	10
4	340	4	3	13	340	4	4
5	420	4	1	14	420	4	2
6	149	3	15	15	149	3	16
7	370	4	11	16	370	4	12
8	357	4	5	17	357	4	6
9	353	4	7	18	353	4	8
OUT	2,766	34		IN	2,766	34	
				TOTAL	5,532	68	
	STANDARD SCRATCH				68		

COURSE INFORMATION

Par 68; SSS 68; Length 5,532 yards.
Visitors: Welcome.
Opening Hours: Sunrise – Sunset.
Avoid: Sunday mornings.
Ladies: Thursdays.
Green Fees: £6 Monday – Friday; £10 Saturday/Sunday.
Clubhouse Hours: 2.00pm – 11.30pm.
Clubhouse Dress: Informal.
Clubhouse Facilities: By prior arrangement.
Open Competitions: Open Week – Early June; Scratch Cups – August; Open Weekend – Mid September.

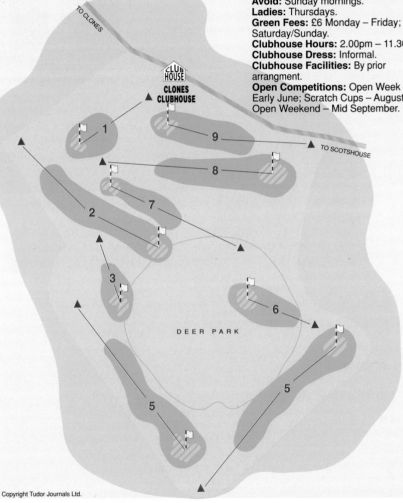

**Carrickmacross, Co. Monaghan.
Tel: (042) 61438 or 62125.**

LOCATION: On the Dublin road, one mile from Carrickmacross.
PROFESSIONAL: Maurice Cassidy.

Three short Par 4's, one Par 4 over the lake. Panoramic views over counties Monaghan, Cavan, Louth, Armagh and Meath. A new eighteen hole championship course opened in August 1991.

COURSE INFORMATION

Par 73; SSS 70; Length 6,246 metres.
Visitors: Welcome everyday.
Opening Hours: Daylight hours.
Avoid: Prior arrangement is preferred.
Green Fees: £16 Weekdays, £20 weekends.
Clubhouse Dress: Casual.
Clubhouse Facilities: Full bar and dining facilities available.
Open Competitions: Open Week – August.

NO.	METRES	PAR	S.I.	NO.	METRES	PAR	S.I.
1	457	5	11	10	309	4	16
2	446	5	15	11	215	3	12
3	379	4	1	12	329	4	8
4	151	3	17	13	351	4	6
5	368	4	3	14	515	5	4
6	171	3	9	15	496	5	10
7	328	4	5	16	125	3	18
8	330	4	7	17	302	4	14
9	337	4	13	18	434	4	2
OUT	2,967	36		IN	3,279	37	
				TOTAL	6,246	73	
				STANDARD SCRATCH		70	

Rossmore Park,
Co. Monaghan.
Tel: (047) 81316/82516.

LOCATION: Two miles south of Monaghan town on the Cootehill Road.
SECRETARY: Jimmie McKenna.
Tel: (047) 81473.
ARCHITECT: Des Smith Golf Design Ltd.

The club has recently undergone an extensive development from a shortish nine hole course to a 6,000 yard eighteen hole course, which is now in operation.

COURSE INFORMATION

Par 70; SSS 68; Length 5,605 metres.
Visitors: Welcome – at all times except on days of major competitions.
Opening Hours: Sunrise – Sunset.
Ladies: Welcome – have priority on Wednesdays.
Green Fees: £10 – any day. (£3 reduction with member).
Juveniles: Welcome any day except Open Days and Major Competition days.

Clubhouse Hours: 11.00am – 12.00pm Tues – Sun; 6.00pm – 11.00pm Mon; Full clubhouse facilities.
Clubhouse Dress: Casual.
Clubhouse Facilities: Full catering availbale from 1.00pm (except Mondays); large parties by prior arrangement.
Open Competitions: Open Week – July; Open Weekend – April, May & August .

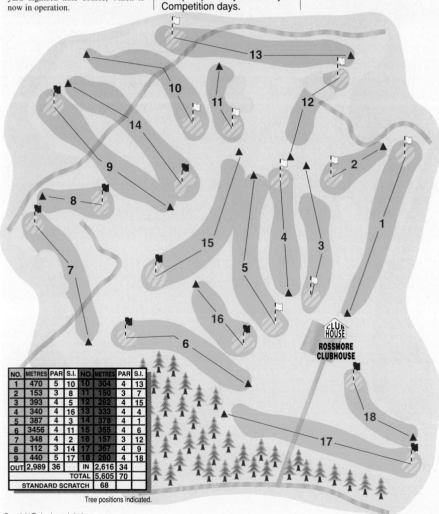

NO.	METRES	PAR	S.I.	NO.	METRES	PAR	S.I.
1	470	5	10	10	304	4	13
2	153	3	8	11	150	3	7
3	393	4	5	12	292	4	15
4	340	4	16	13	333	4	4
5	387	4	3	14	378	4	1
6	3456	4	11	15	355	4	6
7	348	4	2	16	157	3	12
8	112	3	14	17	367	4	9
9	440	5	17	18	280	4	18
OUT	2,989	36		IN	2,616	34	
				TOTAL	5,605	70	
	STANDARD SCRATCH				68		

Tree positions indicated.

DUNGANNON

U L S T E R ▋ **TYRONE**

**34 Springfield Lane,
Dungannon, Co. Tyrone
BT70 1QX.
Tel: (018687) 22098.**

LOCATION: 40 miles west of
Belfast. 1 mile from
Dungannon off B43
Donaghmore Road.
SECRETARY: Mr L. Agnew.
Tel: (018687) 27338.

The Dungannon Golf Club founded in
1890 is a parkland course with tree –
lined fairways. Here, golf is
flourishing with a membership of
about 600. A challenging and pleasant
course and today the visitor could
reiterate the entry in the old handbook
that the greens are 'very good'.

COURSE INFORMATION

**Par 71; SSS 68; Length
5,433 metres.**
Visitors: Welcome any time.
Opening Hours: 9.00am –
Sunset.
Avoid: Saturday.
Ladies: Tuesday.
Green Fees: £10 Mon – Fri;
£13 Sat/Sun/All public
holidays. Ladies £8 Mon – Fri;
£10 Sat/Sun/All public
holidays. £3 Juveniles.
Juveniles: Mon – Fri before
5.00pm. Sat/Sun play after
4.00pm. Lessons by prior
arrangement.

Clubhouse Dress: Casual.
Clubhouse Facilities: By
arrangment. Mon, Tues, Thurs.
7.00pm – 11.00pm; Wed/Fri
4.00pm – 11pm. Sat/Sun
12.00noon – 11.00pm.
Open Competitions: May –
Aughnacloy putter; July -
Mixed foursomes; Aug –
Ladies & Gents open day;
Ladies – Aug; Tyrone Brick
Open – first Sat in September.

NO.	METRES	PAR	S.I.	NO.	METRES	PAR	S.I.
1	485	5	14	10	362	4	9
2	166	3	6	11	190	3	11
3	491	5	16	12	458	4	1
4	346	4	2	13	337	4	7
5	337	4	8	14	382	4	3
6	139	3	12	15	292	4	15
7	496	5	10	16	103	4	13
8	306	4	18	17	500	3	17
9	196	3	4	18	335	5	5
OUT	2,962	36		IN	2,959	4	
				TOTAL	5,433	35	
				STANDARD SCRATCH	68	71	

CLUB
HOUSE

DUNGANNON
CLUBHOUSE

FINTONA

ULSTER   TYRONE

1 Kiln Street, Ecclesville, Demesne, Fintona, Co. Tyrone.
Tel: (01662) 841480/840366.

LOCATION: 8 miles from Omagh.
HONARARY SECRETARY: Gerry McNulty.
Tel: (01662) 841514 (01662) 841480 (H).

An attractive parkland course, its main feature being a trout stream which meanders through the course causing many problems for badly executed shots. Rated one of the top nine hole courses in the province.

COURSE INFORMATION

Par 72; SSS 70; Length 5,765 metres.
Visitors: Welcome Mon – Fri. Sat by arrangement.
Opening Hours: Daylight.
Ladies: Welcome.

Green Fees: £10 Mon – Sun.
Juveniles: Welcome.
Saturday by prior arrangement.
Clubhouse Dress: Casual.
Clubhouse Facilities: Full clubhouse facilities. Bar snacks 5.00pm – 10.00pm.
Open Competitions: Phone club for details.

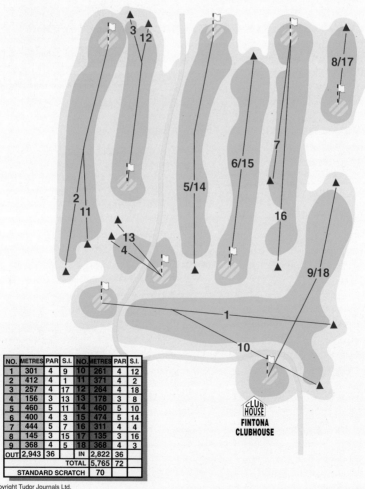

FINTONA CLUBHOUSE

NO.	METRES	PAR	S.I.	NO.	METRES	PAR	S.I.
1	301	4	9	10	261	4	12
2	412	4	1	11	371	4	2
3	257	4	17	12	264	4	18
4	156	3	13	13	178	3	8
5	460	5	11	14	460	5	10
6	400	4	3	15	474	5	14
7	444	5	7	16	311	4	4
8	145	3	15	17	135	3	16
9	368	4	5	18	368	4	3
OUT	2,943	36		IN	2,822	36	
				TOTAL	5,765	72	
	STANDARD SCRATCH	70					

200 Killymoon road, Cookstown, Co. Tyrone BT80 8TW.
Tel: (016487) 62254.

LOCATION: South end of Cookstown, 1 mile from Dungannon roundabout.
HONORARY SECRETARY: Les Hodgett.
Tel: (016487) 63762 / 62976
GOLF SHOP: (016487) 63460.
A parkland course set on high ground with the soil being a sandy consistency. The 1st is the most picturesque hole, which is a dog leg skirting the woods of Killymoon Castle.

COURSE INFORMATION

Par 70; SSS 69; Length 5,488 metres.
Visitors: Welcome Monday, Tuesday, Wednesday, Friday, Sunday. Must have current handicap. Members only Thursday, Saturday.
Ladies: Thursday.
Green Fees: £14 Monday – Friday; £18 Sat (after 5pm) & Sun.
Juveniles: Monday – Friday. Handicap Certificate required for open competitions.

Clubhouse Hours:
Clubhouse Dress: Smart and casual.
Clubhouse Facilities: Bar Snacks Tuesday – Thursday. 12.00 – 9.30pm. Friday/Saturday/Sunday, a la carte 7.00pm – 9.30pm.

NO.	MEDAL METRES	GEN. METRES	PAR	S.I.	NO.	MEDAL METRES	GEN. METRES	PAR	S.I.
1	469	462	5	8	10	327	317	4	9
2	151	139	3	14	11	176	158	3	5
3	454	436	5	6	12	390	382	4	1
4	332	323	4	12	13	157	143	3	17
5	304	292	4	16	14	446	435	5	15
6	276	268	4	18	15	479	470	5	11
7	181	172	3	4	16	175	163	3	13
8	151	139	3	10	17	359	345	4	3
9	336	314	4	2	18	325	300	4	7
OUT	2,654	2,545	35		IN	2,834	2,713	35	
					TOTAL	5,488	5,258	70	
					STANDARD SCRATCH	69	68		

KILLYMOON CLUBHOUSE

229

38 Golf Course Road, Newtownstewart, Omagh, Co. Tyrone BT78 4HU.
Tel: (016626) 61466/6661829.

LOCATION: 2 miles west of Newtownstewart.
SECRETARY/MANAGER: Judy Lafferty.
Tel: (016626) 61466.

Newtownstewart, although only an hour and a half from Belfast lies in a different world in the west of Tyrone. The course is positioned at the confluence of the Strule and the Glenelly rivers and at the foot of the Sperrin Mountains.

CAR PARK

CLUB HOUSE

NEWTOWNSTEWART CLUBHOUSE

COURSE INFORMATION

Par 70; SSS 69; Length 5,341 metres.
Visitors: Welcome any day (phone first).
Opening Hours: 8.30am – 8.30pm.
Avoid: Saturday and Sunday, Wednesday & Thursday.
Ladies: Welcome.
Ladies Day: Thursday.
Green Fees: £10 Mon – Fri (with member £5); £15 Sat/Sun/All public holidays (with member £7.50). £50 weekly; £90 monthly.
Juveniles: Welcome.
Clubhouse Hours:
Clubhouse Dress: Casual except on competition evenings.
Clubhouse Facilities: By prior arrangements.
Open Competitions: Open week – July. Visitors welcome with Handicap Certificate from home club.

NO.	METRES	PAR	S.I.	NO.	METRES	PAR	S.I.
1	277	4	17	10	132	3	18
2	279	4	16	11	321	4	3
3	127	3	12	12	349	4	2
4	347	4	6	13	178	3	13
5	270	4	10	14	460	5	5
6	354	4	1	15	142	3	15
7	194	3	8	16	454	5	11
8	343	4	4	17	332	4	9
9	421	5	14	18	361	4	7
OUT	2,612	35		IN	2,729	35	
				TOTAL	5,341	70	
				STANDARD SCRATCH	69		

Bunker and tree positions indicated.

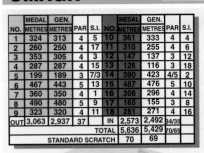

NO.	MEDAL METRES	GEN. METRES	PAR	S.I.	NO.	MEDAL METRES	GEN. METRES	PAR	S.I.
1	324	313	4	5	10	361	333	4	4
2	260	250	4	17	11	310	255	4	6
3	353	305	4	3	12	147	137	3	12
4	287	287	4	15	13	126	116	3	18
5	199	189	3	7/3	14	390	423	4/5	2
6	467	443	5	13	15	487	476	5	10
7	360	350	4	1	16	306	296	4	14
8	490	480	5	9	17	165	155	3	8
9	323	320	4	11	18	281	271	4	16
OUT	3,063	2,937	37		IN	2,573	2,492	34/35	
					TOTAL	5,636	5,429	70/69	
					STANDARD SCRATCH	70	69		

83a Dublin Road, Omagh, Co. Tyrone BT78 1HQ. Tel: (0662) 243160/241442.

LOCATION: 1 mile from town centre on main Omagh – Dublin Road. HONORARYSECRETARY: Joseph A. McElholm. SECRETARY: Florence Caldwell. Tel: (0662) 243160 / 241442. ARCHITECT: Don Patterson.

Attractive course with four of the holes bordering the River Drumragh. The course is split on either side by the Dublin road.

COURSE INFORMATION

Par 71; SSS 70; Length 5,636 metres.
Visitors: Individuals or Societies welcome.
Avoid: Tuesdays, Saturdays and Sundays.
Ladies: Ladies have priority on the 1st Tee, all day Tuesday.
Green Fees: £10 Mon – Fri; £15 Sat/Sun (£2 reduction if playing with a member). O.A.P & Students £5 (weekdays) & £7.50 (weekends).
Clubhouse Hours: 11.30am – 1.30pm and 4.30pm – 11.00pm.
Clubhouse Dress: Casual.
Clubhouse Facilities: By arrangement with caterer.
Open Competitions: Open Week – July.

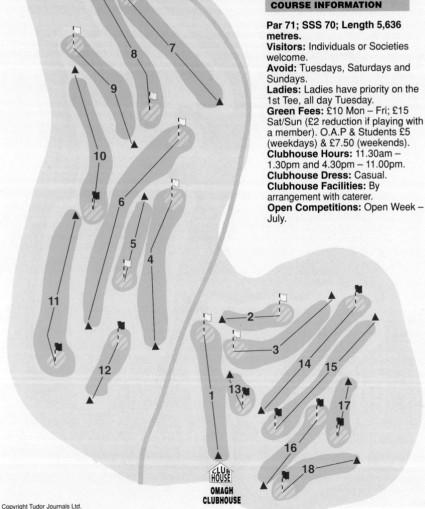

OMAGH CLUBHOUSE

STRABANE

33 Ballycolman Road, Strabane, Co. Tyrone BT82 9PH.
Tel: (01504)382271/382007.

LOCATION: 1 mile from Strabane on the Dublin Road.
SECRETARY/MANAGER: Terry Doherty.
Tel: (01504) 883109.
ARCHITECT: Desmond Hackett.

Rolling parkland intersected by the River Mourne, which runs alongside the 9th fairway, making the 9th one of the most picturesque and feared holes. The course is at the foothills of the Sperrin Mountains which provide an attractive back-drop to the river falls. Agreed by professionals and low handicapped players as an excellent test of golf.

COURSE INFORMATION

Par 69; SSS 69; Length 5,458 metres.
Visitors: Welcome. Telephone appointment advisable.
Opening Hours: 8.00am – Dusk.
Avoid: Saturday.
Ladies: Tuesday.
Green Fees: £10 Monday – Friday; (£8 with member); £12 Saturday/Sunday/All public holidays (£10 with member). £8 Societies (by arrangement).
Juveniles: Welcome. Lessons available by prior arrangements. Caddy servicd available by prior arrangements.

Handicap Certificate required for competition. Prior arrangement required at times.
Clubhouse Hours: 2.00pm – 11.00pm Mon – Fri; 12.00 – 11.00pm Sat; 12.00 – 1.30pm, 5.00pm – 7.00pm and 8.00pm – 10.00pm Sundays.
Clubhouse Dress: Informal but respectable.
Clubhouse Facilities: By arrangement only.
Open Competitions: One Saturday per month; Open week – June.

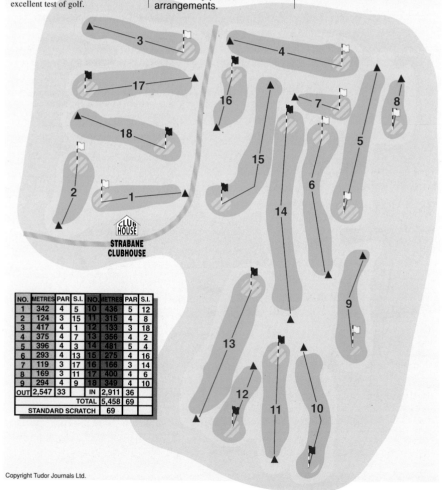

STRABANE CLUBHOUSE

NO.	METRES	PAR	S.I.	NO.	METRES	PAR	S.I.
1	342	4	5	10	436	5	12
2	124	3	15	11	315	4	8
3	417	4	1	12	133	3	18
4	375	4	7	13	356	4	2
5	396	4	3	14	481	5	4
6	293	4	13	15	275	4	16
7	119	3	17	16	166	3	14
8	169	3	11	17	400	4	6
9	294	4	9	18	349	4	10
OUT	2,547	33		IN	2,911	36	
				TOTAL	5,458	69	
	STANDARD SCRATCH					69	

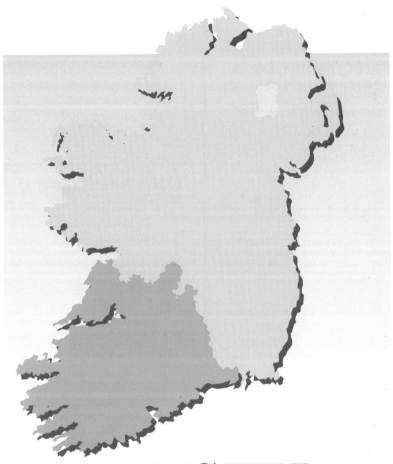

MUNSTER

BY JACK MAGOWAN

If ever there was a name that sounded Irish, it's Ballybunion. And if ever there was a no-frills, absolutely true test of links golf, it is to be found on both Ballybunion courses lapped by the Atlantic winds of an exposed, sometimes inhospitable Shannon Estuary.

Asked to choose one course on which he would be happy to play for the rest of his life, Bob Sommers, a former editor of the *U.S. Golf Journal,* didn't hesitate.

"I'm still working on it," he declared. "But there are two in Ireland high up on my list – Ballybunion and Royal Co. Down. Both are rare jewels (and) difficult to separate. Ballybunion may be the more spectacular test, but

Ballybunion's natural terrain makes it one of the top three courses in Ireland and top ten in the world.

County Down is the more relentlessly demanding. It never stops asking for first-class shot-making."

Sommers then agreed with me on one score. To play golf at Ballybunion is to slide into a blissful vacuum happy in the knowledge that if your hear the phone ring, you'll know the call will be for somebody else!. Waterville, Killarney, Lahinch, Tralee, Shannon, Dingle and Ballybunion ... they string out like green pearls on a jeweller's tray as the loveliest, most inviting part of

Munster welcomes more and more golfers every season.

Today, Ireland's South-West is as closely linked to the Royal and Ancient game as The Curragh is to horses, or Blarney to the Stone. Like O'Connell Street at rush-hour, I once said of the first tee at Killarney, and nothing has changed. The Killeen and Mahony's Point courses now host 40,000 visitors a year, a record for any European club and worth a staggering £1 million-plus in green fees alone.

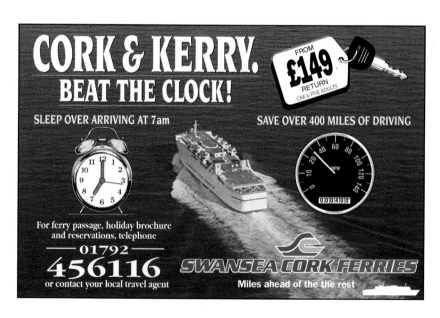

Famous and challenging test of golf — Lahinch, Co. Clare.

Photo: Esler Crawford Photography.

The Killarney club enjoys two excellent courses sharing the majestic Macgillacuddy's Reeks and Lough Leane.

Small wonder some less glamorous neighbours must be green with envy.

Irish golf has a liberating sense of space and freedom, never more so than on the first course Arnold Palmer built outside America – Tralee. It's new, it's scenic, it's tough, and as fresh as tomorrow's milk. Banna Strand, where *Ryan's Daughter* was filmed, is only a nine-iron shot away from the third green, an elusive target on what is the classiest of short holes. Tralee's wind-swept dunes are impressive, yet no bigger than a mole hill compared to those at Ballybunion. Here, as *Golf World* once said, "you're driving over them, into them, up them, and on to them," which might have prompted King Christy's famous remark: "Anybody who breaks 70 on either of these courses on a windy day is playing better than he knows how!".

Full marks, then, to a couple of amateurs called Mulcare and McGimpsey. Record-holder Pat Mulcare (66) is the only man ever to better McGimpsey's gale-lashed round of 67 in the Irish Championship of 1979, the day on which Garth shot five birdies on his way to a flawless outward half of 31. Freak stuff.

Tom Watson fell in love with Ballybunion the first time he ever saw it, and so did the late, great Jimmy Bruen. A burly, overweight Bruen was only 17 and still at school when he won the 'Close' there about 12 months before playing in Britain winning Walker Cup side of 1938. Sadly, he died from cancer at the age of 50.

The tranquility and beauty of Beaufort Golf Course resting at the foot of the famous MacGillycuddy's Reeks. A true test of golf in magnificent surroundings.

Nobody ever swung a golf club the way Bruen did, or with such stunning effect.

"Hogan and Cotton could stir the imagination and command attention," wrote Pat Ward-Thomas in *Masters Of Golf*. "And Thomson and Snead could create an awareness of beauty ...... but the golf of none of these mortals had a greater dramatic appeal for me than that of James Bruen, citizen of Cork."

Ballesteros, Nicklaus, Norman, John Daly—Bruen would have matched them all for magnetism and power-play. Jimmy hit the ball like he had a grudge against it, and in a style that was entirely his own. The 'Bruen loop' was his copyright, clubhead drawn back so much outside the line of flight that at the top of the swing it would be pointed in the direction of the tee-box. The club was then whipped inside and down into the hitting area with animal ferocity.

It's no exaggeration to say there must have been a foot or more between Bruen's arcs. Anybody who didn't know who he was would have been inclined to scoff, Ward-Thomas used to say, but not for long. The action of his hands was identical to that of cracking a whip and was the source of tremendous power.

Henry Cotton once asked Bruen to try swinging normally, and Jimmy hit the ball as well as any scratch player would. Not with the same clubhead speed, however, the key to his great length, especially off the tee.

No rough or hazard was ever tough enough to bold Bruen, yet you could never have said he was erratic.

"There was an almost hypnotic quality about his play," wrote Ward-Thomas. "It's very strangeness was compelling; its power and unusual beauty fascinating. No course, however long or difficult, was safe from destruction when Bruen teed it up. There

**Waterville, on the Ring of Kerry. The eleventh here could well
be the best par 5 in Ireland.**

will never be another like him!"

It was soon after winning the Amateur Championship in 1946 at Royal Birkdale that Jimmy felt a sudden pain in his right wrist while lifting tiles in his garden at home. The explosive violence of a unique but gifted swing had taken its toll. He was never the same player again, and quit tournament golf on the day he lost to Joe Carr in the semi-finals of the Irish Amateur at Killarney. The year: 1963.

All great golf courses are remorseless in the face of sloppy play. Hit the ball badly and the likes of Ballybunion, Lahinch, Waterville or Tralee will devour you. Hit it well, and you'll be rewarded.

Nobody talks of Waterville without mentioning John Mulcahy, the Irish American visionary who gave the course, and resort, a new dimension 25 years ago.

There are so many good holes at Waterville that it's impossible to think of a weak hole. Liam Higgins, the professional there and another prodigious hitter of the ball, once holed out at the 350-yard 16th on his way to a round of 65, but Liam, now 50-plus and playing the Seniors' Tour, almost stands alone among those who can boast of breaking 70. Raymond Floyd still thinks Waterville deserves a top-ten world rating, so who are we to disagree. The eleventh there might be the best par-5 hole in Ireland!.

Golf is a passion, somebody said, that doesn't make a lot of sense, and in Ireland it's completely mad. Was he thinking of Lahinch, I wonder, and the goats there?. For Lahinch is where the barometer on the wall has no hands; just a note saying 'See Goats'. If they are grazing close to the clubhouse, that's a weather warning — wind and rain is on the horizon. Away from the clubhouse, and it'll be a bright and clear day, no rain gear needed.

Don't bank on it. Once a visiting golfer, happy that the goats were nicely placed, set off in short sleeves and summer slacks for a round that was soon washed out by a thunder shower.

"What happened?", he frowned. "How could the goats have got it so badly wrong?"

"Sorry," said the barman "We've just had a delivery of new goats!" Which sums up the laid-back charm of Irish golf very nicely.

KILLIMER / TARBERT CAR FERRY

M.V. "Shannon Willow" (44 cars) loading at Killimer.

From Killimer, Co. Clare
DEPARTURE ON THE HOUR

		FIRST SAILING	LAST SAILING
APRIL / SEPTEMBER.	Weekdays	7.00 a.m.	9.00 p.m.
	Sundays	9.00 a.m.	9.00 p.m.
OCTOBER / MARCH	Weekdays	7.00 a.m.	7.00 p.m.
	Sundays	10.00 a.m.	7.00 p.m.

From Tarbert, Co. Kerry
DEPARTURE ON THE HALF HOUR

		FIRST SAILING	LAST SAILING
APRIL / SEPTEMBER.	Weekdays	7.30 a.m.	9.30 p.m.
	Sundays	9.30 a.m.	9.30 p.m.
OCTOBER / MARCH	Weekdays	7.30 a.m.	7.30 p.m.
	Sundays	10.30 a.m.	7.30 p.m.

SAILINGS
every day of the year except Christmas Day.

TWO FERRY SERVICE
During the peak holiday period both Ferry Boats operate to give half-hourly sailings each side.

Scenic and Direct Routes via Drive-on/Drive-off Car Ferry Service

m.v."Shannon Willow" (44Cars)
m.v."Shannon Dolphin" (52 Cars)

SHANNON FERRY LTD.
KILLIMER, KILRUSH, CO,CLARE
Telephone   Fax
065-53124   065-53125

Newmarket-on-Fergus, Co. Clare.
Tel: (061) 368144/368444.

LOCATION: Six miles North of Shannon Airport. Eight miles South of Ennis.
SECRETARY: John O'Halloran
Tel: (061) 368144
PROFESSIONAL: Philip Murphy
Tel: (061) 368144
ARCHITECT: Robert Trent Jones

This course became affiliated to the Golfing Union of Ireland although it has been in use for some considerable time. It is a course of character with natural lakes and streams, which come into play on a number of holes. Set in the grounds of Dromoland Castle Hotel the course is particularly wooded and very attractive.

COURSE INFORMATION

Par 71; SSS 71; Length 5719 mtrs.
Visitors: Welcome at all times.
Opening Hours: 9am – 9pm.
Avoid: Special event days.
Ladies: Welcome
Green Fees: £20 Mon – Fri; Sat, Sun & Bank Hols £25. (£15 with member).
Juveniles: Welcome.
Lessons available; Club Hire available: Caddy Service available.
Clubhouse Hours: 9.00am – 10.00pm.
Clubhouse Dress: Casual.
Clubhouse Facilities: At Dromoland Castle Hotel.

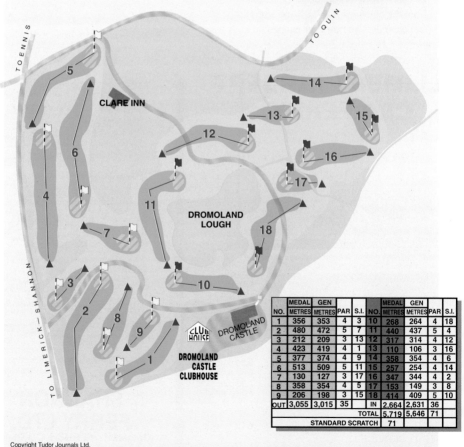

NO.	MEDAL METRES	GEN METRES	PAR	S.I.	NO.	MEDAL METRES	GEN METRES	PAR	S.I.
1	356	353	4	3	10	268	264	4	18
2	480	472	5	7	11	440	437	5	4
3	212	209	3	13	12	317	314	4	12
4	423	419	4	1	13	110	106	3	16
5	377	374	4	9	14	358	354	4	6
6	513	509	5	11	15	257	254	4	14
7	130	127	3	17	16	347	344	4	2
8	358	354	4	5	17	153	149	3	8
9	206	198	3	15	18	414	409	5	10
OUT	3,055	3,015	35		IN	2,664	2,631	36	
					TOTAL	5,719	5,646	71	
					STANDARD SCRATCH	71			

**East Clare Golf Club,
Coolreagh, Bodyke.
Co. Clare.
Tel: (061) 921322.
Fax: (061) 921388.**

Location: One and a half miles from Bodyke Village, situated among the rolling hills and lakes of East Clare.
Secretary: Jim Hogan.
Tel: (061) 921322.
Architect: Arthur Spring.

All weather challenging parkland course with special water features, designed with the players satisfaction, comfort and safety in mind.

COURSE INFORMATION

Par 71; Length 6,664 Yards.
Visitors: Pay as you play.
Opening Hours: As clubhouse.
Ladies: Welcome.
Juveniles: Permitted.

Green Fees: Weekdays £7; weekends £9.
Clubhouse Hours: Winter 9am – 4.30pm; summer 7.30am – 10pm.
Clubhouse Dress: Informal.
Clubhouse Facilities: Light snacks always available, full catering by arrangement.
Open Competitions: Golf/Angling competition, April; Open Week, third week of August.

NO.	YARDS	PAR	S.I.	NO.	YARDS	PAR	S.I.
1	396	4		10	365	4	
2	204	3		11	398	4	
3	398	4		12	515	5	
4	189	3		13	197	3	
5	525	5		14	358	4	
6	510	5		15	432	4	
7	415	4		16	521	5	
8	440	4		17	191	3	
9	175	3		18	435	4	
OUT	3,252	35		IN	3,412	36	
				TOTAL	6,664	71	
STANDARD SCRATCH							

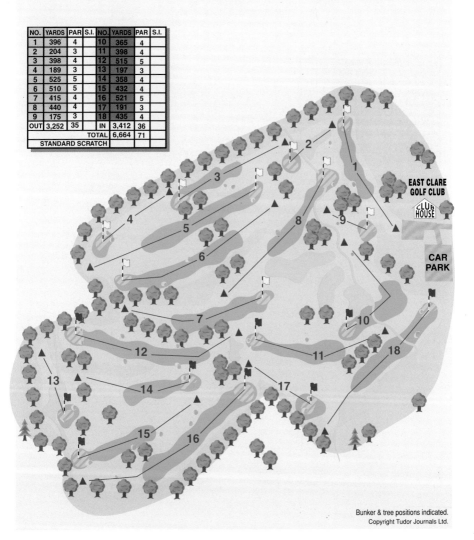

EAST CLARE GOLF CLUB

CLUB HOUSE

CAR PARK

Bunker & tree positions indicated.
Copyright Tudor Journals Ltd.

**Drumbiggle, Ennis,
Co. Clare.
Tel: (065) 24074.**

LOCATION: One mile west of town.
SECRETARY: Maurice Walshe
Tel: (065) 20045
PROFESSIONAL: Martin Ward
Tel: (065) 20690

Rolling parkland course with tree-lined narrow fairways. Playable all year round but can be a bit heavy underfoot in winter. the course overlooks the town of Ennis to the east and the green cliffs of Clare to the west.

COURSE INFORMATION

Par 69; SSS 68; Length 5,275 metres.
Visitors: Welcome Mon – Fri.
Opening Hours: 9.00am-Sunset.
Avoid: Tuesday after 2.00pm.
Ladies: Welcome.
Green Fees: £16.00
Juveniles: Welcome (half green fee is playing with an adult). Lessons available; Club Hire available; Caddy service available by prior arrangements. Telephone

appointment required.
Clubhouse Hours: 9.00am – 11.00pm.
Clubhouse Dress: Casual.
Clubhouse Facilities: Snacks and a la carte.
Open Competitions: Open week August . Handicap certificate required for Open Competitions.

NO.	METRES	PAR	S.I.	NO.	METRES	PAR	S.I.
1	328	4	5	10	160	3	12
2	114	3	18	11	308	4	11
3	296	4	13	12	365	4	2
4	246	4	15	13	158	3	16
5	320	4	7	14	377	4	3
6	417	4	1	15	299	4	6
7	141	3	17	16	180	3	14
8	345	4	4	17	294	4	8
9	468	5	9	18	459	5	10
OUT	2,675	35		IN	2,600	34	
				TOTAL	5,275	69	
				STANDARD SCRATCH	68		

ENNIS GOLF CLUB
CAR PARK

246

Kilkee Golf Club,
East End,
Kilkee, Co. Clare.
Tel: (065) 56048.

LOCATION: Kilkee.
SECRETARY: Mary Haugh.
Tel: (065) 56048
ARCHITECT: Eddie Hackett.

Kilkee Golf Club is proud to welcome you to its new-look 18 hole Golf Links. Situated on the verge of the Atlantic Ocean in a most spectacular setting overlooking Moore Bay and its famous horse-shoe beach.

COURSE INFORMATION

Par 72; SSS 72; Length 6,438 yds, 5,854 mtrs.
Visitors: Welcome.
Opening Hours: Sunrise – Sunset.
Avoid: Competition dates.
Ladies: Welcome.
Green Fees: £12 Mon – Fri; £15 Sat/Sun.
Juveniles: Welcome.
Lessons available by prior arrangement; Clubs and trolleys for hire;

Caddy service available.
Clubhouse Hours: 9.00am – closing.
Clubhouse Dress: Casual.
Clubhouse Facilities: Comfortable bar/snack bar, Restaurant with view over Kilkee Bay and Golf shop.
Open Competitions: During June, July and August. Handicap certificate required for Open Competitions.

NO.	CHAMP METRES	PAR	S.I.	NO.	CHAMP METRES	PAR	S.I.
1	325	4	11	10	264	4	18
2	431	5	5	11	152	3	14
3	292	4	17	12	465	5	10
4	384	4	3	13	355	4	8
5	284	4	15	14	410	4	6
6	154	3	9	15	372	4	2
7	387	4	1	16	122	3	16
8	356	4	7	17	351	4	4
9	421	5	13	18	329	4	12
OUT	3,034	37		IN	2,820	35	
				TOTAL	5,854	72	
				STANDARD SCRATCH		72	

BAY

CLUB HOUSE

PITCH & PUTT

ATLANTIC OCEAN

KILRUSH

M U N S T E R. **CLARE**

NO.	METRES	PAR	S.I.	NO.	METRES	PAR	S.I.
1	220	3	2	10	144	3	14
2	327	4	4	11	238	4	3
3	435	5	9	12	355	4	7
4	131	3	15	13	372	4	1
5	456	5	8	14	220	3	6
6	117	3	18	15	327	4	5
7	308	4	13	16	435	5	10
8	276	4	17	17	131	3	16
9	118	3	7	18	239	4	11
OUT	2,388	34		IN	2,462	34	
				TOTAL	4,850	68	
				STANDARD SCRATCH		66	

Parknamoney,Ennis Road, Kilrush, Co. Clare.
Tel: (065) 51138

Location: One mile on Kilrush – Ennis Road.
Secretary: G O'Malley.
Tel: (065) 51077.

Course with scenic view overlooking Shannon Estuary. Particularly challenging Par 3 especially the 5th hole. The Par 5 will prove very demanding to any golfer. Further developments to both clubhouse and course recently completed. An eighteen hole course is presently under development and is due to open in July 1994.

COURSE INFORMATION

Par 68; SSS 66; Length 4,850 mtrs.
Visitors: Welcome.
Ladies: Welcome.
Ladies Day: Thursday.
Green Fees: £10
Juveniles: Welcome. Club Hire available; Caddy Service available by prior arrangements.
Clubhouse Hours: 11.00am – 11.30pm (summer); Clubhouse facilities.
Clubhouse Dress: Casual.
Clubhouse Facilities: Lunches & evening meals available.
Open Competitions: Captains, Vice Captains and Presidents Prize (confined to members); Open Week: July. Handicap certificate required for Open Competitions.

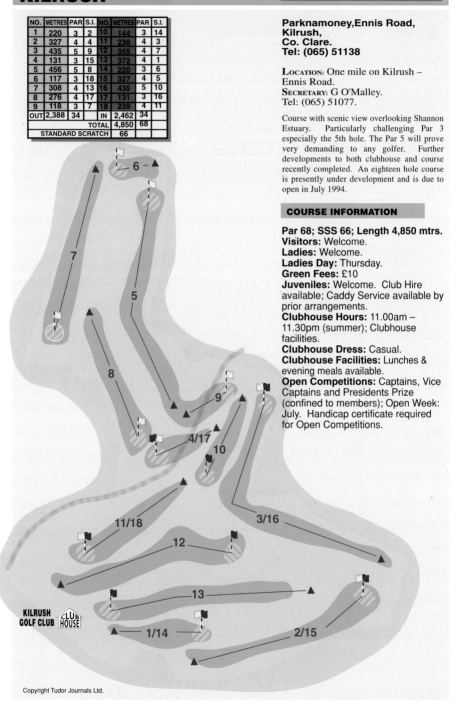

KILRUSH GOLF CLUB

Lahinch, Co Clare.
Tel: (065) 81003.
Fax: (065) 81592.

LOCATION: Half mile from Lahinch town.
SECRETARY: Alan Riordan.
Tel: (065) 81003.
Fax: (065) 81592.
PROFESSIONAL: Robert McCavery.
Tel: (065) 81408.

The second course at the famous Lahinch club and whilst it naturally suffers in prestige compared with 'Old Course', it still provides a fair challenge. A links course which is flat in its aspect but has many streams, small lakes, sea inlets and bunkers to add spice to your game.

COURSE INFORMATION

Par 67; SSS 67; Length 5,236 yds; 4,787 mtrs.
Visitors: Welcome.
Opening Hours: 8.00am – Dusk.

Ladies: Welcome.
Green Fees: £18
Juveniles: Welcome.
Lessons available; Club hire available; Caddy service available.
Clubhouse Hours: 8.00am – 11.00pm.
Clubhouse Facilities:
Lunches, dinners and snacks.
Full clubhouse facilities.
Open Competitions:
Intermediate Scratch Trophy – May; Open Week – June/July.

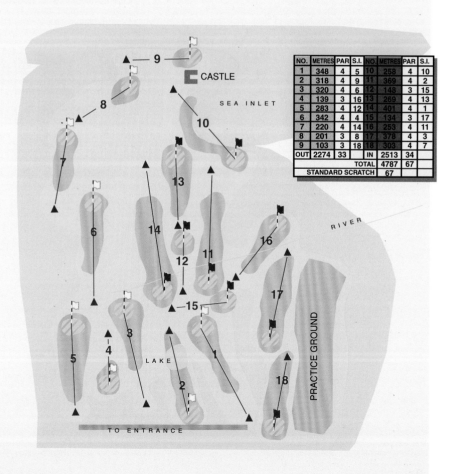

NO.	METRES	PAR	S.I.	NO.	METRES	PAR	S.I.
1	348	4	5	10	258	4	10
2	318	4	9	11	369	4	2
3	320	4	6	12	148	3	15
4	139	3	16	13	269	4	13
5	283	4	12	14	401	4	1
6	342	4	4	15	134	3	17
7	220	4	14	16	253	4	11
8	201	3	8	17	378	4	3
9	103	3	18	18	303	4	7
OUT	2274	33		IN	2513	34	
					TOTAL	4787	67
				STANDARD SCRATCH		67	

249

Lahinch, Co Clare.
Tel: (065) 81003.
Fax: (065) 81592.

Location: 35 Miles North West of Shannon Airport.
Secretary: Alan Riordan.
Tel: (065) 81003 Fax: (065) 81592.
Professional: Robert McCavery.
Tel: (065) 81408.
Architect: Dr Alastair MacKenzie.

Lahinch is steeped in history and has such famous holes such as 'Dell' and 'Klondyke'. The features of this famous course are carved out of natural terrain. The Old Course is the permanent home of the South of Ireland Open Amateur Championship, first played in 1895 and which annually attracts the cream of Ireland's amateur golfers to play for this most coveted title and the magnificent trophy which goes with it. The course also regularly hosts the Irish National Amateur and Professional Championships.

COURSE INFORMATION

Par 72; SSS 73; Length 6696 yds; 6123 mtrs (Old Course).
Visitors: Welcome every day - booking is advisable.
Opening Hours: Sunrise – Sunset.
Ladies: Welcome. Lessons available by prior arrangements; Club Hire available; Caddy service available by prior arrangements; Telephone appointment required.
Green Fees: April – September, Mon – Sun £30; winter months. Mon – Fri £25, Sat/Sun £30 & bank hols £30.
Juveniles: Welcome. Lessons available; Club hire available; Caddy service available.
Clubhouse Hours: Sunrise – Sunset; Catering facilities all day.
Clubhouse Dress: Casual.
Clubhouse Facilities:
Open Competitions: South of Ireland Amateur Open Championship July.

NO.	MEDAL METRES	GEN. YARDS	PAR	S.I.	NO.	MEDAL METRES	GEN. YARDS	PAR	S.I.
1	352	343	4	4	10	412	385	4	3
2	468	455	5	14	11	126	122	3	17
3	138	135	3	16	12	434	418	4	1
4	391	380	4	2	13	250	244	4	11
5	441	435	5	12	14	446	440	5	13
6	142	137	3	18	15	422	403	4	5
7	365	350	4	6	16	178	164	3	15
8	320	318	4	10	17	400	382	4	7
9	351	322	4	8	18	487	457	5	9
OUT	2,968	2,875	36		IN	3,155	3,015	36	
					TOTAL	6,123	5,890	72	
					STANDARD SCRATCH	73	71		

N

LAHINCH GOLF CLUB
CLUB HOUSE PROFESSIONAL
PUTTING GREEN
BEACH
SEA

Bunker positions indicated.
Copyright Tudor Journals Ltd.

SHANNON

M U N S T E R

CLARE

Shannon Airport, Shannon, Co. Clare.
Tel: (061)471849 or 471020/471551

LOCATION: Two Hundred yds beyond Airport terminal building.
PROFESSIONAL: Artie Pyke
Tel: (061) 471551.
Fax: (061) 471507
ARCHITECT: John D. Harris

American styled golf course with plenty of water hazards and bunkers. Tree lined fairways demand accurate tee shots. The greens are largely by protected by mounds and bunkers.

Course is flat and presents a superb challenge for every category of golfer. The par 3, 17th hole is the signature hole with a carry of 185 yds over the Shannon estuary.

COURSE INFORMATION

Par 72; SSS 72: Length 6,874 yds.
Visitors: Welcome at all times, subject to availability.
Opening Hours: Dawn to dusk.
Avoid: Sunday.
Ladies: Welcome.
Ladies Day: Tuesday.
Green Fees: £20 midweek: £25 weekends.
Juveniles: Must be accompanied by an adult.

Lessons by prior arrangement. Club Hire available. Caddy service available by prior arrangement; Telephone appointment required.
Clubhouse Hours: 8.00am – closing (summer); 9.00am – closing (winter); Professional shop; Full clubhouse facilities.
Clubhouse Dress: Casual. No shorts.
Clubhouse Facilities: 10.30am – 9.00pm (summer); 12.00 noon – 2.00pm (winter). Advisable to book for 4 or more.
Open Competitions: Handicap certificate required for Open Competitions. Open week, August.

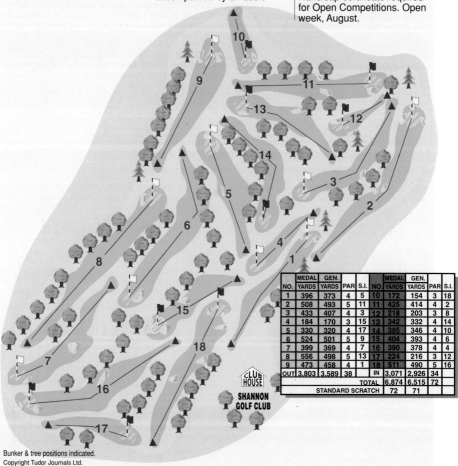

SHANNON GOLF CLUB

NO.	MEDAL YARDS	GEN. YARDS	PAR	S.I.	NO.	MEDAL YARDS	GEN. YARDS	PAR	S.I.
1	396	373	4	5	10	172	154	3	18
2	508	493	5	11	11	425	414	4	2
3	433	407	4	3	12	218	203	3	8
4	184	170	3	15	13	342	332	4	14
5	330	320	4	17	14	385	346	4	10
6	524	501	5	9	15	404	393	4	6
7	399	369	4	7	16	390	378	4	4
8	556	498	5	13	17	224	216	3	12
9	473	458	4	1	18	511	490	5	16
OUT	3,803	3,589	38		IN	3,071	2,926	34	
					TOTAL	6,874	6,515	72	
					STANDARD SCRATCH	72	71		

Bunker & tree positions indicated.
Copyright Tudor Journals Ltd.

SPANISH POINT   M U N S T E R   **CLARE**

Spanish Point, Miltown Malbay, Co. Clare.
Tel: (065) 84198.

LOCATION: Two miles from Miltown Malbay.
SECRETARY: Mr Gerry O'Loughran.
Tel: (065) 84334.

This links . course overlooks the picturesque golden beach at Spanish Point. Playable all year it is renowned for its unique six Par 3's and three Par 4's. The strong Atlantic winds can make life difficult, but it is both fun to play and a challenge for any golf enthusiast.

COURSE INFORMATION

Par 60; SSS 58; Length 3931 yds, 3574 mtrs.
Visitors: Welcome (restrictions on Sundays).
Opening Hours: Sunrise - Sunset.
Ladies: Welcome.
Green Fees: £10; £5 with a member.

Juveniles: Welcome but restricted. Juveniles under 14 are not allowed after 5pm or on Sat/Sun.
Clubhouse Hours: 10.00am – 11.00pm (summer); full clubhouse facilities.
Clubhouse Dress: Casual.
Clubhouse Facilities: Sandwiches and light snacks.
Open Competitions: Open Week in June. Handicap certificate required for Open Competitions.

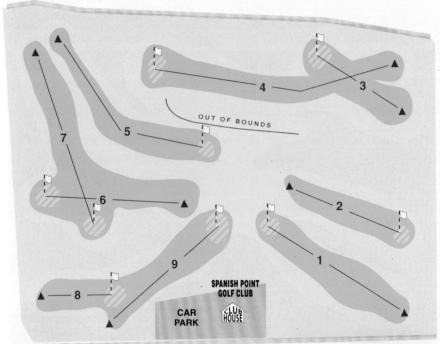

NO.	METRES	PAR	S.I.	NO.	METRES	PAR	S.I.
1	201	3	7	10	201	3	8
2	196	3	11	11	196	3	12
3	176	3	5	12	176	3	6
4	325	4	3	13	325	4	4
5	225	4	17	14	225	4	18
6	180	3	9	15	180	3	10
7	260	4	15	16	260	4	16
8	75	3	13	17	75	3	14
9	202	3	1	18	202	3	2
OUT	1,787	30		IN	1,787	30	
				TOTAL	3,754	60	
				STANDARD SCRATCH	58		

Copyright Tudor Journals Ltd.

252

Woodstock Golf & Country Club, Shanaway Road. Ennis, Co. Clare.
Tel: (065) 29463.
Fax: (065) 20304.

LOCATION: Approx 2 miles from the centre of Ennis off the Lahinch Road.
SECRETARY: Hilary Tonge.
Tel: (065) 29463.
ARCHITECT: Dr. Arthur Spring.

The course is championship standard with green built to the highest standard. It is built on 155 acres of free draining soil and is playable all year round. The course is challenging, yet is built so that it may be enjoyed by all categories of golfers. All who visit Woodstock will be sure of a warm welcome.

COURSE INFORMATION

Par 71; SSS 71; Length 6429 yds, 5879 mtrs.
Visitors: Visitors are welcome all days including week-ends, but are advised to avoid members time at week-end (check with secretary)..
Opening Hours: 8.00am until dusk.
Ladies: No restrictions.

Green Fees: £20 (£10 with member) anyday .
Juveniles: Must be accompanied by an adult.
Clubhouse Hours: 9.00am until closing time.
Clubhouse Dress: Informal but neat.
Clubhouse Facilities: Club shop, practice facilities, clubs, caddy cars and caddies on request. Full bar and Maytree Restaurant.
Open Competitions: Open days as per G.U.I. calender.

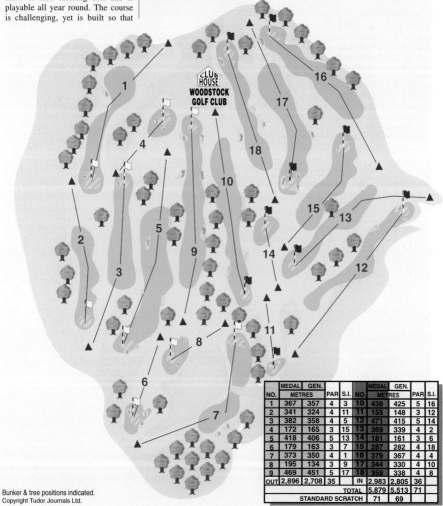

WOODSTOCK GOLF CLUB

NO.	MEDAL METRES	GEN. METRES	PAR	S.I.	NO.	MEDAL METRES	GEN. METRES	PAR	S.I.
1	367	357	4	3	10	438	425	5	16
2	341	324	4	11	11	155	148	3	12
3	382	358	4	5	12	471	415	5	14
4	172	165	3	15	13	369	339	4	2
5	418	406	5	13	14	181	161	3	6
6	179	163	3	7	15	287	282	4	18
7	373	350	4	1	16	379	367	4	4
8	195	134	3	9	17	344	330	4	10
9	469	451	5	17	18	359	338	4	8
OUT	2,896	2,708	35		IN	2,983	2,805	36	
					TOTAL	5,879	5,513	71	
					STANDARD SCRATCH	71	69		

253

Castlebernard, Bandon, Co. Cork.
Tel: (023) 41111 / 42224 / 44690.

LOCATION: Two miles west of Bandon Town.
SECRETARY: B. O'Neill.
Tel: (023) 41111.
PROFESSIONAL: Paddy O'Boyle.
Tel: (023) 42224.

Beautiful parkland course which some consider difficult due to the sloping fairways. It is the only eighteen hole course in West Cork.

COURSE INFORMATION

Par 70; SSS 69; Length 6,193 yds, 5,663 mtrs.
Visitors: Welcome Mon – Fri excluding Wednesday.
Opening Hours: Sunrise – Sunset.
Ladies: Welcome.
Ladies Day: Wednesday.
Green Fees: Mon – Fri £12; Sat/Sun £15.
Juveniles: Welcome.
Lessons available by prior arrangements; Club Hire available; Caddy service available by prior arrangements.
Clubhouse Hours: 10.30am; Full clubhouse facilities; Full catering facilities.
Clubhouse Dress: Casual.
Open Competitions: 1st week in July & Open week – May. Handicap certificate required for Open Competitions.

NO.	MEDAL METRES	GEN. METRES	PAR	S.I.	NO.	MEDAL METRES	GEN. METRES	PAR	S.I.
1	271	260	4	16	10	320	320	4	11
2	337	319	4	8	11	380	372	4	1
3	457	447	5	14	12	179	169	3	7
4	326	316	4	6	13	454	444	5	13
5	155	155	3	12	14	402	392	4	3
6	105	105	3	18	15	348	338	4	5
7	405	395	4	2	16	315	305	4	15
8	363	353	4	4	17	302	292	4	17
9	348	348	4	10	18	176	166	3	9
OUT	2,767	2,698	35		IN	2,896	2,798	35	
					TOTAL	5,663	5,496	70	
					STANDARD SCRATCH	69	68		

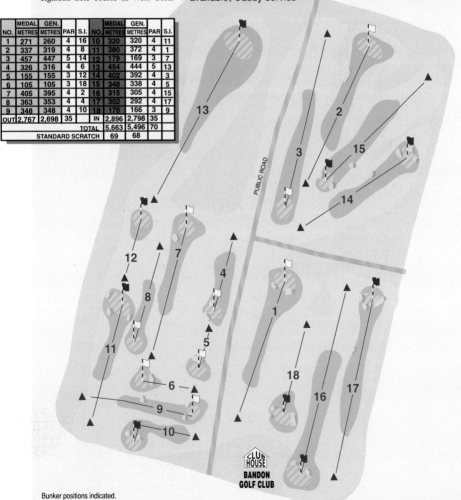

PUBLIC ROAD

CLUB HOUSE
BANDON GOLF CLUB

Bunker positions indicated.
Copyright Tudor Journals Ltd.

Donemark, Bantry, Co. Cork
Tel: (027) 50579.

LOCATION: Two miles from Bantry on Glengarriff Road.
SECRETARY: M Milner.
Tel: (027) 50372.

Bantry Park is considered an interesting and difficult nine holes. Several plantations are steadily coming into play, and are making the course more intriguing.

COURSE INFORMATION

Par 72; SSS 70; Length 6,432 yards; 5,946 metres.
Visitors: Welcome.
Opening Hours: 9.00am – Sunset.
Avoid: Days of major competitions. Prior arrangement only for societies.
Ladies: Welcome.
Green Fees: £13; Society £9 for 18 holes. (£10 in July/Aug).
Juveniles: Welcome. Club Hire available; Caddy service available by prior arrangements; telephone appointment required.
Clubhouse Hours: 9.00am – Sunset during summer months.
Clubhouse Dress: Casual.
Clubhouse Facilities: Bar snacks all day during summer months.

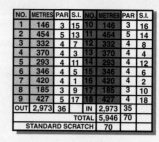

NO.	METRES	PAR	S.I.	NO.	METRES	PAR	S.I.
1	146	3	15	10	146	3	16
2	454	5	13	11	454	5	14
3	332	4	7	12	332	4	8
4	370	4	3	13	370	4	4
5	293	4	11	14	293	4	12
6	346	4	5	15	346	4	6
7	420	4	1	16	420	4	2
8	185	3	9	17	185	3	10
9	427	5	17	18	427	4	18
OUT	2,973	36		IN	2,973	35	
				TOTAL	5,946	70	
STANDARD SCRATCH				70			

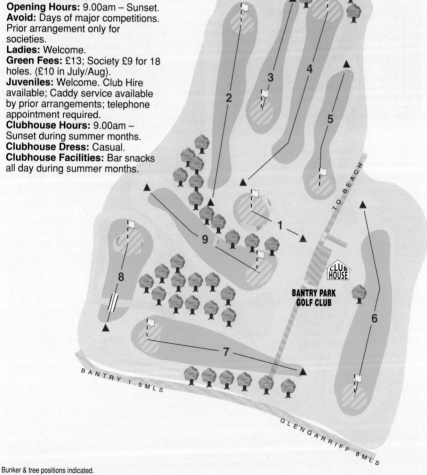

Bunker & tree positions indicated.
Copyright Tudor Journals Ltd.

Millcove, Castletownbere, Co. Cork.
Tel: (027) 70700.

LOCATION: Millcove, Castletownbere.
SECRETARY: Colin Gleeson.

A scenic sea-side links set on the edge of West Cork in a beautiful and quiet location. Water is a feature of the course both visually and in play. The latter features three holes where water comes into play, particularly on the Par 3 9th which requires a tee shot over the water. A new clubhouse was completed in 1994 which has other tourist facilities such as a caravan park, picnic area tennis courts and shingle beach.

COURSE INFORMATION
Par 70; SSS 66; Length 5,207 yards, 4,760 metres.
Visitors: Welcome.
Opening Hours: Dawn–Dusk.

Avoid: Major competitions.
Ladies: Welcome.
Green Fees: £8 midweek: £10 Sat/Sun.
Juveniles: Welcome. Club Hire available.
Clubhouse Facilities: Full facilities from June.
Open Competitions: Paddy Crowley Memorial – July; Open week – July/August.

NO.	METRES	PAR	S.I.	NO.	METRES	PAR	S.I.
1	283	4	13	10	283	4	14
2	428	5	1	11	428	5	2
3	241	4	17	12	241	4	18
4	408	5	11	13	408	5	12
5	274	4	15	14	274	4	16
6	156	3	3	15	156	3	4
7	255	4	5	16	255	4	6
8	166	3	7	17	166	3	8
9	169	3	9	18	169	3	10
OUT	2380	35		IN	2380	35	
				TOTAL	4760	70	
				STANDARD SCRATCH	66		

Bunker & tree positions indicated.
Copyright Tudor Journals Ltd.

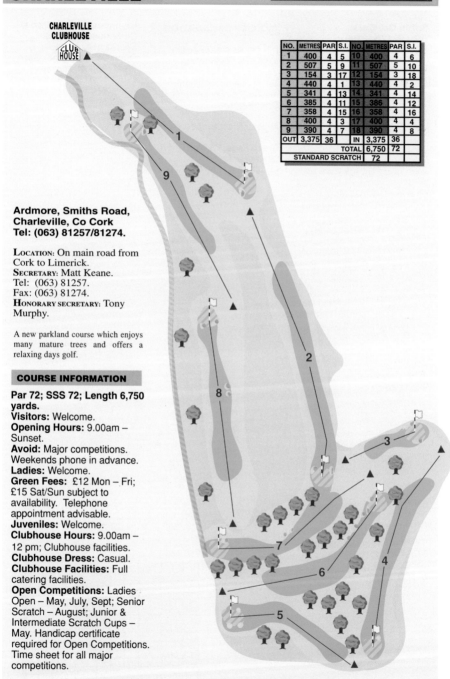

CHARLEVILLE CLUBHOUSE

NO.	METRES	PAR	S.I.	NO.	METRES	PAR	S.I.
1	400	4	5	10	400	4	6
2	507	5	9	11	507	5	10
3	154	3	17	12	154	3	18
4	440	4	1	13	440	4	2
5	341	4	13	14	341	4	14
6	385	4	11	15	386	4	12
7	358	4	15	16	358	4	16
8	400	4	3	17	400	4	4
9	390	4	7	18	390	4	8
OUT	3,375	36		IN	3,375	36	
				TOTAL	6,750	72	
				STANDARD SCRATCH	72		

Ardmore, Smiths Road, Charleville, Co Cork Tel: (063) 81257/81274.

Location: On main road from Cork to Limerick.
Secretary: Matt Keane.
Tel: (063) 81257.
Fax: (063) 81274.
Honorary secretary: Tony Murphy.

A new parkland course which enjoys many mature trees and offers a relaxing days golf.

COURSE INFORMATION

Par 72; SSS 72; Length 6,750 yards.
Visitors: Welcome.
Opening Hours: 9.00am – Sunset.
Avoid: Major competitions. Weekends phone in advance.
Ladies: Welcome.
Green Fees: £12 Mon – Fri; £15 Sat/Sun subject to availability. Telephone appointment advisable.
Juveniles: Welcome.
Clubhouse Hours: 9.00am – 12 pm; Clubhouse facilities.
Clubhouse Dress: Casual.
Clubhouse Facilities: Full catering facilities.
Open Competitions: Ladies Open – May, July, Sept; Senior Scratch – August; Junior & Intermediate Scratch Cups – May. Handicap certificate required for Open Competitions. Time sheet for all major competitions.

Cobh, Co. Cork.
Tel: (021) 812399.

LOCATION: One mile from Cobh Town.
SECRETARY: Diarmuid Kilcullen
Tel: (021) 271361.
ARCHITECT: E. Hackett

A pleasant course on the outskirts of Cobh, noted for the short 2nd hole which is a real card wrecker, with the out-of-bounds only feet away from the back of the green and all down along the right-hand side.

COURSE INFORMATION

Par 66; SSS 63: Length 4796 yds, 4386 mtrs.
Visitors: Welcome. Telephone appointment required for weekend play.
Opening Hours: 9.00am -Sunset.
Avoid: Tuesday (Ladies Day).
Green Fees: £8 Mon — Fri, £9 weekends.
Clubhouse Hours: 12.00

Clubhouse Dress: Casual.
Clubhouse Facilites: Snacks at all times.
Open Competitions: Open Week, August. Handicap certificated required for Open Competitions.

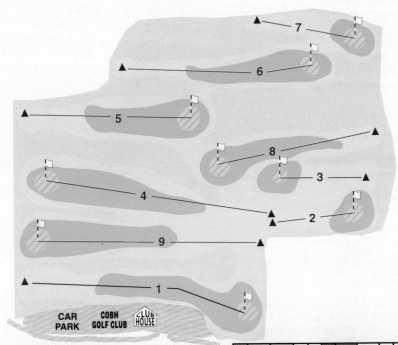

	MEDAL	GEN.				MEDAL	GEN.		
NO.	METRES	METRES	PAR	S.I.	NO.	METRES	METRES	PAR	S.I.
1	240	231	4	13	10	240	231	4	14
2	152	132	3	5	11	152	132	3	6
3	143	134	3	7	12	143	134	3	8
4	270	260	4	17	13	270	260	4	18
5	242	231	4	15	14	242	231	4	16
6	345	330	4	3	15	345	330	4	4
7	146	125	3	11	16	146	125	3	12
8	360	265	4	1	17	360	265	4	2
9	295	278	4	9	18	295	278	4	10
OUT	2,193	1,986	33		IN	2,193	1,986	33	
					TOTAL	4,386	3,972	66	
					STANDARD SCRATCH	63	61		

Coosheen, Schull.
Co. Cork.
Tel: (0281) 28182.

LOCATION: One and a half miles East of Schull.

SECRETARY: Kevin Mullins. Tel: (021) 870823 (evenings only).
ARHITECT: Daniel Morgan.

A nine hole course overlooking beautiful Schull Harbour. The faiways are tight and testing in windy conditions, especially the Par 3's, 8th and 9th holes over water. Renowned for its Par 3's.

COURSE INFORMATION

Par 60; SSS 61; 4,018 Yds.
Visitors: (Restrictions on Sun).
Opening Hours: 8am – Sunset.
Ladies: (Restrictions on Sun).
Juveniles: (Restricted at W/ends).
Green Fees: £6.00 W/days; £8.00 W/ends.
Clubhouse Hours: 9am – 7pm.
Clubhouse Dress: Casual.
Clubhouse Facilities: Bar food available from noon – 4pm, catering by request. Bar open to the Public..
Open Competitions: July, certificates required for Open Competitions.

NO.	YARDS	PAR	S.I.	NO.	YARDS	PAR	S.I.
1	120	3	13	10	120	3	14
2	240	3	3	11	240	3	4
3	100	3	17	12	100	3	18
4	417	4	1	13	417	4	2
5	320	4	11	14	320	4	12
6	130	3	9	15	130	3	10
7	217	3	5	16	217	3	6
8	200	3	15	17	200	3	16
9	265	4	7	18	265	4	8
OUT	2,009	30		IN	2,009	30	
				TOTAL	4,018	60	
	STANDARD SCRATCH		61				

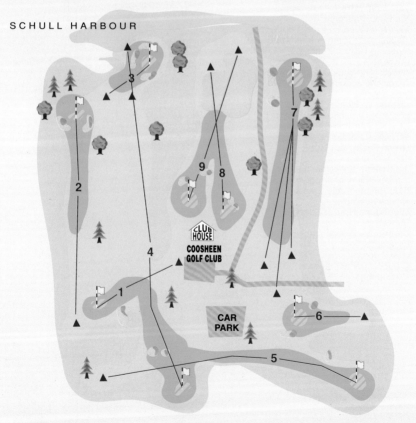

SCHULL HARBOUR

COOSHEEN GOLF CLUB

CAR PARK

Bunker & tree positions indicated.
Copyright Tudor Journals Ltd.

Little Island, Co. Cork.
Tel: (021) 353451/353037
353263.

LOCATION: Five miles East of Cork City on N25 Rosslare Road.
SECRETARY: Matt Sands.
Tel: (021) 353451
Fax: (021) 353410.
ARCHITECT: A McKenzie.

NO.	MEDAL METRES	GEN. METRES	PAR	S.I.	NO.	MEDAL METRES	GEN. METRES	PAR	S.I.
1	340	335	4	7	10	374	358	4	2
2	460	442	5	13	11	454	450	5	14
3	244	244	4	17	12	289	286	4	12
4	411	402	4	1	13	157	149	3	18
5	528	510	5	5	14	397	380	4	8
6	300	272	4	15	15	383	366	4	4
7	169	158	3	9	16	323	315	4	16
8	379	374	4	3	17	360	335	4	10
9	178	170	3	11	18	387	370	4	6
OUT	2,941	2,839	36		IN	3,124	3,009	36	
					TOTAL	6,065	5,848	72	
					STANDARD SCRATCH	72	70		

Not many clubs have such an attractive setting for a golf course with parkland running down to a rocky outcrop of land reaching out into Lough Mahon. An excellent championship test and one of the most attractive courses in Ireland.

COURSE INFORMATION

Par 72; SSS 72; Length 6632 yds, 6065 mtrs.
Visitors: Welcome Mon/Tues/Wed/Fri except from 12.30pm – 2.00pm or after 4pm.
Opening Hours: Sunrise –Sunset.
Avoid: Thursday Ladies Day. Telephone appointment required for wekends.
Ladies: Welcome. Lessons available by prior arrangements; Club Hire available, Caddy service available.
Green Fees: £23 Mon – Fri; £26 Sat/Sun.
Juveniles: Welcome. Lessons available by prior arrangements; Club Hire available, Caddy service available.
Clubhouse Hours: Sunrise – Sunset.
Clubhouse Dress: Jacket and tie after 5.30pm, 1/4 - 31/10 after 7.00pm.
Clubhouse Facilities: 11.00am – 9.00pm.

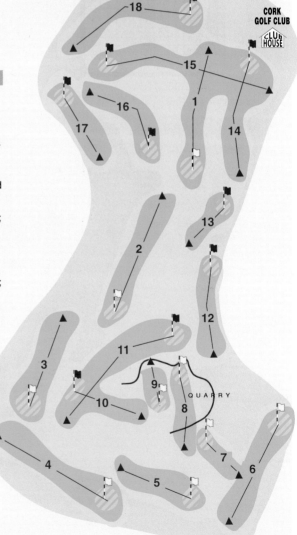

CORK GOLF CLUB

Douglas, Cork.
Tel: (021) 891086 / 895297 / 362055.

LOCATION: Three miles from Cork City.
SECRETARY: Brian Barrett.
Tel: (021) 895297.
PROFESSIONAL: Gary Nicholson.
Tel: (021) 362055

The main attraction of the course is the level terrain on which it stands, this makes it very easy for people of all ages to get around. Douglas has lots of trees and lots of bunkers.

COURSE INFORMATION

Par 70; SSS 69; Length 6194 yds, 5664 mtrs.
Visitors: Welcome Mon, Thurs, Fri all day; Wed morning; Sat/Sun after 2.30pm.
Opening Hours: 9.00am -Sunset.
Avoid: Tuesday (Ladies Day) Sat/Sun until 2.30pm.
Ladies: Welcome.
Green Fees: £19 Mon – Fri; £18 Sat/Sun.

Juveniles: Welcome. Lessons available by prior arrangement; Club Hire available.
Clubhouse Hours: 11.00am – 11.00pm (winter); 11.00am – 11.30 (summer).
Clubhouse Dress: Casual.
Clubhouse Facilities: Full restaurant facilities from 11.00am – 9.30pm; also bar menu.
Open Competitions: Senior Scratch Cup April; Junior Scratch Cup June; Intermediate Scratch Cup July.

NO.	MEDAL METRES	GEN. METRES	PAR	S.I.	NO.	MEDAL METRES	GEN. METRES	PAR	S.I.
1	243	234	4	18	10	307	298	4	15
2	341	295	4	6	11	351	351	4	9
3	409	368	4	2	12	364	357	4	5
4	140	132	3	16	13	341	311	4	11
5	393	384	4	4	14	382	346	4	1
6	346	340	4	8	15	140	125	3	13
7	170	162	3	10	16	370	356	4	3
8	443	438	5	14	17	242	225	4	17
9	297	284	4	12	18	385	377	4	7
OUT	2,782	2,637	35		IN	2,882	2,746	35	
					TOTAL	5,664	5,383	70	
					STANDARD SCRATCH		69	67	

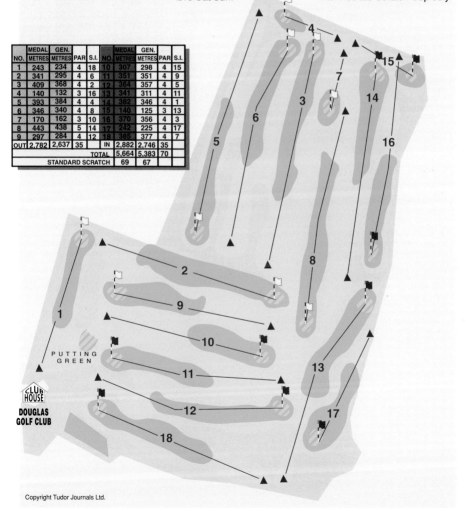

PUTTING GREEN

CLUB HOUSE
DOUGLAS GOLF CLUB

Dunmore, Clonakilty, West Cork.
Tel: (023) 33352.

LOCATION: Three miles south of Clonakilty.
SECRETARY: Ger O'Sullivan.
Tel: (023) 33959.

A short, tight course. Accurate driving is called for as out-of-bounds prevails in six of the nine holes.

COURSE INFORMATION

Par 64; SSS 61; Length 4,482 yds, 4,080 mtrs.
Visitors: Welcome avoid Sundays.
Opening Hours: Sunrise –Sunset.
Avoid: Sat. morning up to noon.
Ladies: Welcome every day.
Green Fees: £8.
Juveniles: Welcome every day – must be accompanied by an

adult after 6.00pm in summer. Handicap Certificate required in competitions.
Clubhouse Hours: 9am – 11pm.
Clubhouse Dress: Casual.
Clubhouse Facilities: In Hotel attached to course – usual trading hours.
Open Competitions: Beginning of July and Aug.

NO.	YARDS	PAR	S.I.	NO.	YARDS	PAR	S.I.
1	270	4	9	10	270	4	10
2	346	4	3	11	346	4	4
3	159	3	13	12	159	3	14
4	440	4	1	13	440	4	2
5	109	3	17	14	109	3	18
6	303	4	11	15	303	4	12
7	275	4	15	16	275	4	16
8	160	3	7	17	160	3	8
9	170	3	5	18	170	3	6
OUT	2,241	32		IN	2,241	32	
				TOTAL	4,482	64	
				STANDARD SCRATCH	61		

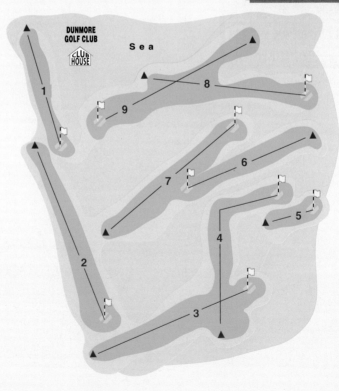

DUNMORE
GOLF CLUB

CLUB HOUSE

Sea

**Gortacrue, Midleton,
Co. Cork.
Tel: (021) 631687.**

LOCATION: Two miles outside town
of Midleton.
SECRETARY: Mr Maurice Moloney.
Tel: (021) 631687.
ARCHITECT: E. Hackett.

A fine eighteen hole course, very tight as
many trees planted in past years, are now
coming into play. A new clubhouse opened
in May 1992.

COURSE INFORMATION

**Par 69; SSS 67; Length 5,694
yards, 5,207 metres.
Visitors:** Welcome.
Opening Hours: 6.00am – 9.00pm.
Avoid: Saturday afternoon; Sunday
morning.
Ladies: Welcome.
Green Fees: £12.00
Juveniles: Welcome.
Clubhouse Hours: 6.00am –
9.00pm.
Clubhouse Dress: Casual.
Clubhouse Facilities: Hot food,
soup, sandwiches, tea and coffee.
Open Competitions: 4 per year from
April – Oct: Friday night open
Fourball, Tues night Invitation Mixed
Foursomes.

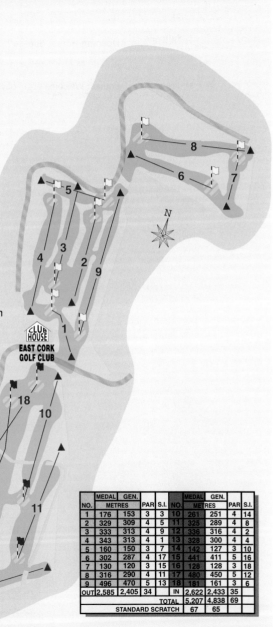

	MEDAL	GEN.				MEDAL	GEN.		
NO.	METRES		PAR	S.I.	NO.	METRES		PAR	S.I.
1	176	153	3	3	10	261	251	4	14
2	329	309	4	5	11	325	289	4	8
3	333	313	4	9	12	336	316	4	2
4	343	313	4	1	13	328	300	4	4
5	160	150	3	7	14	142	127	3	10
6	302	287	4	17	15	441	411	5	16
7	130	120	3	15	16	128	128	3	18
8	316	290	4	11	17	480	450	5	12
9	496	470	5	13	18	181	161	3	6
OUT	2,585	2,405	34		IN	2,622	2,433	35	
					TOTAL	5,207	4,838	69	
					STANDARD SCRATCH	67	65		

**Corrin, Fermoy,
Co. Cork.
Tel: (025) 31472.**

LOCATION: Two miles south west of Fermoy.
SECRETARY: Paddy McCarthy.
ARCHITECT: Commander Harris

Heathland course with undulating terrain approximately 700ft above sea level so wind is a major factor. Plenty of scope with wide fairways. There are two distinct nine holes bisected by a road and the average width of fairways is 25 yards.

COURSE INFORMATION

**Par 70; SSS 70; Length 5825 mtrs.
Visitors:** Welcome.
Opening Hours: 8.30am – Sunset.
Green Fees: £15 Sat/Sun; £12 Mon – Fri
Juveniles: Welcome before 5.00pm. Must be accompanied by an adult.
Clubhouse Hours: 10.00am – 11.30pm.
Clubhouse Dress: Casual.
Clubhouse Facilities: 11.00am – 9.00pm.

FERMOY GOLF CLUB
CLUB HOUSE

NO.	MEDAL METRES	GEN. METRES	PAR	S.I.	NO.	MEDAL METRES	GEN. METRES	PAR	S.I.
1	183	161	3	18	10	458	439	5	15
2	479	479	5	16	11	159	159	3	17
3	305	305	4	8	12	380	380	4	5
4	181	152	3	9	13	339	339	4	3
5	388	348	4	2	14	366	328	4	10
6	320	320	4	14	15	328	310	4	11
7	161	156	3	12	16	158	158	3	13
8	349	308	4	6	17	349	349	4	4
9	395	395	4	1	18	527	464	5	7
OUT	2,761	2,624	34		IN	3,064	2,926	36	
					TOTAL	5,825		69	70
					STANDARD SCRATCH	70			

264

Fota Island, Carrigtwohill, Co. Cork.
Tel: 353 21 883700.

LOCATION: 9 miles from Cork.
MANAGER: Kevin Mulcahy.
Tel: 883700.
PROFESSIONAL: Kevin Morris.
Tel: 883710.

Fota Island Golf Club is located in the heart of 780 acres of landscape. The woodlands are woven into a 72 par championship course which is a natural compliment to the other fine clubs in south west Ireland.

COURSE INFORMATION

Par 72; SSS 74; Length 6,886 yards.
Visitors: Welcome.
Opening Hours: 8.30am – 5.00pm.
Ladies: Welcome.
Ladies Day: Tuesday (members).

Green Fees: £27 (weekdays) £30 (weekends).
Juveniles: Welcome - student rate Mon – Fri..
Clubhouse Hours: 8.30am – 7.30pm.
Clubhouse Dress: Smart /Casual.
Clubhouse Facilities: Full restaurant and bar.

NO.	MEDAL YARDS	GEN. YARDS	PAR	S.I.	NO.	MEDAL YARDS	GEN. YARDS	PAR	S.I.
1	428	412	4	3	10	502	475	5	6
2	435	411	4	9	11	201	142	3	14
3	182	148	3	15	12	425	373	4	4
4	501	486	5	11	13	183	151	3	10
5	577	546	5	5	14	440	404	4	2
6	375	362	4	17	15	445	385	4	12
7	170	146	3	7	16	417	387	4	8
8	484	477	5	13	17	204	139	3	18
9	425	397	4	1	18	492	475	5	16
OUT	3,577	3,385	37		IN	3,309	2,931	35	
					TOTAL	6,886	6,200	72	
					STANDARD SCRATCH	74	70		

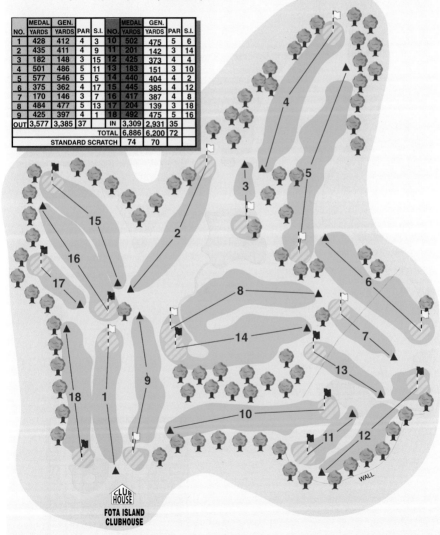

FOTA ISLAND
CLUBHOUSE

**Frankfield,
Cork
Tel: (021) 361199.**

LOCATION: Two miles from
Cork Airport; Three miles
from Cork City.
SECRETARY:Brendan
Early/Mark Ryan.
Tel: (021) 361199.
PROFESSIONAL: David Whyte.
Tel: (021) 363656.
ARCHITECT: M Ryan.

Short, pleasant nine hole course on a
hillside overlooking Cork City. Has
a 30 bay driving range, one of the
best in Muster and is a training
centre used by the Irish Naitonal
Coach in the Muster area.

COURSE INFORMATION

**Par 68 SSS 65; Length
5137yds, 4697 mtrs.
Visitors:** Welcome.
Opening Hours: 9.00am –
Dusk.

Avoid: Sat/Sun morning &
major competitions.
Ladies: Welcome.
Green Fees: £5
Juveniles: Welcome.
Clubhouse Hours: 10.30am –
11.00pm.
Clubhouse Dress: Casual.
Clubhouse Facilities: Lunches
and snacks available at all times.
Lunches Mon – Fri.

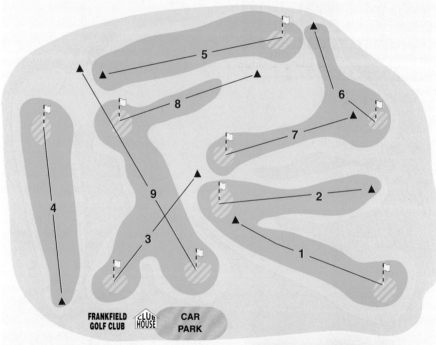

NO.	YARDS	PAR	S.I.	NO.	YARDS	PAR	S.I.
1	336	4	6	10	341	4	5
2	302	4	14	11	302	4	15
3	135	3	17	12	135	3	18
4	179	3	12	13	179	3	13
5	344	4	3	14	344	4	4
6	325	4	10	15	325	4	9
7	355	4	1	16	355	4	2
8	315	4	7	17	315	4	8
9	260	4	16	18	290	4	11
OUT	2,551	34		IN	2,586	34	
				TOTAL	5,137	68	
				STANDARD SCRATCH	65		

Glengarriff, Co. Cork.
Tel: (027) 63150.

LOCATION: One mile from Glengarriff Village.
SECRETARY:John Brooks.
Tel: (027) 63134.

This is a course in a particularly beautiful part of Ireland. There are many breath-taking views of mountains, forestry and sea as most of the holes overlook Glengarriff Harbour and Bantry Bay.

NO.	METRES	PAR	S.I.	NO.	METRES	PAR	S.I.
1	270	4	9	10	270	4	10
2	270	4	5	11	270	4	6
3	149	3	13	12	149	3	14
4	245	4	11	13	245	4	12
5	122	3	17	14	122	3	18
6	259	4	7	15	259	4	8
7	257	4	3	16	257	4	4
8	144	3	15	17	144	3	16
9	331	4	1	18	331	4	2
OUT	2,047	33		IN	2,047	33	
				TOTAL	4,094	66	
		STANDARD SCRATCH	62				

COURSE INFORMATION

Par 66; SSS 62; Length 4477 yds, 4094 mtrs.
Visitors: Welcome at all times.
Opening Hours: 9.00am - Sunset.
Ladies: Welcome.
Green Fees: £10 weekdays & weekends.
Juveniles: Welcome. Club Hire available; Caddy service available by prior arrangement.
Clubhouse Hours: 10.30am - 11.30pm.
Clubhouse Dress: Casual.
Clubhouse Facilities: By prior arrangement. Limited / no catering.
Open Competitions: Team event M. O'Hara C. Blair Classic; June. Scrambles, Mixed Foursomes.

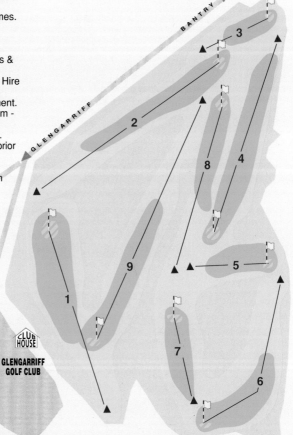

CAR PARK   GLENGARRIFF GOLF CLUB

Clash, Little Island,
Co. Cork.
Tel: (021) 353094.
Fax: (021) 354408.

LOCATION: Seven km from City Centre.
SECRETARY: Niamh O'Connell
Tel: (021) 353094
PROPRIETOR: Sean O'Connell.

Little Island on the banks of the River Lee has a particular rustic charm. Little Island by it topography and setting has all the natural gifts required for a great golf course. In fact it is more than a championship golf course with each fairway tree lined and each green intricately contoured. It is a complex with an in-built 21 bay, all weather and floodlit driving range positioned in acres of ground between the fifth and ninth holes.

COURSE INFORMATION

Par 72; SSS 69; Length 5733 mtrs.
Visitors: Always welcome. Telephone appointment required.

Opening Hours: 8am - 5pm.
Avoid: Sunday before 11am.
Green Fees: £20. £10 with member. Early birds before 11am £10. For group rates please telephone for information.
Juveniles: Welcome.
Clubhouse Hours: 8am - 12pm.
Clubhouse Dress: Neat.
Clubhouse Facilities: Full Restaurant and Bar. Catering hours: 10.30am - 6.00pm (winter). 10.30am - 9.00pm (summer).
Open Competitions: Open weekend, July.

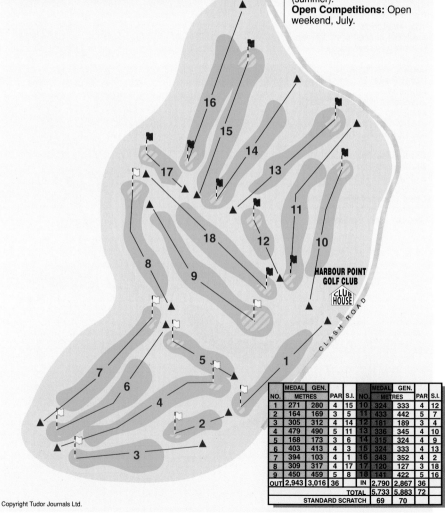

HARBOUR POINT
GOLF CLUB
CLUB HOUSE

NO.	MEDAL METRES	GEN. METRES	PAR	S.I.	NO.	MEDAL METRES	GEN. METRES	PAR	S.I.
1	271	280	4	15	10	324	333	4	12
2	164	169	3	5	11	433	442	5	7
3	305	312	4	14	12	181	189	3	4
4	479	490	5	11	13	336	345	4	10
5	168	173	3	6	14	315	324	4	9
6	403	413	4	3	15	324	333	4	13
7	394	103	4	1	16	343	352	4	2
8	309	317	4	17	17	120	127	3	18
9	450	459	5	8	18	141	422	5	16
OUT	2,943	3,016	36		IN	2,790	2,867	36	
					TOTAL	5,733	5,883	72	
					STANDARD SCRATCH	69	70		

**Ringenane, Belgooly,
Co. Cork
Tel: (021) 772197.**

LOCATION: On main Cork to
Kinsale Road, Two miles out
of Kinsale
SECRETARY: D. J. Cummins.
Tel: (021) 772197.

A picturesque nine hole course on
hillside overlooking Kinsale Harbour
and occupying a small circular
peninsula which cuts into the bay. A
tight course that plays off the natural
slope of the terrain. New course for
August 1995 (18 hole),.

NO.	METRES	PAR	S.I.	NO.	METRES	PAR	S.I.
1	180	3	7	10	180	3	8
2	299	4	15	11	299	4	16
3	312	4	1	12	312	4	2
4	332	4	14	13	332	4	13
5	177	3	6	14	177	3	5
6	326	4	10	15	326	4	9
7	140	3	11	16	140	3	12
8	464	5	18	17	464	5	17
9	436	5	3	18	436	5	4
OUT	2,666	35		IN	2,666	35	
				TOTAL	5,332	70	
STANDARD SCRATCH		68					

COURSE INFORMATION

**Par 70; SSS 68; Length; 5332
mtrs.
Visitors:** Welcome Mon – Fri.
Opening Hours: Sunrise –
Sunset.
Avoid: Weekends.
Ladies: Welcome.
Green Fees: £12.
Juveniles: Welcome.
Clubhouse Hours: 10.00am –
11.30pm; Clubhouse facilities.
Clubhouse Dress: Casual.
Clubhouse Facilities:
Catering facilities all day.

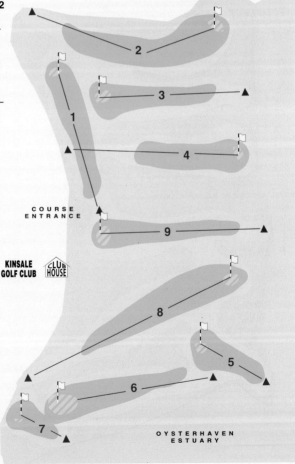

COURSE
ENTRANCE

KINSALE
GOLF CLUB CLUB HOUSE

OYSTERHAVEN
ESTUARY

NO.	MTRS.	PAR	S.I.	NO.	MTRS.	PAR	S.I.
1	439	5	12	10	452	5	11
2	115	3	15	11	140	3	13
3	358	4	1	12	302	4	3
4	296	4	18	13	169	3	7
5	308	4	8	14	315	4	5
6	183	3	6	15	250	4	16
7	444	5	10	16	282	4	17
8	339	4	14	17	460	5	9
9	372	4	4	18	350	4	2
OUT	2,854	36		IN	2,720	36	
				TOTAL	5,574	72	
		STANDARD SCRATCH			70		

**Lackaduv, Macroom,
Co. Cork.
Tel: (026) 41072.**

LOCATION: On grounds of
Castle Demesne in centre
of town.
SECRETARY: Graham McKay.
Tel: 021 334123 (Home).

An undulating scenic 18 hole
parkland course, within the town
and constructed around the River
Sullane, natural water hazards being
a major feature of the course.
Situated on the main Cork /
Killarney Road with entrance
through castle gates.

COURSE INFORMATION

**Par 72; SSS 70; Length 5574
mtrs.**
Visitors: Welcome Mon – Fri
all day – check for weekends.
Opening Hours: Sunrise –
Sunset.
Avoid: Weekends, Wed. &
days of major competitions.
Ladies: Ladies day Wed.
Ladies full m/ship.
Green Fees: £10.00, Mon –
Fri; £12, weekends.
Juveniles: Cannot play after
6.00pm or at weekends.
Caddy service available by
prior arrangements;
Telephone appointment
required.
Clubhouse Hours: 11.00am
– 11.30pm from Easter to Nov;
weekend service from Nov –
April. Full catering facilities.
Clubhouse Dress: Casual.
Open Competitions: About
six in the year as advertised in
newspapers – dates vary due
sometimes to sponsorship.
Open week, May.

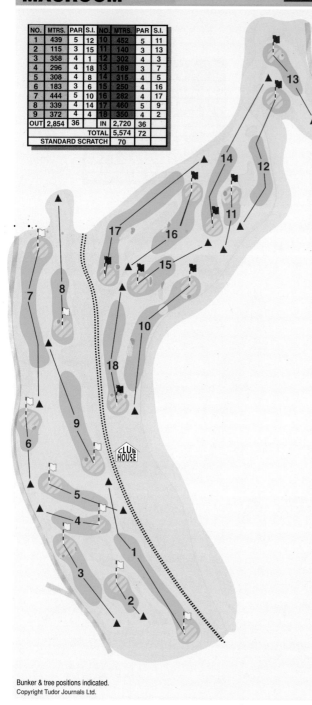

Bunker & tree positions indicated.
Copyright Tudor Journals Ltd.

Skehard Road, Cork.
Tel: (021) 362480.

LOCATION: Skehard Road
(Three miles from city).
HONORARY SECRETARY: Ashley
Hennessy
Tel: (021) 362727.
SECRETARY: Tim O'Connor.

Mahon is a municipal course and is
administered by Cork Corporation. It
is built on the very edge of the River
Douglas Estuary and because of this
has many interesting holes, the 9th
especially is not a place for the
faint-hearted, with a tee shot over
water.

COURSE INFORMATION

**Par 68; SSS 66; Length 4818
mtrs.**
Visitors: Welcome. Should
ring in advance.
Opening Hours: Sunrise -
Sunset.
Avoid: Friday mornings.
Ladies: Welcome.
Green Fees: £8.50 Mon - Fri;
£9.50 Weekends/Bank
Holidays; Pensioners £3.50;
Students £3.00 Mon - Fri.
Juveniles: £3.00 Mon - Fri. All
clubhouse facilities. Club hire
available.
Clubhouse Dress: Casual.
Clubhouse Facilities: Bar and
catering facilities available at
the Cloverhill House.
Tel: 358311
Open Competitions:
Throughout the year.

DOUGLAS
RIVER

GOAT
ISLAND

NO.	METRES	PAR	S.I.	NO.	METRES	PAR	S.I.
1	339	4	4	10	437	5	11
2	134	3	18	11	279	4	15
3	324	4	8	12	341	4	3
4	192	3	2	13	274	4	13
5	252	4	12	14	180	3	5
6	99	3	16	15	248	4	17
7	166	3	6	16	145	3	9
8	282	4	14	17	334	4	1
9	444	5	10	18	348	4	7
OUT	2,232	33		IN	2,586	35	
				TOTAL	4,818	68	
	STANDARD SCRATCH	66					

Copyright Tudor Journals Ltd.

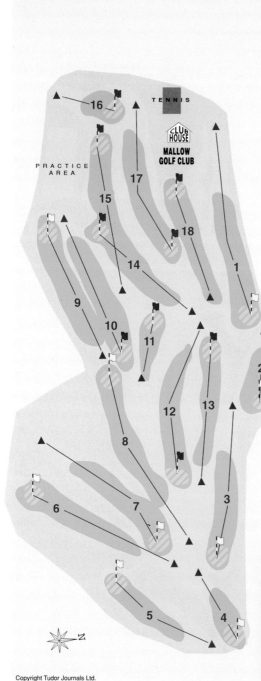

**Ballyellis, Mallow,
Co Cork.
Tel: (022) 21145. Answering
service: (022) 42501.**

LOCATION: One mile from centre of Mallow town on the Kilavullen Road.
SECRETARY: Michael O'Sullivan. Tel work: (022) 22591.
PROFESSIONAL: Sean Conway. Tel: (022) 21145.
ARCHITECT: Commander John D Harris.

True championship course, this is a tree lined parkland with excellent view of the Blackwater Valley and the distant Galtee Mountains. The 12th, is a well known feature hole which has a mound running down its length and is appropriately named "The Spine".

COURSE INFORMATION

Par72; SSS 71; Length 5874 mtrs.
Visitors: Welcome to play on all weekdays. Tuesday is traditionally Ladies day, but there are times available. Weekends are very busy up to approximately 6.00pm.
Opening Hours: 9am to late evening.
Avoid: Saturday and Sunday. Prior arrangement is advisable, especially if there is a group of more than six.
Green Fees: £10 per day; £12 weekends. Caddy car hire available by prior arrangment.
Clubhouse Hours: 10.00am - 11.00pm.
Clubhouse Dress: Casual.
Clubhouse Facilities: 3 tennis courts, 2 squash courts, snooker room, television lounge and sauna. Snacks at all times. Full meals by prior arrangments.
Open Competitions: Open week, July.

NO.	MEDAL METRES	GEN.	PAR	S.I.	NO.	MEDAL METRES	GEN.	PAR	S.I.
1	363	350	4	5	10	380	375	4	6
2	174	166	3	9	11	159	148	3	8
3	412	402	5	13	12	481	468	5	12
4	171	166	3	11	13	378	353	4	1
5	348	340	4	3	14	291	282	4	14
6	480	457	5	7	15	355	347	4	4
7	396	380	4	2	16	125	115	3	18
8	443	437	5	17	17	437	435	5	16
9	302	295	4	15	18	179	171	3	10
OUT	3,089	2,993	37		IN	2,785	2,694	35	
					TOTAL	5,874	5,687	72	
					STANDARD SCRATCH	71	70		

Gurrane, Mitchelstown, Co. Cork.
Tel: (025) 24072.

LOCATION: One mile on Limerick road from Mitchelstown.
SECRETARY: Dennis Nolan.
Tel: (025) 24519.

A level course which appears easy, but should not be under estimated.

The main attraction to visitors are the nearby Galtee Mountains. Additional holes opening soon.

COURSE INFORMATION

Par 67; SSS 67; Length 5,148 mtrs.
Visitors: Welcome.
Opening Hours: Sunrise – Sunset.
Avoid: Sunday.

Green Fees: £10.00
Juveniles: Welcome.
Clubhouse Hours: 9.00am – 11.30pm.
Clubhouse Dress: Casual.
Clubhouse Facilities: Bar only in evenings. Snacks available in evenings.
Open Competitions: Open week July . Various open weekends throughout the year, generally on bank holidays.

	MEDAL METRES	GEN. PAR	S.I.	NO.	MEDAL METRES	GEN. PAR	S.I.
	384	375	4	3	10	164	145	3	10
	192	182	3	9	11	359	349	4	2
	348	348	4	11	12	353	333	4	4
	325	314	4	13	13	143	128	3	12
	175	175	3	7	14	272	258	4	6
	328	328	4	15	15	322	308	4	8
	137	126	3	17	16	451	434	5	16
	357	340	4	1	17	109	107	3	18
	376	258	4	5	18	353	353	4	14
	2,622	2,546	33	IN		2,526	2,415	34
				TOTAL		5,148	4,961	67
	STANDARD SCRATCH		67			66	

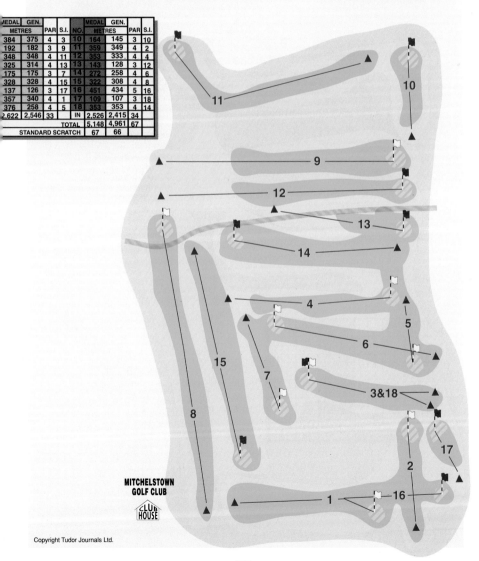

MITCHELSTOWN
GOLF CLUB

CLUB
HOUSE

Parkgariffe, Monkstown, Co. Cork.
Tel: (021) 841225.

LOCATION: Seven miles from City.
SECRETARY: Tony Finn. Tel: (021) 841376.
PROFESSIONAL: Mr B. Murphy . Tel: (021) 841686.
ARCHITECTS: Peter O'Hare/Tom Carey/B. Murphy.

A testing parkland course where, because of many trees and bunkers, accuracy is at a premium. All greens are well protected. From the first nine there are many scenic views of Cork Harbour, and on the back nine, water features on four holes. 85 bunkers have recently been newly built or remodelled offering a great golfing challenge.

COURSE INFORMATION

Par 70; SSS 69; Length 6199 yards, 5669 metres.
Visitors: Welcome. Telephone bookings in advance advisable.
Opening Hours: 8.00am-Sunset.
Avoid: Tues (Ladies Day); Wed afternoon; Sat/Sun mornings.
Ladies: Welcome at quiet times.
Green Fees: £20 Mon - Thurs; £23 Fri/Sun.
Juveniles: Must be accompanied by an adult. Lessons available by prior arrangements; Club Hire available; Telephone appointment advisable.
Clubhouse Hours: 8.00am - 11.30pm.
Clubhouse Dress: Casual. No denims or sneakers.
Clubhouse Facilities: Breakfast, Lunch, Dinner, a la carte. Last orders 9.00pm Tel: 841098.
Open Competitions: Intermediate, Junior and Senior Scratch Cups.

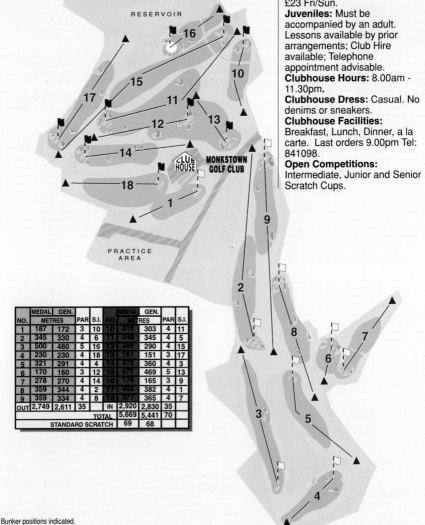

NO.	MEDAL METRES	GEN.	PAR	S.I.	NO.	MEDAL METRES	GEN.	PAR	S.I.
1	187	172	3	10	10	316	303	4	11
2	345	330	4	6	11	348	345	4	5
3	500	480	5	16	12	298	290	4	15
4	230	230	4	18	13	161	151	3	17
5	321	291	4	4	14	375	360	4	3
6	170	160	3	12	15	477	469	5	13
7	278	270	4	14	16	176	165	3	9
8	359	344	4	2	17	382	382	4	1
9	359	334	4	8	18	377	365	4	7
OUT	2,749	2,611	35		IN	2,920	2,830	35	
					TOTAL	5,669	5,441	70	
					STANDARD SCRATCH	69	68		

RESERVOIR

CLUB HOUSE

MONKSTOWN GOLF CLUB

PRACTICE AREA

Bunker positions indicated.
Copyright Tudor Journals Ltd.

Carrigrohane, Co. Cork.
Tel: (021) 385104.

LOCATION: Eight miles north west of Cork City; Two miles west of Blarney.
SECRETARY: J. J. Moynihan
Tel: (021) 385297 Fax: (021) 381445.
PROFESSIONAL: M. Lehane
Tel: (021) 385104.

Undulating on three levels. The 6th hole could be described as good a Par 3 as will be found anywhere. Last four holes provide a most challenging finish, the last two crossing a river. Precise clubbing and accuracy are demanded on this course.

COURSE INFORMATION

Par 71; SSS 70; Length 6327 yards, 5786 metres.
Visitors: Welcome: Mon & Tue all day; Wed up to 11.00am; Thurs 12.30pm; Fri up to 4.00pm; Sat/Sun enquire. Telephone in advance each day.
Opening Hours: 9.00am-Sunset.
Ladies: Welcome.
Ladies Day: Thursday.
Green Fees: £15.00.
Juveniles: Welcome.
Lessons available by prior arrangement; Club Hire

available; Caddy service available by prior arrangements; Telephone appointment required for weekends.
Clubhouse Hours: 9.00am - 11.30pm.
Clubhouse Dress: Casual.
Clubhouse Facilities: By prior arrangement.
Open Competitions: Senior, Junior and Intermediate Scratch Cups.

NO.	MEDAL METRES	GEN. METRES	PAR	S.I.	NO.	MEDAL METRES	GEN. METRES	PAR	S.I.
1	381	368	4	2	10	292	292	4	11
2	243	241	4	18	11	360	338	4	9
3	354	348	4	10	12	154	141	3	13
4	450	437	5	12	13	373	347	4	1
5	338	328	4	4	14	451	444	5	15
6	183	173	3	6	15	156	138	3	17
7	445	436	5	14	16	394	378	4	5
8	157	143	3	16	17	390	362	4	3
9	308	284	4	8	18	357	352	4	7
OUT	2,859	2,758	36		IN	2,927	2,802	35	
					TOTAL	5,786	5,560	71	
					STANDARD SCRATCH	70	69		

MUSKERRY GOLF CLUB

ROAD

RIVER

**Ringaskiddy, Co. Cork.
Tel: (021) 378430.**

LOCATION: Ten miles from Cork.
SECRETARY: Des Fitzgerald.
PROFESSIONAL: David Harrington.
ARCHITECT: E. Hackett.

A scenic course whose special features are tough over-water shots. Straight, accurate play will get best results. The 8th and 9th are two fearsome holes with the Lake coming into play.

COURSE INFORMATION

**Par 70; SSS 68; Length
5575 yards, 5098 metres.
Visitors:** Welcome.
Opening Hours: Sunrise-Sunset.
Avoid: Competition times; Sat/Sun mornings.
Ladies: Welcome Mon - Fri.

Green Fees: £12 Mon – Fri; £14 Sat/Sun, £8 early morning Mon – Friday.
Juveniles: Welcome Tues-Fri up to 6.00pm. Telephone appointment required.
Clubhouse Hours: 9.00am - 11.30pm.
Clubhouse Dress: Casual.
Clubhouse Facilities: Snacks available, full meals by prior arrangement.

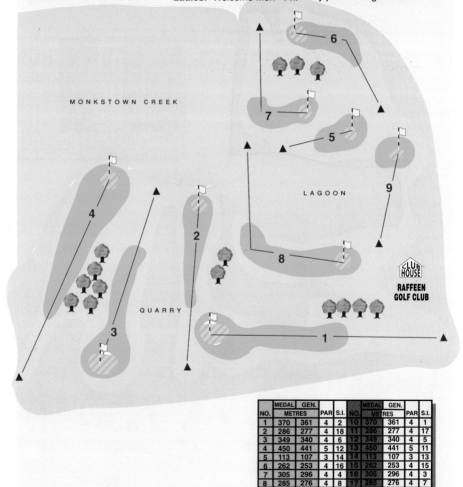

NO.	MEDAL METRES	GEN.	PAR	S.I.	NO.	MEDAL METRES	GEN.	PAR	S.I.
1	370	361	4	2	10	370	361	4	1
2	286	277	4	18	11	286	277	4	17
3	349	340	4	6	12	349	340	4	5
4	450	441	5	12	13	450	441	5	11
5	113	107	3	14	14	113	107	3	13
6	262	253	4	16	15	262	253	4	15
7	305	296	4	4	16	305	296	4	3
8	285	276	4	8	17	285	276	4	7
9	129	120	3	10	18	129	120	3	9
OUT	2,549	2,471	35		IN	2,549	2,471	35	
					TOTAL	5,098	4,942	70	
					STANDARD SCRATCH	68	67		

Tree positions indicated.
Copyright Tudor Journals Ltd.

Licknavar, Skibbereen.
Co. Cork.
Tel: (028) 21227.

LOCATION: Approx. two miles Skibbereen.
SECRETARY: John Hutchins.
Tel: (028) 21227.
CAPTAIN: John McNamara.
Tel: (028) 21700.

A course with very few hazards and wide open fairways, excellent for the high handicapper. Extra nine holes opened in late 1993.

Par 71; SSS 68; Length 5967 yards, 5279 metres.
Visitors: Welcome.
Opening Hours: Sunrise – Sunset.
Avoid: Thursday (Men's Competition); Friday (Ladies Day).
Green Fees: £12 (£15 July/Aug).

Clubhouse Hours: 10.00am – 10.00pm (summer); irregular hours in winter.
Clubhouse Dress: Casual.
Clubhouse Facilities: All day, drinks, soups, sandwiches (summer). Full restaurant & bar food.
Open Competitions: At fixed dates during summer and at Bank Holiday weekends.

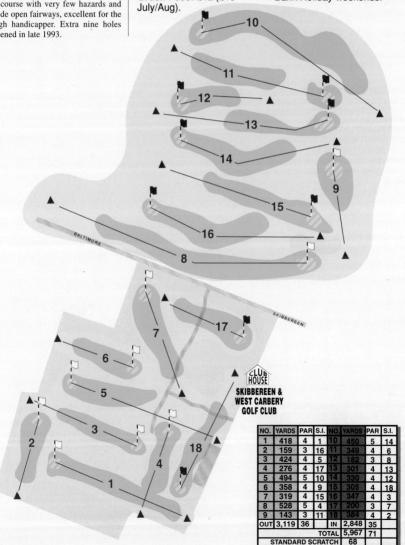

SKIBBEREEN & WEST CARBERY GOLF CLUB

NO.	YARDS	PAR	S.I.	NO.	YARDS	PAR	S.I.
1	418	4	1	10	450	5	14
2	159	3	16	11	349	4	6
3	424	4	5	12	182	3	8
4	276	4	17	13	301	4	13
5	494	5	10	14	330	4	12
6	358	4	9	15	305	4	18
7	319	4	15	16	347	4	3
8	528	5	4	17	200	3	7
9	143	3	11	18	384	4	2
OUT	3,119	36		IN	2,848	35	
				TOTAL	5,967	71	
				STANDARD SCRATCH		68	

**Knockaveryy, Youghal,
Co. Cork.
Tel: (024) 92787.
Fax: (024) 92641.**

LOCATION: Knockaverry,
Youghal.
SECRETARY: Margaret
O'Sullivan.
Tel: (024) 92787.
PROFESSIONAL: Liam Burns.
ARCHITECT: Commander Harris.
Meadowland course offering
panoramic views of Youghal Bay and
Blackwater estuary. It is enjoyable for
high handicap golfers while still
offering a good test for the low
handicap golfer.

COURSE INFORMATION

**Par 70; SSS 70; Length 5,664
Metres.**
Visitors: Welcome every day
except Wednesday; telephone
appointment required for
week-ends.
Opening Hours: 9.00am-
Sunset.
Green Fees: £14; £5 Student;
£3 Juvenile; Advisable to phone
the Club in advance.
Juveniles:
Clubhouse Hours: 9.30am -
11.30pm. Variable in winter
months; full clubhouse facilities.
Clubhouse Dress: Casual.
Clubhouse Facilities: Snacks
available at all times; full meals
served from 10.30am - 9.00pm.
Open Competitions: One
week in July and first two
weeks in August.

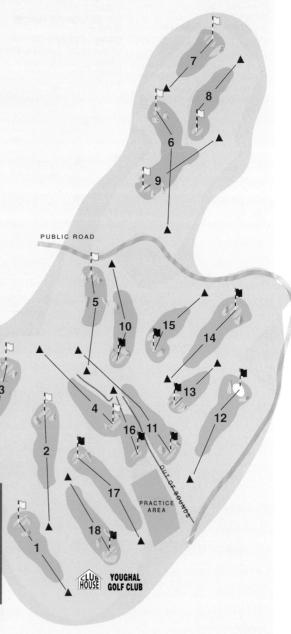

NO.	CHAMP METRES	MED. METRES	PAR	S.I.	NO.	CHAMP METRES	MED. METRES	PAR	S.I.
1	275	252	4	10	10	370	359	4	4
2	451	438	5	12	11	328	320	4	11
3	160	142	3	16	12	302	289	4	15
4	371	358	4	3	13	151	140	3	17
5	401	390	4	5	14	381	369	4	2
6	320	309	4	7	15	335	322	4	13
7	281	268	4	14	16	183	174	3	9
8	381	362	4	1	17	349	340	4	8
9	243	240	4	18	18	381	373	4	6
OUT	2883	2759	36		IN	2781	2686	34	
					TOTAL	5664	5445	70	
	STANDARD SCRATCH		70	69					

Bunker positions indicated.
Copyright Tudor Journals Ltd.

**Ardfert Golf Club,Sacksville, Ardfert, Tralee. Co. Kerry.
Tel: (066) 34744.**

LOCATION: Six miles from Tralee.
SECRETARY: Siobhán O'Sullivan. Tel: (066) 34744.

A nine hole parkland course greatly compliments the scenic countryside with a river and lake featured in its design. It has 12 all weather driving range bays lessons available by appointment. Club hire is also available.

COURSE INFORMATION

Par 68; SSS 60; Length 5,116 Yards.
Visitors: Welcome, telephone for weekends.
Opening Hours: 9am – Sunset.
Ladies: Welcome.

Juveniles: Welcome, lessons available.
Green Fees: £7 Weekdays & £8 Weekends.
Clubhouse Hours: 9.00am – 9.30pm.
Clubhouse Dress: Casual.
Clubhouse Facilities: Tea, coffee & light snacks.

NO.	YARDS	PAR	S.I.	NO.	YARDS	PAR	S.I.
1	175	3	9	10	175	3	10
2	308	4	13	11	308	4	14
3	502	5	1	12	502	5	2
4	355	4	11	13	355	4	8
5	340	4	7	14	340	4	4
6	315	4	3	15	315	4	12
7	166	3	11	16	166	3	16
8	238	4	15	17	238	4	18
9	159	3	5	18	159	3	6
OUT	2,558	34		IN	2,558	34	
				TOTAL	5,116	68	
				STANDARD SCRATCH	60		

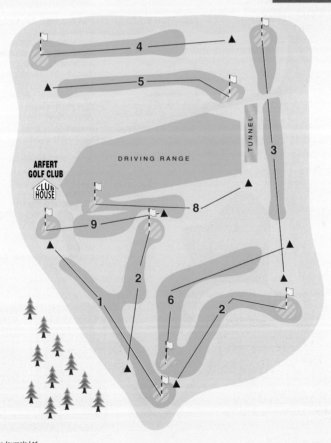

Ballybunion Co Kerry.
Tel: (068) 27146.

Location: **Ballybunion.**
Secretary: **Jim McKenna.**
Tel: (068) 27146.
Professional: **Brian O'Callaghan.**
Tel: (068) 27146.

The 'Old Course' at Ballybunion is world famous and is consistently rated amongst the top ten courses in the world. A magnificent course with several holes right on the shore and towering sandhills coming into play on all. One of Ireland's greatest golfing challenges it regularly receives golfing accolades from all over the world. (The Cashen Course was designed by Robert Treant Jones and is every bit as demanding (if not more) as the Old Course).

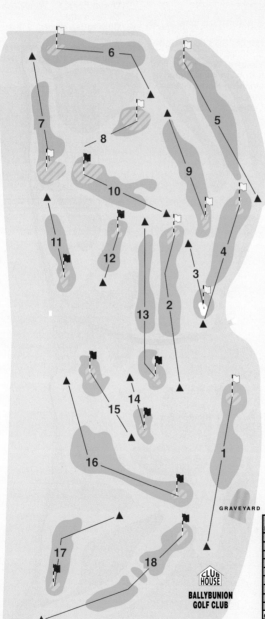

COURSE INFORMATION

Par 71; SSS 72; Length 6542 yrds.
Visitors: Welcome.
Opening Hours: 7.00am – 4.30pm.
Avoid: Weekends.
Ladies: Welcome
Green Fees: £35 (Old Course); £50 (Both Courses).
Juveniles: Welcome. Lessons available by prior arrangement; Club Hire available by prior arrangement; Caddy service available; Handicap Certificate required; Telephone appointment required for open competitions.
Clubhouse Hours: 7.00am – 11.00pm; Professional Chop Open; Full clubhouse facilities; Full catering facilities 9.00am – 9.00pm.
Clubhouse Dress: Neat.

GRAVEYARD

BALLYBUNION
GOLF CLUB

CLUB
HOUSE

NO.	MEDAL YARDS	GEN. YARDS	PAR	S.I.	NO.	MEDAL YARDS	GEN. YARDS	PAR	S.I.
1	392	366	4	9	10	359	336	4	10
2	445	394	4	1	11	449	400	4	2
3	220	211	3	11	12	192	179	3	16
4	498	490	5	15	13	484	480	5	8
5	508	489	5	13	14	131	125	3	18
6	364	344	4	7	15	216	207	3	4
7	423	400	4	5	16	490	482	5	14
8	153	134	3	17	17	385	368	4	12
9	454	430	4	3	18	379	366	4	6
OUT	3,457	3,258	36		IN	3,085	2,943	35	
					TOTAL	6.542	6,201	71	
					STANDARD SCRATCH	72	70		

Ballybunion, Co Kerry.
Tel: (068) 27146.

LOCATION: Ballybunion.
SECRETARY: Jim McKenna.
Tel: (068) 27146.
PROFESSIONAL: Brian
O'Callaghan.
Tel: (068) 27146.

The 'Cashen Course' at Ballybunion
was designed by Robert Trent
Jones and is every bit as
demanding - if not more - than the
'Old Course'. Both courses enjoy
the benefit of the Atlantic coastline.
The remote location of the course
is instrumental in reducing the
number of casual players leaving
those on 'pilgrimage' with more
solitude.

COURSE INFORMATION

**Par 72; SSS 73; Length 6278
yards.**
Visitors: Welcome.
Opening Hours: 7.00am –
5.30pm.
Avoid: Weekends.
Ladies: Welcome.
Green Fees: £25 (Cashen
Course); £50 (Both Courses).
Juveniles: Welcome.
Lessons available by prior
arrangement; Club Hire
available by prior
arrangement; Caddy service
available; Handicap Certificate
required; Telephone
appointment required for open
competitions.
Clubhouse Hours: 7.00am -
11.00pm; Professional shop
open; Full clubhouse facilities;
Full catering facilities 9.00am -
9.00pm.
Clubhouse Dress: Neat.

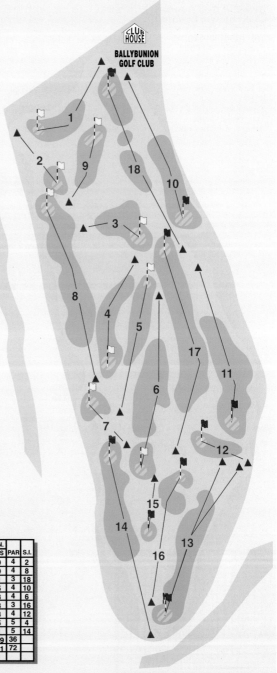

BALLYBUNION
GOLF CLUB

NO.	MEDAL YARDS	GEN. YARDS	PAR	S.I.	NO.	MEDAL YARDS	GEN. YARDS	PAR	S.I.
1	324	312	4	11	10	432	399	4	2
2	146	140	3	17	11	377	359	4	8
3	237	223	4	13	12	154	141	3	18
4	395	374	4	1	13	350	325	4	10
5	400	355	4	7	14	378	373	4	6
6	487	476	5	3	15	155	143	3	16
7	199	145	3	15	16	314	303	4	12
8	479	476	5	9	17	605	585	5	4
9	368	361	4	5	18	478	451	5	14
OUT	3.035	2.826	36		IN	3.243	3.079	36	
					TOTAL	6.278	5.941	72	
					STANDARD SCRATCH	73	72		

Beaufort Golf Course, Churchtown, Beaufort, Killarney. Co. Kerry.
Tel: (064) 44440.
Fax: (064) 44752.

LOCATION: Seven miles west of Killarney, just off the R562.
SECRETARY: Colin Kelly.
Tel: (064) 44440.
ARHITECT: Arthur Spring.

Parkland, 6,605 Yds. Par 71. Situated in the centre of South West Ireland's golfing mecca. Just five miles from the world famous Killarney Golf Club. Course is surrounded by Kerry mountains and the back nine is dominated by the ruins of Castle Core.

COURSE INFORMATION

Par 71; SSS 72; Length 6,605 Yards.
Visitors: Avoid 1.00pm –

2.30pm (members only).
Opening Hours: 7.30am until darkness.
Ladies: Welcome.
Juveniles: Permitted.
Green Fees: £25 Weekdays, £28 Weekends.
Clubhouse Hours: 7.30am.
Clubhouse Dress: Neat, Informal.
Clubhouse Facilities: Bar & Bar food.

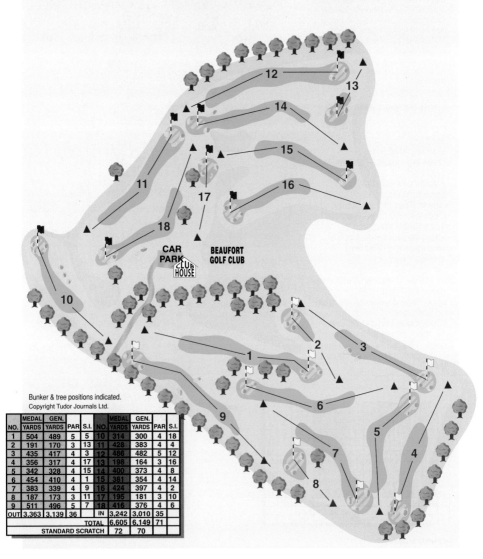

Bunker & tree positions indicated.
Copyright Tudor Journals Ltd.

NO.	MEDAL YARDS	GEN. YARDS	PAR	S.I.	NO.	MEDAL YARDS	GEN. YARDS	PAR	S.I.
1	504	489	5	5	10	314	300	4	18
2	191	170	3	13	11	428	383	4	4
3	435	417	4	3	12	486	482	5	12
4	356	317	4	17	13	198	164	3	16
5	342	328	4	15	14	400	373	4	8
6	454	410	4	1	15	381	354	4	14
7	383	339	4	9	16	424	397	4	2
8	187	173	3	11	17	195	181	3	10
9	511	496	5	7	18	416	376	4	6
OUT	3,363	3,139	36		IN	3,242	3,010	35	
					TOTAL	6,605	6,149	71	
					STANDARD SCRATCH	72	70		

**Ballyoughterach,
Ballyferriter, Co. Kerry.
Tel: (066) 56255/56408.
Fax: (066) 56409.**

LOCATION: Dingle Penisula.
SECRETARY: Garry Partington.
HONORARY SECRETARY: Tomás
Ó Sé.
PROFESSIONAL: Dermot
O'Connor.
Tel: (066) 56255/56408.
ARCHITECT: E. Hackett /
Christy O'Connor Jnr.

A links course with wind proving a
big factor as it sweeps in from the

Atlantic Ocean. The design of the
course uses the natural terrain and
has the advantage of the area's
marvellour turf.   A setting for
traditional golf with panoramic
surroundings.

COURSE INFORMATION

**Par72; SSS 71; Length
6,550 yards, 6,074 metres.
Visitors:** Welcome at all
times.
Opening Hours: Sunrise –
Sunset.
Avoid: Sunday afternoons.
Ladies: Welcome.

Green Fees: £20 Sat, Sun &
Bank Hols. Lessons available
by prior arrangements; Club
Hire available, Caddy service
available by prior
arrangements.
Juveniles: Welcome
(accompanied by adult).
Clubhouse Hours: 8.00am -
9.00pm; Professional shop
open.
Clubhouse Dress: Casual.
Clubhouse Facilities: Full
clubhouse facilities.
Open Competitions: All
Sundays in July/August; Sept.

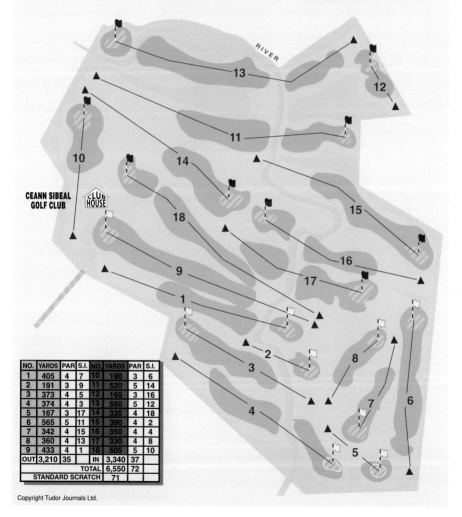

NO.	YARDS	PAR	S.I.	NO.	YARDS	PAR	S.I.
1	405	4	7	10	190	3	6
2	191	3	9	11	520	5	14
3	373	4	5	12	160	3	16
4	374	4	3	13	560	5	12
5	167	3	17	14	335	4	18
6	565	5	11	15	390	4	2
7	342	4	15	16	350	4	4
8	360	4	13	17	330	4	8
9	433	4	1	18	505	5	10
OUT	3,210	35		IN	3,340	37	
				TOTAL	6,550	72	
				STANDARD SCRATCH	71		

Copyright Tudor Journals Ltd.

**Dooks, Glenbeigh,
Co. Kerry.
Tel: (066) 68205/68200.**

LOCATION: Four miles from Killorglin.
SECRETARY: M. Shanahan, Tel: (066) 67370.

Dooks-a word derived from Gaelic 'drumhac' meaning sand-bank - is a testing 18 hole links situated in one of the most picturesque corners of the Ring of Kerry. The golf course is laid out on one of three stretches of sand-dunes at the head of picturesque Dingle Bay.

COURSE INFORMATION

**Par 70; SSS 68; Length 6572 yds, 6010 mtrs.
Visitors:** Welcome.
Opening Hours: Sunrise - Sunset.
Avoid: Weekends.
Ladies: Welcome. Caddy service available; Handicap

Certificate required.
Green Fees: £16 any day.
Clubhouse Hours: 9.00am - 11.00pm.
Clubhouse Dress: Casual.
Clubhouse Facilities: 11.00am - 7.00pm.
Open Competitions: By invitation.

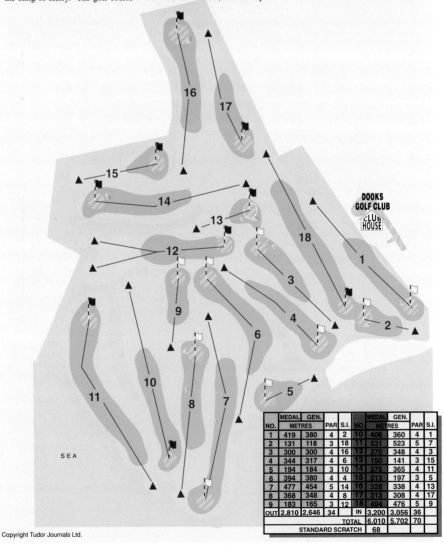

NO.	MEDAL METRES	GEN. METRES	PAR	S.I.	NO.	MEDAL METRES	GEN. METRES	PAR	S.I.
1	419	380	4	2	10	406	360	4	1
2	131	118	3	18	11	531	523	5	7
3	300	300	4	16	12	370	348	4	3
4	344	317	4	6	13	150	141	3	15
5	194	184	3	10	14	375	365	4	11
6	394	380	4	4	15	213	197	3	5
7	477	454	5	14	16	328	338	4	13
8	368	348	4	8	17	313	308	4	17
9	183	165	3	12	18	494	476	5	9
OUT	2,810	2,646	34		IN	3,200	3,056	36	
					TOTAL	6,010	5,702	70	
					STANDARD SCRATCH		68		

Kenmare, Co. Kerry.
Tel: (064) 41291.

LOCATION: Turn left at top of town.
SECRETARY / MANAGER: M. MacGearailt.
Tel: (064) 41291 & 41636.
SECRETARY for bookings: Siobhan O'Connor.

The course was increased recently from nine to eighteen holes. It is picturesque and mainly very sheltered which leaves it playable in all kinds of weather. It also has the advantage of being sited in one of Ireland's areas of outstanding scenery.

COURSE INFORMATION

Par 71/70; SSS 69/68; Length 6,003 yds.
Visitors: Welcome at any time. Booking in advance is advisable (especially weekends).
Opening Hours: Everyday, peak time May – Sept 6am – 7pm. Off peak time 9am – 6pm.
Ladies: Welcome.
Juveniles: Welcome, to be accompanied by adult.
Green Fees: £15 Weekdays & Saturdays, £18 on Sunday. Club hire £5, Pullcart £1.
Clubhouse Hours: 8.00am - sunset.
Clubhouse Dress: Casual.
Clubhouse Facilities: Tea, coffee & snacks 8.00am – sunset.
Open Competitions: Ladies Open April; Ladies Scratch Cup July; Mitsubishi fourball June; Kenmare open day July; Scratch Cups July; GAA Classic July / Aug; The Brothers Classic Sept.

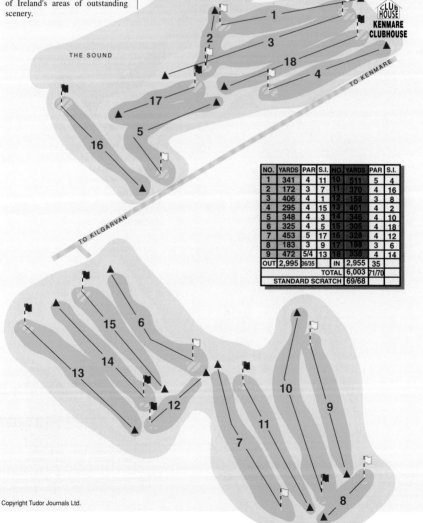

NO.	YARDS	PAR	S.I.	NO.	YARDS	PAR	S.I.
1	341	4	11	10	511	5	4
2	172	3	7	11	370	4	16
3	406	4	1	12	158	3	8
4	295	4	15	13	401	4	2
5	348	4	3	14	346	4	10
6	325	4	5	15	305	4	18
7	453	5	17	16	328	4	12
8	183	3	9	17	198	3	6
9	472	5/4	13	18	338	4	14
OUT	2,995	36/35		IN	2,955	35	
				TOTAL	6,003	71/70	
				STANDARD SCRATCH	69/68		

285

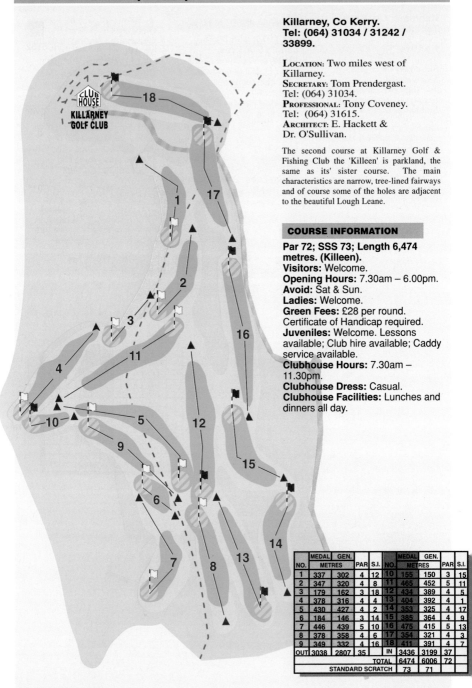

Killarney, Co Kerry.
**Tel: (064) 31034 / 31242 /
33899.**

LOCATION: Two miles west of
Killarney.
SECRETARY: Tom Prendergast.
Tel: (064) 31034.
PROFESSIONAL: Tony Coveney.
Tel: (064) 31615.
ARCHITECT: E. Hackett &
Dr. O'Sullivan.

The second course at Killarney Golf &
Fishing Club the 'Killeen' is parkland, the
same as its' sister course.   The main
characteristics are narrow, tree-lined fairways
and of course some of the holes are adjacent
to the beautiful Lough Leane.

COURSE INFORMATION

**Par 72; SSS 73; Length 6,474
metres. (Killeen).**
Visitors: Welcome.
Opening Hours: 7.30am – 6.00pm.
Avoid: Sat & Sun.
Ladies: Welcome.
Green Fees: £28 per round.
Certificate of Handicap required.
Juveniles: Welcome. Lessons
available; Club hire available; Caddy
service available.
Clubhouse Hours: 7.30am –
11.30pm.
Clubhouse Dress: Casual.
Clubhouse Facilities: Lunches and
dinners all day.

NO.	MEDAL METRES	GEN.	PAR	S.I.	NO.	MEDAL METRES	GEN.	PAR	S.I.
1	337	302	4	12	10	155	150	3	15
2	347	320	4	8	11	465	452	5	11
3	179	162	3	18	12	434	389	4	5
4	378	316	4	4	13	404	392	4	1
5	430	427	4	2	14	353	325	4	17
6	184	146	3	14	15	385	364	4	9
7	446	439	5	10	16	475	415	5	13
8	378	358	4	6	17	354	321	4	3
9	349	332	4	16	18	411	391	4	7
OUT	3038	2807	35		IN	3436	3199	37	
					TOTAL	6474	6006	72	
					STANDARD SCRATCH	73	71		

**O'Mahoney's Point,
Killarney,
Co. Kerry.
Tel: (064) 31034 / 31242 /
33899.**

LOCATION: Two miles west of Killarney.
SECRETARY: Tom Prendergast. Tel: (064) 31034 Fax: (064) 33065.
PROFESSIONAL: Tony Coveney. Tel: (064) 31615.
ARCHITECT: Sir Guy Campbell - O'Mahony's Point.

Two parkland courses occupying a site of great natural beauty, both courses adjacent to Lough Leane, with the mountains of Kerry rising on the other side of the lake. The additional eighteen holes were completed in 1971 and the new holes were mixed with the old to form the two courses – 'Killeen' and 'O'Mahony's Point'

COURSE INFORMATION

Par 72; SSS 72; Length 6152 mtrs (O'Mahony's Point).
Visitors: Welcome..
Opening Hours: 7.30am – 6.00pm.
Avoid: Sunday.
Ladies: Welcome to play every day.
Green Fees: £28 per round. Certificate of Handicap required.
Juveniles: Welcome to play every day.
Clubhouse Hours: 7.30am – 11.30pm.
Clubhouse Dress: Casual.
Clubhouse Facilities: Professional shop. Lunches and dinners all day.

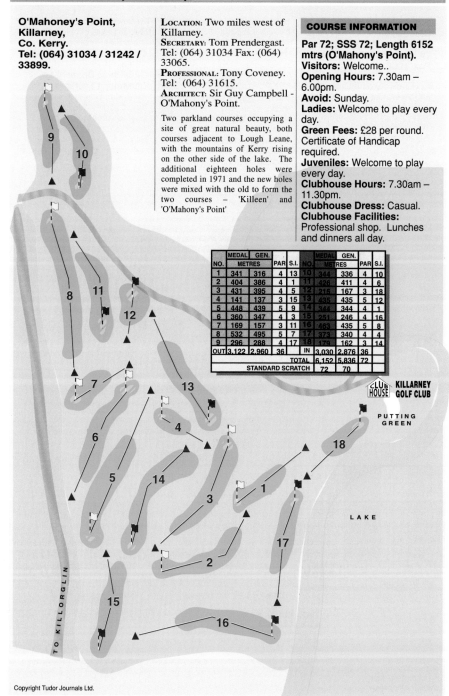

NO.	MEDAL METRES	GEN. METRES	PAR	S.I.	NO.	MEDAL METRES	GEN. METRES	PAR	S.I.
1	341	316	4	13	10	344	336	4	10
2	404	386	4	1	11	426	411	4	6
3	431	395	4	5	12	215	167	3	18
4	141	137	3	15	13	435	435	5	12
5	448	439	5	9	14	344	344	4	1
6	360	347	4	3	15	251	246	4	16
7	169	157	3	11	16	463	435	5	8
8	532	495	5	7	17	373	340	4	4
9	296	288	4	17	18	179	162	3	14
OUT	3,122	2,960	36		IN	3,030	2,876	36	
					TOTAL	6,152	5,836	72	
					STANDARD SCRATCH	72	70		

KILLARNEY GOLF CLUB

**Killorglin Golf Club,
Steelrue,
Killorglin. Co. Kerry.
Tel: (066) 61979/62078.
Fax. (066) 61437.**

LOCATION: Two miles from
Killorglin, on Tralee Road, 14
miles from Kilarney.
SECRETARY: Barry Harmon.
Tel: (066) 61979.
ARCHITECT: Eddie Hackett.

Eddie Hackett has made marvellous
use of the dramatic physical features

of the lands in providing golf shots
that are delightful & challenging
territory in Ireland. It offers a new &
exciting challenge to visiting golfers.

COURSE INFORMATION

**Par 72; SSS 71; Length 6464
yds.
Visitors:** Welcome at all
times.
Opening Hours: Sunrise -
Sunset.
Ladies: Welcome at all times.

Green Fees: Mon - Fri £12;
Sat, Sun & Bank Hols £14.
Juveniles: Welcome.
Clubhouse Hours: 8.30am –
11.30pm.
Clubhouse Dress: Casual.
Clubhouse Facilites:
Pro-shop, Bar and Food all
day. Caddies available by
prior arrangement. For
reservations Tel: Eileen or
Billy.

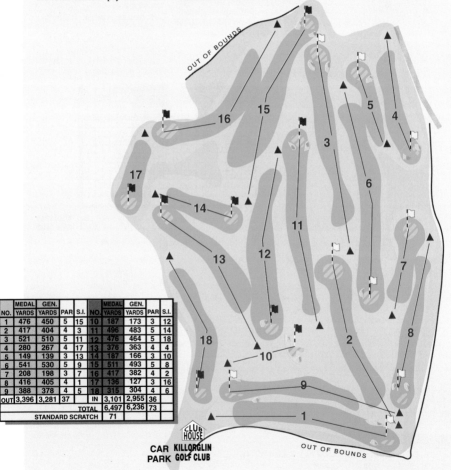

NO.	MEDAL YARDS	GEN. YARDS	PAR	S.I.	NO.	MEDAL YARDS	GEN. YARDS	PAR	S.I.
1	476	450	5	15	10	187	173	3	12
2	417	404	4	3	11	496	483	5	14
3	521	510	5	11	12	476	464	5	18
4	280	267	4	17	13	376	363	4	4
5	149	139	3	13	14	187	166	3	10
6	541	530	5	9	15	511	493	5	8
7	208	198	3	7	16	417	382	4	2
8	416	405	4	1	17	136	127	3	16
9	388	378	4	5	18	315	304	4	6
OUT	3,396	3,281	37		IN	3,101	2,955	36	
					TOTAL	6,497	6,236	73	
					STANDARD SCRATCH	71			

CLUB HOUSE

CAR **KILLORGLIN**
PARK **GOLF CLUB**

Bunker positions indicated.
Copyright Tudor Journals Ltd.

Parknasilla Great Southern Hotel, Sneem, Co. Kerry.
Tel: (064) 45122.

LOCATION: Parknasilla.
SECRETARY: Mr. J. Feeney.
Tel: (064) 45122.
PROFESSIONAL: Charles McCarthy.
Tel: (064) 45172.

Well laid out course in beautiful scenery overlooking Kenmare Bay. The course is part of the Parknasilla Great Southern Hotel and golfers have the added advantage of having these facilities available to them.

COURSE INFORMATION

Par 69; SSS 64; Length 4886 yds, 4467 mtrs.
Visitors: Welcome..
Opening Hours: 8.00am - 7.00pm.
Ladies: Welcome.
Green Fees: £10.
Juveniles: Welcome.
Lessons available by prior arrangement; Club Hire available; Caddy Service available by prior arrangment; Telephone appointment required.
Clubhouse Facilities: Limited catering facilities at hotel.
Open Competitions: Small competitions throughout the year. Open weekend, August.

NO.	YARDS	PAR	S.I.	NO.	YARDS	PAR	S.I.
1	314	4	7	10	269	4	10
2	116	3	17	11	116	3	18
3	432	4	3	12	477	5	6
4	279	4	13	13	278	4	14
5	275	4	11	14	275	4	12
6	251	4	5	15	255	4	4
7	96	3	15	16	101	3	16
8	383	4	1	17	392	4	2
9	283	4	9	18	294	4	8
OUT	2,429	34		IN	2,457	35	
				TOTAL	4,886	69	
				STANDARD SCRATCH	64		

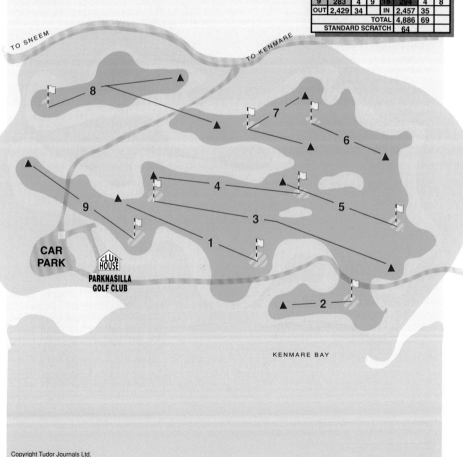

TO SNEEM

TO KENMARE

8   7   6   4   5   9   3   1   2

CAR PARK

CLUB HOUSE

PARKNASILLA GOLF CLUB

KENMARE BAY

**West Barrow, Ardfert,
Co. Kerry.
Tel: (066) 36379.
Fax: (066) 36008.**

LOCATION: Barrow.
SECRETARY: Peter Colleran.
ARCHITECT: Arnold Palmer.
Tel: (066) 36379.

Challenging course with the first nine relatively flat holes, set on cliff top; the second nine by contrast are built on dunes. The course is set amidst the beautiful scenery associated with the Kerry region. Tralee is the first Arnold Palmer designed course in Europe.

COURSE INFORMATION

Par 71; SSS 73; Length 6252 mtrs.
Visitors: Welcome up to 4.30pm.
Limited green fees Weds/Weekends.
Opening Hours: 8.00am – Sunset
(summer); 9.00am – Sunset (winter).
Members: Wednesday.
Green Fees: £25 Mon – Fri; £30
Sat/Sun.
Juveniles: Welcome. Caddy
Service available by prior
arrangement; Handicap Certificate
required. Telephone appointment
required.
Clubhouse Hours: 10.00am –
10.00pm (summer); 10.00am –
6.00pm (winter) Golf Shop open.
Clubhouse Dress: Casual – no
beach wear.
Clubhouse Facilities: Lunch, dinner,
snacks available all day.

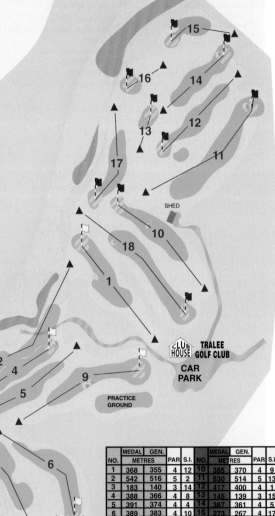

NO.	MEDAL METRES	GEN.	PAR	S.I.	NO.	MEDAL METRES	GEN.	PAR	S.I.
1	368	355	4	12	10	385	370	4	9
2	542	516	5	2	11	530	514	5	13
3	183	140	3	14	12	417	400	4	1
4	388	366	4	8	13	145	139	3	15
5	391	374	4	4	14	367	361	4	5
6	389	383	4	10	15	273	267	4	17
7	143	135	3	18	16	181	152	3	11
8	354	339	4	6	17	323	304	4	7
9	451	443	5	16	18	422	403	4	3
OUT	3,209	3,051	36		IN	3,043	2,910	35	
					TOTAL	6,252	5,961	71	
					STANDARD SCRATCH	73	71		

Bunker & tree positions indicated.
Copyright Tudor Journals Ltd.

Ring of Kerry, Waterville, Co. Kerry.
Tel: (0667) 4102
Fax: (0667) 4482.
LOCATION: One mile outside village.
SECRETARY: Noel J. Cronin. Tel: (066) 74102/74545.
PROFESSIONAL: Liam Higgins. Tel: (0667) 4237.
ARCHITECT: J. A. Mulcahy/E. Hackett.

Waterville features finely manicured fairways and greens with limited water on the course. Panoramic views from the back nine of the Atlantic Ocean and Kerry Mountains. Spectacular Par 3's. Driving Range on course. The course is long, however not hilly, so a pleasant 18 hole walk is enjoyed. Each hole has individual characteristics and every club in the bag will be needed.

COURSE INFORMATION

Par 72; SSS 74;
Length 7184 yds.
Visitors: Welcome any day.
Opening Hours: 7.30am – 7.30pm.
Ladies: Welcome.
Green Fees: £40 inc VAT.
Juveniles: Welcome. Lessons available by prior arrangements; Club Hire available; Caddy service available (May – Sept); Handicap Certificate required for open competitions; Telephone appointment advised.
Clubhouse Hours: 7.00am – 11.00pm; Full clubhouse facilities.
Clubhouse Facilities: Breakfast on request; Dining room facilities available from 11.30am – 7pm. Snacks served through the day.
Open Competitions: June/July by invitation.

(Course map showing holes 1–18, with labels: SHELTER, TOILET, PRACTICE GROUND, PUTTING GREEN, WATERVILLE GOLF CLUB, CLUB HOUSE, PRO SHOP)

NO.	MEDAL YARDS	GEN. YARDS	PAR	S.I.	NO.	MEDAL YARDS	GEN. YARDS	PAR	S.I.
1	430	395	4	11	10	475	450	4	2
2	469	425	4	1	11	496	477	5	10
3	417	362	4	3	12	200	154	3	18
4	179	160	3	15	13	518	480	5	14
5	595	525	5	9	14	456	410	4	4
6	371	343	4	13	15	392	365	4	6
7	178	155	3	17	16	350	330	4	12
8	435	410	4	5	17	196	153	3	16
9	445	405	4	7	18	582	550	5	8
OUT	3,519	3,180	35		IN	3,665	3,369	37	
					TOTAL	7,184	6,549	72	
					STANDARD SCRATCH	74	72		

Adare Golf Club, Adare, Co. Limerick.
Tel: (061) 396566.
Fax: (061) 396124.

ARHITECT: Robert Trent Jones Snr.

Adare Manor has entered a new era with the introduction of the Adare Golf Club, a world class Championship Golf Course. The Golf Course measuring 7,138 yards off the Championship tees will open in July 1995. The design of the course with four tees on each hole ensures that every level of golfer will enjoy their game.

COURSE INFORMATION

Par 72; Length 7,138 Yards.
Visitors: Welcome.
Opening Hours: Dawn – Dusk.
Green Fees: £33.75 (residents) £28.14 (non residents); Group rate (minimum 30) £30 per person.
Clubhouse Dress: Formal.

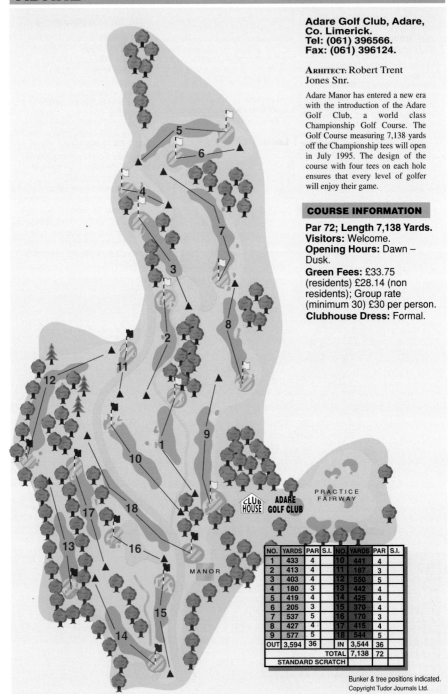

NO.	YARDS	PAR	S.I.	NO.	YARDS	PAR	S.I.
1	433	4		10	441	4	
2	413	4		11	187	3	
3	403	4		12	550	5	
4	180	3		13	442	4	
5	419	4		14	425	4	
6	205	3		15	370	4	
7	537	5		16	170	3	
8	427	4		17	415	4	
9	577	5		18	544	5	
OUT	3,594	36		IN	3,544	36	
				TOTAL	7,138	72	
STANDARD SCRATCH							

PRACTICE FAIRWAY

CLUB HOUSE ADARE GOLF CLUB

MANOR

Bunker & tree positions indicated.
Copyright Tudor Journals Ltd.

Adare, Co. Limerick.
Tel: (061) 396204.

LOCATION: Ten miles from Limerick City.
SECRETARY: T. P. Healy.
Tel: (061) 396407.

Adare is a parkland course, which is particularly scenic. The Abbey and Desmond Castle are unique features to the course. There are three Par 5's and six Par 3's over the eighteen holes. The fairways are narrow and well maintained.

COURSE INFORMATION

Par 70; SSS 69; Length 5706 mtrs.
Visitors: Welcome all days. Booking required for weekends.
Opening Hours: 9.00am – Sunset.
Ladies: Welcome.
Ladies Day: Thursday, although anyone can play.
Green Fees: £15 Mon – Fri. & £20 Weekends.

Juveniles: Welcome, but accompanied by an adult. Club Hire available; Caddy service available by prior arrangements.
Clubhouse Hours: 10.00am closing time.
Clubhouse Dress: Casual – no shorts.
Clubhouse Facilities: Snacks, fast food and meals (booked in advance). Pro – shop.
Open Competitions: June & August.

ADARE MANOR GOLF CLUB

CLUB HOUSE

CEMETARY

ABBEY

RIVER MAIGUE

NO.	MEDAL YARDS	GEN. YARDS	PAR	S.I.	NO.	MEDAL YARDS	GEN. YARDS	PAR	S.I.
1	138	127	3	15	10	168	150	3	18
2	402	383	4	3	11	335	318	4	12
3	460	440	5	9	12	143	128	3	16
4	315	304	4	17	13	515	499	5	8
5	376	335	4	1	14	190	174	3	10
6	167	147	3	11	15	360	353	4	6
7	383	366	4	5	16	421	412	4	2
8	215	193	3	7	17	272	262	4	14
9	476	454	5	13	18	370	351	5	4
OUT	2,932	2,749	35		IN	2,774	2,647	35	
					TOTAL	5,706	5,396	70	
		STANDARD SCRATCH	69				67		

Castletroy,
Co. Limerick.
Tel: (061) 335261.

LOCATION: Less than three miles from Limerick City on N7 to Dublin.
SECRETARY: Laurence Hayes.
Tel: (061) 335753.

Parkland course with out of bounds on the left for the first two holes. Well maintained fairways are tree lined demanding accuracy off the tee. The long Par 5 10th features a narrow entrance to the green with a stream to catch the more adventurous. The par 3 13th features a panoramic view from the tee while the picturesque 18th is a stern test to finish with the green guarded by bunkers on both sides.

COURSE INFORMATION

Par 71; SSS 71; Length 6335 yds, 5793 mtrs.
Visitors: Welcome most weekday mornings. Some afternoons may be booked by societies (check in advance).
Avoid: Thursday afternoon; Weekends; Tuesday is Ladies Day (some restriction).
Green Fees: £20 (£12 with a member). Group rate on request.
Juveniles: Must be accompanied by an adult. Lessons available by prior arrangements; Club Hire available; Caddy service available by prior arrangements.
Clubhouse Hours: 8.00am – 11.30pm.
Clubhouse Dress: Casual.
Clubhouse Facilities: Bar snacks available all day; last orders for full meals 9.30pm. Bar service as per licencing hours.

NO.	METRES	PAR	S.I.	NO.	METRES	PAR	S.I.
1	339	4	4	10	458	5	11
2	323	4	10	11	326	4	9
3	337	4	8	12	306	4	5
4	335	4	12	13	159	3	15
5	396	4	2	14	312	4	13
6	420	5	18	15	407	4	1
7	134	3	16	16	116	3	17
8	330	4	6	17	367	4	7
9	329	4	14	18	399	4	3
OUT	2,943	36		IN	2,850	35	
				TOTAL	5,793	71	
				STANDARD SCRATCH	71		

CAR PARK

CLUB HOUSE

STREAM

CASTLETROY GOLF CLUB

Bunker positions indicated.
Copyright Tudor Journals Ltd.

KILLELINE

MUNSTER **LIMERICK**

**Killeline golf Club, Cork Road, Newcastle West, Co. Limerick.
Tel: (069) 62853.**

LOCATION: 25 miles from Limerick City, off Killarney Road.
SECRETARY: John Devine.
Tel: (069) 61600.

Killeline is an 18 hole parkland course. Wooded with over 3000 decidious trees giving all fairways a clear definition, two good par '5's and four challenging par '3's.

COURSE INFORMATION

**Par 70; Length 5,724 yards.
Visitors:** Welcome.
Opening Hours: 9am – sunset.
Avoid: Sundays.
Ladies: Welcome.
Green Fees: £10 Mon – Fri.
Juveniles: Welcome but accompanied by adult.
Clubhouse Hours: 10am – closing time.
Clubhouse Dress: Casual, no shorts.
Clubhouse Facilities: Bar food, full meals (booked in advance) & pro-shop.
Open Competitions: June,. July & August.

NO.	YARDS	PAR	S.I.	NO.	METRES	PAR	S.I.
1	282	4		10	331	4	
2	127	3		11	361	4	
3	277	4		12	341	4	
4	336	4		13	470	5	
5	404	4		14	144	3	
6	451	5		15	330	4	
7	409	4		16	180	3	
8	432	4		17	282	4	
9	160	3		18	407	4	
OUT	2,878	35		IN	2,846	35	
				TOTAL	5,724	70	
STANDARD SCRATCH							

Bunker and tree positions indicated.
Copyright Tudor Journals Ltd.

295

Ballyclough, Limerick.
Tel: (061) 414083/415146.

LOCATION: Three miles South of Limerick City.
SECRETARY: Declan McDonogh.
Tel: (061) 415146.
PROFESSIONAL: John Cassidy.
Tel: (061) 412492.

A parkland course with tree lined fairways. Pleasant surroundings, situated on a hill overlooking the city of Limerick.

COURSE INFORMATION

Par 72; SSS 71; Length 6551 yds, 5656 mtrs.
Visitors: Welcome up to 4.00pm Mon, Wed, Fri; Thurs am only.
Opening Hours: 8.30am - Sunset.
Avoid: Tuesday (Ladies Day) and weekends.
Ladies: Welcome. Lessons available by prior arrangements; Club Hire available; Caddy service available by prior arrangements; Telephone appointment advisable.
Green Fees: £20 (with member £12).
Clubhouse Hours: 9.30am - 11.00pm; Full clubhouse facilities.
Clubhouse Dress: Casual.
Clubhouse Facilities: Full service from 12.00 noon.
Open Competitions: Mainly holiday weekends.

NO.	MEDAL METRES	GEN. METRES	PAR	S.I.	NO.	MEDAL METRES	GEN. METRES	PAR	S.I.
1	326	309	4	9	10	397	379	4	2
2	439	426	5	15	11	341	328	4	11
3	427	419	4	1	12	372	370	4	6
4	349	337	4	5	13	280	273	4	17
5	158	153	3	16	14	140	132	3	14
6	466	456	5	7	15	344	297	4	4
7	378	369	4	3	16	305	287	4	10
8	122	110	3	18	17	344	318	4	8
9	450	438	5	13	18	316	312	4	12
OUT	3,115	3,017			IN	2,841	2,696	35	
					TOTAL	5,956	5,713		
					STANDARD SCRATCH	71	70		

REAR ENTRANCE

CLUB HOUSE

LIMERICK GOLF CLUB

MAIN ENTRANCE

Bunker positions indicated.
Copyright Tudor Journals Ltd.

Limerick County Golf & Country Club, Ballyneety. Co. Limerick.
Tel: (061) 351881.
Fax: (061) 351384.

LOCATION: 5 miles south of Limerick City on the R512, direction Kilmallock..
SECRETARY: Vari McGreevy. Tel: (061) 351881.
PROFESSIONAL: Philip Murphy. Tel: 061 351881.
ARCHITECT: Des Smyth & Associates.

18 hole championship standard golf course, set on 230 acres of undulating sand-based terrain, ensuring that it is playable 12 months of the year. The course boasts many interesting sand and water hazards. A uniquely-shaped circular clubhouse provides panoramic views of over 50% of the course and the surrounding countryside. Other facilities include riving range, three hole short-game area, 4 star luxury holiday cottage accommodation.

COURSE INFORMATION

Par 72; SSS 74; Length 6712 yds, 6137 mtrs.
Visitors: Welcome seven days a week. Weekdays 9am – 1pm and 2pm – 5pm. Weekends 10am – 1.30pm.
Opening Hours: 7am to Sunset.
Avoid: After 1.30pm

weekends.
Ladies: Max. handicap 36.
Green Fees: For 1996: £20 per round all week. £12.50 before 9.30am and after 6pm all week. Group rates available.
Juveniles: Welcome.
Clubhouse Hours: 8am – 12pm.
Clubhouse Dress: Jacket or smart casual wear.
Clubhouse Facilities: Full bar & restaurant services. Clubhouse tuition available. Clubs, caddy cars and caddies on request.

NO.	MEDAL METRES	GEN. METRES	PAR	S.I.	NO.	MEDAL METRES	GEN. METRES	PAR	S.I.
1	373	352	4	9	10	330	307	4	12
2	145	119	3	17	11	444	421	5	18
3	367	354	4	5	12	288	285	4	6
4	489	452	5	7	13	448	420	5	16
5	408	384	4	1	14	350	326	4	14
6	169	145	3	15	15	178	164	3	4
7	283	261	4	13	16	370	349	4	10
8	386	364	4	3	17	321	301	4	8
9	379	353	4	11	18	409	381	4	2
OUT	2,999	2,784	35		IN	3,138	2,954	37	
					TOTAL	6,137	5,738	72	
					STANDARD SCRATCH	74	72		

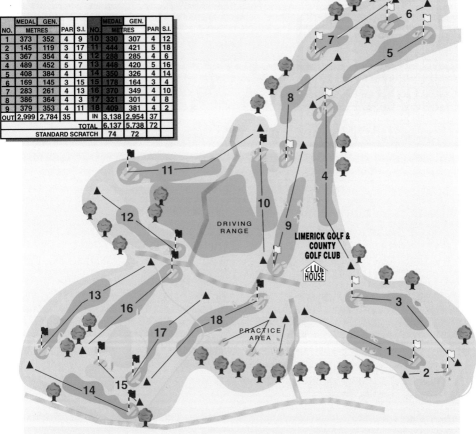

Bunker & tree positions indicated.

Newcastle West Golf Club,
Ardagh, Co. Limerick.
Tel: (069) 76500.
Fax: (069) 76511.

LOCATION: Three miles from Newcastlewest.
SECRETARY: Patrick Lyons.
Tel: (069) 76500.
ARCHITECT: A. Spring.
Set in 150 acres of unspoilt rolling West Limerick countryside. Newcastle West comprises an 18 hole championship course built to the highest standards on sandy free raining soil which will be playable all the year round. A practice ground and driving range are included.

COURSE INFORMATION

Par 71; SSS 73; Length 5,905 metres.
Visitors: Welcome.
Opening Hours: 9.00am – Sunset.

Avoid: Thursday evenings and Sunday mornings.
Ladies: Welcome.
Ladies Day: Play any day.
Green Fees: £15.
Clubhouse Hours: 10.00am - 11.00pm.
Clubhouse Dress: Casual.
Clubhouse Facilities: Full meals, snacks & Pro-shop.
Open Competitions: Open Fourball, June & other times.

NO.	MEDAL METRES	GEN. METRES	PAR	S.I.	NO.	MEDAL METRES	GEN. METRES	PAR	S.I.
1	434	446	5	13	10	162	176	3	14
2	319	329	4	15	11	323	365	4	16
3	157	179	3	17	12	284	337	4	18
4	287	309	4	9	13	286	296	4	8
5	359	383	4	7	14	463	469	5	6
6	158	179	3	11	15	296	311	4	10
7	318	358	4	1	16	347	373	4	12
8	459	469	5	3	17	162	160	3	2
9	321	340	4	5	18	384	406	4	4
OUT	2,812	2,992	36		IN	2,709	2,913	35	
					TOTAL	5,521	5,905	71	
					STANDARD SCRATCH		73		

NEWCASTLE WEST CLUBHOUSE

Tree positions indicated.
Copyright Tudor Journals Ltd.

Ballykisteen Golf Club, Monard, Co. Tipperary.
Tel: (062) 33333.
Fax: (062) 33668.

LOCATION: Centrally located on the M24 – two miles from Tipperary Town and within a twenty minute drive of Limerick City.
SECRETARY: Josephine Ryan. Tel: (062) 33333.
PROFESSIONAL: David Reddan.
ARCHITECT: Ryder Cup star Des Symth.

A parkland course, nestled in emerald green countryside in the heart of the Golden Vale. A very interesting and clever design has made this a course suitable to the high and low handicap golfer.

COURSE INFORMATION

Par 72; SSS 74; Length 6,765 Yards.
Green Fees: £20

Juveniles: Club hire available, Caddy service available by prior arrangement, Fully equipped Professional shop, Group and individual tuition and a Floodlit driving range.

Clubhouse Facilities: Elegant restaurant and bar – open to the general public.

NO.	CHAMP YARDS	MEDAL YARDS	PAR	S.I.	NO.	CHAMP YARDS	MEDAL YARDS	PAR	S.I.
1	371	353	4	6	10	415	392	4	1
2	446	409	4	2	11	417	393	4	3
3	171	171	3	18	12	509	493	5	15
4	534	510	5	8	13	169	155	3	13
5	395	345	4	10	14	394	354	4	11
6	513	490	5	12	15	226	168	3	7
7	394	357	4	14	16	389	346	4	17
8	335	314	4	4	17	371	362	4	5
9	170	156	3	16	18	546	516	5	9
OUT	3,329	3,105	36		IN	3,436	3,179	36	
					TOTAL	6,765	6,284	72	
					STANDARD SCRATCH	74	72		

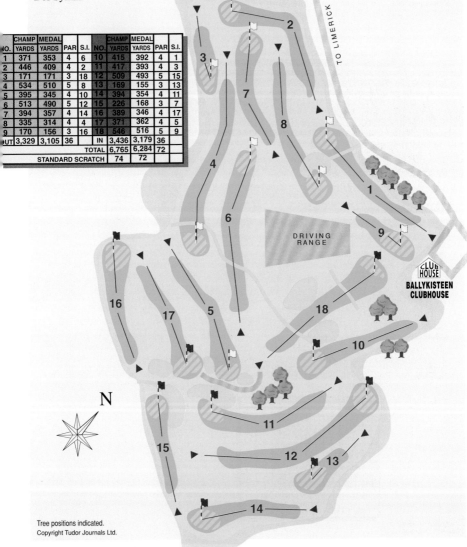

DRIVING RANGE

CLUB HOUSE

BALLYKISTEEN CLUBHOUSE

TO LIMERICK

N

Tree positions indicated.
Copyright Tudor Journals Ltd.

Kilcommon,
Cahir,
Co. Tipperary.
Tel: (052) 41474.

LOCATION: One mile from town centre.
SECRETARY: Michael Fitzgerald.
PROFESSIONAL: Dominic Foran. Tel: (062) 62111.
ARCHITECT: E. Hackett.

Prime parkland, part of old Cahir Park Estate. Sloping down to River Suir which runs along the right hand side of the 7th hole, this hole is rated as one of the most difficult on the course.

COURSE INFORMATION

Par70; SSS 69; Length 5,740 mtrs.
Visitors: Welcome.
Opening Hours: Sunrise - Sunset.
Avoid: Major club competition days. Sat/Sun in June/Aug.
Green Fees: £10.

Green Fees: £10
Juveniles: Welcome at times when course is available.
Clubhouse Hours: 10.30am - 11.00pm.
Clubhouse Dress: Casual.
Clubhouse Facilities: Full clubhouse facilites, tea coffee and snacks most days. Meals by prior arrangement.
Open Competitions: Open week (May); Bank holiday weekends.

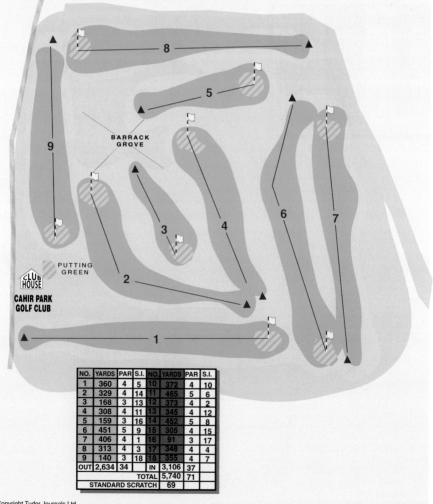

NO.	YARDS	PAR	S.I.	NO.	YARDS	PAR	S.I.
1	360	4	5	10	372	4	10
2	329	4	14	11	465	5	6
3	168	3	13	12	373	4	2
4	308	4	11	13	345	4	12
5	159	3	16	14	452	5	8
6	451	5	9	15	305	4	15
7	406	4	1	16	91	3	17
8	313	4	3	17	348	4	4
9	140	3	18	18	355	4	7
OUT	2,634	34		IN	3,106	37	
				TOTAL	5,740	71	
				STANDARD SCRATCH	69		

**Garravoone,
Carrick-On-Suir
Co. Tipperary.
Tel: (051) 640047.**

LOCATION: 1 mile from
Carrick-On-Suir on
Dargarvan Road.
SECRETARY: Gerard Grant.
Tel: (051) 95323.
ARCHITECT: E.Hackett.

Carrick on Suir is a scenic nine hole
course on elevated ground close to
the town. The Comeragh Mountains
are on one side as a backdrop to the
first five holes and the River Suir in

the valley winds its way to the sea at
Waterford. The scenery will keep the
golfer occupied if the game is not
going to plan.

COURSE INFORMATION

**Par 70; SSS 68; Length
5948 yds.**
Visitors: Welcome Mon-Sat.
Opening Hours: Sunrise -
Sunset.
Avoid: Mon-Wed in summer
after 5.00pm; Wed Ladies
Day.
Ladies: Welcome. Caddy
service available; Handicap
Certificate required.

Green Fees: £10 Mon-Sat.
Juveniles: Welcome,
telephone appointment
required.
Clubhouse Hours:
10.00pm –11.00pm Mon-Fri;
9.00am – 11.00pm Sat/Sun
(summer); Thurs 2.00pm –
7.00pm; Sat/Sun 9.00am –
9.00pm (winter).
Clubhouse Dress: Casual
but neat.
Catering Facilities: Full
meals and snacks available
by prior arrangement.
Open Competitions:
Tipperary Crystal Open
Week, August .

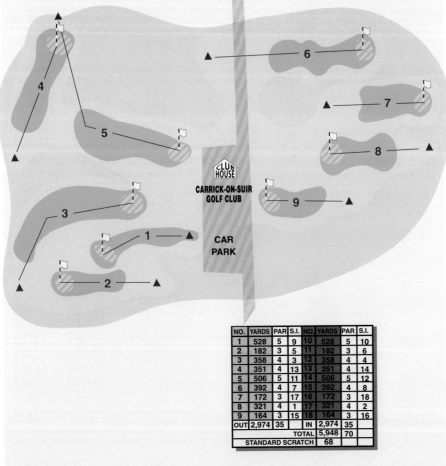

CARRICK-ON-SUIR
GOLF CLUB

CAR
PARK

NO.	YARDS	PAR	S.I.	NO.	YARDS	PAR	S.I.
1	528	5	9	10	528	5	10
2	182	3	5	11	182	3	6
3	358	4	3	12	358	4	4
4	351	4	13	13	351	4	14
5	506	5	11	14	506	5	12
6	392	4	7	15	392	4	8
7	172	3	17	16	172	3	18
8	321	4	1	17	321	4	2
9	164	3	15	18	164	3	16
OUT	2,974	35		IN	2,974	35	
				TOTAL	5,948	70	
				STANDARD SCRATCH		68	

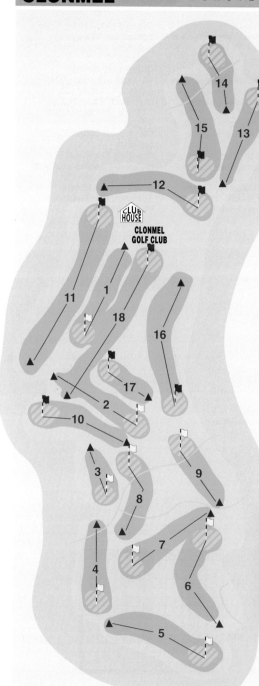

Lyneanearla, Mountain Road, Clonel, Co. Tipperary. Tel: (052) 21138.

LOCATION: 3 miles from Clonmel.
SECRETARY/MANAGER: Aine Myles-Keating.
Tel: (052) 24050.
PROFESSIONAL: Robert Hayes.
ARCHITECT: Eddie Hackett.

Clonmel is a very pleasant inland course with lots of open space and plenty of variety. There is a stream that crosses three fairways and has the advantage of a picturesque setting on the scenic slopes of the pine and fir covered Comeragh Mountains overlooking the plains of Tipperary.

COURSE INFORMATION

Par 71; SSS 70; Length 5,785 Metres.
Opening Hours: 8am – 10pm.
Visitors: Welcome.
Green Fees: £13 Mon – Fri ; £15 Sat,Sun & Bank Hols (with member £10).
Ladies: Welcome.
Juveniles: Welcome. Lessons by prior arrangement. Club hire available. Caddies by prior arrangement. Telephone appointment required for societies.
Clubhouse Hours: 8.30am – 11pm.
Clubhouse Facilities: Catering – soup and sandwhiches. Lunch and dinner bt prior arrangements.
Clubhouse Dress: Casual.

NO.	MEDAL METRES	GEN. METRES	PAR	S.I.	NO.	MEDAL METRES	GEN. METRES	PAR	S.I.
1	343	332	4	12	10	355	344	4	11
2	368	357	4	4	11	456	441	5	13
3	131	120	3	18	12	273	262	4	17
4	448	429	5	14	13	385	370	4	1
5	341	322	4	10	14	174	163	3	3
6	344	333	4	6	15	347	317	4	7
7	306	295	4	16	16	382	371	4	5
8	347	317	4	2	17	170	159	3	9
9	167	137	3	8	18	448	415	5	15
OUT	2,795	2,642	35		IN	2,990	2,824	36	
					TOTAL	5,785	5,484	71	
					STANDARD SCRATCH	70	69		

NENAGH

**Beecwood, Nenagh,
Co. Tipperary.
Tel: (067) 31476.**

LOCATION: 4 miles from
Nenagh town.
SECRETARY: L. Cashhell.
Tel: 412229.
ARCHITECT: R. Stillwell/J.
Paramour.

This course features panoramic views
from some tees, and requires driving
and approach shots to several sloping,

two tier greens. It is playable all year
except in extremely adverse weather
conditions.

COURSE INFORMATION

**Par 69; SSS 68; Length 5,491
Metres.
Visitors:** Welcome Mon-Fri
Avoid: Tuesday
Opening Hours: Sunrise –
Sunset.
Ladies: Welcome.
Ladies Day: Thursday.

Green Fees:£12 Mon-Fri. £16
Sat-Sun; £5 for students and
juveniles.
Juveniles: Welcome.
Clubhouse Hours:
10.00am-11.00pm;
Clubhouse Dress: Casual.
Clubhouse Facilities: All
catering facilities available.
Open Competitions: Open
week – 1st week in JUne;
Semi-opens – all Bank Holiday
Weekends.

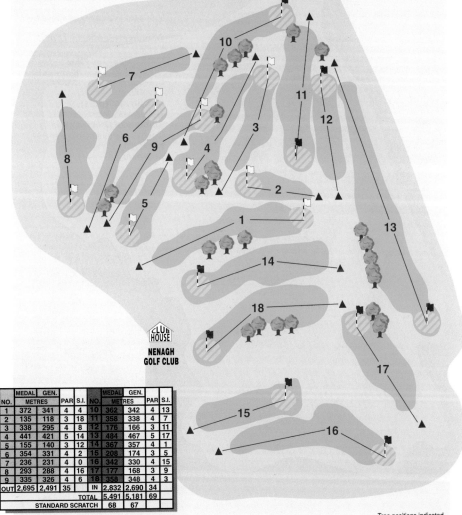

NENAGH
GOLF CLUB

NO.	MEDAL METRES	GEN.	PAR	S.I.	NO.	MEDAL METRES	GEN.	PAR	S.I.
1	372	341	4	4	10	362	342	4	13
2	135	118	3	18	11	358	338	4	7
3	338	295	4	8	12	176	166	3	11
4	441	421	5	14	13	484	467	5	17
5	155	140	3	12	14	367	357	4	1
6	354	331	4	2	15	208	174	3	5
7	236	231	4	0	16	342	330	4	15
8	293	288	4	16	17	177	168	3	9
9	335	326	4	6	18	358	348	4	3
OUT	2,695	2,491	35		IN	2,832	2,690	34	
					TOTAL	5,491	5,181	69	
					STANDARD SCRATCH		68	67	

Copyright Tudor Journals Ltd.

Tree positions indicated.

303

Derryvale, Roscrea.
Co. Tipperary.
Tel: (0505) 21130.

LOCATION: 2 miles east of Roscrea on the N7.
SECRETARY: K. McDonnell.
Tel: (0505) 21130.

A fine 18 hole course with some excellent Par 3's. The last six holes are particularly challenging.

COURSE INFORMATION

Par 71; SSS 70; Length 5,708 mtrs.
Visitors: Welcome Sundays by arrangement.
Opening Hours: 8am to dusk.
Ladies: Welcome.
Ladies Day: Tuesday.
Green Fees:£10 Mon–Fri. £12 Sat–Sun.
Juveniles: Welcome.
Clubhouse Hours: 10.30am-11.30pm;
Clubhouse Dress: Casual.
Open Competitions: Open week, July. Bank holiday weekends.

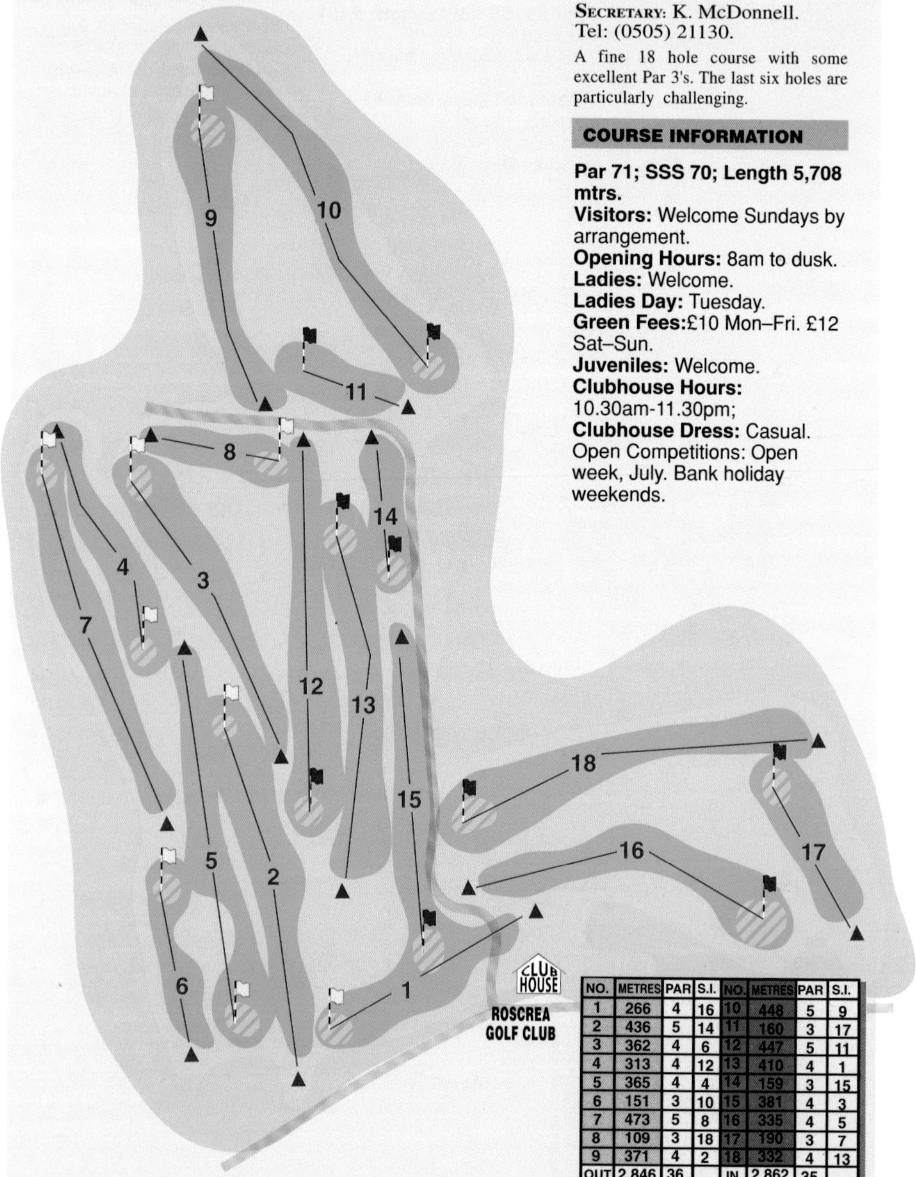

ROSCREA
GOLF CLUB

NO.	METRES	PAR	S.I.	NO.	METRES	PAR	S.I.
1	266	4	16	10	448	5	9
2	436	5	14	11	160	3	17
3	362	4	6	12	447	5	11
4	313	4	12	13	410	4	1
5	365	4	4	14	159	3	15
6	151	3	10	15	381	4	3
7	473	5	8	16	335	4	5
8	109	3	18	17	190	3	7
9	371	4	2	18	332	4	13
OUT	2,846	36		IN	2,862	35	
				TOTAL	5,708	71	
		STANDARD SCRATCH			70		

**Manna South,
Templemore.
Co Tipperary.
Tel: (0504) 31400.**

LOCATION: 1/2 mile from town centre.
SECRETARY: John Moloughney.
Tel: (0504) 31522/31720.

This course provides a pleasant test of golf, starting with a 385 mtrs Par

4. The course has six Par 3's, finishing with a very good Par 5 at the 9th and 18th. It has a very compact layout requiring only short walks from green to tees.

COURSE INFORMATION

Par 68; SSS 67; Length 5112 mtrs.
Visitors: Welcome Mon – Fri.

Avoid: Tuesday.
Opening Hours: 8.00am – Sunset.
Ladies: Welcome
Green Fees: £5 Mon – Sat. £10 Sun & Bank Holidays.
Juveniles: Welcome, new members welcome, apply Honorary Secretary.
Clubhouse Hours: 8.00am – Sunset.
Clubhouse Dress: Casual.
Clubhouse Facilities: By prior arrangement.
Open Competitions: Open week July.

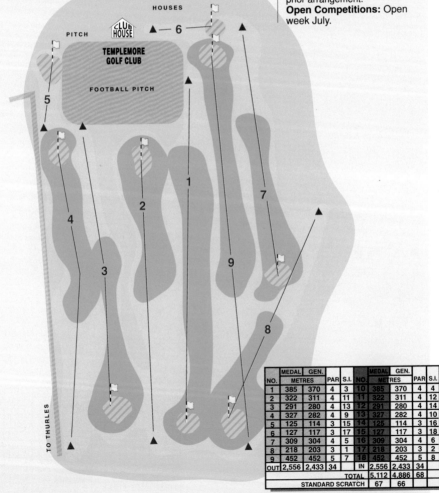

NO.	MEDAL METRES	GEN. METRES	PAR	S.I.	NO.	MEDAL METRES	GEN. METRES	PAR	S.I.
1	385	370	4	3	10	385	370	4	4
2	322	311	4	11	11	322	311	4	12
3	291	280	4	13	12	291	280	4	14
4	327	282	4	9	13	327	282	4	10
5	125	114	3	15	14	125	114	3	16
6	127	117	3	17	15	127	117	3	18
7	309	304	4	5	16	309	304	4	6
8	218	203	3	1	17	218	203	3	2
9	452	452	5	7	18	452	452	5	8
OUT	2,556	2,433	34		IN	2,556	2,433	34	
					TOTAL	5,112	4,886	68	
					STANDARD SCRATCH	67	66		

Turtulla, Thurles.
Co. Tipperary.
Tel: (0504) 22466.

LOCATION: 1 mile from Thurles
town.
SECRETARY: Thomas Ryan.
Tel: (0504) 23787.
PROFESSIONAL: Sean Hunt.
Tel: (0504) 21983.
ARCHITECT: Lionel Hewson.

Fine parkland course, with the main
features being the four excellent Par
3 holes and the fearsome 18th with
the out-of-bounds all the way down
the left. Unusual beginning to your
round with two Par 5's in a row.

COURSE INFORMATION

Par 72; SSS 71; Length
6,456 yds, 5,904 mtrs.
Visitors: Welcome.
Opening Hours: 9.00am –
11.30pm.
Ladies: Welcome.
Avoid: Limited availablity at
weekends.
Green Fees: £15 (£8 with
member).
Juveniles: Welcome, club
hire available; caddy service
and lessons available by prior
arrangement, telephone
appointment required.

Clubhouse Hours: 10.00am
– 11.00pm. Full clubhouse
facilities which include two
championship squash courts.
Limited availability at
weekends.
Clubhouse Dress: Casual.
Clubhouse Facilities: Snacks
at all times; full meals as
ordered..
Open Competitions: June;
Open four ball, July; Open
Week, Aug; Guinness Open
four ball, September.

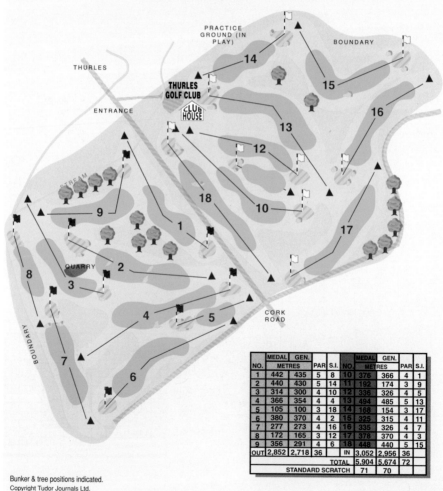

NO.	MEDAL METRES	GEN. METRES	PAR	S.I.	NO.	MEDAL METRES	GEN. METRES	PAR	S.I.
1	442	435	5	8	10	376	366	4	1
2	440	430	5	14	11	192	174	3	9
3	314	300	4	10	12	336	326	4	5
4	366	354	4	4	13	494	485	5	13
5	105	100	3	18	14	168	154	3	17
6	380	370	4	2	15	325	315	4	11
7	277	273	4	16	16	335	326	4	7
8	172	165	3	12	17	378	370	4	3
9	356	291	4	6	18	448	440	5	15
OUT	2,852	2,718	36		IN	3,052	2,956	36	
					TOTAL	5,904	5,674	72	
					STANDARD SCRATCH	71	70		

Bunker & tree positions indicated.
Copyright Tudor Journals Ltd.

306

**County Tipperary Golf &
Country Club,
Dundrum, Co. Tipperary.
Tel: (062) 71116.
Fax: (062) 71366.**

DIRECTOR OF GOLF: William
Crowe. Tel: (062) 71116.

Parkland course playable all year
round subject to weather.

COURSE INFORMATION

**Par 72; SSS 72; Length
6,709 Yards, 6,150 Metres.
Visitors/Societies:** Welcome
anytime.
Opening Hours: 8am –
Sunset.
Ladies: Welcome.
Weekends: Advisable to
book.
Green Fees: £17 midweek,
£20 Weekends.
Juveniles: Welcome
Clubhouse Hours: 11am -
11pm.
Clubhouse Dress: Casual.
Open Competitions: Open
Week, July.

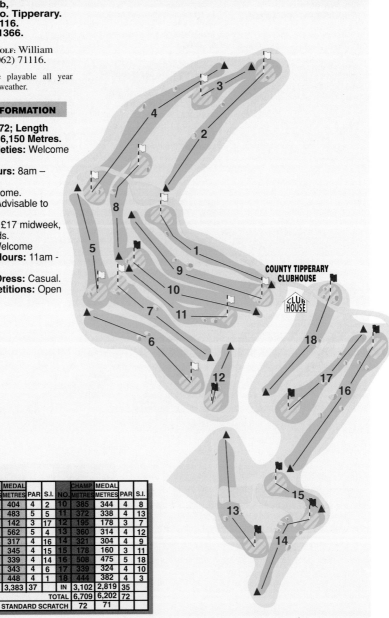

COUNTY TIPPERARY
CLUBHOUSE

CLUB HOUSE

NO.	CHAMP METRES	MEDAL METRES	PAR	S.I.	NO.	CHAMP METRES	MEDAL METRES	PAR	S.I.
1	432	404	4	2	10	385	344	4	8
2	510	483	5	5	11	372	338	4	13
3	168	142	3	17	12	195	178	3	7
4	584	562	5	4	13	360	314	4	12
5	342	317	4	16	14	321	304	4	9
6	366	345	4	15	15	178	160	3	11
7	357	339	4	14	16	508	475	5	18
8	378	343	4	6	17	339	324	4	10
9	470	448	4	1	18	444	382	4	3
OUT	3,607	3,383	37		IN	3,102	2,819	35	
					TOTAL	6,709	6,202	72	
		STANDARD SCRATCH				72	71		

**Knocknagrannagh,
Co. Waterford.
Tel: (058) 41605/43310.
Fax: (058) 44113.**

LOCATION: Dungarvan 2 miles.
On N25 route.
AMINISTRATOR: Tom Whelan.
Tel: (058) 41605/43310.
Fax: (058) 44113.
ARCHITECT: Maurice Fives.

Dungarvan Golf Club is set against
the backdrop of the Comeragh
Mountains and runs adjacent to

Dungavan Bay. This 6,700 yd Par 72
championship course has been
architecturally designed with nine
lakes and man-made hazards
strategically placed to test all levels
of golfer.

COURSE INFORMATION

**Par 72; SSS 73; Length
6708 yds, 6134 mtrs.
Visitors:** Welcome.
Opening Hours: 7.00am –
sunset.
Ladies: Welcome.

Green Fees: Weekdays £14;
Sat/Sun/Bank Holidays £18.
Society outings are welcome.
Special offer for mid-week
reservations.
Juveniles: Welcome.
Clubhouse Hours: 9.00am –
12.00pm.
Clubhouse Dress: Neat at all
times.
Clubhouse Facilities: Include
light meals & full dining room
service.
Open Competitions: Open
weeks, July and September.

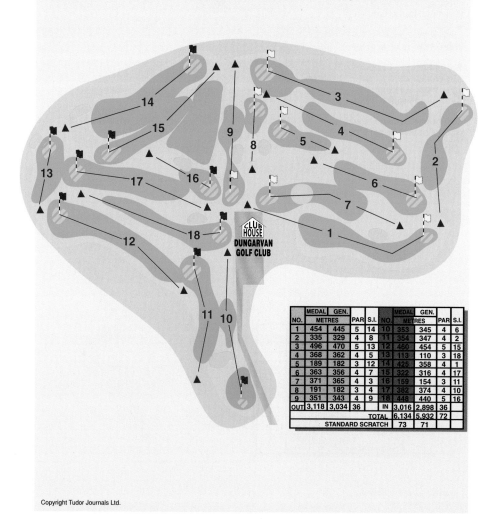

NO.	MEDAL METRES	GEN. METRES	PAR	S.I.	NO.	MEDAL METRES	GEN. METRES	PAR	S.I.
1	454	445	5	14	10	353	345	4	6
2	335	329	4	8	11	354	347	4	2
3	496	470	5	13	12	460	454	5	15
4	368	362	4	5	13	113	110	3	18
5	189	182	3	12	14	425	358	4	1
6	363	356	4	7	15	322	316	4	17
7	371	365	4	3	16	159	154	3	11
8	191	182	3	4	17	382	374	4	10
9	351	343	4	9	18	448	440	5	16
OUT	3,118	3,034	36		IN	3,016	2,898	36	
					TOTAL	6,134	5,932	72	
					STANDARD SCRATCH	73	71		

**Dunmore East Golf & Country Club,
Dunmore East,
Co. Waterford.
Tel: (051) 383151.**

Location: Ten miles from Waterford City in Dunmore East village.
Secretary: Mary Skehan.
Tel: (051) 383151.
Arhitect: William Henry Jones.

This 18 hole course overlooks the village of Dunmore East with panoramic views of the bay and harbour. The course offers challenging golf, in idyllic surroundings, with five holes on the waters edge.

COURSE INFORMATION

Par 72; Length 6,655 Yds.
Visitors: No restrictions.
Opening Hours: Dawn – Dusk.
Ladies: Welcome no restrictions.
Juveniles: Welcome, avoid Sun. mornings.

Green Fees: £10 Weekdays £12 Weekends.
Clubhouse Hours: 10am – 12pm.
Clubhouse Dress: Neat / casual.
Clubhouse Facilities: Full bar, light snacks. Club hire available, caddy by prior arrangement.
Open Competitions: Every Tuesday.

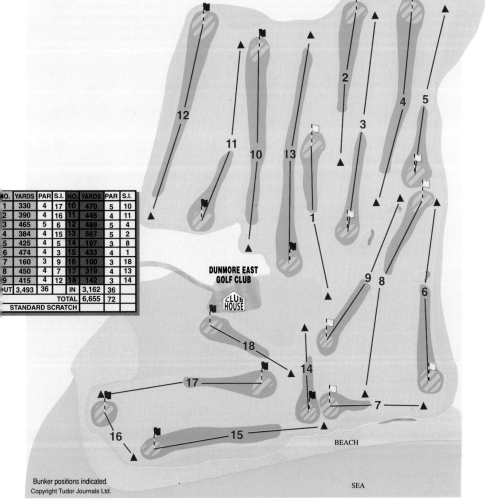

NO.	YARDS	PAR	S.I.	NO.	YARDS	PAR	S.I.
1	330	4	17	10	470	5	10
2	390	4	16	11	445	4	11
3	465	5	6	12	489	5	4
4	384	4	15	13	567	5	2
5	425	4	5	14	197	3	8
6	474	4	3	15	433	4	1
7	160	3	9	16	100	3	18
8	450	4	7	17	319	4	13
9	415	4	12	18	142	3	14
OUT	3,493	36		IN	3,162	36	
				TOTAL	6,655	72	
STANDARD SCRATCH							

DUNMORE EAST
GOLF CLUB

CLUB HOUSE

BEACH

SEA

Bunker positions indicated.
Copyright Tudor Journals Ltd.

FAITHLEGG

M U N S T E R **WATERFORD**

**Faithlegg Golf Club,
Faithlegg House.
Co. Waterford.
Tel: (051) 382241.
Fax: (051) 382664.**

LOCATION: Six miles from
Waterford City, from
Waterford take Dunmore East
road for Cheekpoint village
SECRETARY: Ted Higgins.
Tel: (051) 382241.
PROFESSIONAL: Ted Higgins.
Tel: (051) 382241.
ARCHITECT: Patrick Merrigan.

Some wicked slopes and borrows on
the immaculate greens and a
dog-legged approach to the two tier
18th green are just some of the novel
features incorporated into the course.
The architect sensitively integrated the
course into a landscape textured with
mature trees, flowing parkland and no
less than five lakes. This is a golfing
tour-de-force.

COURSE INFORMATION

**Par 72; SSS 72; Length
6633 yds, 6057 mtrs.**

Visitors: Welcome.
Societies always welcome.
Opening Hours: 7.30am –
Sunset.
Ladies: Welcome.
Green Fees: £20 weekdays,
£22 weekends per person,
£16 before 9.00am (except
Saturdays).
Juveniles: Permitted.
Clubhouse Hours: 8.00am –
11.30pm.
Clubhouse Dress: Casual
but neat.
Clubhouse Facilities: Full
bar and catering facilities
available, mens & ladies
locker rooms, proshop.
Open Competitions: Open
Week mid August; Canada
Life Pro-Am June, Open
parent & child foursomes
July.

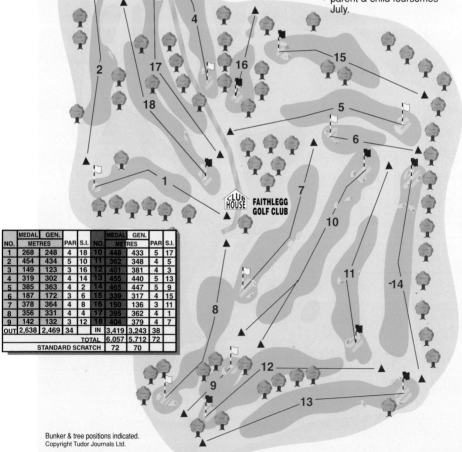

NO.	MEDAL METRES	GEN. METRES	PAR	S.I.	NO.	MEDAL METRES	GEN. METRES	PAR	S.I.
1	268	248	4	18	10	448	433	5	17
2	454	434	5	10	11	362	348	4	5
3	149	123	3	16	12	401	381	4	3
4	319	302	4	14	13	455	440	5	13
5	385	363	4	2	14	465	447	5	9
6	187	172	3	6	15	339	317	4	15
7	378	364	4	8	16	150	136	3	11
8	356	331	4	4	17	395	362	4	1
9	142	132	3	12	18	404	379	4	7
OUT	2,638	2,469	34		IN	3,419	3,243	38	
					TOTAL	6,057	5,712	72	
					STANDARD SCRATCH		72	70	

Bunker & tree positions indicated.
Copyright Tudor Journals Ltd.

Gold Coast Golf Club,
Ballinacourty,
Dungarvan.
Co. Waterford.
Tel: (058) 42249.
Fax: (058) 43378.

LOCATION: Three miles East of
Dungarvan.
SECRETARY: John Murphy.
Tel: (058) 41811.
ARCHITECT: Moss Fives.

Presently a nine hole course.
Adjacent land has been purchased to
extend present course to Eighteen
holes. Present course – parkland,
bordered by Atlantic Ocean, scenic
background – Dungarvan Bay &
Comeragh Mountains.

COURSE INFORMATION

Par 72; SSS 70; Length
5,786 mtrs.

Visitors: Welcome.
Opening Hours: Sunrise –
Sunset.
Avoid: Advisable to book in
advance for weekends.
Ladies: Welcome.
Green Fees: £12.
Juveniles: Welcome.
Clubhouse Hours: 8.00am –
12.00pm.
Clubhouse Dress: Casual,
neat.
Clubhouse Facilities: New
clubhouse opening June '95
will include all hotel &
catering services, including
leisure centre & swimming
pool.

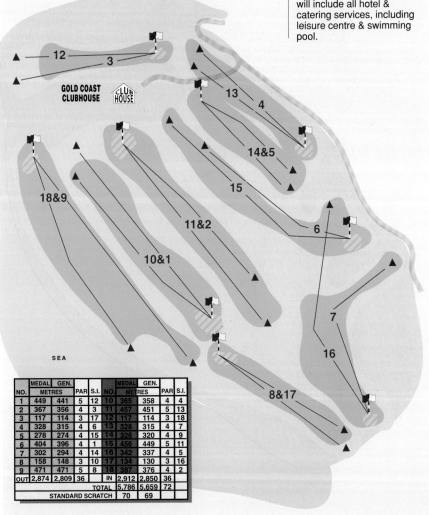

	MEDAL	GEN.				MEDAL	GEN.		
NO.	METRES		PAR	S.I.	NO.	METRES		PAR	S.I.
1	449	441	5	12	10	365	358	4	4
2	367	356	4	3	11	457	451	5	13
3	117	114	3	17	12	117	114	3	18
4	328	315	4	6	13	328	315	4	7
5	278	274	4	15	14	326	320	4	9
6	404	396	4	1	15	456	449	5	11
7	302	294	4	14	16	342	337	4	5
8	158	148	3	10	17	134	130	3	16
9	471	471	5	8	18	387	376	4	2
OUT	2,874	2,809	36		IN	2,912	2,850	36	
					TOTAL	5,786	5,659	72	
	STANDARD SCRATCH		70	69					

Copyright Tudor Journals Ltd.

**Newtown Hill,
Tramore.
Co Waterford.**

LOCATION: On the Dungarvan
coast road.
SECRETARY: J. Cox.
Tel: (051) 386170.
PROFESSIONAL: P. McDaid.
Tel: (051) 381706.

Eighteen hole championship course
with generous fairways. In a recent
survey, by Sports Columnist John
Cowyn, two holes — the 4th and the
6th were rated in the top eighteen in
Ireland.

COURSE INFORMATION

Par 72; SSS 71; Length 6559

yds, 6155 mtrs.
Visitors: Welcome.
Ladies: Welcome.
Green Fees: £17 Mon – Fri.
£20 Weekends.
Juveniles: Welcome, lessons
available by prior
arrangements; club hire
available; caddy service
available by prior
arrangements; telephone
appointments required.
Clubhouse Hours: 11.00am –
11.30pm;
Clubhouse Dress: Casual.
Open Competitions: Aug,
Sept.

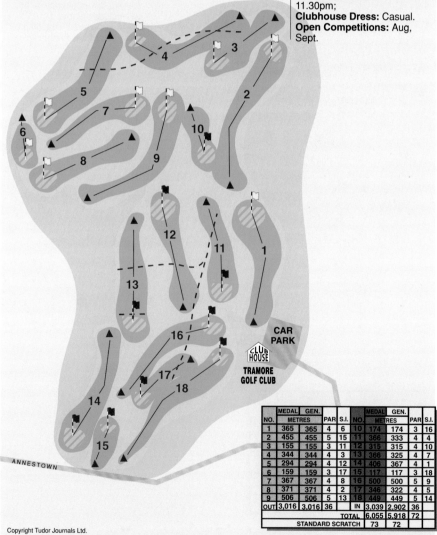

NO.	MEDAL METRES	GEN. METRES	PAR	S.I.	NO.	MEDAL METRES	GEN. METRES	PAR	S.I.
1	365	365	4	6	10	174	174	3	16
2	455	455	5	15	11	366	333	4	4
3	155	155	3	11	12	315	315	4	10
4	344	344	4	3	13	366	325	4	7
5	294	294	4	12	14	406	367	4	1
6	159	159	3	17	15	117	117	3	18
7	367	367	4	8	16	500	500	5	9
8	371	371	4	2	17	346	322	4	5
9	506	506	5	13	18	449	449	5	14
OUT	3,016	3,016	36		IN	3,039	2,902	36	
					TOTAL	6,055	5,918	72	
					STANDARD SCRATCH	73	72		

ANNESTOWN

CAR PARK

CLUB HOUSE

TRAMORE GOLF CLUB

Waterford Castle Golf Club, The Island, Ballinakill, Waterford.
Tel: (051) 71633.
Fax: (051) 79316.

Location: Waterford City.
Secretary: Dick Brennan.
Tel: (051) 71633.
Architect: Des Smyth & Associates.

Parkland, wooded, four artificial lakes, surrounded by River Suir. Sand based Tees & greens.

An excellent test of golf in most enjoyable surroundings. Heated swimming pool & tennis available.

COURSE INFORMATION

Par 72; SSS 73; Length 6,209 Metres.
Visitors: Welcome.
Opening Hours: 8am.
Avoid: 8.30am – 10.00am (members times).

Ladies: Welcome.
Juveniles: Permitted with adult.
Green Fees: £20 midweek. £22 weekends.
Clubhouse Hours: 8.00am –
Clubhouse Dress: Casual, no jeans etc.
Clubhouse Facilities: Limited bar food – soup, sandwiches, tea/coffee. Full meals with pre-booking.
Open Competitions: July.

NO.	MEDAL MTRS	GEN. MTRS	PAR	S.I.	NO.	MEDAL MTRS	GEN. MTRS	PAR	S.I.
1	385	361	4	7	10	160	152	3	18
2	176	154	3	15	11	346	318	4	6
3	372	346	4	3	12	415	397	4	2
4	356	338	4	5	13	463	427	5	12
5	476	432	5	13	14	343	306	4	10
6	315	303	4	17	15	468	454	5	14
7	193	176	3	9	16	187	173	3	8
8	452	443	5	11	17	368	344	4	4
9	381	360	4	1	18	353	326	4	16
OUT	3,106	2,913	36		IN	3,103	2,897	36	
				TOTAL	6,209	5,810	72	
	STANDARD SCRATCH		73	71					

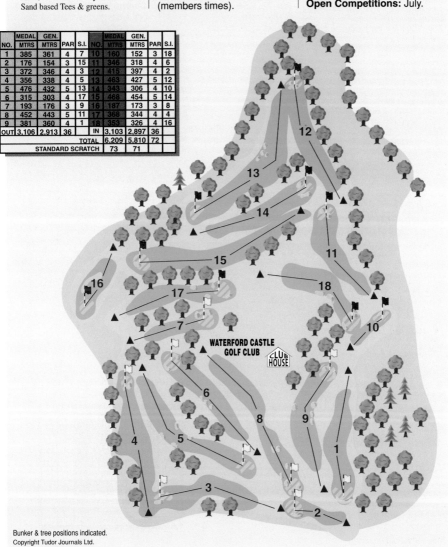

WATERFORD CASTLE GOLF CLUB
CLUB HOUSE

Bunker & tree positions indicated.
Copyright Tudor Journals Ltd.

**Coolcormack,
Dungarvan.
Co. Waterford.
Tel: (058) 43216.
Fax: (058) 44343.**

LOCATION: 3 miles from Dungarvan, 30 miles from Waterford city.
SECRETARY: Nora Spratt.
ARCHITECT: Eddie Hackett.

The course extends over 150 acres of magnificent rolling topography taking in the beautiful panoramic views of Co. Waterford. An interesting feature of the course is that the first nine holes are laid out on a large plateau featuring a lovely stream which comes into play at the 3rd and 4th holes. The course extends to 6900 yds, but it was built to suit a wide range of players with a minimum interference to the natural characteristics and vegetation. Playable all year round.

COURSE INFORMATION

**Par 72; SSS 74: Length 6,192 mtrs.
Visitors: Welcome.**

Opening Hours: Sunrise – sunset.
Green Fees: £15 Mon-Fri. £20 Sat-Sun. Discount for societies.
Juveniles: Welcome. Clubs and caddy cars available for hire.
Clubhouse Hours: 8am – Sunset.
Clubhouse Dress: Casual/neat.
Clubhouse Facilities: Full bar & catering facilities all day, every day.

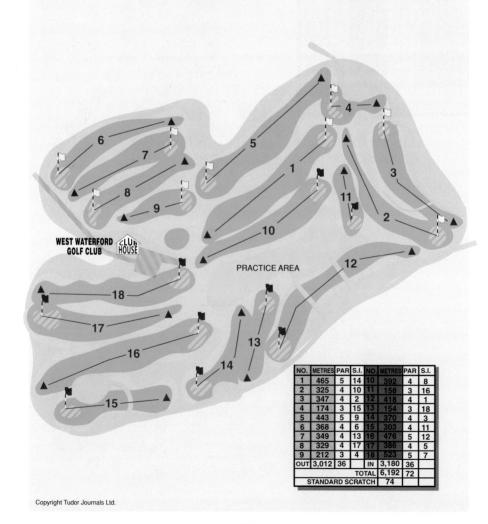

WEST WATERFORD GOLF CLUB

CLUB HOUSE

PRACTICE AREA

NO.	METRES	PAR	S.I.	NO.	METRES	PAR	S.I.
1	465	5	14	10	392	4	8
2	325	4	10	11	158	3	16
3	347	4	2	12	418	4	1
4	174	3	15	13	154	3	18
5	443	5	9	14	370	4	3
6	368	4	6	15	303	4	11
7	349	4	13	16	476	5	12
8	329	4	17	17	386	4	5
9	212	3	4	18	523	5	7
OUT	3,012	36		IN	3,180	36	
				TOTAL	6,192	72	
				STANDARD SCRATCH	74		

CONNACHT

BY JACK MAGOWAN

Cecil Ewing was a big man — feisty, humorous, opinionated and hopelessly in love with golf. He wore an 'extra large' label in personality, and was the kind you thought would live for ever. When he died at 63, it was as though the game had lost a grand uncle.

Cecil had not only played in six Walker Cup teams and for Ireland over 90 times, he won the West of Ireland championship ten times and was beaten finalist on another eight occasions, a record almost without parallel in the days when the BBC of amateur golf, Burke, Bruen and Carr, were in their prime.

Ewing could play left-handed as well as right, and often did, usually for a happy wager.

Nobody loved an audience as much as he did, and his favourite party piece

Galway course has an attractive mixture of tree-lined fairways and superb views

would be to challenge somebody to a match over the last three holes of his beloved Rosses Point links.

If the reply was "no thanks, you're too good,", Cecil would propose a compromise, "OK. I'll play left-handed and you right-handed," he would tease. And nine times out of ten the result would be the same — he won!.

Like O'Connor Senior, he revelled, too, in wind and rough weather. "I learned the game in a good school," he used to say. "When it blows at Rosses Point, the only hiding place is in the clubhouse!"

Cecil had a gift for making the game look easy, and was 45, and over 17 stone, when he played against the United States for the last time in the Walker Cup at St Andrews. Three years later he was Irish Close champion again, a surprise winner over one of the toughest courses in the game, Ballybunion.

Ewing was also a Cup selector and captained Ireland to two European championship victories, one of them in Italy. The ball he used for an exciting win against Ray Billows in Britain's historic Cup victory of 1938 is on display in Sligo's splendid new clubhouse and still spark many potent memories, especially of some of the great names who've played under the shadows of Ben Bulben.

Like Walter Hagen, who took two days to get there from London. And Bobby Locke and Henry Cotton, and more recently Bernhard Langer. "I went there to play one round and stayed two weeks," says Langer of the 100 per cent links course that would almost surely covet a world rating were it not so isolated.

If it wasn't the sea air and scenery that captivated Langer, then it must have been the loudest silence in golf. Along the corridors of these exposed and barren fairways, all you hear is the grass growing!.

Sligo can boast several star-studded holes, but the pick of them by far is the 17th. Tucked among high dunes, this classic hole spans 450 yards off the tiger tee, and in O'Connor Senior's book is one of the finest two-shot holes in the country. "It carries a knock-out punch like Mike Tyson," smiles fight-fan O'Connor.

Ireland now has over 250 golf courses, and if there's a bad one

anywhere, somebody once said, they're keeping it a secret. Inexpensive, underplayed and welcoming – that's how they beat the drums for Connacht courses, the cream of which are always special.

Nothing beats the birth of a new course, and if two here could be awarded a rosette for quality they are Carn, in Co. Mayo, and O'Connor Junior's wonderfully ambitious layout at Galway Bay.

Have you ever been to Belmullet?. That's where Carn is – in the back of beyond. Or as *Golf World* so aptly put it in their choice of Britain's top – 10 new courses, "it's not the sort of place you can pop in to on the way to somewhere else!"

Some holes there are truly majestic, and there's the odd one or two that push the realms of respectability a bit too far. But it's a challenge and fun to play.

German and French golfers are drawn to Ireland's west coast like fruit flies to a ripening. The piano in the lounge at Connemara is a gift from a German diplomat who came for a fishing holiday some years ago, but never even got rod and line out of his car. Instead, he hired a set of clubs and had a ball in the company of some of the most remote, yet hospitable, people on earth.

Connemara, like Waterville, is an Eddie Hackett creation, and, like Waterville, the second nine there are better than the first. In fact, the last six holes at Clifden is as tough a finishing stretch as there is anywhere, a veritable no-man's land of sand and wilderness. In May and June, the links are a tapestry of yellows, blues and purples.

It will surprise many golfers that Enniscrone is not in Ireland's top-30 rankings, for here, too, is a links course that can both exhilarate and terrify. It's about ten miles from Ballina on the shore of Killala Bay, and looks like a lunar landscape among dunes that dip and roll and disappear out of sight.

Eddie Power won the Irish title there in '93, beating Liam Higgins' son, David in a thrilling final, and calls Enniscore 'a sleeping giant'. It's the real thing, that's what he means!.

Westport has also hosted the Close championship and makes a fuss over visitors in a town where hotel beds are not expensive, and there are plenty of them.

After a benign start, Westport picks up momentum with the long 15th the pinnacle hole. The tee-shot here is not for the faint-hearted, not with a carry over an inlet of Clew Bay that must be all of 170 yards. And just for added mischief, there's an out of bounds fence along the port side.

Again, the welcome at Westport has been known to trip up the unsuspecting, so go prepared.

No two golf courses play the same, and in the west of Ireland they are all different. From Achill to Athlone to the sylvan setting of Athenry—they're all nature's own design, a playground for those who like to compliment their golf with scenery and atmosphere. As Henry Longhurst once wrote, Irish golf has that indefinable something which makes you relive again and again the days you played there!.

**Athenry Golf Club,
Palmerstown, Oranmore,
Co. Galway.
Tel: (091) 794466.**

LOCATION: 5 miles from Athenry town. 8 miles from Galway.
HONORARY SECRETARY: Padraic Klattery. Tel: (091) 751405.
ARCHITECT: Eddie Hackett.

This eighteen hole parkland course sports two ruined forts amidst dense wooded backdrop. It was extended from a nine hole to an eighteen hole course in 1991 taking on a completely different layout, but not detracting from its sylvan setting.

COURSE INFORMATION

**Par 70; SSS 69; Length 5,463 Metres.
Visitors:** Welcome.
Opening Hours: Sunrise – Sunset.
Avoid: Sundays.
Green Fees: £12 (with member £7.

Juveniles: Permitted.
Clubhouse Hours: Flexible.
Clubhouse Dress: Casual.
Clubhouse Facilities: Full meals at all times.
Open Competitions: Easter & July. Open Week – July.
Handicap certificate required for open competitions.

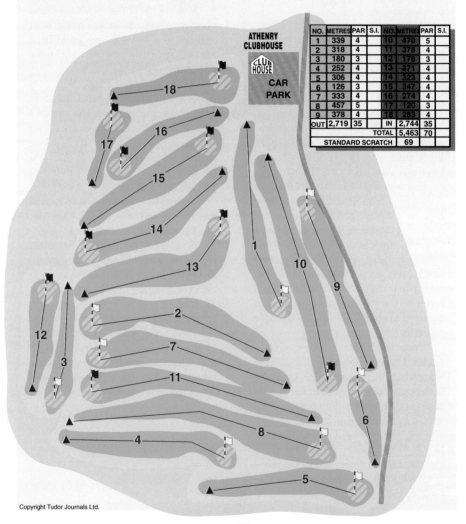

ATHENRY CLUBHOUSE

CAR PARK

NO.	METRES	PAR	S.I.	NO.	METRES	PAR	S.I.
1	339	4		10	470	5	
2	318	4		11	378	4	
3	180	3		12	178	3	
4	252	4		13	371	4	
5	306	4		14	323	4	
6	126	3		15	347	4	
7	333	4		16	274	4	
8	457	5		17	120	3	
9	378	4		18	283	4	
OUT	2,719	35		IN	2,744	35	
				TOTAL	5,463	70	
		STANDARD SCRATCH		69			

BALLINASLOE

C O N N A C H T

GALWAY

**Rossgloss, Ballinasloe,
Co. Galway.
Tel: (0905) 42126,
Fax: (0905) 42538.**

LOCATION: Off the Ballinasloe
Portumna road. Two miles
from the town centre.
SECRETARY: Mr John Millane.
Tel: (0905) 42904.
PROFESSIONAL: Shane O'Grady.
ARCHITECT: Eddie Hackett.

Ballinasloe Golf Club was established
on the Cloncarty Estate, now
Garbally College, in 1894. Originally
a nine hole parkland course, major

redevelopment of the club was
undertaken in 1970 and the course
was extended to eighteen holes in
1984. The course is invariably
playable all year round.

COURSE INFORMATION

**Par 72; SSS 70; Length
5,868 Metres.**
Visitors: Welcome.
Opening Hours: 8am – Dusk.
Avoid: Major Sunday
competitions.
Ladies: Welcome.

Ladies Day: Tuesday.
Green Fees: £12 all week.
Clubhouse Dress: Neat and tidy.
Clubhouse Facilities: Catering
– snacks during the week
(meals in evenings). Full
catering on Saturday & Sunday.
Open Competitions:
Open weeks June & July. Other
open days throughout the year.

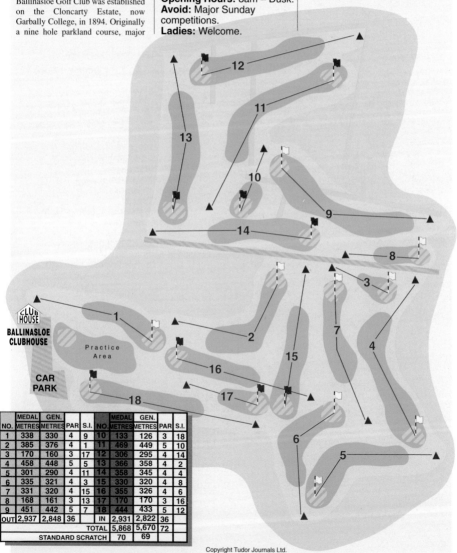

NO.	MEDAL METRES	GEN. METRES	PAR	S.I.	NO.	MEDAL METRES	GEN. METRES	PAR	S.I.
1	338	330	4	9	10	133	126	3	18
2	385	376	4	1	11	469	449	5	10
3	170	160	3	17	12	306	295	4	14
4	458	448	5	5	13	366	358	4	2
5	301	290	4	11	14	358	345	4	4
6	335	321	4	3	15	330	320	4	8
7	331	320	4	15	16	355	326	4	6
8	168	161	3	13	17	170	170	3	16
9	451	442	5	7	18	444	433	5	12
OUT	2,937	2,848	36	IN		2,931	2,822	36	
TOTAL						5,868	5,670	72	
STANDARD SCRATCH						70	69		

Copyright Tudor Journals Ltd.

321

Ballyconneely, Co. Galway.
Tel: (095) 23502,
Fax: (095) 23662.

LOCATION: Nine miles from Clifden.
SECRETARY: John McLaughlin.
Tel: (095) 23503.
ARHITECT: Eddie Hackett.

Situated on the edge of the Atlantic Ocean in a spectacular setting with the Twelve Bens Mountains in the background, this championship course is a challenge as good as any golfer would wish for. Established in 1973 the course has a popular reputation with big hitters, who relish the long meandering fairways.

COURSE INFORMATION

Par 72; SSS 73; Length 6,173 Metres.
Visitors: Welcome.
Opening Hours: Dawn – Dusk.
Avoid: Sunday mornings.
Green Fees: £25 May – Sep, £16 Oct – April. Lessons available by prior arrangement. Club hire and caddy car available. Golf carts available.
Juveniles: Welcome but may not play Weekends, Bank Holidays or Open Weeks.
Clubhouse Hours: 8am – 11pm.
Clubhouse Dress: Casual (no spikes).
Clubhouse Facilities: Snacks and A la carte restaurant.
Open Competitions: June and September. Pro-Am – October. Handicap certificates required for open competitions.

LAKE

CONNEMARA CLUBHOUSE

NO.	CHAMP METRES	MEDAL METRES	PAR	S.I.	NO.	CHAMP METRES	MEDAL METRES	PAR	S.I.
1	349	331	4	6	10	398	383	4	7
2	385	366	4	8	11	171	151	3	17
3	154	145	3	18	12	416	399	4	1
4	358	335	4	14	13	196	180	3	5
5	360	342	4	12	14	483	460	5	15
6	193	175	3	10	15	367	349	4	9
7	531	482	5	16	16	417	370	4	3
8	438	418	4	2	17	491	468	5	11
9	408	344	4	4	18	496	475	5	13
OUT	3,176	2,938	35		IN	3,435	3,235	37	
					TOTAL	6,611	6,173	72	
					STANDARD SCRATCH	75	73		

Galway Golf Club, Blackrock, Galway.
Tel: (091) 523038.

LOCATION: 3 miles west of Galway city.
SECRETARY: Padraic Fany.
PROFESSIONAL: Don Wallace.
Tel: (091) 522033.

A tight tree lined course. Some tiered greens make it very important to accurately place your drives and a good short game is necessary to score well. The course has excellent views of Galway Bay, the Burren and the Arran Islands.

COURSE INFORMATION

Par 70; SSS 70; Length 5,816 Metres.
Visitors: Welcome.
Opening Hours: 8am – Dusk.
Avoid: Tuesday, Saturday and Sunday.

Ladies: Welcome.
Juveniles: Welcome.
Green Fees: £16 weekdays, £20 weekends; Group rate (minimum 25) £12.
Clubhouse Hours: 11.00am –
Clubhouse Dress: Informal.
Clubhouse Facilities: At all times.
Open Competitions: Open Week – June; Race Week – July; Guinness Open – June; Open Weekend – October.

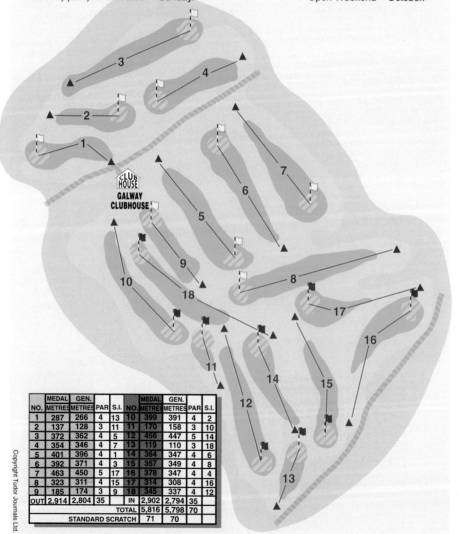

GALWAY CLUBHOUSE

NO.	MEDAL METRES	GEN. METRES	PAR	S.I.	NO.	MEDAL METRES	GEN. METRES	PAR	S.I.
1	287	266	4	13	10	399	391	4	2
2	137	128	3	11	11	170	158	3	10
3	372	362	4	5	12	456	447	5	14
4	354	346	4	7	13	119	110	3	18
5	401	396	4	1	14	364	347	4	6
6	392	371	4	3	15	357	349	4	8
7	463	450	5	17	16	378	347	4	4
8	323	311	4	15	17	314	308	4	16
9	185	174	3	9	18	345	337	4	12
OUT	2,914	2,804	35		IN	2,902	2,794	35	
					TOTAL	5,816	5,798	70	
					STANDARD SCRATCH	71	70		

Renville, Oranmore, Co. Galway.
Tel: (091) 90500.
Fax: (091) 90510.

LOCATION: Six miles south of Galway City.
SECRETARY: Eamonn Meagher.
Tel: 091 90500.
PROFESSIONAL: Eugene O'Connor.
Tel: 091 90503.
ARCHITECT: Christy O'Connor Jnr.

Christy O'Connor Jnr, Ryder & world cup player, designed this 18 hole course to highlight and preserve the ancient historic features of the Renville Peninsula. The spectacular setting on Galway Bay is distractingly beautiful and the cleverly designed mix of holes presents a real golfing challenge which demands total concentration.

COURSE INFORMATION

Par 72; Length 6,533 yards.
Visitors: Welcome.
Opening Hours: 7am–7.30pm.
Ladies: Welcome.
Green Fees: £20 weekdays; £25 weekends.
Juveniles: Restricted - Before 8.30am, 11am–12noon & 3pm–4pm (weekdays).
Clubhouse Hours: 7am–11pm.
Clubhouse Dress: Informal.
Clubhouse Facilities: Restaurant, Spike Bar & Cocktail Bar – all day.
Open Competitions: June/July – by invitation.

NO.	MEDAL METRES	GEN. METRES	PAR	S.I.	NO.	MEDAL METRES	GEN. METRES	PAR	S.I.
1	506	486	5	14	10	411	367	4	5
2	409	362	4	2	11	377	356	4	7
3	387	370	4	10	12	400	372	4	1
4	155	136	3	16	13	158	148	3	15
5	336	363	4	8	14	501	464	5	9
6	481	434	5	12	15	172	160	3	17
7	138	126	3	18	16	496	481	5	11
8	418	386	4	6	17	349	323	4	13
9	400	374	4	4	18	439	423	4	3
OUT	3,230	2,997	36		IN	3,303	3,094	36	
					TOTAL	6,533	6,091	72	
					STANDARD SCRATCH	73	71		

GALWAY BAY CLUBHOUSE

Bunker positions indicated.

Gort Golf Club,
Laughtyshaughnessy,
Gort, Co. Galway.
Tel: (091) 31336.

LOCATION: Tubber Road, Gort.
HONORARY SECRETARY: Sean
Devlin. Tel: (091) 31281.

A parkland course with out-of-bounds areas on numerous holes. The course has several unusual features including a railway line, which is flanked on either side, by the 3rd and 8th holes.

COURSE INFORMATION

Par 68; SSS 67; Length 5,174 Metres.
Visitors: Welcome to play everyday.
Opening Hours: All day.
Avoid: Sunday mornings until 1pm.
Ladies: Welcome.
Juveniles: Welcome.
Green Fees: £9.
Clubhouse Hours: Mon – Fri normally 9.30am – 11.30pm;

Sunday 12.00 – 4.00pm closed. Sunday evenings.
Clubhouse Dress: Casual.
Clubhouse Facilities: Light snacks during opening hours.
Open Competitions: Open Week – June / July.

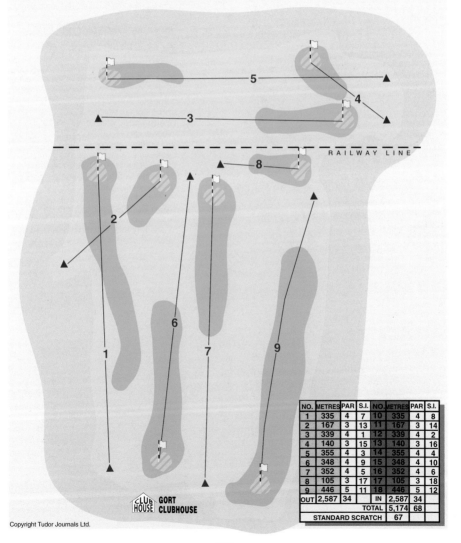

GORT CLUBHOUSE

NO.	METRES	PAR	S.I.	NO.	METRES	PAR	S.I.
1	335	4	7	10	335	4	8
2	167	3	13	11	167	3	14
3	339	4	1	12	339	4	2
4	140	3	15	13	140	3	16
5	355	4	3	14	355	4	4
6	348	4	9	15	348	4	10
7	352	4	5	16	352	4	6
8	105	3	17	17	105	3	18
9	446	5	11	18	446	5	12
OUT	2,587	34		IN	2,587	34	
				TOTAL	5,174	68	
				STANDARD SCRATCH		67	

NO.	MEDAL METRES	GEN. METRES	PAR	S.I.	NO.	MEDAL METRES	GEN. METRES	PAR	S.I.
1	336	330	4	11	10	368	351	4	2
2	375	347	4	8	11	146	124	3	12
3	392	381	4	3	12	445	427	5	7
4	187	178	3	9	13	307	291	4	6
5	388	383	4	1	14	134	121	3	18
6	354	340	4	5	15	267	242	4	4
7	260	243	4	14	16	421	415	5	13
8	120	105	3	15	17	160	135	3	16
9	259	242	4	17	18	342	332	4	10
OUT	2,671	2,549	34		IN	2,590	2,438	35	
					TOTAL	5,261	4,987	69	
					STANDARD SCRATCH	69	69		

Loughrea Golf Club, Craigu, Loughrea, Co. Galway.
Tel: (091) 841049.

LOCATION: One mile south east on the Loughrea to Bullaun road.
SECRETARY: Jackie Burke.
Tel: (091) 841049.
ARCHITECT: Eddie Hackett.

The course has wide grassy fairways with smooth greens and has a generally quiet atmosphere. The main course difficulties are the lush rough and the fact that second shots need great accuracy.

COURSE INFORMATION

Par 69; SSS 67; Length 5,261 Metres.
Visitors: Welcome.
Opening Hours: 9am – Dusk.
Avoid: Sunday, Wednesday & major competition days.
Ladies Day: Wednesday.
Green Fees: Weekdays – £10; Weekends – £12.
Juveniles: Welcome (before 6pm). Lessons available by arrangement.
Clubhouse Hours: Open all day.
Clubhouse Dress: Casual.
Clubhouse Facilities: Snacks (sandwiches).
Open Competitions: Most Bank Holiday weekends and Open Week in June. Handicap certificate required.

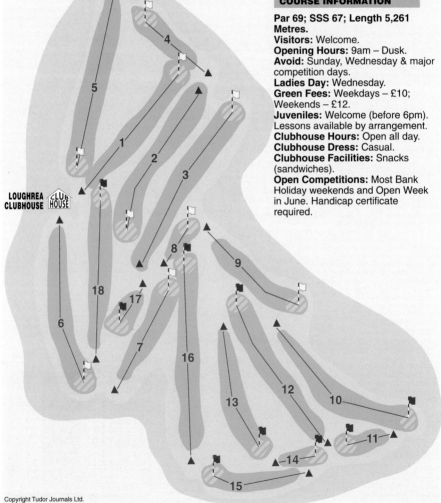

LOUGHREA CLUBHOUSE

**Mountbellew Golf Club,
Mountbellew, Ballinasloe,
Co. Galway.
Tel: (0905) 79259.**

LOCATION: Ballinasloe 17 miles,
Galway 30 miles and
Roscommon 20 miles.
CAPTAIN: L.Challower
Tel: (0905) 79573.
HON. SEC: Padraic Costello.

Parkland course in sylvan setting. Ideal
for a casual, leisurely round or a day of
golf. Generous fairways on all

holes with the greens always in good
condition.

COURSE INFORMATION

**Par 69; SSS 66; Length 5,143
Metres.**
Visitors: Wecome to play, no
special arrangements required.
Opening Hours: Daylight
hours.
Avoid: Saturday afternoons
(Ladies competitions). Sunday
all day (Mens competitions).

Green Fees: £7 Mon – Fri & £10
Weekends. £25 per week.
Clubhouse Hours: 3pm – 9pm.
Clubhouse Dress: Informal.
Clubhouse Facilities: Light
snacks in bar. Outings catered
for by arrangement.
Open Competitions: Open
Week – June.

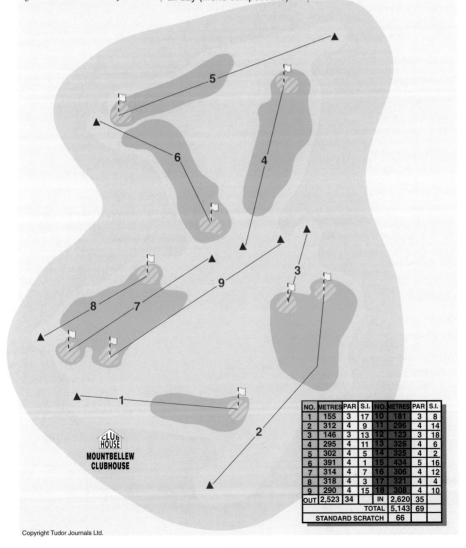

MOUNTBELLEW
CLUBHOUSE

NO.	METRES	PAR	S.I.	NO.	METRES	PAR	S.I.
1	155	3	17	10	181	3	8
2	312	4	9	11	296	4	14
3	146	3	13	12	123	3	18
4	295	4	11	13	326	4	6
5	302	4	5	14	325	4	2
6	391	4	1	15	434	5	16
7	314	4	7	16	306	4	12
8	318	4	3	17	321	4	4
9	290	4	15	18	308	4	10
OUT	2,523	34		IN	2,620	35	
				TOTAL	5,143	69	
STANDARD SCRATCH		66					

Gortreevagh, Oughterard, Co. Galway
Tel: (091) 82131.

LOCATION: Fifteen miles west of Galway City en route to Connemara.
SECRETARY: John Waters.
Tel: (091) 82131,
Fax: (091) 82377.
PROFESSIONAL: Michael Ryan.
Tel: (091) 82626.
ARCHITECT: Dr Harris/E Hackett.

A beautiful and mature parkland course on the shores of Lough Corrib, Oughterard is renowned for its friendly and welcoming atmosphere. Always in pristine condition with a variety of trees and shrubs to punish wayward shots to otherwise generous and lush fairways.

COURSE INFORMATION

Par 70; SSS 69; Length 5,506 Metres.
Visitors: Welcome. Restricted at weekends, due to competitions.
Opening Hours: Sunrise – Sunset.
Avoid: Telephone in advance.
Ladies: Wednesday.
Green Fees: £13; £22 for Husband & Wife; £7 Juveniles.

Juveniles: Welcome.
Clubhouse Hours: 8.00am-12.00pm (except Winter). Full clubhouse facilities.
Clubhouse Dress: Casual.
Clubhouse Facilities: Breakfast from 8.00am – 10.30am; full dinner menu all day until 10.00pm.
Open Competitions: Open week in June. Many open weekends throughout the year. Handicap certificate required for Open Competitions.

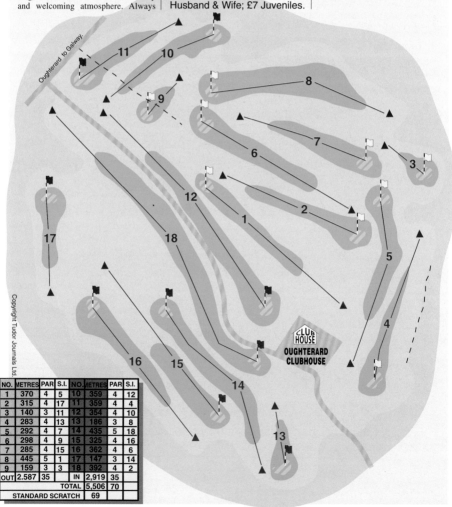

NO.	METRES	PAR	S.I.	NO.	METRES	PAR	S.I.
1	370	4	5	10	359	4	12
2	315	4	17	11	359	4	4
3	140	3	11	12	354	4	10
4	283	4	13	13	186	3	8
5	292	4	7	14	435	5	18
6	298	4	9	15	325	4	16
7	285	4	15	16	362	4	6
8	445	5	1	17	147	3	14
9	159	3	3	18	392	4	2
OUT	2,587	35		IN	2,919	35	
				TOTAL	5,506	70	
	STANDARD SCRATCH				69		

PORTUMNA

Portumna, Co. Galway.
Tel: (0509) 41059.

LOCATION: Less than two miles west of Portumna on the Woodford Road
SECRETARY: Gerard Ryan.
Tel: (0509) 41021.

Located in Portumna Forest Park, this is a very attractive woodland course with plenty of mature trees. Deer can sometimes be found on the course. The finishing Par 3 hole is the most difficult of the round, playing to an elevated green.

COURSE INFORMATION

Par 68; SSS 67; Length 5,205 Metres.
Visitors: Welcome to play every day.
Opening Hours: 9am – Dusk.
Avoid: Sunday.
Ladies: Wednesday.
Green Fees: £10 (w/m £6).
Juveniles: Welcome
Clubhouse Hours: 9.00am - 10.00pm. (Summer).
Clubhouse Dress: Casual.

Clubhouse Facilities:
Catering facilities by prior arrangement.
Open Competitions:
Handicap certificate required for Open Competitions. Open week – July.

NO.	METRES	PAR	S.I.	NO.	METRES	PAR	S.I.
1	406	4	3	10	267	4	15
2	166	3	11	11	297	4	13
3	405	4	1	12	332	4	2
4	292	4	14	13	149	3	4
5	140	3	17	14	368	4	12
6	321	4	10	15	449	5	7
7	341	4	6	16	156	3	18
8	271	4	16	17	368	4	5
9	317	4	8	18	160	3	9
OUT	2,659	34		IN	2,546	34	
				TOTAL	5,205	68	
	STANDARD SCRATCH			67			

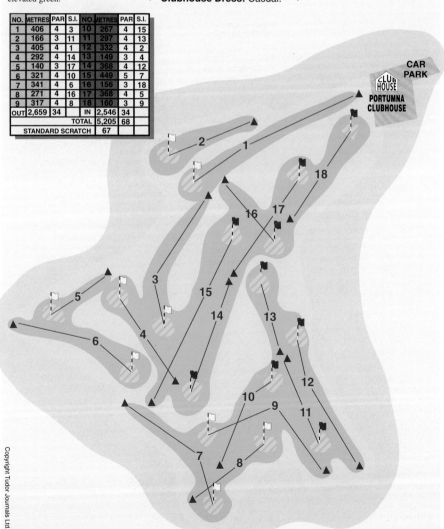

CAR PARK

CLUB HOUSE

PORTUMNA CLUBHOUSE

NO.	CHAMP METRES	MEDAL METRES	PAR	S.I.	NO.	CHAMP METRES	MEDAL METRES	PAR	S.I.
1	362	312	4	4	10	318	310	4	18
2	475	439	5	17	11	342	330	4	12
3	379	326	4	3	12	187	178	3	8
4	300	286	4	11	13	467	449	5	14
5	452	436	5	15	14	309	302	4	4
6	171	165	3	7	15	317	299	4	10
7	390	368	4	1	16	157	138	3	6
8	134	130	3	13	17	479	448	5	16
9	339	330	4	9	18	366	358	4	2
OUT	3,002	2,792	36		IN	2,942	2,812	36	
					TOTAL	5,944	5,604	72	
					STANDARD SCRATCH	71	69		

Tuam Golf Club, Barnacurragh, Tuam, Co. Galway.
Tel: (093) 24354.

LOCATION: Twenty miles north of Galway.
SECRETARY: Mary Tierney.
Tel: (093) 28993.
CAPTAIN: Brian Flesk.
HON. SEC: Tom Canavan.
PROFESSIONAL: Henry Reynolds.
Tel: (093) 24091.

There is on-going development on this course. The fairways are guarded by plantations and trees, with greens well bunkered. Tuam just recently completed their new clubhouse development.

COURSE INFORMATION

Par 72; SSS 69; Length 5,944 Metres.
Visitors: Welcome any weekday.
Opening Hours: 8.00am – Sunset.
Avoid: Weekends.
Ladies: Welcome.
Ladies Day: Tuesday.
Green Fees: £10
Juveniles: Welcome (accompanied by an adult). Lessons available. Club hire; Caddy service and cars available by prior arrangement.
Clubhouse Hours: 9.00am – 12 midnight (except winter).
Clubhouse Dress: Casual.
Clubhouse Facilities: Catering facilities and full restaurant.
Open Competitions: Open Week – May / June. Open week – July.

TUAM CLUBHOUSE

Bunker positions indicated.

Ballinamore Golf Club, Ballinamore, Co. Leitrim
Tel: (078) 44346.

LOCATION: Two miles north west of Ballinamore
SECRETARY: Padraig Reyolds.
Tel: (078) 44346.

Members will confirm there is a large degree of difficulty with the course. Things are made interesting with a canal alongside the 3rd hole and the back of the 9th green.

COURSE INFORMATION

Par 68; SSS 66; Length 5,192 Metres.
Visitors: Welcome except on Captain's or President's Day.
Opening Hours: 8.00am – Sunset.
Avoid: Sundays.
Ladies: Welcome.
Green Fees: £5. A handicap certificate is required.
Clubhouse Hours: 9.00am – 11.00pm.

Clubhouse Dress: Casual.
Clubhouse Facilities: Catering facilities – soup and sandwiches.
Open Competitions: Open week and certain weekends.

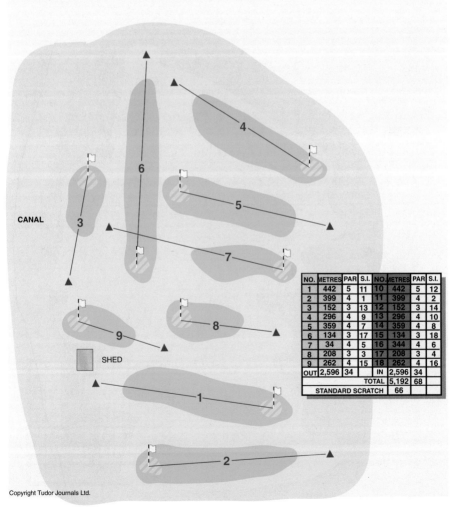

NO.	METRES	PAR	S.I.	NO.	METRES	PAR	S.I.
1	442	5	11	10	442	5	12
2	399	4	1	11	399	4	2
3	152	3	13	12	152	3	14
4	296	4	9	13	296	4	10
5	359	4	7	14	359	4	8
6	134	3	17	15	134	3	18
7	34	4	5	16	344	4	6
8	208	3	3	17	208	3	4
9	262	4	15	18	262	4	16
OUT	2,596	34		IN	2,596	34	
				TOTAL	5,192	68	
			STANDARD SCRATCH		66		

CANAL

SHED

**Achill Golf Club, Keel,
Co. Mayo.
Tel: (098) 43456.**

LOCATION: Keel, Achill.
SECRETARY/MANAGER: P.
Lavelle.

A scenic links course situated beside
a large beach. Achill course is of a
level and open nature – continuously
grazed by sheep. Fairways marked by
white stones.

COURSE INFORMATION

**Par 70; SSS 66; Length
5,446 Yards.**
Visitors: Welcome.
Opening Hours: Dawn – Dusk.
Ladies: Welcome.
Green Fees: £4 per day & £16
per week.
Juveniles: Must be
accompanied by an adult.
Clubhouse Hours: Same as
course.

Clubhouse Dress: Casual.
Open Competitions: Handicap
certificate required for open
competitions.

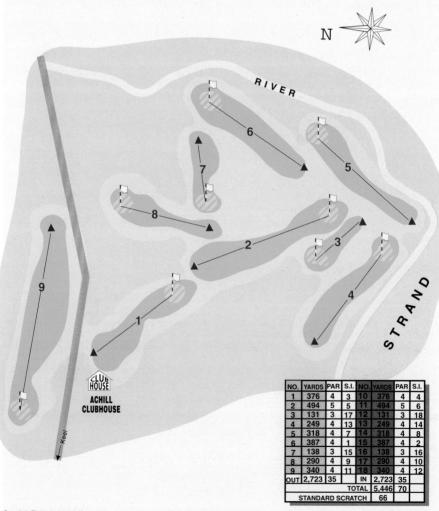

NO.	YARDS	PAR	S.I.	NO.	YARDS	PAR	S.I.
1	376	4	3	10	376	4	4
2	494	5	5	11	494	5	6
3	131	3	17	12	131	3	18
4	249	4	13	13	249	4	14
5	318	4	7	14	318	4	8
6	387	4	1	15	387	4	2
7	138	3	15	16	138	3	16
8	290	4	9	17	290	4	10
9	340	4	11	18	340	4	12
OUT	2,723	35		IN	2,723	35	
				TOTAL	5,446	70	
				STANDARD SCRATCH		66	

BALLINA

Ballina Golf Club,
Mossgrove, Shanaghy,
Ballina, Co. Mayo.
Tel: (096) 21050.

Location: Shanaghy, Ballina.
Secretary: V. Frawley.
Tel: (096) 21795/21050.

A flat inland course, with fairways
guarded by plantations.

COURSE INFORMATION

**Par 70; SSS 67; Length
5,700 Yards.**
Visitors: Welcome.
Opening Hours: 9am–10pm.
Avoid: Sundays.
Ladies: Welcome.
Green Fees: £12 (£8 with a
member). Lessons and caddy
service available by prior
arrangement.
Juveniles: Welcome.
Clubhouse Hours: 9am–11pm.

Clubhouse Dress: Informal.
Clubhouse Facilities:
Catering facilities by
arrangement.
Open Competitions: Whit
weekend; August weekend.
Handicap certificate required
for open competitions.

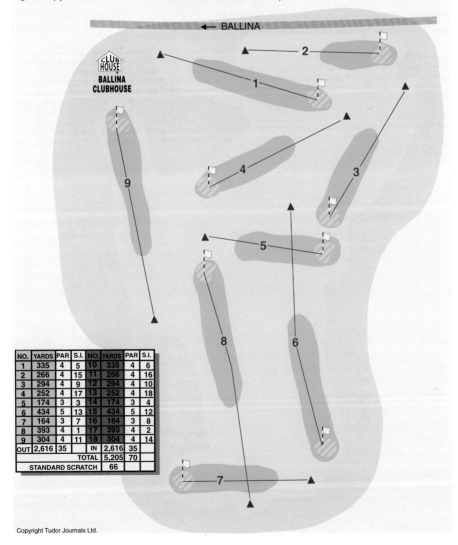

NO.	YARDS	PAR	S.I.	NO.	YARDS	PAR	S.I.
1	335	4	5	10	335	4	6
2	266	4	15	11	266	4	16
3	294	4	9	12	294	4	10
4	252	4	17	13	252	4	18
5	174	3	3	14	174	3	4
6	434	5	13	15	434	5	12
7	164	3	7	16	164	3	8
8	393	4	1	17	393	4	2
9	304	4	11	18	304	4	14
OUT	2,616	35		IN	2,616	35	
				TOTAL	5,205	70	
STANDARD SCRATCH		66					

Copyright Tudor Journals Ltd.

Ballinrobe Golf Club,
Castlebar Road,
Ballinrobe, Co. Mayo.
Tel: (092) 41448.

LOCATION: 30 miles from Galway. 20 miles from Castlebar and Westport. SECRETARY: Pat Holian. Tel: (0092) 41659.

Ballinrobe is a flat, nine hole course that actually plays across a race track. Well suited to high handicappers.

COURSE INFORMATION

Par 72; SSS 68; Length 5,214 Yards.
Visitors: Welcome.
Opening Hours: 7am – 8pm (summer) & 9am – 3.00pm (winter).
Avoid: Sundays and Tuesday evenings.
Ladies: Welcome.
Green Fees: £8 per round, £30 per week.
Juveniles: Welcome.
Clubhouse Hours: 10am – 6pm (June – Aug.).

Clubhouse Dress: Casual.
Clubhouse Facilities: Tea, coffee, snacks, soup and sandwiches.
Open Competitions: Open week in July.

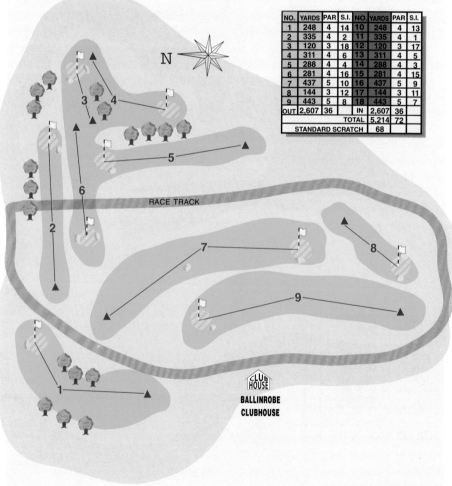

NO.	YARDS	PAR	S.I.	NO.	YARDS	PAR	S.I.
1	248	4	14	10	248	4	13
2	335	4	2	11	335	4	1
3	120	3	18	12	120	3	17
4	311	4	6	13	311	4	5
5	288	4	4	14	288	4	3
6	281	4	16	15	281	4	15
7	437	5	10	16	437	5	9
8	144	3	12	17	144	3	11
9	443	5	8	18	443	5	7
OUT	2,607	36		IN	2,607	36	
				TOTAL	5,214	72	
STANDARD SCRATCH					68		

N

RACE TRACK

BALLINROBE
CLUBHOUSE

Bunker and tree positions indicated.

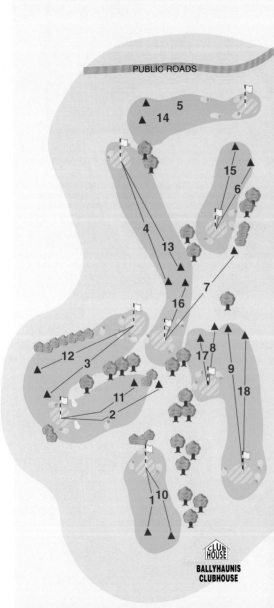

PUBLIC ROADS

BALLYHAUNIS
CLUBHOUSE

Ballyhaunis Golf Club, Coolnaha, Co. Mayo.
Tel: (0907) 30014.

LOCATION: 2 miles north of Ballyhaunis on the Charlstown Road. 7 miles from Horan International Airport.
SECRETARY/MANAGER: John G. Forde.
Tel: (0907) 30013.

An interesting parkland course situated close to the famous Knock Shrine. The main features of Ballyhaunis are its pleasant elevated greens protected with well positioned bunkers.

COURSE INFORMATION

Par 70; SSS 69; Length 5,801 Yards, 5,413 Metres.
Visitors: Welcome at all times.
Opening Hours: 9am – Sunset.
Avoid: Members competitions on Sundays & Thursdays.
Ladies: Welcome.
Green Fees: £8 per day.
Juveniles: Welcome (handicap certificate required). Caddy service available by prior arrangement.
Clubhouse Hours: Licencing hours.
Clubhouse Dress: Casual. During presentations – jacket and tie.
Clubhouse Facilities: Full catering facilities by prior arrangement.
Open Competitions: Open weeks in May and August. Handicap certificate required for Open Competitions.

NO.	MEDAL METRES	GEN METRES	PAR	S.I.	NO.	MEDAL METRES	GEN METRES	PAR	S.I.
1	359	355	4	3	10	372	364	4	4
2	309	304	4	9	11	337	334	4	6
3	447	442	5	11	12	412	410	5	14
4	360	355	4	1	13	354	347	4	2
5	282	278	4	15	14	273	269	4	16
6	153	149	3	13	15	149	145	3	18
7	322	317	4	7	16	301	295	4	10
8	126	121	3	17	17	148	143	3	12
9	359	354	4	5	18	350	345	4	8
OUT	2,717	2,675	35		IN	2,696	2,652	35	
					TOTAL	5,413	5,327	70	
					STANDARD SCRATCH		69		

Bunker/hedge and tree positions indicated.
Copyright Tudor Journals Ltd.

Carn Golf Club, Carn, Belmullet, Co. Mayo.
Tel: (097) 81051,
Fax: (097) 81477.

LOCATION: On the Mullet Peninsula near Belmullet, Co. Mayo. 2.5KM from Belmullet.
SECRETARY: Liam McAndrew.
ARCHITECT: Eddie Hackett.

This new exciting links has a natural setting of incomparable beauty. Splendid sand dunes on ancient commonage. Elevated tees and plateau greens exploit the magnificent backdrops over Blacksod Bay.

NO.	MEDAL METRES	GEN METRES	PAR	S.I.	NO.	MEDAL METRES	GEN METRES	PAR	S.I.
1	362	352	4	5	10	468	435	5	18
2	182	147	3	17	11	318	287	4	8
3	374	367	4	7	12	270	263	4	14
4	472	458	5	15	13	481	446	5	10
5	377	327	4	11	14	135	130	3	12
6	361	351	4	3	15	362	354	4	4
7	163	155	3	9	16	141	131	3	16
8	369	362	4	2	17	404	397	4	1
9	324	316	4	13	18	495	485	5	6
OUT	2984	2835	35		IN	3074	2928	37	
					TOTAL	6058	5763	72	
					STANDARD SCRATCH	73	72		

COURSE INFORMATION

Par 72; SSS 73; Length 6,058 metres.
Visitors: Welcome Anytime.
Green Fees: £17.
Club Facilities: Practice range, caddy and car hire.
Clubhouse Facilities: Bar and Restaurant.

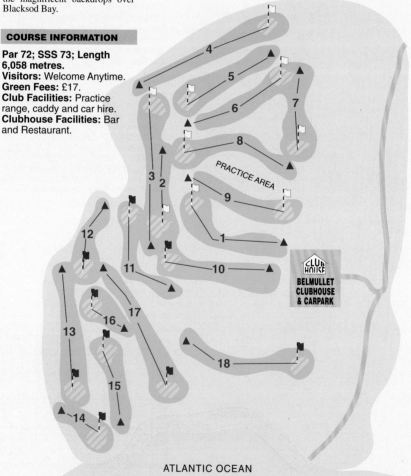

ATLANTIC OCEAN

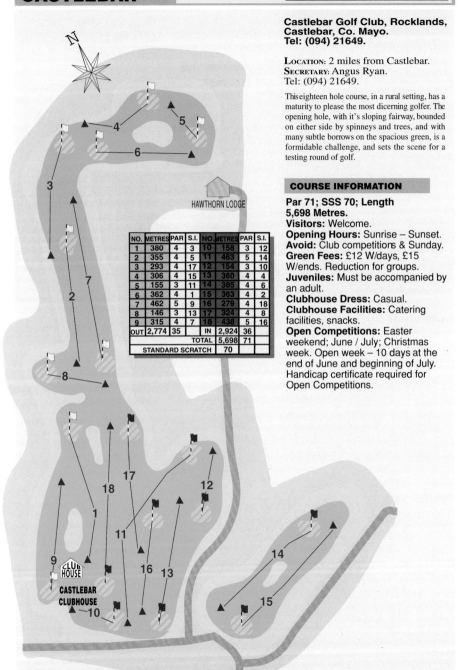

**Castlebar Golf Club, Rocklands, Castlebar, Co. Mayo.
Tel: (094) 21649.**

LOCATION: 2 miles from Castlebar.
SECRETARY: Angus Ryan.
Tel: (094) 21649.

This eighteen hole course, in a rural setting, has a maturity to please the most dicerning golfer. The opening hole, with it's sloping fairway, bounded on either side by spinneys and trees, and with many subtle borrows on the spacious green, is a formidable challenge, and sets the scene for a testing round of golf.

HAWTHORN LODGE

COURSE INFORMATION

Par 71; SSS 70; Length 5,698 Metres.
Visitors: Welcome.
Opening Hours: Sunrise – Sunset.
Avoid: Club competitions & Sunday.
Green Fees: £12 W/days, £15 W/ends. Reduction for groups.
Juveniles: Must be accompanied by an adult.
Clubhouse Dress: Casual.
Clubhouse Facilities: Catering facilities, snacks.
Open Competitions: Easter weekend; June / July; Christmas week. Open week – 10 days at the end of June and beginning of July. Handicap certificate required for Open Competitions.

NO.	METRES	PAR	S.I.	NO.	METRES	PAR	S.I.
1	380	4	3	10	158	3	12
2	355	4	5	11	463	5	14
3	293	4	17	12	154	3	10
4	306	4	15	13	360	4	4
5	155	3	11	14	385	4	6
6	362	4	1	15	363	4	2
7	462	5	9	16	279	4	18
8	146	3	13	17	324	4	8
9	315	4	7	18	438	5	16
OUT	2,774	35		IN	2,924	36	
				TOTAL	5,698	71	
	STANDARD SCRATCH				70		

CASTLEBAR CLUBHOUSE

**Claremorris Golf Club,
Castlemagarrett,
Claremorris, Co. Mayo.
Tel: (094) 71527.**

LOCATION: Galway Road, 2 miles from town.
SECRETARY/MANAGER: Willy Feely.
Tel: (094) 71868.

A difficult nine hole course. Very hilly and usually very undercrowded except for competitions which are played mostly on Sundays. Claremorris Golf Club was formed in 1918 and some members still recall Christy O'Connor Senior giving lessons in the 1940's at 2/6d per half hour.

COURSE INFORMATION

Par 70; SSS 69; Length 5,264 Metres.
Visitors: Welcome to play at any time.
Avoid: Competitions for members.
Ladies: Welcome.
Juveniles: Welcome
Green Fees: £8 per day; £6 with a member. Students half price.

Clubhouse Dress: Casual.
Clubhouse Facilities:
Catering facilities by prior arrangement.

NO.	YARDS	PAR	S.I.	NO.	YARDS	PAR	S.I.
1	380	4	3	10	158	3	12
2	346	4	5	11	463	5	14
3	293	4	17	12	154	3	10
4	306	4	15	13	360	4	4
5	155	3	11	14	283	4	6
6	357	4	1	15	363	4	2
7	462	5	9	16	279	4	18
8	146	3	13	17	324	4	8
9	315	4	7	18	438	5	16
OUT	2,760	35		IN	2,822	36	
				TOTAL	5,582	71	
				STANDARD SCRATCH		69	

CLUB HOUSE

**CLAREMORRIS
CLUBHOUSE**

**Swinford Golf Club,
Barbazon Park, Swinford,
Co. Mayo.
Tel: (094) 51378.**

LOCATION: Beside Swinford
town.
SECRETARY: Mary Horkan.
Tel: (094) 51378.
HEAD GROUNDSMAN: Michael
Farrelly.

There are quite a number of trees on the
course which adds considerably to the
difficulty of wayward shots.

COURSE INFORMATION

**Par 70; SSS 68; Length 5,237
Metres.
Visitors:** Welcome
Opening Hours: All day every
day.
Ladies: Welcome.

Green Fees: £7 per day; £17 per
weekend & £35 per week.
Juveniles: Permitted.
Clubhouse Hours: Open all day.
Clubhouse Dress: Casual.
Clubhouse Facilities: Bar.
Catering by request.
Open Competitions: Open week
– 1st week in August; Handicap
certificate required for Open
Competitions.

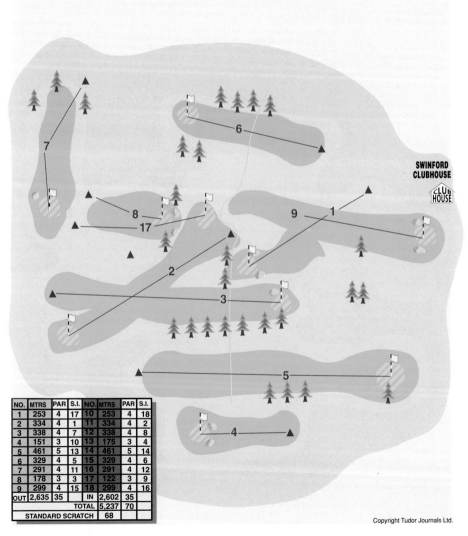

NO.	MTRS	PAR	S.I.	NO.	MTRS	PAR	S.I.
1	253	4	17	10	253	4	18
2	334	4	1	11	334	4	2
3	338	4	7	12	338	4	8
4	151	3	10	13	175	3	4
5	461	5	13	14	461	5	14
6	329	4	5	15	329	4	6
7	291	4	11	16	291	4	12
8	178	3	3	17	122	3	9
9	299	4	15	18	299	4	16
OUT	2,635	35		IN	2,602	35	
				TOTAL	5,237	70	
STANDARD SCRATCH					68		

NO.	CHAMP YARDS	MEDAL YARDS	PAR	S.I.	NO.	CHAMP YARDS	MEDAL YARDS	PAR	S.I.
1	348	335	4	16	10	517	498	5	11
2	343	330	4	10	11	433	420	4	1
3	162	149	3	18	12	220	208	3	7
4	501	488	5	14	13	455	442	4	3
5	356	343	4	12	14	189	180	3	9
6	453	445	4	4	15	580	515	5	5
7	524	511	5	8	16	363	350	4	15
8	468	455	4	2	17	316	303	4	17
9	202	196	3	6	18	520	499	5	13
OUT	3,357	3,252	36		IN	3,593	3,415	37	
					TOTAL	6,959	6,667	73	
					STANDARD SCRATCH	75	73		

**Westport Golf Club,
Carrowholly, Westport,
Co. Mayo.
Tel: (098) 25113/27070.**

LOCATION: 2½ miles from Westport
town.
SECRETARY: Dermit Ruddy.
Tel: (098) 25113.
PROFESSIONAL: Alex Mealia.
Tel: (098) 25113.
ARCHITECT: Fred Hawtree.

Situated on the shores of Clew Bay and set in
260 acres of parkland, Westport offers golfers a
memorable challenge. The course commands a
wonderful view of Clew Bay and is dominated
by the Holy Mountain, Croagh Patrick. The best
known hole on this course is the Par 5 fifteenth
which reaches 580 yards (535 metres) and
features a long carry from the tee over an inlet
of Clew Bay. Designed by the noted golf
architect Fred Hawtree, who also designed the
new course at St Andrews.

COURSE INFORMATION

**Par 73; SSS 75; Length
6,959 Yards.**
Visitors: Welcome (phone first).
Opening Hours: Sunrise to Sunset.
Avoid: Competition days.
Ladies: Welcome.
Green Fees: Weekdays – £18;
weekends & Bank holidays – £22.50
Special rates for societies.
Juveniles: Welcome. Lessons and
caddy service available by prior
arrangement. Club hire available.
Clubhouse Hours: 9.00am –
11.30pm.
Clubhouse Dress: Informal.
Clubhouse Facilities: Catering
facilities – meals available 9am –
10pm.
Open Competitions: Open weeks in
June & August. Handicap certificate
required for Open Competitions.

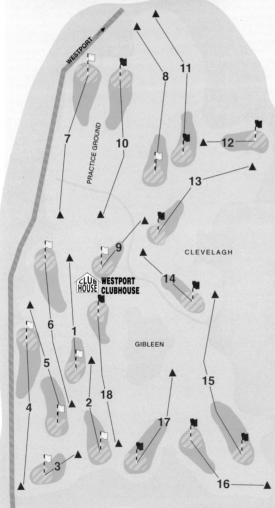

ATHLONE

CONNACHT **ROSCOMMON**

Athlone Golf Club, Hodson Bay, Athlone, Co. Roscommon.
Tel: (0902) 92073/92235.

LOCATION: Four miles from Athlone.
HON. SECRETARY: John Kinahan.
Tel: (0902) 92073.
PROFESSIONAL: Martin Quinn.
Tel: (0902) 92073/92868.
CAPTAIN: Joe Walsh.

Athlone has a commanding view of Lough Ree from an elevated Clubhouse. Fairways are guarded by trees and a further large tree plantation recently undertaken should come into play soon. Out of bounds exists on the right of ten fairways. Course well equipped with strategically placed bunkers.

COURSE INFORMATION

Par 71; SSS 70; Length 5,935 Metres.
Visitors: Welcome.
Opening Hours: 7.30am – 10.00pm.
Ladies Day: Tuesday.
Green Fees: £15 Mon - Fri; £18 Sat/Sun/Bank Holidays.
Juveniles: Must play with an adult before 3.30pm. Special times on noticeboard. Lessons available by prior arrangements. Club Hire available. Caddy service available by prior arrangements. Handicap Certificate required.

Clubhouse Hours: 7.30am – 11.30pm.
Clubhouse Dress: Casual – no shorts.
Clubhouse Facilities: Full catering facilities available, Restaurant hours 9.30am – 10.00pm open all year round.
Open Competitions: Open week first week in June; Lough Ree Open July and August.

NO.	MEDAL METRES	GEN. METRES	PAR	S.I.	NO.	MEDAL METRES	GEN. METRES	PAR	S.I.
1	348	339	4	7	10	332	322	4	10
2	155	149	3	11	11	457	447	5	12
3	268	261	4	15	12	404	392	4	3
4	380	372	4	4	13	326	316	4	8
5	503	493	5	9	14	300	291	4	16
6	432	421	5	17	15	171	163	3	14
7	392	382	4	5	16	412	397	4	1
8	381	373	4	2	17	120	111	3	18
9	176	166	3	13	18	365	378	4	6
OUT	3,035	2,956	36		IN	2,887	2,817	35	
					TOTAL	5,922	5,773	71	
		STANDARD SCRATCH					71	70	

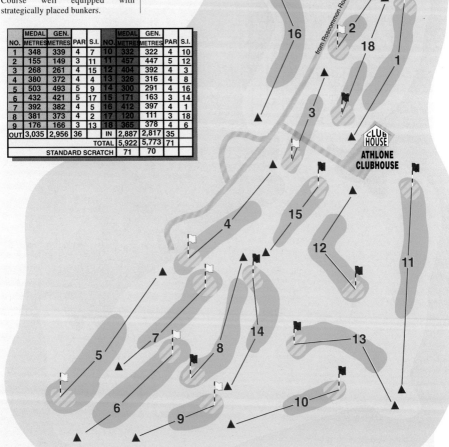

Copyright Tudor Journals Ltd.

**Ballaghadereen Golf Club,
Aughalustia,
Ballaghadereen,
Co. Roscommon.
Tel: (0907) 60358.**

LOCATION: Three miles from
Ballaghadereen town.
SECRETARY: Basil Clancy.
Tel: (0907) 60029.

A relatively flat course but trees
which are maturing are becoming a
great asset both visually and also

coming into play. A trip to the rough
can quite easily cost a shot. The 2nd
hole in particular requires great
accuracy to a very small green, well
protected with bunkers.

COURSE INFORMATION

**Par 70; SSS 66; Length
5,180 Metres.
Visitors:** Welcome at all
times.
Opening Hours: 9am – Dusk.
Ladies: Welcome.

Green Fees: £6 daily.
Handicap Certificate required
for open competitions.
Juveniles: Welcome. Caddy
service available by prior
arrangement.
Clubhouse Hours: Evenings
Saturday & Sunday.
Clubhouse Dress: Casual.
Clubhouse Facilities: Bar.
Catering by prior
arrangement.
Open Competitions: Open
week – June.

NO.	METRES	PAR	S.I.	NO.	METRES	PAR	S.I.
1	342	4	3	10	335	4	4
2	145	3	9	11	105	3	18
3	426	5	16	12	367	4	1
4	150	3	10	13	150	3	11
5	238	4	17	14	284	4	13
6	313	4	7	15	313	4	8
7	353	4	2	16	421	5	12
8	304	4	14	17	305	4	15
9	314	4	5	18	315	4	6
OUT	2,585	35		IN	2,595	35	
				TOTAL	5,180	70	
	STANDARD SCRATCH					66	

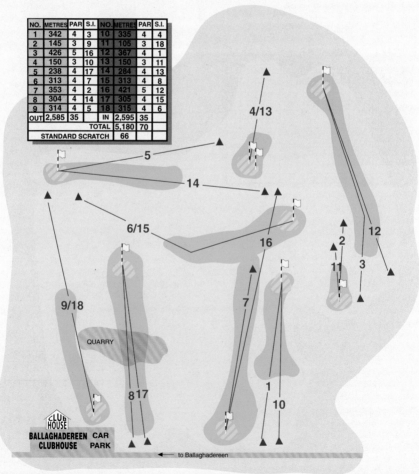

QUARRY

CLUB HOUSE

BALLAGHADEREEN   CAR
CLUBHOUSE   PARK

← to Ballaghadereen

Boyle Golf Club, Knockadoobrusna, Boyle, Co. Roscommon.
Tel: (079) 62594.

Location: One mile from Boyle.
Secretary: Paddy Nangle.
Tel: (079) 63288.
Handicap Sec: Bartly Moran.
Tel: (079) 62102.

A feature of the course is the views of Lock Key, Curlew Mountains, Sligo Mountain and the Mayo Mountains from the 8th green and 2nd tee. The course is also within easy reach of Loch Key and Forest Park, Boyle.

COURSE INFORMATION

Par 67; SSS 66; Length 4,865 Metres.
Visitors: Welcome at all times.
Opening Hours: Sunrise – Sunset.
Ladies: Welcome.
Green Fees: £5 per day. Special rate for Families £12; Gentleman & lady £10; Juvenile £2.
Juveniles: Welcome, with restrictions. Club Hire available; Caddy service available by prior arrangement.

Clubhouse Hours: 4pm – 10pm.
Clubhouse Dress: Casual.
Clubhouse Facilities: Catering facilities: snacks.
Open Competitions: Open Week July; 12 hole open every Thurs from May – Dec; Open Scramble every Friday from May – Sept.

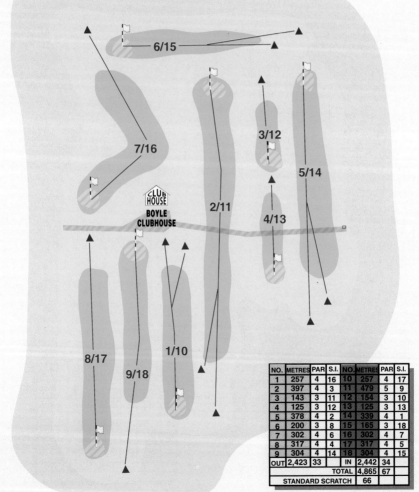

NO.	METRES	PAR	S.I.	NO.	METRES	PAR	S.I.
1	257	4	16	10	257	4	17
2	397	4	3	11	479	5	9
3	143	3	11	12	154	3	10
4	125	3	12	13	125	3	13
5	378	4	2	14	339	4	1
6	200	3	8	15	165	3	18
7	302	4	6	16	302	4	7
8	317	4	4	17	317	4	5
9	304	4	14	18	304	4	15
OUT	2,423	33		IN	2,442	34	
				TOTAL	4,865	67	
				STANDARD SCRATCH		66	

**Carrick-on-Shannon,
Co Roscommon.
Tel: (079) 67015.**

LOCATION: Beside N4 route four miles west of Carrick-on-Shannon.
HOUSE SEC: L. McCarthy.
Tel: (079) 67015.
CLUB SEC: Diarmuid Croghan.

A pleasant inland course overlooking the River Shannon, that provides a good test of golf for any low or high handicappers.

COURSE INFORMATION

Par 70; SSS 68; Length 5,545 Metres.
Visitors: Welcome to play at any time.
Opening Hours: Daylight hours.
Ladies: Welcome.
Green Fees: £10 per day.
Juveniles: Welcome.
Clubhouse Hours: 9.30am – 11.00pm.

Clubhouse Dress: Informal.
Clubhouse Facilities: Coffee and snacks at bar.
Open Competitions: Open Week – July. Open Weekends April, June, July & August. Handicap certificate required for Open Competitions.

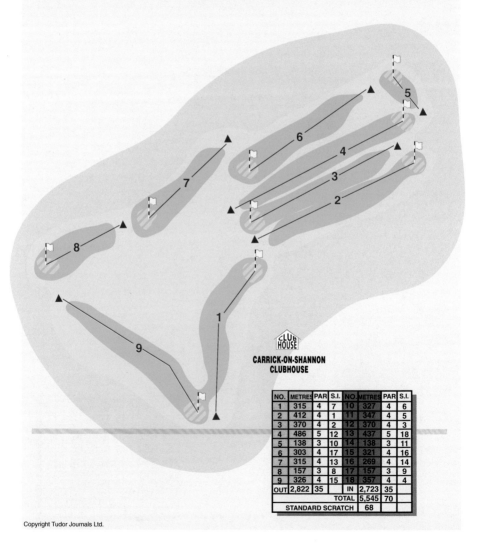

**CARRICK-ON-SHANNON
CLUBHOUSE**

NO.	METRES	PAR	S.I.	NO.	METRES	PAR	S.I.
1	315	4	7	10	327	4	6
2	412	4	1	11	347	4	5
3	370	4	2	12	370	4	3
4	486	5	12	13	437	5	18
5	138	3	10	14	138	3	11
6	303	4	17	15	321	4	16
7	315	4	13	16	269	4	14
8	157	3	8	17	157	3	9
9	326	4	15	18	357	4	4
OUT	2,822	35		IN	2,723	35	
				TOTAL	5,545	70	
				STANDARD SCRATCH		68	

**Castlerea Golf Club,
Clonailis, Castlerea,
Co. Roscommon.
Tel: (0907) 20068.**

LOCATION: Town of Castlerea.
Between Castlebar and
Roscommon.
SECRETARY:Mr D.T. Murray.
Tel: (0907) 20791.

This is a short parkland course with
three Par 3 holes. River comes into
play on 4th, 5th and 8th holes.
Narrow fairways make accuracy
important, although the light rough
does not cause too much frustration
for errant shots.

COURSE INFORMATION

**Par 72; SSS 66; Length
4,974 Metres.**
Visitors: Welcome.
Opening Hours: Sunrise –
Sunset.
Ladies: Welcome.
Green Fees: Mon – Fri £8;
Sat & Sun £10.
Juveniles: Welcome. Caddy
service available by prior
arrangement.
Clubhouse Hours: 10.30am
to closing time.
Clubhouse Dress: Casual.

Clubhouse Facilities: By
prior arrangment.
Open Competitions: Open
Week June; Intermediate
Scratch Cup July; Open
Mixed Foursomes. Handicap
certificate required for Open
Competitions.

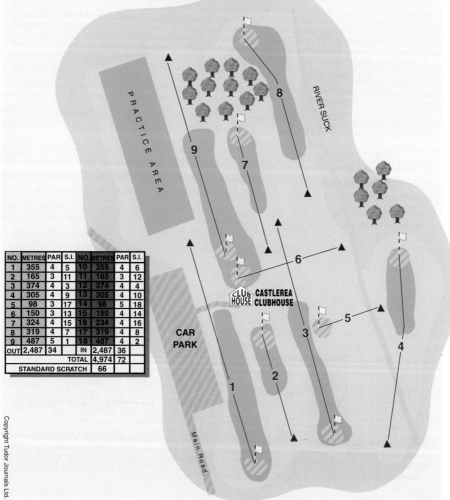

NO.	METRES	PAR	S.I.	NO.	METRES	PAR	S.I.
1	355	4	5	10	355	4	6
2	165	3	11	11	165	3	12
3	374	4	3	12	374	4	4
4	305	4	9	13	305	4	10
5	98	3	17	14	98	5	18
6	150	3	13	15	150	4	14
7	324	4	15	16	234	4	16
8	319	4	7	17	319	4	8
9	487	5	1	18	487	4	2
OUT	2,487	34		IN	2,487	36	
				TOTAL	4,974	72	
STANDARD SCRATCH		66					

Roscommon Golf Club, Mote Park, Roscommon, Co Roscommon.
Tel: (0903) 26382.

LOCATION: Roscommon Town.
SECRETARY: Cathal McConn.
Tel: (0903) 26062.

Though a nine hole course, Roscommon is one of the more challenging golf tests in the Midlands and West. With a standard scratch score of 70, it requires long and accurate hitting on some holes, while others will test the short game skills of the golfer. Extension to 18 holes due to open in Autumn '95.

COURSE INFORMATION

Par 72; SSS 69 Length 5,784 Metres.
Visitors: Welcome to play any time except Tuesdays and Sundays.
Opening Hours: Sunrise – Sunset.
Avoid: Summer evenings.
Ladies: Tuesday.
Green Fees: £10.00 per day, £6.00 for Societies, £40 for a week.
Clubhouse Hours: 2.00pm – 11.30pm.

Clubhouse Dress: Informal.
Clubhouse Facilities: Bar, catering.
Open Competitions: Open Week June /July. Easter Weekend and Bank Holidays.

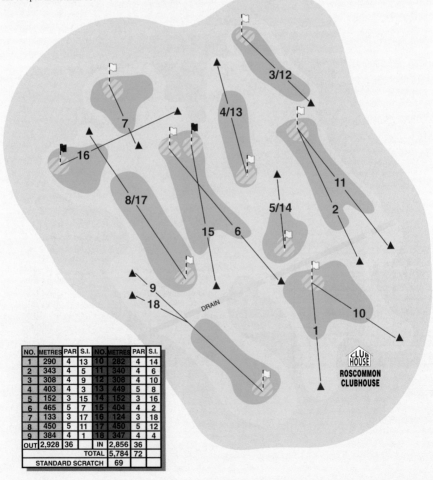

NO.	METRES	PAR	S.I.	NO.	METRES	PAR	S.I.
1	290	4	13	10	282	4	14
2	343	4	5	11	340	4	6
3	308	4	9	12	308	4	10
4	403	4	3	13	449	5	8
5	152	3	15	14	152	3	16
6	465	5	7	15	404	4	2
7	133	3	17	16	124	3	18
8	450	5	11	17	450	5	12
9	384	4	1	18	347	4	4
OUT	2,928	36		IN	2,856	36	
				TOTAL	5,784	72	
	STANDARD SCRATCH			69			

ROSCOMMON CLUBHOUSE

County Sligo Golf Club, Rosses Point, Co Sligo.
Tel: (071) 77186/77134
Fax: (071) 77460.

LOCATION: Eight km. west of Sligo.
SECRETARY: Anda Lanergan.
Tel: (071) 77134.
PROFESSIONAL: Leslie Robinson.
Tel: (071) 77171.
ARCHITECT: Colt & Allison.

Situated under the shadow of famous Benbulben, the County Sligo Golf Club, or Rosses Point as it is more popularly known, is one of Ireland's great championship links. Home of the West of Ireland Championship held each year since 1923. Set among vast sand dunes on the cliffs overlooking three large beaches. Constant winds are an added factor to its many challenges, not least of which are some of its elevated tees. A burn meanders through the course and comes into play on a number of holes.

COURSE INFORMATION

Par 71; SSS 72; Length 6,003 Metres.
Visitors: Welcome to play, except during major competitions.
Opening Hours: Daylight.
Avoid: Advisable to check tee time available before travel.
Ladies: Welcome.

Green Fees: IR£18 weekdays; Sat/Sun/Bank Holidays IR£25; Societies: Weekdays IR£15; Weekend/Bank Holidays IR£23. Lessons available by prior arrangement. Club hire available. Caddy service available by prior arrangement. Clubhouse Hours: 8.00am - 11.30pm.
Clubhouse Dress: (Casual Neat).
Clubhouse Facilities: Full facilities. Snacks during day, a la carte after 6pm, and any other requirements by arrangement.
Open Competitions: Open week July/ August. Handicap certificate required for open competitions.

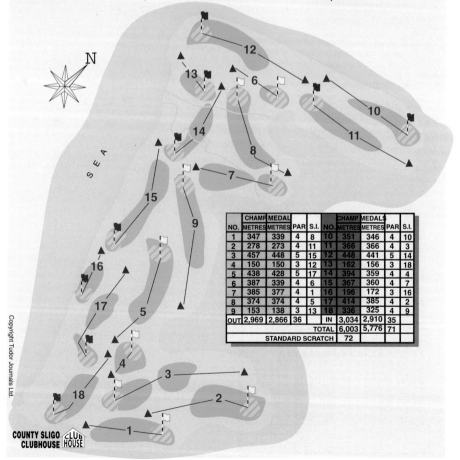

NO.	CHAMP METRES	MEDAL METRES	PAR	S.I.	NO.	CHAMP METRES	MEDALS METRES	PAR	S.I.
1	347	339	4	8	10	351	346	4	10
2	278	273	4	11	11	366	366	4	3
3	457	448	5	15	12	448	441	5	14
4	150	150	3	12	13	162	156	3	18
5	438	428	5	17	14	394	359	4	4
6	387	339	4	6	15	367	360	4	7
7	385	377	4	1	16	196	172	3	16
8	374	374	4	5	17	414	385	4	2
9	153	138	3	13	18	336	325	4	9
OUT	2,969	2,866	36		IN	3,034	2,910	35	
					TOTAL	6,003	5,776	71	
					STANDARD SCRATCH	72			

COUNTY SLIGO CLUBHOUSE

Enniscrone Golf Club, Enniscrone, Co. Sligo. Tel: (096) 36297.

LOCATION: Ballina Road, south of Enniscrone.
SECRETARY: John Fleming.
Tel: (096) 36243/21472.
PROFESSIONAL: Charles McGolderick.
ARCHITECT: E. Hackett

This links, on the shore of Killala Bay, is one of the many marvellous tests of golf which can be found in Ireland. The quality of the golf is matched by the surroundings, with the Ox Mountains close at hand. Killala Bay reaches out to the broad Atlantic within miles of sandy beaches surrounding the course. *"This is certainly a course not to be missed... the club is very keen to encourage visitors so a warm welcome is assured"* (Golf World). Enniscrone is also the venue for the Irish Close Championships.

COURSE INFORMATION

Par 72; SSS 72; Length 6,620 Yards.
Visitors: Always welcome. (telephone at weekends).
Opening Hours: Sunrise – Sunset.
Avoid: Bank Holidays; Sundays 8.00am – 10.30am and 1.30pm – 3.30pm.
Ladies: Welcome.
Green Fees: £18 per day. £22 weekends (includes vat). £10 Societies (12 or more people).
Juveniles: Must be accompanied by an adult. Club Hire is available. Caddy service available by prior arrangements. Telephone appointment required for weekends.
Clubhouse Hours: Mid April – mid October open at all times. Mid-week winter months restricted opening.
Clubhouse Dress: Casual.
Clubhouse Facilities: Catering facilities: snacks at all times. Meals must be ordered before play commences.
Open Competitions: All Bank Holidays; Open Week last week August.

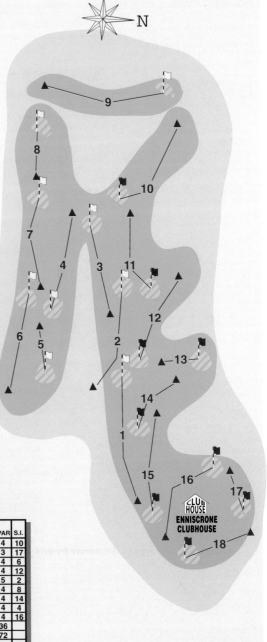

NO.	MEDAL YARDS	GEN. YARDS	PAR	S.I.	NO.	MEDAL YARDS	GEN. YARDS	PAR	S.I.
1	370	370	4	15	10	370	318	4	10
2	411	411	4	3	11	411	172	3	17
3	352	352	4	13	12	352	316	4	6
4	419	419	4	9	13	419	398	4	12
5	514	514	5	1	14	514	523	5	2
6	374	374	4	11	15	374	401	4	8
7	359	359	4	7	16	359	351	4	14
8	166	166	3	18	17	166	461	4	4
9	307	307	4	5	18	307	354	4	16
OUT	3,272	3,272	36		IN	3,272	3,294	36	
					TOTAL	6,620	6,566	72	
					STANDARD SCRATCH	72	72		

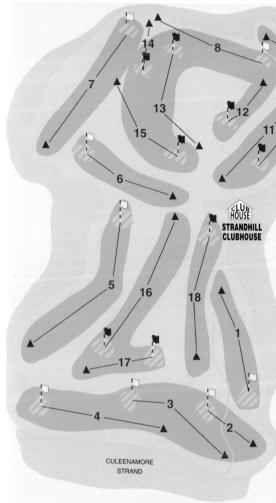

STRANDHILL
CLUBHOUSE

CULEENAMORE
STRAND

**Strandhill Golf Club,
Strandhill, Co. Sligo.
Tel: (071) 68188.**

LOCATION: Five miles west of
Sligo City.
SECRETARY: John Gillen.
Tel: (071) 69734.
ARCHITECT: E. Hackett

Strandhill is a links course, playable all
year round and situated in a most scenic
area with views of Knocknarea and
Benbulben Mountains. It has some very
interesting holes, with the final three
providing a sting in the tail.

COURSE INFORMATION

**Par 69; SSS 68; Length 6,032
Yards, 5,516 Metres.
Visitors:** Welcome.
Opening Hours: 8.30am –
Sunset.
Ladies: Thursday.
Green Fees: £12 Mon – Fri; £15
Sat/Sun & All public holidays; plus
VAT. Groups £2 less.
Juveniles: Welcome. Prior
arrangement is required for
groups only (or for individuals on
Thursdays).
Clubhouse Hours: 8.30am –
11.30pm.
Clubhouse Dress: Casual.
Clubhouse Facilities: Snacks at
any time, lunch by prior
arrangement.
Open Competitions: Most
weekends April - September.

NO.	MEDAL METRES	GEN. METRES	PAR	S.I.	NO.	MEDAL METRES	GEN. METRES	PAR	S.I.
1	397	380	4	1	10	304	285	4	12
2	158	155	3	13	11	300	263	4	16
3	375	330	4	15	12	304	260	4	14
4	291	270	4	7	13	338	305	4	6
5	480	460	5	17	14	132	111	4	18
6	355	336	4	5	15	306	270	4	8
7	352	335	4	3	16	386	362	4	2
8	308	275	4	9	17	178	141	3	10
9	186	140	3	11	18	384	329	4	4
OUT	2,902	2,681	35		IN	2,614	2,326	34	
					TOTAL	5,516	5,007	69	
					STANDARD SCRATCH	68	67		

GOLF CLUBS IN IRELAND

(NORTH & SOUTH – LISTED ALPHABETICALLY)

ADVERTISERS INDEX

GOLF DAYS GRATEFULLY ACKNOWLEDGES THE SUPPORT OF ADVERTISERS AND RECOMMENDS THAT READERS TAKE ADVANTAGE OF THEIR SERVICE WHEREVER POSSIBLE.

ACKNOWLEDGEMENTS

GOLF DAYS WOULD LIKE TO RECORD ITS THANKS AND APPRECIATION TO THE MANY GOLF CLUBS AND STAFF WHO GREATLY ASSISTED THE PUBLISHERS IN COMPILING THIS BOOK.

PUBLISHERS NOTE

THIS IS THE SEVENTH EDITION OF GOLF DAYS AND IN COMPILING THE INFORMATION WE ARE AWARE THAT IT IS NOT POSSIBLE TO ENSURE COMPLETE ACCURACY. WE WOULD WELCOME COMMENTS FROM READERS AND OBSERVATIONS FROM CLUB OFFICIALS TO ASSIST US IN OUR PROGRAMME OF CONTINUALLY UPDATING.